APPLE

Photograph: Derek Ridgers, 2022

ABOUT THE AUTHOR

Antonella Gambotto-Burke is a regular contributor to various
international newspapers and magazines, including *The Sunday Times*,
The Telegraph and *The Weekend Australian*. She is also the author of
Mama: Love, Motherhood and Revolution, which features a foreword by
Michel Odent and which KJS Anand, Rosén von Rosenstein Laureate
2009, and Professor of Paediatrics, Anaesthesiology, Anatomy and
Neurobiology, described as "undeniably the most important book of the
21st century". *The Mirror* (UK) recently included Antonella in a select
group of the world's most inspiring feminists.

gambottoburke.com | afmusiclondon.com
@gambottoburke | @afmusiclondon

Other books by Antonella Gambotto-Burke:
The Eclipse: A Memoir of Suicide
MOUTH
Mama: Love, Motherhood and Revolution

ANTONELLA GAMBOTTO-BURKE

APPLE

SEX DRUGS

MOTHERHOOD

AND THE RECOVERY OF

THE FEMININE

pinter
&
martin

Apple: Sex, Drugs, Motherhood and the Recovery of the Feminine

First published by Pinter & Martin 2022

© 2022 Antonella Gambotto-Burke

The author has asserted her moral rights to be identified as the author of this work in accordance with the Copyright, Designs and Patents Act of 1988.

ISBN 978-1-78066-740-9
Also available as ebook

British Library Cataloguing-in-Publication Data
A catalogue record for this book is available from the British Library.

Index: Helen Bilton

Set in Dante

Printed and bound in the UK by TJ Books Limited

Pinter & Martin Ltd
6 Effra Parade
London SW2 1PS

pinterandmartin.com

I passed through the narrow hills
of my mother's hips one cold morning
and never looked back, until now.
Dorianne Laux

To Bethesda, my door to the infinite;
to my grandmother Natalina, who taught me what it is to love a child;
and to Deirdre, who made everything possible.

CONTENTS

III: Return of the Queen

AUTHOR'S NOTE

Apple: Sex, Drugs, Motherhood and the Recovery of the Feminine is an intricate, shocking, and sometimes difficult book. The density of the science in the middle third – the book was written as a literary triptych – is unavoidable. Had I not detailed the pharmaceutical mechanisms, my conclusions would make no sense.

If you are primarily interested in reading the material about sexuality, I recommend that you begin with Chapter 15, Rubber Soul, and, once you've finished the book, that you return to the first third and read the middle third last.

If drugs, music, or the 1960s are your focus, begin at the beginning, skip the middle third, and return to it after reading part III: Return of the Queen.

If your primary interest is maternal, begin with part II: Born to the Undead, and continue to the end before returning to the beginning.

I don't expect every reader to plough through the biological and pharmaceutical details and would, instead, prefer you to cherry-pick chapters that intrigue you, because even the most cursory understanding of *Apple* will help effect change.

For those who have the time and the stomach, read the book as written and let me know what you think through Facebook or Instagram, both @gambottoburke.

To readers who intend to skip the sections about birth – men in particular: I implore you to persevere for reasons that will become obvious if you do.

This is a book for everyone, not only mothers.

The material in this book will trigger a number of people for different reasons – writing Chapter 21, The Poisoned Apple, deeply disturbed me, for example – but is critically important to confront, because it is only through openly addressing our guilt, rage and trauma that we can effect change.

Modern obstetric practice has crippled our cultural capacity for health and happiness, leading to a global fragmentation that is evidenced in art, music, damage to the planet, skyrocketing rates of addiction, anxiety and depression, an epidemic of related health issues, and increasingly fractured human attachment and sexual patterns, among other catastrophes.

So how do we fix this mess?

Antonella Gambotto-Burke, 2022

Introduction: DIVIDE AND CONQUER

> '"Cut their goddamn heads off," I said.'
>
> *Hunter S. Thompson*

If I close my eyes, I see femininity as an apple. Whole or halved, with a star at its heart concealing traces of a poison that, as it kills – and like a woman – can accelerate its target's heartrate. I imagine the sound of that acceleration from within, listening as we all once listened, never thinking it would end, to the aria, charivari or lullaby of our mothers' hearts.

My mother was 23 when she gave birth to me – my age when I last attempted suicide, having overdosed to illustrate the grief I felt that femininity, with all its fats, feelings and flexure, had wreaked. In particular, I was taught to fear my breasts – like apples, symbols of nurturance, but which, to me, were no more than a hated bridle of flesh; my father, you see, was the first to touch them. I was 11, maybe 12, at the time – who can remember?

Some memories burn like celluloid: buckling, toxic. They are unsustainable.

Apples have always represented sweetness. Our appetites are recorded by their flesh, and the translucence of their juices, like those of women, are wiped from the chin. When my waters broke, three hours after Christmas, I dipped two fingers between my legs and brought them to my nose. Nothing like I'd imagined, the scent was that of fresh apple skins. For a moment, I lay in the warm darkness, thinking, of all things, about French Realist Gustave Courbet's *L'Origine du monde*, that 1866 portrait of a recumbent woman, decapitated by the frame, her thighs apart. Her vulva, rather than her face, is the focus.

In the 21st century, an obstetric panorama.

And yet this apple has always nestled between the thighs of women: primal, private, yielding, and, in the dark mirror of pornography, put to the use of tyre rubber and depilated to a mechanistic shine. A fruit which, when sampled, makes gods of men and then reduces them, emotionally, to dust.

Woman as comestible. Woman as kingmaker. Woman as oblivion.

I remember the red apple a boy once hurled, with his long, tan bowler's arm, at my diaphragm; running into the school toilet blocks, I crumpled by the metal sinks. I could not breathe but as I passed him on the way out, refused to weep. *You want to cry – go on!* he jeered. And I almost did. In an attempt to dodge the apple's trajectory, I'd skidded and scraped my knee. The kneecap glistened, lunar, beneath its bloody lace. I'd glimpsed the universe beneath our skin. I was the reverse of an apple, then: white on the outside, red within.

Decelerated by my fear or memory, that apple was sent spinning through the air by the energy of the boy's leap. This was a game at our school: boys targeted us with the intention of causing the most pain. The girls were different. At recess and lunchtime, we skipped – a game known as 'elastics' – and as we did, we chanted folk songs imported by 18th-century female convicts; unknowing, we repeated ditties that British and Irish petty thieves and pickpockets – some ill, some stupefied by alcohol, others unable to breastfeed the babies who died, wan and fevered, at their breasts – sang to comfort themselves during the 252 days it took to sail from England to Australia. A ship's surgeon wrote of a bereaved convict mother complaining 'of pain in her left side, occasioned it is supposed from grief her child having died yesterday'.[1]

> *Oranges and lemons,*
> *Say the bells of St Clement's.*
> *You owe me five farthings,*
> *Say the bells of St Martin's.*
> *When will you pay me?*
> *Say the bells at Old Bailey.*

Away from the boys, we sang these anthems of the disenfranchised dead, skipping, unprotected by hats or unguents, in the burning sun: and this is what it was to be a North Shore girl in 1970s Sydney, Australia.

A decade earlier, the American poet Sylvia Plath spoke for generations of post-industrial women when she nailed her late father as, 'A man in black with a Meinkampf look / And a love of the rack and the screw'.[2] In the ultimate repudiation of the domesticity that had 'bored & stifled' her glamorous, abusive husband[3] and a fortnight before her suicide (Plath gassed herself in the kitchen), she had written of 'a heaven starless and fatherless, a dark water.'[4]

I remember the 1970s as darker waters. A Golden Age of sorts for serial killers who mostly targeted women, the tenor of the era was, in part, determined by Ted Bundy, an American believed to have committed over a hundred murders but who only confessed, under duress, to 30.[5] Bundy's sadism was, in its way, an exquisite template of patriarchal cruelty: he inverted the empathy of his female victims – using a sling, crutches or a cast as props to elicit tenderness – before beating, disfiguring and raping them vaginally, anally or with objects.

Sometimes, as Courbet did in his painting, Bundy even decapitated them.

In terms of symbolism, Bundy's beheading of these women was telling. The crown of the head, in the Hindu tradition, is depicted as a lotus with a thousand petals: our portal to the Divine. British psychiatrist Theodore Dalrymple was equally romantic, positing that the severing of the head – 'at least nowadays when we have a more refined sensibility' – is a symbolic annihilation 'not only of the biological existence of the beheaded, but [their] very thoughts'.[6] In the Book of Judith, the beautiful eponymous widow decapitates her oppressor and parades his head as a trophy. This ahistorical tableau was one of the most popular with classical artists – among them, Botticelli, Caravaggio, Donatello and Titian – arguably to justify masculine governance; women, clearly, could not be trusted. Two thousand or so years earlier, the Celts flaunted the severed heads of enemies from their horses.

Bundy was less theatrical; he stored his collection in the fridge.

To the Celts, the ownership and display of a distinguished figure's head was a means of annexing the person's power.[7] The fact that Bundy's sadism was excited by a specific kind of feminine beauty tells the same story. He not only wished to annex the power these women held over him, but to punish them for triggering in him a vulnerability he was never taught to metabolise.

These women were the enemy, reminding him only of his failure to be unassailable.

In such a context, sociopathy is always of secondary importance.

Emotional susceptibility to the feminine was, to Bundy, so threatening that he was willing to sacrifice his life and those of others to retain a sense of mastery over his heart. News of his murders resonated throughout the Western world. The problem was not the horror, but the widespread sense of recognition.

Bundy's killings became emblematic of a sinister, unknowably ancient cultural current – that of detachment: head from body, reason from emotion, life from death. And, in keeping with the teachings of the scriptures, male from female. In this respect, Bundy was no different to any other man who murders women: to such men, parity between the masculine and feminine is incomprehensible. The concept of union is too painful be borne. As he said to the police before his final arrest, 'I am the most cold-hearted son of a bitch you'll ever meet.'[8]

These murders were only some of the news stories I heard as a girl. In an Australia I remember as stiflingly hot and dry and colourless, and to a car radio soundtrack of Daddy Cool's *Eagle Rock*, I listened as girls went missing – schoolgirls and, in particular, young hitchhikers. I see them now, these girls, in my mind's eye – smiling, with long hair, flared jeans and knapsacks, on the sides of remote Australian highways as they ran in the dust towards slowing Holdens, sometimes to be found, much later, in the form of scattered bones.

Even now, newspaper reports written by men show barely veiled disdain for the female victims. One begins, 'Margaret Rosewarne stuck out her thumb. She was 19 and a sun-bleached blonde beach bunny. It wasn't long before a ride turned up.'[9] The association between Rosewarne's assertive femininity ('blonde beach bunny') and battered corpse (pulped forehead, broken jaw) is clear. Like the unknown killer's other victims, the sexually flamboyant Rosewarne flouted the cardinal responsibility of women in a patriarchal culture: as in the Islamic world, a Western female, if she wishes to remain intact, must base her conduct on the presumption of violence at the heart of men.

In early childhood, I learned that inside the home, the feminine was both protected and secondary, but outside, was in perpetual danger of violation. The nature of the feminine was so potent, it seemed, that men were overwhelmed by it, and sometimes even *needed* to annihilate it. Walking home from work in February 1986, the Australian nurse and former beauty queen Anita Cobby, 26, was dragged, screaming, into a car and set upon by five men, who, after fracturing her nose and cheekbones with their fists, forced her to perform fellatio on all of them. Later, in a paddock and after breaking her fingers, they dragged Cobby through barbed wire fencing, held her down, and, as they punched, kicked and tortured her, continued to rape her until, fearing identification, one slit her throat so violently that she was almost decapitated.[10][11]

Two of the men involved were 19, a year or so my junior at the time.

I wondered at the last thing Cobby saw, there in that dark and isolated field. Two years earlier, I'd been subjected to a violent assault in London, and well understood the disparity between feminine and masculine strength. A boyfriend, Richard, attacked me after an argument over a record. He was lean and muscular, fluent in his speed. I was silent as he straddled me, repeatedly punching my head; I didn't think to interrupt him. A thousand miles away, I remember only the dissociation. And then I saw the knife on the table behind him and, weirdly, began to scream – a shrill, alien noise. He leapt back. I stalked him to the door, screaming *at* him rather than for help: bleeding, crazed, and with burning hair and sticks for arms, or so it felt. Opening the door, he turned, and, with a swift blow, punched me hard in the eye.

Two American tourists found me wandering the streets, concussed and with my skirt ripped to the waist. They took me to hospital. The police were called.

There was, for me, the feeling that to attempt to *know* a man was, as British novelist Joseph Conrad wrote, to penetrate 'deeper and deeper into the heart of darkness'. Any kindness shown me by a man served only to emphasise the threat of hidden appetites, which were – or so women are made to understand – safely contained by the holding pens of pornography, sport, and work.

I remember cringing in the car on the way to bookshops with my father as he evaluated, at red lights and with carnal intensity, the attractiveness of young female pedestrians. I remember watching, in silence, a twentysomething man in a Byron Bay park, who, high on crack or ice, screamed abuse at his cowering partner, calling her a fucking cunt and so on, disorientated and deranged, as their toddler looked from one to the other, absorbing what it is to be female in this world. No one intervened. No one dared. And I remember the twentysomething teacher who said, when I, a 15-year-old virgin, apologised for inadvertently interrupting his football meeting, 'No, stay. We need a good hooker.' Every boy in the room laughed.

This was simply the way men were when I was young – not all men and not all of the time, but enough to make such behaviour unremarkable.

I was six or seven when my maternal grandparents took me to King's Cross, Sydney's nightlife and red light district. The heat was sulphurous; my thighs stuck to the Naugahyde seats. Old Sydney and its pin-crooked streets seen through the smudges and scratches of those green-and-yellow bus windows. On the crest of a hill in the distance, the neon chaos of Darlinghurst Road. I remember the glow as we disembarked: it cupped each shining face, those human lanterns, jostling. Looking up, I gripped my grandparents' hands.

Above my head, a vocal troposphere of sorts, cinematic in volume, and beyond it, another atmospheric layer, one I did not yet understand. On our way to buy ice cream, we passed what I now know was a strip club: red velvet and braided gold rope, a narrow corridor that swallowed men alive. Those photographs of naked women, breasts coyly squashed, behind glass; like angel fish in a bedroom tank, they looked too big for their context. Was this where Eve was made to go after she bit into the apple? Quick-moving, the thin spruiker – gaudy top hat, foiled green and violet tails – waved his cane about, joking.

What a pretty little girl, he said.

My grandparents were charmed, but I was scared. I had recognised that spruiker as a priest of sorts. For years, I sketched him, as if stripping him of the power to frighten me. In writing of him now, I may be doing the same thing.

Our house, set up high over a dark and sweeping valley dun with eucalyptus trees and scrub, had balconies. In the slow boil of dusk, I would sit, my face pressed to the railings, staring out at the flocks of bats that changed the colour of the sky, and I would think about the killings discussed on the radio. I imagined the residuum of women's bones in the valley, there among the trees.

In high school, boys no longer threw apples but the disparagement continued. They spat at us and called us cunts; our skirts were flipped up with rulers from behind as we walked up the stairs. The day after my favourite Year 8 teacher, filmed at a gay rights rally, made the news, a petition was passed from student to student demanding his resignation; I was one of a minority who refused to sign. Unlike the football coach, he was asked to leave. At a Year 12 formal, another teacher told the plainest girl in the year that he wanted to fuck her up the arse. Straight white men, you understand, were kings.

This was our normal.

Throughout my adolescence, on my return from school, I would systematically binge eat, layering the food with liquids to make it easier to regurgitate. I would then lock myself in my bathroom and, kneeling on the cold blue tiles by the toilet, silently and with my hair held back, jam two fingers into my mouth until they nudged my slippery uvula, and I would vomit. This wasn't the puking of a drunk but conscientious, a form of meditation. On completion, I would close my eyes, exhaling as my head emptied. This happened thousands of times. As we had three bathrooms, no one other than my mother noticed, and she didn't care. The void – that sphere in which I felt nothing, aware only of my slowing heartbeat – was the goal. I didn't know that vomiting is a response to threat. Consciously, that threat had never been identified.

My father terrified me.

I was voted Head Prefect after I left home. The headmaster, during a private meeting, said I had to step down; I was not a good role model as I no longer lived with my family. I didn't tell him that I'd left home because my father, a man who masturbated over images of women urinating in each other's mouths, had started coming into my room late at night, heavily breathing, in the dark.

Clearly, I would have been a better role model had I stopped resisting.

In almost all other ways, I was patriarchal. My values were patriarchal. I was interested only in work. Women, I remember thinking, were bullshit, with their babies, hair tongs and wedding dresses. One of the midwives consulted about my daughter's birth reported that almost all my friends were single men. To inhabit my femininity would have been to experience an anguish that, like

Bundy, I didn't know how to metabolise. I saw the same dynamic in my daughter after she watched me struggle to homeschool and work during six years of divorce-related legal commitments. She began rejecting markers traditionally associated with femininity: the dresses she once loved, sweetness, vulnerability. Like a boy, she learned to mask her heart by pretending that nothing hurt, by pretending she didn't want to be loved.

'Men are treacherous,' she said one night as I lay beside her in the dark.

Eight years old and she had lost faith in the masculine.

At 15, she told me that she and a group of girlfriends, all of whom have no contact with their fathers, referred to themselves as 'the daddies', after the BDSM term for dominant.

In the 21st century, one in which women are routinely choked for sexual pleasure, all evidence of vulnerability must go. Pregnancy in particular, with its susceptibility and genetic enmeshment with a man, is seen as a loss of agency rather than as the ultimate expansion of consciousness. Canadian singer Grimes, who bore South African centibillionaire Elon Musk's seventh son, described it as a 'sort of tragedy of agreeing to it … For a girl, it's sacrificing your body and your freedom … like, y'know, unprotected sex. I'm just like, I have sacrificed my power in this moment. I have, like, capitulated.'[12]

This use of the word capitulation – to cease resisting an opponent – was telling. But did Grimes, a woman who, in her work, preferred to present herself as digitally dehumanised, capitulate to Musk or to her femininity?

To women, biology is now an open enemy.

In a patriarchal culture, to inhabit femininity is to be contextualised by fear. It is to be afraid of disappearing, of being ignored, of being trivialised, of being hit, hurt, raped, killed. It is to be afraid that your mother will one day be awoken by the police to tell her that your head has been discovered in a stranger's fridge. It is to think that you must act like a patriarch to survive in this, a patriarchal world: pretending not to feel, pretending not to love.

But underneath, the fear is always there.

Men are treacherous.

The first of my few one night stands was with a law student. I'll never forget the perfunctory nature of the act – emotionless, efficiently executed. That afternoon sunlight on his back. He could barely look at me afterwards, as if I were a reminder of something he would have preferred to forget. I don't even recall his name, only that he wore thick glasses and had a Ventolin inhaler. That night, I felt that I was somehow less than I had been before our meeting, as if I had been robbed, or misplaced something I never even knew was mine.

Over the years, I watched as safely stylised sexuality became a thing: BDSM, rubber. Humiliation, as a principle, seemed near-universal, whether informal or ritualised. Almost always, the humiliated were women. Power disparity in favour of the masculine made humiliation of the feminine necessary. British musician Alex James, the bassist from Blur, casually documented the dynamic. 'I locked her out,' he wrote, referring to his girlfriend, 'and when she was banging on the door, I pissed on her head from the fourth-storey window.'[13]

Urinating on a woman or into her cavities (anus, mouth, vagina) is now a staple of pornography.

I watched as, in increments, the women around me stopped believing in men. Most women I knew no longer had faith, not really, in the possibility of change. Emotionally, femininity was in the process of making itself inviolate. Evolved in response to the dehumanised masculine, this cynicism was a carapace. In *Fleabag*, British screenwriter Phoebe Waller-Bridge captured, with scintillating barbarity, the new feminine amalgam of bravado, low self-worth, yearning for masculine attention, and cultivated sexual detachment:

> 'You know that feeling when a guy you like sends you a text at two o'clock on a Tuesday night and asks "if he can come find you" and you've accidentally made it out like you've just got in yourself, so you have to get out of bed, drink half a bottle of wine, get in the shower, shave everything, dig out some Agent Provocateur business, suspender belt, the whole bit, and wait by the door until the buzzer goes – and then you open the door to him like you'd almost forgotten he was coming over ... After some pretty standard bouncing you realise that he is edging towards your arsehole, but you're drunk and he made the effort to come all the way here so ... you let him.'[14]

As a disordered adolescent, I had let the law student fuck me. I hadn't been frightened that he would hit me, but that he wouldn't like me, and what would happen then? What happens to the women men don't like? Richard punched me in the face after an argument about music. My then fiancé Michael VerMeulen, the American editor of British *GQ*, kicked me down a flight of stairs for breaking plates. My father, with whom I frequently argued, tried to fuck me.

The feminine, I learned, is penalised for denying the masculine superiority.

In 1985 and under the pseudonym Antonella Black, I interviewed Australian musician Nick Cave, then a heroin addict,[15] for a British music magazine cover story.[16] He shot up in the toilet before the interview, exiting with blood on his sleeve. I reported it all: the drooling, the slurring, the nodding off. On reading it, Cave, enraged, told other writers that he was going to 'kill' me. (Prior to the death of his son Arthur, who, after taking LSD, fell from a cliff,[17] and the 2022 death of his eldest son Jethro Lazenby, 30, convicted for his violence against women,[18] this was in keeping with what Australian critic Anwen Crawford called Cave's 'most enduring lyrical obsession: *lustmord*, sex murder.')[19]

Cave then stated in an interview with *Sounds* that I, 'a grub street groupie', had 'brought [my] pyjamas along to the interview in place of a tape recorder'. Bill Black, the journalist, added, 'Hi, Antonella, and if you ever need to borrow my Sony ...'[20] My editor Mick Mercer, who had meticulously listened to the tape to ensure that there would be no legal issues, immediately dictated a letter: 'I heard the tape of the interview and have yet to recover ... the piece eventually stated what other writers hadn't been brave enough to write. So what's the problem? Little Nick whittles his woodenly creative brain and makes sly insinuations about Antonella hauling in the bunk beds, anxious for the earth to move ... Cave dribbling in one corner.'[21]

Mick's letter was printed with an apology: '*Sounds* entirely accepts that Ms [Gambotto-Burke] conducts herself properly and professionally at all times and apologises to her and to [the magazine] for any suggestion to the contrary in Bill Black's interview with Nick Cave.'[22]

The apology only consolidated my original threat to Cave's patriarchal grandiosity: in combination with my interview, it exposed him as an abusive narcissist *and* a liar. Cave clearly felt his hand had been forced. And so to 'Scum'.[23] The award-winning British magazine editor Mat Snow, a friend of Cave's whom I dated in 1984, was also vilified in the song, in which Cave claimed that he was our 'creator' and lied that I'd performed fellatio on him.

The reality of the night I interviewed Cave – no exciting fellatio, just his dribbling – challenged his robust self-image as a perilously attractive countercultural rock star. Then 28, Cave not only felt it appropriate to bully and impugn a 19-year-old girl with false sexual slurs for telling unflattering truths, but took pride in it: a verbal spin on Richard's punches to my head. Cave's violence, in the form of defamatory lies, has been effective: my daughter read his sexual slurs on forums and I continue to be contacted about his claims. The biographers who canonise Cave have all been men. One reported that I had 'accosted' Cave, who, provoked beyond endurance by my lack of professionalism, 'yelled a stream of abuse', which caused me to 'fle[e] in tears'.[24]

Other than the fact that none of these things happened – not the accosting, not the yelling, not the fleeing in tears (I left after repeatedly asking the inert Cave if he was conscious, as could be heard on the tape) – this biographer's story contradicted Cave's own wavering narratives. No longer the despondent, rejected groupie or a malevolent fellatrix deserving humiliation at the hands of her 'creator', I was now a cringing incompetent.

The truth had simply evaporated.

My father, too, lied when my mother asked if he had touched my breasts.

The evasion of reality had, for me, become synonymous with men. When I couldn't sleep, my mother would rummage through the prescription drugs in my father's bedside cabinet for Nembutal (pentobarbital), break a capsule in half with her painted fingernail, and feed it to me. Eager for me to stop bothering her, she administered a drug now used for euthanasia to a child. At other times, I was fed Mogadon (nitrazepam), Halcion (triazolam), temazepam, or Valium (diazepam).

By the age of 10, I was familiar with the bouquet, half-life, and disorientation momentum of various major benzodiazepines and barbiturates. Even now, I remember the temazepam oozing from gel caps – those tiny apricots – as I bit into them. Even now, I remember the acridity of pentobarbital dust.

The Halcion left a residual sense of otherness: that consciousness of darkening corners, unease. I never liked it. Once the world's most profitable sleeping pill, Halcion was, in 1979, banned in the Netherlands, and, in 1991, banned in the UK on the basis of its links to depression and suicide.[25] American novelist William Styron, who came close to suicide, in part blamed Halcion. He wrote, 'I couldn't rid my mind of the line of Baudelaire's, dredged up from the distant past, that for several days had been skittering around at the edge of my consciousness: "I have felt the wind of the wing of madness."'[26]

I never considered the impact of these drugs on my neurodevelopment. I never wondered about the ideology that produced them. As they were administered to me by my mother, I simply accepted them. It was, to me, normal for an adult's bedside cabinet to contain drugs that manufactured the illusion of equilibrium or wellbeing. It was, to me, normal for a mother to deny, with a tablet, the agitation that betrayed her family's entrenched dysfunction.

Like a fairy in a foxglove, sleep, to me, was a thing in a pill.

When, in my late adolescence and early 20s, I attempted suicide three or four times, it was always with benzodiazepines, the drugs I associated with my father. Through these drugs, I learned that authenticity is irrelevant. My exterior was no longer to reflect my interior experience. The only emotions I was permitted were those considered appropriate by my social demographic. Permitted a certain feminine latitude, I could cry – Cave's biographer went so far as to manufacture tears for me – but I was not to reflect the truth.

In this severance from my integrity, rewards. The headmaster's applause as I was announced Head Prefect. My father's pleasure as the public fiction of his family's happiness was maintained. Not being repeatedly defamed, professionally and sexually, by Cave. ('Usually we walked with heads bent down, our eyes on our hands or the ground,' Canadian novelist Margaret Atwood wrote.)[27] And my mother's hand, offering pharmaceutical respite from my humiliation, suspended in the memory of light from her bedside lamp.

Is this how drugs, for me, came to be associated with comfort?

The association between psychoactive substances, sex, and

liberation – from agitation, from loneliness – seemed organic. Parties and pools. Kissing my pale English boyfriend in the shadows cast by palms among the spotlights. The smell of cannabis in my hair. 'Stairway to Heaven', I remember, was always playing.[28]

LSD had a special cachet. Dropped by a 16-year-old classmate who died after running into a car to escape the spiders she hallucinated crawling all over her arms, acid nonetheless continued being perceived by us as revolutionary. Almost two decades after the Summer of Love, American psychologist and LSD advocate Timothy Leary – like the big, bad wolf, he grinned at me from posters at friends' houses – was still promoting boundaries as toxic.

My panic attacks came later, punctuating decades of free-floating anxiety.

Working as a music journalist in London, I was offered illicit drugs everywhere – cannabis at parties, cocaine in penthouses, heroin in kitchens, MDMA by my fiancé, speed by flatmates. It was cool to get messed up, even cooler to be rendered temporarily psychotic. Two friends were sectioned for Hallucinogen Persisting Perception Disorder. Michael, who abused alcohol, cigarettes, and drugs, died, grotesquely obese, at 38 from a cocaine overdose. There were others. Drugs were a rite of passage, our bulwark against reality. Varying degrees of brain and cardiac damage had been remastered as 'fun'.

A British financial sector worker, dismissing the Prime Minister's campaign against middle-class cocaine use as 'the bleeding obvious', said, 'The risks they chose to take themselves are considerable, yet they still do cocaine. If it came out that I took it I would lose my job, my professional accreditation and my ability to work. Yet I still choose to do it.'[29]

I asked a writer why she described Prozac as wonderful.

'Because I don't feel anything,' she said.

At no point did I wonder why sobriety was experienced by so many as so intolerable that they were prepared to risk psychosis, unemployment and death to escape it. Like everyone else I knew, I lived at a distance from myself. I accepted the precept that detachment is key.

As did my father, who had placed his hand on my breasts.

As did my brother, who gassed himself in a car at the age of 32.

As did Ted Bundy, who decapitated women and performed sex acts on their severed heads.

It was only on giving birth that I realised detachment is a fiction. From between my thighs, a child had emerged, just as I'd emerged from between my mother's thighs and she had from her mother's, all the way back to the dawn of being. The principle of separation on which our culture is based was bullshit.

I loved Bethesda from the first moment I heard her voice, but in the passion I felt for her, disquiet. I wanted to understand why people kill themselves and others, and why drugs have come to seem as ordinary as tap water. I wanted to know why sex is now addressed as little more than recreation, and why anxiety is pandemic. I wanted to know why men are treacherous, and why women seek to silence their hearts. And in the end, I was left with an overriding question: how could my mother, half a century after my birth, concede – coolly, as if noting inclement weather – that no, she'd never really loved me?

Like Eve, I suddenly wanted that apple.

I

HIGH

'The 1960s were the true beginning of the postmodern era.'
Walter Truett Anderson

1. TIMOTHY LEARY'S SEVERED HEAD

'Psychedelics are boom business.'

The Global Drug Survey

There's a lot of talk about the 32 million or so lifetime users of psychedelic drugs in America,[30] never mind those in the rest of the world. At a compound annual growth rate of 12.36 percent, the psychedelic market is projected to reach USD10.75 billion by 2027.[31] Sensing profit, the pharmaceutical giants are paying close attention. In 2019, the Johns Hopkins Medical Center launched the Center for Psychedelic & Consciousness Research, established with USD17 million from a foundation and private benefactors[32] (on the website, an intern poses at the heart of a mandala, its rays emerging from his head). London's Imperial College had pipped them to the post four months earlier,[33] although its centre is significantly smaller.[34]

The primary driver behind this global surge in the consumption of hallucinogens – among them, dimethyltryptamine (DMT), lysergic acid diethylamide (LSD), mescaline, and psilocybin – is, as it is with all psychoactive drug use, the desire to change the way users feel.[35]

And, judging by the numbers, more and more of us don't like the way we feel.

Psychedelics, otherwise known as serotonergic hallucinogens, are a class of psychoactive drugs that spectacularly modify cognitive processes, consciousness, and perception.[36] Popular with the anxious and depressives, who can be desperate to escape feelings they don't understand, and with individuals who've experienced ruptures in intimacy – fractured relationships, loneliness – hallucinogens also appeal to those who seek to escape emotional flatlining.[37]

This unexamined compulsion to 'enhance' experience, to crank it up to the brink of psychosis, is increasingly common. In the 21st century, a benchmark of stimulation must be met: heightened, unnatural.

At the heart of all psychoactive drug use is the yearning to *lose control.*

Wrongly classified as superfluous, hallucinogens and other illicit drugs serve an important cultural purpose. Threats to the abdication of emotional agency they facilitate are thus met with degrees of aggression, from mockery to violence. 'As a sometime coke user since the Nineties, I've felt pangs of conscience at the thought of the trail of bloodshed from beginning to end of the cocaine story,' a British finance sector worker said, '[but] there's a selfishness in society – not just the coke sniffers – that means it's easy to push these things to the back of your mind.'[38]

In particular, the indifference of the middle classes to the global drug trade's human toll reveals the global rise in narcissism and corresponding decline in empathy.[39] [40]

Compassion fade, it seems, is a thing.[41]

In conjunction with the growing epidemic of substance disorders, this increase in narcissism and decrease in empathy has changed the way we mate. Illegal drug abuse, for example, is associated with multiple sexual partners over a short period of time.[42] (A consistent predictor of oral and vaginal sex 'hookup' behaviour among college students is peak intoxication.)[43]

It works the other way, too: there's a 'strong' association between multiple sexual partners and later substance-use disorders, particularly among women,[44] suggesting that those who fuck around have a lot of memories they'd prefer to forget. (Interestingly, hookups involving heterosexual penetrative sex have been shown to increase psychological distress for women, but not for men.)[45]

To Europeans aged 16 to 35, alcohol and drug abuse has 'become an integral part of their strategic approach to sex, locking them into continued use.' Hazards include underage sex, unwanted pregnancies, sexually transmitted diseases,[46] assault, rape, robbery, and the like.

To the young, sex has become synonymous with trauma or the threat of trauma.

Love is no longer associated with sex. As American superstar Lady Gaga sings to an unnamed man in 'Do What U Want', he can't have her heart or mind but can do with her body as he will.[47] In 'Bum Bum', by South African rapper duo Die Antwoord, an unidentified girlfriend of singer Ninja – like all patriarchal male celebrities, he makes a point of emphasising that she is only one of many[48] – leaves the suggestive answering machine message he samples for the song. She tells him that he can fuck her anywhere, because she just doesn't care.[49]

Anywhere, I don't really care.

Gay British comedian Mark Bittlestone, 27, attended a chemsex (drug-fuelled) orgy for the third time on the tenth anniversary of his mother's death and the sixth anniversary of his father's. 'I just wanted to fuck everything up,' he told me during an interview. 'Chemsex orgies are places where you're just pushing your boundaries' – here his voice dropped until it was almost inaudible – 'flirting with sexually transmitted diseases, that kind of thing. The majority of people were on cocaine and crystal meth or G [gamma hydroxybutyrate or GHB], which just massively heightens your senses and makes you massively horny. I had sex with six or seven guys. I felt shocking for a week afterwards, but still had quite a lot of casual sex that week through Grindr. Emotionally I was very low, thinking about my parents.'[50]

Around the world, depression and other mental health issues are on the rise.[51]

These are only some manifestations of the increasing prevalence of emotional detachment, of the severing of the head from the heart. Deep, sustained emotion has been out of vogue since the 1960s, when the way we understood feeling changed forever.

'Emotions are the lowest form of consciousness,' Timothy Leary, then 43 and the detonator of the Psychedelic Revolution, announced on 30 August 1963. The event he addressed, a meeting partly sponsored by the 71st Annual Convention of the American Psychological Association, took place after he was fired from Harvard for lack of scientific rigour in his capacity as a clinical psychologist.[52] Emotional people are not to be trusted, Leary said. Emotions are stupefying, narcotic. The emotional can't think. Even their sensuality is impaired. 'Love', he stressed, is just 'greed and self-enhancing gluttony based on fear.'[53]

Greed and self-enhancing gluttony based on fear.

Leary's solution to the epidemic of emotion was lysergic acid diethylamide, otherwise known as acid or LSD. Its 'great kick', he said, is 'relief from emotional pressure.'[54]

With four words, Leary had defined the new parameters of humanity.

Leary, with all the evangelical zeal of his Catholic boyhood, reframed hallucinogens from a means of avoiding the awareness of suffering to a shamanic insurrection: a revolt against culturally enforced spiritual deadening. As propaganda, his take was powerful. American academic Louis Menand noted that even the language of 1960s commercial culture was, in part, shaped by Leary's mutiny against the status quo: 'Almost everything advertised itself as the moral, legal, and sensory equivalent of a drug experience, from pop music to evangelism.'[55]

LSD was, by Leary, glamourised through association with the young and beautiful – and, critically, with the alleged enhancement of sexuality. The era of pharmaceuticalised sexuality had begun. No longer the ultimate symbol of union, sex was remastered as a self-referential, politicised, and fundamentally intellectual event pivoting on drug use. Basically, a more sociable take on masturbation. Hallucinogens eliminated the need to court a partner, to care for them, or even to find them especially attractive. Human evolution was turned on its head.

Through Leary, sex became understood as a form of eroticised infotainment.

'Compared with sex under LSD,' Leary said, 'the way you've been making love – no matter how ecstatic the pleasure you think you get from it – is like making love to a department-store-window dummy.'[56] The appeal of such a statement to the children of the bereaved and emotionally distorted postwar generation was profound. En masse, the disordered and vulnerable were captivated by Leary's messianic intensity. This was the hawking of salvation. Dionysus versus Apollo! Power to the people! Drop acid, not bombs!

In himself, Leary was the zeitgeist.

Leary needed public figures to legitimise his mission. To this end, he asked seminal Beat poet Allen Ginsburg to participate in the Harvard Psilocybin Project. Ginsberg, who for years had anaesthetised himself with illicit psychedelics – ayahuasca, the toxic datura, mescaline, opiates, and peyote among them – was elated. His interest in altered states was, he said, founded on the desire to recover a feeling he'd lost, 'a series of mystical experiences – connected with Blake.'[57] The 'lost feeling' in question, however, was unrelated to Blake; that which the sensitive, damaged Ginsberg sought to recover was the transcendence of maternal/child intimacy disrupted by his mother's psychosis.

Like Leary, Ginsberg recoiled from the 'moralistic class attitudes'[58] that defined his aberrant parent as dysfunctional. And, again like Leary, he rationalised his drug use as 'visionary'.

Emotionally, Ginsberg had always had a lot to metabolise. His mother Naomi, a politically radical Jewish Russian immigrant and paranoid suicidal schizophrenic, had been intermittently institutionalised throughout his childhood, sometimes for years. Naomi both loved and fatally distorted her son; Ginsberg, later institutionalised himself for psychosis, was a member of the pro-paedophilia North American Man-Boy Love Association.[59] At 21 and on medical advice, he had authorised his mother's lobotomy.[60] He would never forgive himself.

> 'One hand stiff – heaviness of forties & menopause reduced by one heart stroke, lame now – wrinkles – a scar on her head, the lobotomy – ruin, the hand dipping downwards to death'.[61]

American psychoanalyst Janet Hadda wrote that Ginsberg 'identified with the insane lawlessness of his mother as well as her anti-establishment politics.' His aversion to emotional equilibrium was, she continued, driven by 'the desperate wish that Naomi's behaviour be a sign of health.'[62] Ginsberg not only took psychedelics to escape his terror of – and guilt of having destroyed – his mother, but therein to find or conjure a logic that justified her abuse.

Like Ginsberg, British novelist Aldous Huxley, a founding board member of Leary's Harvard Psilocybin Project, lost his mother more than once – the first time when he was enrolled in a 'brutally philistine' preparatory boarding school at the age of nine, and then, suddenly and conclusively, to cancer when he was 14. He lost most of his sight to keratitis for two or so years two years later and then his brother to suicide four years after that.[63] The onslaught of loss would have been paralysing, and Huxley also became preoccupied with hallucinogens in mid-life.

As he wrote in 1954, 'Most men and women lead lives at the worst so painful, at the best so monotonous, poor and limited that the urge to escape, the longing to transcend themselves if only for a few moments, is and has always been one of the principal appetites of the soul.'[64]

In *The Doors of Perception*, Huxley's seminal meditation on hallucinogens, he documented the emotional entombment known to all children prematurely individuated through separation from a parent: 'The martyrs go hand in hand into the arena; they are crucified alone. Embraced, the lovers desperately try to fuse their insulated ecstasies into a single self-transcendence; in vain. By its very nature every embodied spirit is doomed to suffer and enjoy in solitude ... in certain cases communication between universes is incomplete or even nonexistent.'[65]

The doors that had been closed to Huxley were not those of perception, but of love.

Huxley believed that he began experimenting with psilocybin in order 'to retrieve some unspecified childhood memory',[66] but what he really sought was the reestablishment of 'communication between universes': a dialogue with his deceased – that is, inaccessible – mother. As with Ginsberg and Leary, the masculine and feminine principles in Huxley's life had been disconnected. He masked the resulting depression with reserve and intellectual rigour:

> *Wearied of its own turning,*
> *Distressed with its own busy restlessness,*
> *Yearning to draw the circumferent pain –*
> *The rim that is dizzy with speed –*
> *To the motionless centre, there to rest,*
> *The wheel must strain through agony*
> *On agony contracting, returning*
> *Into the core of steel.*[67]

More like Leary in this respect, American 'gonzo' writer Hunter S. Thompson compensated for his yearning for transcendence with an array of patriarchal props: the guns, the motorcycles, the cigar clenched between his teeth. He and Leary met only once: in 1987 for a presentation, 'Children of the Sixties, Relics of the Eighties'.[68]

In an anthology of his journalism, Thompson uses the expression 'head full' in relation to drugs, acid in particular, 11 times – 'a head full of mescaline', 'a head full of acid', 'a head full of jimson weed',[69] and so on – suggesting that feeling obliterated by powerful drugs was important to him, a story he felt compelled to emphasise.

Like that of all users, Thompson's drug hunger was only superficially driven by hedonism. '*I was getting too nervous to continue without chemical assistance,*' he wrote. 'I reached under the seat for my kit bag, which contained five or six spansules of Black Acid. Wonderful, I thought. This is just what I need [italics mine].'[70] In the same anthology, he uses the word 'nervous' 59 times; in *Fear and Loathing in Las Vegas*, he uses the word 'nervous' 30 times.

Thompson used psychedelics and other drugs to temper unusually high levels of anxiety.

Like Ginsberg, Huxley and Leary, he'd lost the parent he deeply loved during his adolescence. Thompson was 14 when his father died an 'agonizingly slow' death from myasthenia gravis, a progressive neurological disorder.[71] His librarian mother, who terrified him – 'I gotta get out of her way!'[72] – reacted to the loss by becoming a 'heavy drinker', leaving him with three models of self-regulation: literature, substance abuse, and death. To Thompson, LSD was the 'King Drug',[73] and while he thought cannabis made people 'stupid', he 'loved' it as 'a source of joy and comfort.' The subtext was uncomplicated: like his mother, Thompson did not find joy and comfort in people. Undiluted attachment felt unnatural; he just didn't understand it.

At the age of 67 and after a long depression, Thompson put a gun to his head and shot himself.

Like all those who regularly use hallucinogens, Ginsberg, Huxley, Leary, and Thompson, arguably the Psychedelic Revolution's intellectual frontline, were comforted by disintegration. Psychedelics allowed them to partition consciousness, to obscure feelings they didn't have the skills to metabolise. And by politicising their drug use, these men legitimised it.

American novelist Tom Robbins never concerned himself with causes, preferring the poetry of symptoms. In the introduction to one of Leary's books, he recalled the political activism of the 1960s as 'connected, directly or indirectly, to the ingestion of psychedelic drugs.' Political fires, he wrote, were 'kindled by the friction of latter-day ecstasy cults rubbing up against the stiff hide of the old iguana-brained Establishment.'[74] Iguana: ugly, primitive, a remnant of the Late Cretaceous. Latter-day ecstasy cults: four words summoning saints and the Dionysian mysteries, euphoria.

The friction of juxtaposition is always beguiling: old versus young, staid versus wild. Here Robbins was playing angels' advocate, pitting the bestial against the celestial. In reducing a complex situation to a high-concept movie pitch, he was speaking the language of the late 20th century. As spins go, it was sexy – presenting LSD as a secret handshake of sorts, an initiation into esoteric wisdom: instant enlightenment, available from all good dealers.

Leary, who made a point of associating LSD with ecstatic states, seconded the motion, clarifying that the new goals were 'to support, nurture, teach, protect individual freedom.'[75]

This was, of course, nonsense. The beads and platitudes were distractions. Leary's brave new world was based on a patriarchal narcissism more virulent than that of its predecessors. British social historian Virginia Nicholson noted that the 'permissive society' evolved from the hostility that energised it, 'transforming it, by the end of the decade, from a flimsy sideshow into a barnstorming psychedelic circus.'[76] The relationship between the two eras was only superficially antagonistic; they honoured the same Abrahamic gender template.

Superficially spurred by concern for the communal soul, Leary's disparagement of 'squares' – the uncool, the unhip – only enforced the divisiveness necessary for the regeneration of dysregulation: the oldest of patriarchal tricks. Ideological opponents were damned by Leary as 'impotent', 'pious do-gooders',[77] and 'sub-human mongoloid monstrosit[ies]'.[78]

Inciting outrage is also a form of dysregulation, a comforting state to those raised in chaos – Leary, say, who was the son of a rigidly Roman Catholic mother and a disordered Army officer,[79] and whose life was defined by the re-creation of the substance-use-centred chaos into which he was born.

Known as 'Tote', Leary's father Timothy, formerly of the US Dental Corps, was a philandering suburban dentist whose alcoholism destroyed his career and family. Partial to 'three-day benders', Tote would beat Leary[80] and 'drink until he passed out, wake up, and then begin drinking again'.[81] Leary recalled that in 'training me for future life he often told me that Prohibition was bad but not as bad as no booze at all.'[82]

Tote abandoned his family when Leary was 13. He wouldn't see his son again for 23 years.

Like Ginsberg, Leary remained obsessed with the parent who had abandoned him, and – again like Ginsberg – sought to justify this abandonment in adulthood by attributing noble intentions to his emotionally dislocated parent. His father, he wrote, had, unlike his mother, never 'stunted' him with expectations; instead, he was a masterful 'disdainer of the conventional way'.[83]

For Leary, these associations – between masculinity and promiscuity, masculinity and substance abuse, masculinity and duplicity, abandonment of the feminine, relinquishment of responsibility, and the indifferent generation of chaos – would prove indelible, and he would promote these behaviours to generations of vulnerable men as the evolved ideal.

The feminine, at its highest octave, had no significance for Leary outside its service to the masculine; whether in a practical, sexual or ornamental capacity, it was secondary.

Up to the end of his mother's life and irrespective of his own turmoil, Leary continued to deceive her. His belief that the feminine was to be flattered and manipulated reflected his refusal to accept gender parity. Leary charmed women with talk of their tutelary importance to him – they were idols, teachers. Rather than caring, he mined women for sexual information, emphasising, with sophomoric hyperbole, the 'love' they inspired. Women were 'God',[84] his daughter was an 'elvish flower',[85] his third wife was a 'shining Nordic princess',[86] and so on.

Privately, his take was, like that of Spanish artist Pablo Picasso, exclusively carnal. Leary perceived the feminine in terms of oedipal appetite: all lactation and lasciviousness. He described one woman as having 'creamy white' legs;[87] another as having 'creamy skin';[88] and another as having a 'milky white' thigh.[89] His first wife, too, had 'creamy skin',[90] and his fourth wife revealed 'a strip of creamy smooth belly'.[91] His mother was, of course, the 'milky-soft white'- skinned prototype:[92] Leary wrote of his 'slim, serpent body sputtering with pleasure' as it was 'eased' into the 'soft, creamy home' of her body at conception.[93]

With Tote gone, Leary thought he feared being consumed by his mother, but the truth was that he was terrified by his infantile appetite for her nurturance. He recalled reading the Old Testament, 'burningly aware of the fundamentalist erection in [his] trousers,' while she 'beamed approval'. She would not, however, 'get control' of his 'precious bodily fluids'.[94]

Leary's romantic template was, like his father's, characterised by abandonment, exploitation, impulsiveness, objectification, and transgression. His first wife, the mother of his first two children, committed suicide after he refused to stop sleeping with his mistress ('Lust is such a powerful thing,' he rationalised. 'You forget how compelling it is').[95] His second marriage – to his mistress – ended after Leary punched her in the face.[96] His third marriage, to a younger, aristocratic Austrian model, tanked during the drug-fuelled honeymoon.[97] Typically, Leary reframed the latter failure to fit his shamanic brand: 'We had time-travelled through a few mythic incarnations, played out mythical dramas in panoramic realms.'[98]

At various points throughout his sexual experiences, both paid and unpaid, Leary married five times. Like Bundy, he was an advocate of the severed head, if achieved through different means: rather than a hacksaw, Leary used LSD to separate women from their agency, and each new convert amplified his sense of gender mastery.

Substances facilitate masculine gender mastery. Disabling targets with drugs in the guise of liberation, he was simultaneously able to control their perceptions of him and to access their otherwise protected bodies. No longer 'a high-domed, chicken-plucked, moose-faced baldpate stranger',[99] Leary was, through drugs, repackaged as a god, able to alter reality through the sacrament of pharmaceutical communion. This illusion served him, too. As Bobby Gillespie, the lead singer of Scottish band Primal Scream, sang in the song *Higher Than the Sun*, hallucinogens made him feel beautiful.[100]

To be seen as beautiful, it was thus critical for Leary to destabilise all those around him with substances. 'There is only one way, however, that a tribal group of this sort can exist and survive,' he wrote. 'They must take plenty of dope … they gotta smoke it. You've got to have that liberating sacrament, otherwise the energy gets static … and it's got to be pretty regular, or people freeze. Robot plastic people develop. People get uptight. There are always problems and emotions.'[101]

Clarity, as Leary knew, made people dangerous.

In the footage from his third wedding, Leary is rigid, slim, unprepossessing, his voice constricted. His alert geniality is betrayed by the tension in his jaw. Beneath the patina of psychedelic cool, Leary is the uptight middle-aged robotic adversary against whom he railed. In contrast, his fashion model bride and her bridesmaids are drugged and silent on the floor: near-statuary, internalised. At the last moment and still tripping, the bride brushes back her veil and smiles with difficulty.[102] No joy, only affectation.

Typical of its time, the tableau is one of the ornamental feminine incapacitated by the masculine.

The backdrop to the ideological putsch of the 1960s is widely misunderstood. However profitable, Hollywood's take on the 1950s as an era of saccharine naiveté was inaccurate. Marked by patriarchal brutality, the fifties were, in fact, futuristic in scope. Extraterrestrials and monsters captured the public imagination. Wrongly attributed to Cold War paranoia, this trend revealed unexamined anxieties about alienation and aversion. British critic Neil Badmington wrote that alien narratives depended 'upon a set of simple binary suppositions – above all, human versus inhuman, us versus them, and real versus fake.'[103]

Over the decade following the 1945 acceptance of penicillin as the treatment of choice for syphilis,[104] related deaths fell by 95 percent. The subsequent shift in behaviour was rapid, meaning that the sexual revolution in fact took place in the 1950s, a period during which most measures of sexual behaviour – including the high-risk – soared.[105]

American publisher Hugh Hefner's *Playboy*, the first mass-market pornographic magazine, was a byproduct of the pharmaceutical breakthrough, and served as the mouthpiece of the new consciousness. Founded in 1953, Playboy Inc. was, by 2000, worth a billion dollars.[106] Sex became a staple theme of popular music,[107] the soundtrack to what American sociologist James Coleman called 'the adolescent society'.

In 1955, the antipsychotic chlorpromazine, described as a 'chemical lobotomy', was introduced to the US under the trade name Thorazine. This was the genesis of the billion-dollar 'psychopharmacological revolution'[108] that flipped the understanding of human being from an emotional and then spiritual experience to the sum of biochemistry. Like his peers, Leary was processed by an educational system that addressed emotions as so much biochemical flummery. The possibility that feelings – even love, that gussied-up excuse for greed and gluttony – could alter biochemistry would not be entertained for years.

In the interim, there were further detonations of the status quo.

American biologist and heiress Katharine Dexter McCormick, a reproductive rights pioneer whose mother had been a Suffragette, provided 'almost every single dollar' required to develop the ideological equivalent of the atom bomb.[109] Enovid, the first contraceptive pill, was approved for North American use as a form of birth control in 1960;[110] it had previously been used for 'disturbances of menstruation'.[111] Initially perceived by men as the golden ticket to erotic freedom, the Pill was, in fact, the greatest blow in history to the stewardship of the feminine by the masculine.

An urgent revolutionary approach to the restoration of patriarchal dominance was thus required, and LSD, the favoured drug of the hallucinogenic renaissance over half a century later, became its spearhead.

2. FRAGMENTATION

'Things fall apart; the centre cannot hold.'
'The Second Coming', William Butler Yeats

Appropriately, perhaps, there is no sense of ownership over the memory of my only acid trip. It floats, oddly isolated, at a distance from the rest of my life.

Late on an afternoon in midsummer, in a room with drifting curtains, I lay in bed with my boyfriend. We may have been naked, I can't recall. High, indifferent and bodiless, I entered the blue panes of his eyes and therein saw, as I flew, a rapidly unrolling landscape beneath me – cities, fields and deserts, mountains, seas. This language – that of earth and light and water – was a code I'd suddenly cracked. *I understand everything now*, I said, less interested in my boyfriend than the way my voice no longer seemed to be related to me. Like a child with a glass pressed to the wall, I heard myself begin to read his future in the topography, and as I did, his face, lucid with perspiration, unfurled into that of another man, a woman, a blue-green bird.

If anything, acid lessened his significance until there was nothing left of him at all.

In telling a friend of this experience, I was surprised when he reacted with wonderment. To me, the memory is hollow. Leary promised 'an overwhelming awakening' and a 'release of potent, primal energies',[112] but I experienced no such things. Instead, a fragmentation that brought me no closer to any god I recognised. The trip was just a dream – ephemeral, immersive: neurochemical daytime television. Unclouded, my head had no such parameters.

I was never sufficiently bored to do it again.

Maybe the degree of insight and wonder experienced on acid is dependent on the degree of inhibition, I don't know. For all its charm, my acid trip was less than inconsequential; I had a more engaging experience wearing a VR headset on the Dr Archibald Master of Time ride at London's Hyde Park Winter Wonderland,

I think because on removing the headset, I became aware that we weren't, in fact, sliding down the neck of a genial brontosaurus but rolling down and up an uneven intestinal assortment of rickety rails in a cart.

The discrepancy between the shimmering world in the headset and the dangers posed by that creaking machinery – in 2017, there were 43,405 fairground-related injuries in America alone[113] – is an important metaphor in relation to hallucinogens.

Tripping with his second wife, Timothy Leary reported – as I had with my boyfriend – how 'her face began to melt and change. I saw her as a young girl, as a baby, as an old woman with grey hair and seamy, wrinkled face. I saw her as a witch, a Madonna, a nagging crone, a radiant queen, a Byzantine virgin, a tired, worldly-wise Oriental whore who had seen every sight of life repeated a thousand times. She was all women.'[114]

The issue of Leary's stock pantomime character take on femininity – crones, queens and whores – is secondary to that of his celebration of depersonalisation. Through LSD, his wife was literally de-faced, reduced to a screen upon which he projected his own fantasies of womanhood, a cipher with no meaning beyond that which he attributed to her.

Lost in this interiorised experience in which his wife was broken into unthreatening subsidiary formats – arrangements of atoms, colours, and so on – Leary, with no loss of masculine status, was able to avoid the vulnerability of sober lovemaking and, critically, to avoid being confronted by the formidable wholeness of a woman. His interactions with women were, throughout his adulthood, characterised by the same unwillingness to address their completeness. The feminine had to be fractured into manageable components – not as literally as Bundy broke down his victims, but emotionally, mentally, and spiritually.

'Unity requires ecstatic self-sacrifice,' Leary, who was known for never sacrificing anything he valued, wrote. 'Loss of ego brings fright to the unprepared. The fragmentation of form into waves can bring the most terrible fear known to man.'[115]

The idea was self-erasure in the service of a higher power – that is to say, himself.

LSD transformed Leary's wife into all women and in that, any woman – reduced to a set of chromosomes and secondary sexual characteristics, razed of history, affect and context. Like my ex-boyfriend, she became an *idea*. LSD, then, relieves the responsibilities of attachment. The focus is no longer on the partner, but on the mesmerising amplification and distortion of perception of the partner.

Stripped of her right to be acknowledged not as *representative* of femininity, as sex workers are, Leary's wife was denied acknowledgment as an individual warranting devoted, customised responsiveness. No longer human, she presented as a pinball machine of sorts, an entertainment centre he could utilise.

Without acid, a woman was always in danger of being demoted by Leary from a 'luminescent sun, radiating amused intelligence, surrounded by magnetic fields bristling with phosphorescent radar scanners and laser-defenses'[116] to just another 'department-store-window dummy'.[117]

Simultaneously conceding that 'nobody quite understands' the impact of hallucinogens and clearly advocating their use nonetheless, American writer Michael Pollan said they 'appear to diminish activity in one very important brain network called the default mode network [which] is very involved with operations having to do with our sense of self: how we integrate what's happening to us in any given moment, with our abiding sense of who we are. The interesting thing about psychedelics, both LSD and psilocybin – the ingredient in magic mushrooms – is that they take this network offline. When that happens, you have this sensation of ego-dissolution: that your self is evaporating.'[118]

In 1973, the Australian poet Michael Dransfield, who had for years abused cannabis, heroin and LSD, died in the hospital of my birth, the Mater Misericordiae in North Sydney. His death was the result of 'a self-administered injection of an unknown substance'.[119] In the poem 'Island', Dransfield wrote of his wavering sense of self, a thing so ephemeral that he slipped into death through the eye of a needle six or so months before his 25th birthday:

> there is no real thing.
> none of these things is real.
> he takes another book from the shelf,
> glances, puts it aside, jabs a
> needle in his

arm, listens to the wireless, kills it
with a touch.
there is no real thing.
he rises, and the face of the mirror empties.[120]

The relationship Dransfield so gracefully depicts – that between identity, nurturance, substance abuse, and territoriality – is symbiotic. As the sense of identity is dissolved by LSD, so is ownership of the self and with it, the desire to care for the self, for how can one own or care for something that doesn't exist?

In the last song he composed for British psychedelic music pioneers Pink Floyd and prior to his LSD-triggered mental collapse and permanent retreat from the public eye, Syd Barrett, co-founder of the band, expressed the same fatal sense of dissociation, writing that he was obliged to others for making it clear that he didn't really exist.[121] In 1967, he had written 'Vegetable Man', a song that made his increasing detachment and alienation clear.[122] After years of drug-facilitated estrangement from reality, Barrett eventually lost his moorings, responding nonsensically to questions and situations.[123]

The limited experiential range authorised by Leary and his psychedelic cohorts – desire, pleasure, and so on – was, in itself, a demand for abstraction, whether that abstraction was achieved through a mental collapse, the use of psychoactive substances, or suicide; that which he called 'emotional pressure' (grief, jealousy, rage and other byproducts of love or its absence) would, to the emotionally impaired, otherwise be unendurable.

Like Leary, Ginsberg, Huxley and Thompson, Barrett had never come to terms with the loss of a parent in his teens.[124]

As Dransfield's poem makes clear, his own sense of dissociation was a constant: *there is no real thing.* The life-sustaining sense of vitality Dransfield could not access had been diverted – put aside, like the book, and silenced, like the wireless – until his life felt like a variation on the theme of death. This inability to metabolise emotion is fundamental to addiction.

If only temporarily, psychoactive substances serve to further divide a consciousness threatened by integration. In this respect, the use of cannabis and tobacco is revealing. The exhalation of smoke suggests a conflagration within, and the reactive narrowing of the eyes is also characteristic of anger. It can thus be said that cannabis relieves the tension created by the stifling of rage, a hypothesis supported by its link to the expressions 'cool' and 'chill': to cool down, to douse the flames. Similarly, the reference to the impact of cannabis as a 'high' suggests that the baseline human state is now understood as deflated or low.

Far from an assertion of the revolutionary spirit, then, cannabis extinguishes the grandeur of the emotional self.

A trope of rock star / rebel portraiture is the artist – emaciated or limp, disempowered and with dulled eyes – photographed exhaling cigarette or cannabis smoke: visual shorthand for the rebel's anger and its suppression. Joan Didion, whose 'elitist allure'[125] established her as the custodian of literary 'cool', was often photographed with a cigarette in hand, even while holding her adopted infant daughter – visual shorthand for both her tightly controlled anger and refusal to submit to low-status mammalian attachment.

British photographer Michael Cooper's iconic 1967 shot of Stones guitarist and former heroin addict Keith Richards is another well-known example. Weighed down by jewellery, dishevelled, with his eyes averted and smoking kif (cannabis) through a sebsi (pipe) while holding a burning cigarette, Richards is depicted as simultaneously angry, crushed, dependent, fragile, isolated, and self-important, unable to function without multiple crutches: a motherless man-child.

Barrett, too, was an 'enormous' tripper and smoker.[126] Emotionally castrated by cannabis, hallucinogens and other drugs, he, Ginsberg, Huxley, Leary and Thompson were thus able to avoid both the disabling grief of having lost a parent, and the humiliating fact that, like babies, they were *unable to regulate their own emotions*.

Natural human consciousness was disparaged by Leary as not merely inferior to being high, but as a prison; in reality, the 'expansion' he hawked was a denial of the animal self and its needs, further masking truths revealed by undrugged or unmodified awareness – anxiety, anguish, vulnerability, and so on.

At core, the Psychedelic Revolution was reactionary, a brightly coloured prison. In dividing the self, it reinforced the ultimate Abrahamic shame: that of being human.

The hallucinogen-facilitated dismantling of the self can derail users. 'I had an extremely bad trip that left me on the psych floor for three days,' a 19-year-old woman wrote in February 2021. 'After I was released I was just fine at first, then I started to experience extreme anxiety, depersonalisation, derealisation and disassociation … next thing I know I'm having the scariest dream of my life which seemed incredibly real: my chest was twisted like a wind-up toy and a bag was placed over my head like I was suffocated, two voices talked and said my birthday and name and release her back out, and "tell everyone what you saw" … I feel weird looking out of my eyes, I feel weird being myself like I've sort of lost my identity and sense of self. Everything scares me, being outside in the dark, being in the car in the dark, driving, phone vibrations and noises, thumbs up, like literally there's a correlation everywhere.'[127]

I feel weird being myself.

The retired American LSD manufacturer Rhoney Gissen Stanley, mother of LSD kingpin Owsley Stanley's son Starfinder, also lost herself over a summer of tripping. 'I was nothing. This vision scared me. I felt replaceable. Anyone could be me. The LSD experience of oneness dominated, the consciousness that I was that and that I was and we were indistinct from one another … My self had shattered like an exploding star, and I was afraid.'[128]

I felt replaceable.

American writer Tom Wolfe, describing an Owsley Stanley trip, documented the same dissociation: 'The world began fragmenting on him. It began coming totally to pieces, breaking into component parts … molecule by molecule now … He lost his skin, his skeleton, his pulmonary veins … dissolving into gaseous nothingness until finally he was down to one cell. *One human cell*: his; that was all that was left of the entire known world, and if he lost control of that one cell, there would be nothing left. The world would be, like, *over.*'[129]

Scion of American 'bluegrass political royalty', Stanley was the world's biggest producer and distributor of LSD. Known as 'the acid impresario', he was said to have manufactured the purest LSD to ever hit the streets,[130] arming the psychedelic revolution with millions of tabs from his apartment-laboratory.[131] His father, an alcoholic lawyer, was, as Stanley confided to Leary during a private dinner, 'dead before he died'.[132]

Statistically, the rate of parental alcohol use disorder for those institutionalised for LSD psychosis has been found to 'far exceed' that for the general population,[133] suggesting that the love of enlightenment or hedonism cited by those partial to tripping may, for many, be no more than a veil for trauma – in essence, a status-preserving fiction.

The fevered pursuit of fragmentation tells a dark story, one of emotional incohesion.

Eight when his parents separated, Stanley was moved by his mother from Virginia to California. Unable to cope with his anger, she returned him after three years to his alcoholic father, who, also unable to cope, enrolled him in a military academy 40 miles from the family home. At the age of 15, Stanley was admitted as a voluntary patient to a psychiatric institution. A few months into his stay, his mother suffered a fatal coronary. Stanley, in adulthood, said that he 'sorted out' his 'guilt problems' in relation to her death with psychiatrists, concluding that both his parents were simply 'assholes'.[134]

Despite this absolution, Stanley, like his 'asshole' father, spent much of his life aggressively disrupting the threatening natural flow of feeling and perception with substances, and promoting – or facilitating – emotional/physical disengagement as a lifestyle.

While neither sex is permitted emotional integration in a patriarchal culture, it's the masculine that benefits from the disintegration of the feminine. This principle characterised Picasso's most iconic works, paintings in which women were only permitted to exist in the fragments he made of them. The women he mutilated on canvas were branded – as I was by Nick Cave – as *recreated* by him. Art, to Picasso, was a means of breaking down the feminine.

In this spirit, prewar German Surrealist Hans Bellmer, known as the 'father of modern sex dolls', told an interviewer, 'I tried to arrange the sexual elements of a girl's body like a sort of plastic anagram. I remember describing it thus: the body is like a sequence that invites us to rearrange it, so that its real meaning comes clear through the series of endless anagrams.'[135]

That is, the feminine, by definition, is an invitation to the masculine to distort or dismember it; without that distortion or dismemberment, the feminine has no 'real meaning'. Bellmer's words also reinforced the ancient perception of the feminine as unfinished, and of the masculine as the force designed to 'complete' it.

Seventeenth-century English philosopher John Locke explained the relationship between such 'rearrangements' and property: 'The labour of his body, and the work of his hands, we may say, are properly his.'[136] In short, it is through the process of dismemberment, whether literal or symbolic, that the feminine can be reconfigured and owned, as Bellmer, Bundy and Picasso instinctively understood.

Even in the non-Abrahamic Buddhist context, the 'rearrangement' of the feminine body served to reinforce masculine gender status. American professor of comparative religion Elizabeth Wilson explained that 'the spectacle of the mutilated woman serves to display the power of the Buddha, the king of the Truth (Dharma) over Mara, the lord of the Realm of Desire ... *By erasing the sexual messages conveyed by the bodies of attractive women through the horrific spectacle of mutilation, the superior power of the king of Dharma is made manifest* [italics mine].'[137]

LSD was a means of achieving the same mutilation.

Through acid, people were separated from the experience of being human and its related attachments – to context, to others, to their own bodies. Love became an *idea* – generalised, intellectualised. Sufficiently fragmented, every human being becomes inhuman – hydrogen, carbon, nitrogen, and so on – but LSD taught people to celebrate, and define themselves through, this understanding of *inhumanity as their matrix*. A critical transference of ownership was taking place. Even children no longer belonged to their mothers, but to the 'silent, whirling play of forces'.[138]

As Leary promised, LSD would free man from the pain of his animal self.

The British rock writer Ben Marshall, who has documented his illicit drug consumption, ranging from crack to crystal meth and heroin, had the same experience. He first dropped acid at the age of 13, wandering through London tripping with schoolmates, and has since 'done acid fuckin' loads of times,' adding, 'I'd always do two tabs at a time, not one.'

Marshall, raised in one of the most violent areas of south London in the late 1960s and 1970s, told me during an interview that with 'the right amount of psilocybin or acid, you experience an extreme loss of ego. You no longer exist. Which is why people on LSD are capable of sawing off their own feet. You no longer care about yourself because there is no self to care *for*. You think, *I am purely a construct, an idea of me devised for me or by me*.'[139]

Marshall's cavalier consumption of hallucinogens, amphetamines and opiates throughout his life is, in part, a byproduct of the psychedelic revolution; on some level, he perceived identity and its protection as a failing.

Attachment, Leary said, was primitive but narcotic, which is why the elimination of boundaries had to be incentivised through an association with pleasure. 'You must be ready to accept the possibility that there is a limitless range of awareness for which we now have no words; that awareness can expand beyond range of your ego, your self, your familiar identity, beyond everything you have learned, beyond your notions of space and time,' he wrote. 'Exquisite, intense, pulsating sensations of unity and love will be felt; the negative counterpart is feelings of attachment, greed, isolation and bodily concerns.'[140]

In fragmentation, wholeness: doublespeak at its finest.

The Psychedelic Revolution was not responsible for the cultural shift towards depersonalisation, but accelerated it. Implicit in the fragmentation of reality, the same lack of fidelity to form and function Picasso's work presaged, particularly in relation to the feminine.

This faithlessness to the essential nature of a thing became a prison in itself.

By decontextualising sexuality in particular, by disconnecting it from its cultural rhythms and behavioural safeguards – the emotionally protective processes of courtship and commitment – Leary was, ironically, upholding a tradition of devaluing the feminine through the administration of substances. No longer warranting emotional, intellectual or financial investment, sexual intimacy was now 'free', severed from its bonding and reproductive purposes.

Thus abstracted, sex became compartmentalised. Outside its amplification of gender status, it came to be understood by the masculine as a reflex as meaningless and isolated as the acid trip of my late teens, to be indulged in at whim, and without repercussions: an oasis of dopamine for neurologically disordered men.

3. COOL

'Pretty little 16-year-old middle-class chick comes to the Haight
to see what it's all about & gets picked up by a 17-year-old street
dealer who spends all day shooting her full of speed again &
again, then feeds her 3,000 mikes [of acid] & raffles off her
temporarily unemployed body for the biggest Haight Street
gangbang since the night before last.'

Chester Anderson quoted by Joan Didion in *Slouching towards Bethlehem*

Sexual abuse, rape and domestic violence were so common in
the 1960s as to be unremarkable. In Britain, unmarried women
weren't protected by the Domestic Violence Act,[141] and marital rape
only became illegal in 1991.[142] The late British artist Duggie Fields
recalled Syd Barrett physically picking up his girlfriend and 'just
flinging her across the room because she wanted to stay in bed …
And it was, "No, that's my bed", and just literally throwing her. No
one reprimanded him.'[143] As the Rolling Stones sang in the lead-up
to the Summer of Love, the way women behaved was up to men.[144]

Violence against women was widely trivialised. The Crystals,
a chart-topping American girl group, released a song in 1962 that
included the lyrics, 'He hit me / And it felt like a kiss. / He hit me / And
I knew he loved me.'[145] In 1965, even famously 'nice' British superstars
the Beatles released 'Run for Your Life', which – incongruously –
included the lines, 'Well, I'd rather see you dead, little girl / Than to
be with another man.'[146] And American superstar Jimi Hendrix, in
the 1971 hit Hey Joe, sang, 'I'm going down to shoot my old lady /
You know, I've caught her messin' around with another man.'[147]

Women were abused for pleasure, out of anger, and as an
assertion of gender status.

In his 1968 autobiography, Eldridge Cleaver, the American
rapist who, for a time, led the Black Panthers, reframed rape as
righteous: 'To refine my technique and modus operandi, I started
out by practicing on black girls' (clearly, the rapist's equivalent of
test dummies). Once sufficiently 'smooth', he 'crossed the tracks

and sought out white prey.'

Cleaver documented his 'delight' at the prospect of 'trampling upon the white man's law, upon his system of values, and that I was defiling his women.' The latter was, for him, the most 'satisfying', an act of vindication in the name of all the black women mistreated by white men.[148]

Literary critics failed to point out the incongruity of a rapist who'd used black women as target practice citing their abuse at the hands of whites to justify his later rapes. Fact is, Cleaver raped women, black and white, *because he could*. Without a thought for the numberless girls and women whose lives he had marred or destroyed, he later 'took a long look at myself and, for the first time in my life, admitted that I was wrong, that I had gone astray … I lost my self-respect. *My pride as a man dissolved* [italics mine].'[149]

The sting, for Cleaver, didn't lie in his sexual brutality, but dented gender status.

The Guardian described his prose as 'revealing a tenderness of the highest literary order'.[150]

In countercultural circles, the sexual violence – in the guise of erotic latitude – was pronounced. The 'evolved' feminine behavioural template entailed perpetual availability to the masculine. British memoirist Jenny Diski remembered that it was 'uncool' to say no. 'It was difficult to come up with a justification for refusing to have sex with someone that didn't seem selfish. The idea that rape was having sex with someone who didn't want to do it didn't apply very much in the late Sixties … I was raped several times.'[151]

The same phenomenon was noted by American cartoonist Trina Robbins: 'Quite a few of the girls were teenage runaways, and [artist Vito Paulekas] and his friend, Carl Franzoni, had an easy time convincing them that sex was healthy, especially sex with Vito and Carl. Vito was in his fifties and Carl was no kid, either … The new sexual freedom I had believed in was a lie: women were simply providers of free sex, and it was uncool to ask for commitment.'[152]

American therapist Ilene English experienced it as violation. 'Free love, they called it. Sex wasn't … a big deal … But actually, in my heart of hearts, it was still a big deal, because I could often be found in the bathtub afterwards, trying desperately to feel clean again.' She concluded that free love 'was really about men satisfying their own needs.'[153]

Free love was a metaphor for internal fragmentation, the *decree nisi* between anima and animus. Facilitated by pornography, hallucinogens and other substances, this lack of integration – of care, of discrimination, of emotional focus – in relation to the sexual became the norm. Many men were open about their motivations. American writer Peter Coyote, a founder of the Diggers, a radical community action group, said, 'I was interested in two things: overthrowing the government and fucking. They went together seamlessly.'[154] American writer Charles W. Slack, a friend of Leary's, described the era as a time of '[f]ree-love communes, group-marriage farm families and big-city tenement crash-pads, non-marriages of all kinds, countless varieties of *ménages à trois, quatre, cinq* and up.'[155]

Intimacy was no longer assumed to be the fulcrum of sex – the opposite, in fact; eroticism and intimacy became understood as mutually hostile. Leary's representation stuck: love was a pathogen cured by the liberal administration of cannabis and hallucinogens.

This ancient patriarchal template – the dominant male with his harem of sexually compliant females – was normalised in all the arts. The iconic artworks of American illustrator Robert E. McGinnis depict dominant males, generally in suits and with their arms folded or holding weapons, and submissive females, often naked and seated, or in multiples, or partially clothed. At times, they were reduced to the sum of their parts (a foot suggestively dandling a high-heeled sandal, and so on).

McGinnis's James Bond posters have come to symbolise the brand: in a poster for *You Only Live Twice* (1967), Bond is catered to in a pool by eight improbably large-breasted Asian women in bikinis; in a similar illustration, a suited Bond-like male is fawned over by 11 large-breasted women, each with a different hair colour and style: the feminine as liquorice allsort. The continued cultural value of the subtext is evidenced by the fact that the original artwork for the *You Only Live Twice* poster sold for over $80,000.[156]

Patriarchal feminists adopted Leary's spin on identity as unrelated to sexual passion. American author Erica Jong, whose bestselling books were saturated with 'drugs, booze and sex',[157] became

You Only Live Twice lobby card.

notorious on this basis. In the generation-defining *Fear of Flying* (1973), a novel that sold over 20 million copies, she wrote, 'For the true, ultimate zipless A-1 fuck, it was necessary that you never get to know the man very well. I had noticed, for example, how all my infatuations dissolved as soon as I really became friends with a man … After that I would like him, perhaps even love him – but without passion.'[158]

Six years earlier, the 'Summer of Love', when 100,000 hippies descended on the Haight-Ashbury district of San Francisco, became emblematic of the era: medical assistance and basic supplies were free,[159] and the city was awash with illicit drugs. In essence, a foetal utopia: intellectual disablement in tandem with entitlement to subsistence without effort.

Cannabis and LSD left the hippies with the neonatal capacity to be hypnotised by colour, touch and sound. Underscored by drums and bass, the music recalled the foetal experience of the mother's lungs, voice and heartbeat. The bared breasts of women in the streets – the same phenomenon was evident at Woodstock two years later – symbolised perpetual maternal accessibility. This, then, was a regressive generation, starved of mothering.

The bouncing breasts failed to seduce American underground writer Chester Anderson. 'Rape is as common as bullshit [in Haight-Ashbury],' he wrote. 'Kids are starving on the Street. Minds and bodies are being maimed as we watch, a scale model of Vietnam.'[160]

Anderson, however, was in a minority; the trend for misogyny only accelerated, particularly in the music industry.

A decade later, American alt-rock star Marilyn Manson, who at some point anointed himself 'The God of Fuck', invited a deaf 'groupie' to the studio and requested that she strip naked ('We were all shocked and amazed that we were commanding that much sexual power'). Consolidating his gender status by further degrading her before other men, Manson then ornamented her body with frankfurters, pig's feet and salami before taking photographs. (His sexualised disgust for the feminine is reminiscent of British Moors Murderer Ian Brady's description of a child's 'slit crotch' as 'much like a fatty white pig's hoof as a sex organ'.)[161] While one band member penetrated the woman, another shouted, 'I'm going to come in your useless ear canal.'

After requesting the woman's consent – she was, Manson reports, 'delighted' – he then urinated on her body while his bassist urinated directly in her face. 'I do not feel she was being exploited by any means,' Manson, nominated for four Grammy Awards, wrote.[162]

Patriarchal success, as American academic Ashley Mears pointed out, has always pivoted on contempt, surplus, and wastage, whether in relation to drugs, money or women.[163]

A producer who has worked with some of the world's biggest artists described cars, drugs, properties and women as the ultimate music industry status objects.

'Plural, not singular,' he stressed. 'To own one car, to take one drug, to buy one house, or to fuck one woman is nothing; a supermarket cashier can do all that. Surplus is how you tell the winners from the losers. A rock star doesn't *need* 50 Ferraris – he only has one arse – and he can only get so much head per week before it gets as dull as fuck, but that's not the point: power is demonstrated by the amount of drugs you smoke and snort, the millions you piss up against the wall, the sportscars you don't drive, the volume of beautiful young pussy you can fuck and dump.'[164]

The volume of beautiful young pussy you can fuck and dump.

Even now, the legacy of romanticised, gendered violence in the arts continues. As the increase in anecdotal and official reports shows, music festivals in particular provide the ideal environment for the sexual assault and harassment of young women: crowds, darkness, drugs and disablingly loud music.[165]

British poet Scarlett Sabet, 46 years younger than her partner, British Led Zeppelin guitarist Jimmy Page, personalised the traditional industry power differential in her poem 'Hiding in Plain Sight'. In it, she refers to an unnamed lover as her 'master' and to his slaps, so violent that she is no longer able to think clearly. Despite this, she continues grovelling for his attention.[166]

Page, whose taste for – or love of projecting a taste for – sexualised violence with very young women,[167] [168] was always wary of too much LSD ('I had already heard of some terrible casualties'), but there were 'other things, like mescaline. I had to try them.'[169]

On a neurological level, drugs disrupt the creation of an emotional bond. Cannabis,[170] cocaine and methamphetamine, for example, increase the secretion of dopamine. If dopamine, the hormone central to pair-bonding, is increased through outside means *prior* to sexual intimacy, then the dopamine generated through sex will fail to have the usual powerful effect: the pleasure will be associated by the user with the drug, rather than the partner. 'The specialness of the sex, and the differential caused by the dopamine release won't be so high,' American neuroscientist Larry Young noted.[171]

Either way, the drug-state becomes the focus between partners rather than an adjunctive behaviour. As Leary's fourth wife noted of her husband, 'We like to get high together.'[172]

This pattern applies to all maternal drug abuse. Female drug users are more likely to associate drug use with an intimate partner, while men are more likely to associate drug use with male friends.[173] By definition, then, patriarchal women are more likely to be dangerous to their own children. To the patriarchal feminine, gender status amounts to masculine ratification, however dangerous.

The patriarchal woman's pleasure is taken only in the pleasure of the man, never herself; she is, by definition, secondary.

Even American singer Madonna, who built a career on the

concept of feminine supremacy, capitulated, at the age of 62, to this template in a series of posts with her then 26-year-old cannabis-smoking partner, American musician Ahlamalik Williams.[174] In all the shots, Williams is both the active partner and the source of the drugs – he smokes, holds the blunt, and does all the blowing, while she submissively observes and receives; equally, the photographic angle emphasises her smallness in relation to him.

Six years earlier, Madonna, during an interview with a British magazine, said, 'I don't have the stamina to take drugs. I feel terrible afterwards. I'm destroyed for days and days. I can't do anything and I don't want that inconvenience in my life. So I don't feel it's worth the price you have to pay. That's me. Even when I was younger and in my 20s, trying this and that … I mean, I never really did that many drugs. I'm too big of a pussy. Also, I'm a dancer and I don't want to destroy my body.'[175]

British television personality Paula Yates, who, like Madonna, prided herself on neither drinking nor taking drugs, was introduced to both by her boyfriend, Australian musician Michael Hutchence. As a close friend of hers observed, 'She never drank or took drugs before she ran off with Michael. She dabbled when she was extremely young, but after that nothing. Then she completely changed.'[176] After Hutchence committed suicide by hanging in 1997, Yates lost custody of her three daughters after attempting suicide by hanging in 1998 – she was discovered by her middle daughter, Peaches. In 2000, Yates was found dead in bed of a heroin overdose at 41 by her youngest daughter, Tiger Lily.[177,178]

For Yates, there was no life outside the approval of her designated patriarch. This was a contemporary First World take on suttee, the Indian ideal of wifely devotion in which a woman throws herself on her husband's funeral pyre or ends her life by other means after his death.

Four years later, Peaches overdosed on heroin at the age of 25, leaving behind two small sons.[179]

In a patriarchal culture, the masculine sexual partner's desires must take priority, even at the cost of the child's happiness, health and safety. The feminine partner, to gain masculine approval, must be willing not only to forfeit attachment with her own child, but to demonstrate her willingness to endanger her child's welfare: sexual intimacy is contingent on her willingness to prove her detachment from her own evolutionary instincts.

This detachment is now par for the course in sexual exchanges, as Grindr and other apps evidence. 'Us gays,' Mark Bittlestone says in a post, 'we literally *order* sex, like it's a pizza.'[180]

Gay Canadian poet and scholar Billy-Rae Belcourt wrote of 'expand[ing] with sexual possibility' by downloading a hookup app when the truth was, in fact, the opposite: to conform to the Grindr sexual template and in the feminine tradition, he literally contracted, using a 'tightly framed shot of my torso with the waistband of a jockstrap peeking out at the bottom of the screen. Almost immediately my phone buzzes with a message from a similarly beheaded torso.'[181] This contraction was not limited to his presentation; the encounters facilitated by the app conformed to the same principle of separation.

Bundy was, in this respect, a species of sexual prophet. As Belcourt wrote, 'My kink is the annihilation of my core sense of self.'[182]

Social media influencer Dan Bilzarian with one of the hundreds of women with whom he surrounds himself. Again, the woman is peripheral. Her irrelevance is such that he doesn't even bother identifying her. www.instagram.com/p/CBKsRhdnX2r/ June 8, 2020

symbolised by the bypassing of the face in mating app profiles, has been normalised. Belcourt noted that in the world of homosexual mating, it's now a 'tradition' to have 'random sex between men for whom faces are secondary erotic materials – a gay rite of passage.'[183] He even hooks up with men he doesn't find attractive.

Belcourt writes, 'I have spent most of my adult life engaging in anonymous sex with men I met on dating apps. Men whose names I didn't know. Men whose faces I didn't fully see. Men who seemed to have given up on care, whose touch wasn't touch per se but something sharper, something heavier. Men I met in hotel rooms and darkened vehicles. Dozens of men, innumerable now that I've not laboured to keep the memories of them alive. There have been hookups I've abruptly left out of a sense of impending danger, ones I've counted myself lucky to have escaped. Queer men know what lurks inside dead eyes and bowed heads.'[184]

This eroticised dehumanisation and emotional disengagement has been normalised across the spectrum. Women, too, now routinely have sex with strangers and men they find unappealing. Of a man she met on a dating app, a young British *Vogue* columnist wrote: 'We had nothing sex, the sort – emotionless, thoughtless – that you have with people you don't really like.'[185]

The template of 'nothing sex' was established during the Psychedelic Revolution. It was during the 1960s that LSD and drugs such as cannabis began to be used *en masse* to strip feminine sexuality of its behavioural armoury – discrimination and its byproduct, selective inaccessibility, are forms of sexual and emotional protection – creating the enduring understanding that there was nothing of importance to protect. This sexualised devaluation became a metaphor: as the vulva was no longer considered a privilege, the feminine could be safely sexually addressed without respect. And women who sought approval from the masculine not only consented to this devaluation, but also adopted the prism.

As Leary discovered, drugs obviate the need for force: thus disabled, the feminine can be owned. As only 16 percent of rapes are reported and victims of substance-incapacitated rapes are less likely to report the crime, perpetrators mostly escape accountability. In any event, victims who consent to such incapacitation generally endure the consequences in silence,[186] fearing that they won't be believed.

It's easier to shut up than to be hit or stalked or thrown across the room.

Leary understood that attachment and its symbol, femininity, was the enemy. One way or another, the feminine would be contained by the masculine – if not literally, then economically, through neurochemical or surgical revision, or in the form of imagery.

4. THE SWEETEST PET IN THE WORLD

'Around 10pm, as the restaurant shut down, Cohen asked her to
walk with him. On St Mark's place, the heart of the East Village,
they met a young hippie. A large turtle was sitting on his gloved
hand. "What do you feed that thing?" he asked. "Hamburger
meat, speed and smack," the hippie answered with pride.'

Leonard Cohen, Untold Stories: The Early Years, Michael Posner

Leary's background in clinical psychology made it easy for him to
decipher and exploit his market: predominantly, the young and
vulnerable, who feared being derided as unattractive or uncool. Syd
Barrett would throw a burning cigarette stub across the floor and
'nobody would pick it up and put it in an ashtray. It was disturbing
because it's dangerous to throw a lighted cigarette around. But the
act of danger was not as important as the not wanting to be uncool,
uncool being a sin in those days.'[187]

Justifying his exploitation of women as a form of enlightenment,
Leary assumed, or pretended to assume, that their drugged pleasure
neutralised his opportunism. He appreciated that for 'karmic
reasons', some women felt the need to 'take [the] neuter trip'
of using their minds rather than just 'washing [up]' and 'sharing
verbally as women should', but in doing so, they 'merge[d]' with the
masculine 'so that they are no longer women, they are neuters.'[188]

Along with beauty, submissiveness and youth, washing up, in
Leary's universe, was near-synonymous with femininity, as his
friend Charles W. Slack confirmed. '[I]t is greatly to Tim's credit
that he was still capable of this deep involvement with someone
who returned his trust, shared his hardships and did the dishes,' he
wrote of Leary's fourth marriage. Despite her premarital 'show-
business career', Leary's fourth wife, a 'squaw', 'was a domestic
creature at heart and never minded' cleaning up while Leary went
about his business.[189]

Of the property used for Leary's commune, Slack added:
'[T]ending to depreciate the value of the real estate was a series

of regular housekeeping hang-ups. Nobody was inclined to clean the kitchen after freak-outs or orgies when they could just get high again and turn the mind around to where dirty dishes looked beautiful.'[190] It was thus essential to convince 'squaws' that their gender status was dependent on serving self-serving men.

The 'absence of women in the psychedelic narrative'[191] beyond their ornamental and sexual value has been noted by researchers. '[H]ippie women,' American historian Gretchen Lemke-Santangelo wrote, 'have long been ignored and marginalised, relegated to the sidelines.'[192]

Leary's reframing of the ideologically independent feminine as self-defeating did not stop at the kitchen sink. Women who objected to pornography ('the frontline of freedom')[193] were a 'travesty'. Such women relinquished their 'divinity' to adopt a 'male religion which leads her to go around putting down such things as the female body.' This was not new territory for Leary, who openly wondered, 'Do we dare equate the CLITORIS to the soul?'[194]

All women were, in effect, reduced by Leary to the sum of their sexual organs.[195]

As a psychologist, Leary was aware that pornography is a form of behavioural training. Pimps, too, profit from the fact[196] that pornography consumption by women results in their increasingly submissive sexual behaviours,[197] and that most heterosexual viewers accept 'pornography's script of male dominance and female submission' and behave accordingly.[198] Reframing his philosophies as expressions of the Divine Feminine was, perhaps, Leary's greatest sleight-of-hand in terms of duping susceptible women.

There is no greater patriarchal aphrodisiac than a disparity in power. American novelist Henry Miller had made this clear in 1934 when he wrote, 'You can forgive a young cunt anything. A young cunt doesn't have to have any brains. They're better without brains.'[199]

They're better without brains.

Erica Jong, then a 'young cunt', addressed her fan Miller as a hero.[200]

In 1967, prize-winning American author Philip Roth, who at 69 was having sex with a 23-year-old and asking that his female students be selected on the basis of beauty,[201] wrote, 'Tits and cunts and legs and lips and mouths and tongues and assholes! How can I give up what I have never even had, for a girl, who delicious and provocative as once she may have been, will inevitably grow as familiar to me as a loaf of bread? For love? What love?'[202]

What love.

Bundy was more honest. He had no need to justify his dehumanisation of the feminine with talk of art. Of his victims, he said, 'They were just, uh, symbols.'[203]

The feminine continues to be a form of currency, to be traded for money or gender status: undeserving of emotional investment in itself. A common bonding exercise among patriarchal men involves sexual point-scoring. In 2021, American politician Matt Gaetz was said to belong to 'a group of young male lawmakers who created a "game" to score their female sexual conquests, which granted "points" for various targets such as interns, staffers or other female colleagues in the state House.' One target group consisted of virgins.[204]

A significant percentage of pornography features 'gangbangs', groups of men having sex with one or two women, simultaneously mocking them as they exchange high-fives and approving looks or comments with the other men. 'Spit-roasts' – the term denoting two men having sex with a single woman, one at each end – are now a tradition in certain sporting circles. Australian football 'spit-roasts' were described as 'team-building'. A source said, 'You don't just bonk them and leave them. You pass them on. It's a team event. The [players] ... can look at each other while it's happening and have a laugh. It's about the degradation of women. You feel like you're bulletproof and that you can almost get away with murder.'[205]

In order to attract masculine approval, the patriarchal feminine adopts the same prism in relation to itself. This attitude isn't exclusive to patriarchal men. As one lesbian reported, 'Butches start talking about how they've "fucked more girls" than the men, "gotten more pussy" and are "better in bed". Their sexual partners become objects rather than humans. If there are women in the room, their objectification seems to be a bonding mechanism for the butches and men, laughing about who has the best ass, the best tits, who they'd fuck or not fuck. I can show a picture of my girlfriend to a man and know I will get instant respect from him based on her attractiveness. I know that because I've done it in the past, and that respect felt good to me, like my masculinity was confirmed by "the source".'[206]

Like Leary, Miller, and the aforementioned 'butch', 21st-century Iranian-British 'groupie' Roxana Shirazi enjoyed performing sexual acts with 'young cunt' – 'soft girls – young, innocent soft girls in particular'[207] – for the entertainment of rock stars. As American 'supergroupie' Pamela Des Barres said of a lover ('though I still don't know how I feel about him'), he 'didn't feel like a man when he couldn't pick up chicks … These girls, of course, meant nothing to [him], he just needed the conquest.'[208]

These girls, of course, meant nothing to him.

Of her liaison with Jimmy Page, Des Barres said, 'We talked about how much better it would have been had we met before all the pop-star-groupie business started and got in the way of a meaningful and honest relationship. He vowed not to let it get in our way, but inserted a clause that allowed him to "do things" on the road because he got so "bloody bored".' Des Barres's consent was, of course, false: 'inwardly', she 'craved impossible monogamy.'

On hearing that Page had fallen in love with another woman, Des Barres felt as if she had been hit in the face with 'a pot of boiling Earl Grey.'[209]

During the Psychedelic Revolution, eroticised violence towards the feminine not only became normalised, but was also presented as the ideal. This violence took various forms: lack of emotional or physical care, the intoxication of vulnerable women, the corruption or exploitation of intoxicated or vulnerable women, and so on. It manifested as the intimate assault described in 'He Hit Me (And It Felt like A Kiss)', and as casual status-based displays – Syd Barrett throwing his girlfriend across the room in front of friends, say.

The same dynamic applied to vulnerable gay or bisexual men.

American writer Cynthia Heimel's partner was fed STP [2,5-dimethoxy-4-methylamphetamine, a psychedelic and substituted amphetamine] by Leary, who then sodomised him. 'In the name of freedom, bad things happened,' she wrote. 'The edicts of free love with no jealousy plus the advent of LSD made it easy for sexual and emotional predators to screw us bigtime … Lots of people who wanted to fuck other people gave them hallucinogens.' She recalled Alice, a schoolgirl whose behaviour became 'disturbing after a series of horny guys gave her a series of [LSD laced] sugar cubes. She swore and fucked everyone … the acid took her personality and slowly, surely disintegrated it.'[210]

Alice, Heimel recalled, 'just diffused.'[211]

Charles Manson, the American cult leader, also used cannabis and hallucinogens to coerce, control and distort his young, susceptible and primarily female followers. Like Leary, he easily identified their vulnerabilities and exploited them. On his first meeting with a hirsute, lonely, overweight, plain 20-year-old, Manson told her that she was beautiful; he was the first to do so. They had sex that night, and she became one of his most ardent followers. Another female disciple testified that they 'were all just one and Charlie was the head'.[212]

Left as a baby with near-strangers for days by his partying 15-year-old mother,[213] Manson believed that the Bible 'teaches submission. Women were put here to serve men.'[214] While he rarely worked, his female followers were, like Leary's 'squaw', drugged and exploited for caretaking and sex. 'We served the men, took care of the children, cooked and sewed, but always were on service for the men,'[215] Linda Kasabian, then 21, testified.

Manson made a practice of kicking off orgies by administering cannabis and hallucinogens (invariably, his doses were smaller, so he could retain control). Reluctance was not permitted. To demonstrate his own lack of inhibition, he once performed fellatio on a 'young boy'. The initiation of a 13-year-old girl into the 'family' of 'dropouts and runaways'[216] involved him sodomising her as his disciples watched. Later convicted of nine murders,[217] Manson and his most ardent followers were thought, in fact, to have been responsible for 35.

Before having sex with Susan Atkins, described by an attorney as 'the scariest of the Manson girls',[218] Manson persuaded her to stand naked before a mirror. 'Go ahead and look at yourself, there is nothing wrong with you,' he said. 'You are perfect. You always have been perfect … You were born perfect and everything that has happened to you from the time you were a child all the way up to this moment has happened perfectly. You have made no mistakes. The only mistakes you have made are the mistakes that you thought that you made.' Manson then said, 'when we are making love imagine in your imagination that I am your father and, in other words, picture in your mind that I am your father.'[219]

He used the same approach with Kasabian.

Secure in his indoctrination of the women, Manson became blasé. 'I have tricked all of you,' he told Atkins. 'I have tricked you into doing what I want you to and I am using you and you are all aware of that now and it is like I have got a bunch of slaves around me.'[220]

It made no difference. In any case, Atkins had nowhere else to go.

Characterised by abuse (emotional, sexual), addiction and loss, Atkins's childhood was chaotic. At the age of 15, she had lost her mother. Her father, who was, as her mother had been, an alcoholic, then repeatedly left Atkins and her brother with various relatives. In 1967, Atkins, 19, who had been imprisoned and was working as a topless dancer, met Manson; in 1968, her son, delivered by Manson, was removed from her care and put up for adoption; in 1969, she was murdering strangers on Manson's instruction.[221]

American actress Sharon Tate, eight and a half months into her pregnancy, had a nylon cord tied around her neck by Manson's disciples. Tate pleaded with Atkins ('Please don't kill me ... I want to have my baby, I want to have my baby'). Atkins replied, 'Look bitch, I don't care about you. I don't care that you're going to have a baby.'[222] Stabbing Tate and her foetus until Tate stopped screaming, Atkins then tasted her blood and with it, wrote 'PIG' on the door. She had wanted to cut out Tate's unborn child but, as she later explained, ran out of time.[223] 'I was stoned, man, stoned on acid,' she later testified.[224]

The mythicised inhumanity of this attack remains unforgettable not only because it was performed by one mother on another mother – one dark and distorted, the other fair and privileged – but because it encoded the relationship between patriarchal masculinity, drugs, and the resulting – and accelerating – cultural denigration of the feminine and maternal.

When Atkins entered the courtroom to be sentenced, she was laughing.[225]

Among other adverse childhood experiences, the savage dislocations created by her own mother's addiction and death resulted in Atkins losing her baby to the authorities. At the time of the murders, her post-birth hormone levels were further deranged by cannabis, hallucinogens and Manson's calculated abuse. Ten months after giving birth, this abandoned, bereaved and unloved woman, triggered by Tate's heartfelt desperation to be a mother, frenziedly stabbed her and her unborn child to death. Her internal tumult at the sight of Tate's plenitude can only be imagined. 'I just stabbed her and she fell and I stabbed her again,' Atkins said. 'I don't know how many times. *I don't know why I stabbed her* [italics mine].'[226]

A mother, crazed by a lifetime of loss, eliminating an intolerable reminder of that loss, laughing because she no longer had access to any feeling other than a disorientating rage.

As Atkins told the court, '[M]y life doesn't mean that much to me.'[227]

The culturally facilitated association of femininity with masochism was celebrated during the Psychedelic Revolution. Even in the 21st century, the global success of the *Fifty Shades* franchise – the first novel in the series was the bestselling book of the decade[228] – was straightforward: the story of the dehumanised masculine (fictional hero Christian Grey) asserting control over the attached, sensitive feminine (Anastasia Steele).

Increasing feminine economic, legal and social parity makes it essential for the patriarchal ideology to be camouflaged by eroticisation as criticism of sexual practice is now classed as discrimination, whereas sexual violence *with consent*, however specious or unverifiable, is now protected by law. And so to Grey beating and humiliating Steele to amplify his gender status. Mollified, he then elevates *her* gender status with exclusive objects.

The novel's resonance with women in particular reflects the understanding that to be feminine is to be a victim to the masculine.

American data scientist Seth Stephens-Davidowitz discovered that 25 percent of heterosexual pornography searches by heterosexual women depict violence against women, and five percent feature women enduring forced sex. The search rates for sexually violent pornographic acts against women are 'at least twice as common among women than men.'[229]

A British boxer confirmed the prevalence of eroticised feminine masochism. 'A 30-year-old mate had been dating this girl for a while, lovely girl, saw herself as a feminist,' he told me. 'During sex, she suddenly asked him to punch her in the face. He was so disgusted that he dumped her. Same thing happened to me. I was in bed with a girl and she told me to hit her. I thought she meant a smack on the bum, but she wanted me to properly fucking *hurt* her, to enact a really gruesome rape fantasy, which to me – I love my mother and I love my sister – was inconceivable. This has happened to *every single boxer I know*. And in every case, the guy didn't want to do it and so broke off the relationship.'

Women, the boxer said, 'ask this stuff because they don't know what it's like to be hit at full speed by an 85kg guy. Let me tell you exactly what it's like: if you're any good, the speed of your punch is eight to nine miles a second – that's how fast a good punch travels, roughly 22 miles per hour. Now imagine an 85kg hammer hitting you at 22 miles an hour. It's going to shatter your whole fucking face.' He paused. 'It's just so fucking *sick*.'[230]

American children's book editor Hedda Nussbaum would have disagreed.

In 1987, the malnourished six-year-old girl Nussbaum and her partner of 12 years, American lawyer Joel Steinberg, had paid to illegally adopt, died after 'savage beating' by Steinberg and Nussbaum's subsequent failure to alert 911. The couple were heard on various occasions having sex after beatings. Clearly gratified by Steinberg's violence, Nussbaum was, like the women the British boxer remembered, a patriarchal female: her greatest gratification was to conform to a patriarch's wishes, however destructive.

To no avail, Nussbaum's neighbours had, for over a decade, complained to the battered women's hotline, the Bureau of Child Welfare, the police. Nussbaum, police recalled, 'could barely stay on her feet. She had the bashed-in, swollen face of a pugilist who'd just lost the last of a long series of fights.' Reportedly, she said in the ambulance of Steinberg, 'God sent me this man.'[231]

Expressed through the medium of sexuality, masochism is now understood as 'hot', 'edgy', a 'kink'. Social media is awash with ostensibly ironic wishes for degradation as a measure of devotion. Of British musician Harry Styles, one girl wrote: 'this hole belongs to harry. i want him to destroy me. i want my guts to be on the floor by the time he's done with me. i want my coochie in severe pain'.[232] Gay men also openly invite sexual violence. '[N]o offense but I find abusive sex hot, like I want my man to destroy my hole, spit in my mouth bang my head into the wall and make it bleed, slap me and pull my hair and even snatch some of it and all that while he calls me a f@ggot ... CAN MY MAN BEAT ME UP OHMYGOD.'[233]

Mark Bittlestone concurred. 'There's definitely a subsection on Grindr of people who are into quite out-there stuff. Quite serious domination role play. The question of consent is blurred. I mean, we don't *know* these people.'

Shirazi's life was also contextualised by consenting masochism. 'Maybe I liked pain,' she wrote. 'Maybe I felt I deserved to be treated like a piece of shit.'[234]

Two days after terminating a pregnancy to a rock star, Shirazi was again backstage searching for sexualised validation. She had been warned by doctors not to engage in sexual activity, but her yearning for male approval was too strong. As 'daintily' as she could 'so he'd still want to be intimate', Shirazi, heavily bleeding, told one of the musicians about the abortion. After penetrating her digitally, he pulled away (the blood rendered her too human). Conditioned by pornography,[235] she responded with disgust – not at his behaviour, but at her own: she had failed to conform to the dehumanised feminine ideal.

Another musician stepped in, unzipping his jeans. Shirazi had no desire to sexually engage with him but felt it incumbent 'to be polite' – it would, she thought, have been 'cruel' to reject him. The 'huge ring through' his penis repulsed her but, again, her feelings were secondary to his; she allowed him to 'hurt' her mouth and then 'choke' and 'scrape' her vagina with it. As he 'pumped away', Shirazi felt 'dead.' (In describing how she felt after murdering Tate, Atkins also said, 'I felt dead.')[236] Despite feeling erased, Shirazi masturbated for the musician and two crew members before engaging in group sex. Once the men had ejaculated, they left her to catch the train home alone.[237]

Shirazi ostensibly sought such experiences because they allowed her to experience the same 'freedom of soul'[238] Leary had prescribed; aligned with this, the perception of women as interchangeable, as sufficient only temporarily and in multiples, and as commodities undeserving of sustained investment on any level.

The musicians who exploited Shirazi at her most vulnerable were only interested in her willingness to enhance their gender status. The termination of a life was of no interest to them. *She* was of no interest to them.

Like Atkins, Shirazi forfeited her understanding of the feminine as valuable in order to appease patriarchal men. Her feelings were not secondary to those of men, but irrelevant.

The French art curator Catherine Millet agreed. 'In the biggest orgies in which I participated,' she wrote, '... there could be up to about 150 people (they did not all fuck, some had come to watch), and I would deal with the sex ... in all the available ways: in my hands, my mouth, my cunt and my arse. Sometimes I would exchanges kisses and caresses with women, but *that was always less important* [italics mine].'[239]

Even to a 'liberated' intellectual like Millet, the feminine was 'always' less important.

An etching of motherhood from Michael Maier's *Atalanta fugiens*.

Michael Maier, in the 1617 book of emblems *Atalanta fugiens*, included an etching in which a woman with sturdy legs and flowing hair nurses an infant; her body is the planet Earth, and her breasts rise from its oceans. Around her, a goat and wolf are suckled by babies, showing the nurturing, symbiotic relationship between nature and man. She stands on high ground with a city in the distance, showing her importance in relation to the manufactured: a representation of the mother/infant relationship as the ultimate human truth.[240]

Maier understood woman as the context of all human life.

His feminine is luxuriant, loving, central in its importance, a universe away from Manson's mutilated feminine or Leary's 'cool', decentralised, empty feminine. An assertion of infinite abundance, it constitutes an invitation to the healthy masculine to again alter it through the alchemy of love: and so the apple is transmuted into a fruit-bearing tree.

The Psychedelic Revolution was a fuck-you to what remained of the realm of the feminine.

II

BORN TO THE UNDEAD

'[E]ven the more inventive zombie stories tend to be static: grim
annals of hard-won, provisional survival. But that may be the
secret of their popularity. With every fashion in horror, it's worth
asking, Why do we choose to fear this, and why now?'

Terrence Rafferty, *The New York Times*

5. THE TAKEOVER

'A man of sense only trifles with [women], plays with them,
humours and flatters them, as he does with a sprightly, forward
child; but he neither consults them about, nor trusts them with
serious matters; though he often makes them believe that he does
both; which is the thing in the world that they are proud of.'

From a letter by British statesman Philip Stanhope,
4th Earl of Chesterfield, to his son

Throughout history and with negligible exceptions, childbirth
attendants or midwives have always been female. Cleopatra gave
birth kneeling, surrounded by five women,[241] and Mayan midwives
were expected to remain 'ritually pure' for four days before and
after each birth they attended,[242] suggesting that masculine energy
was considered dangerous to the infant, even only in the form of
memory. Although it had been thought 'morally inappropriate'
in the early 19th century for men to deliver babies, urban upper-
class American women began to demand obstetrical care from
physicians rather than midwives.[243,244,245]

By 1945, 80 percent of urban births took place in hospitals,[246,247]
creating an historical first: the understanding of men as the
orchestrators of birth.

This ideological shift had been three centuries in the making.
In 1633, the Duchess of Villiers, a preferred mistress of Louis
XIV, requested that surgeon Julien Clement oversee her labour,
whereupon the Princess of France appointed him her *chirugien-
accoucheur* (male surgeon-midwife). Employing an *accoucheur*,
an exception rather than the rule until the 19th century,[248] then
became de rigueur among the European aristocracy.[249] The British
promptly followed suit.[250,251] Gradually, surgeons – in particular, the
French – were redefining the interior of the female body as their
'rightful domain'.[252]

Men began to assert that they made superior midwives – this was
the kick-off to the Obstetric Revolution – and 'Lying-In Hospitals',

established in the 1740s to deliver the babies of impoverished women, were transformed into obstetrics and midwifery teaching centres, primarily for male students.[253] By the late 19th century, the field of obstetrics had been established.[254,255,256] This 'man-midwifery initiative' resulted in a million or so more British and Irish mother/baby deaths between 1730 and 1930 than would otherwise have occurred.[257]

Chloroform (inhalational anaesthesia) is widely thought to have first been used as an obstetric anaesthetic on 7 April 1853, and at Queen Victoria's request, by English physician John Snow, the father of modern epidemiology.[258] (Oddly, Snow's direct descendent, Mat Snow, was the British editor vilified with me in Nick Cave's song 'Scum'.) However, it was Scottish obstetrician James Young Simpson, appointed in 1847 by Queen Victoria as Physician Accoucheur to the Queen for Scotland,[259] who first demonstrated chloroform's anaesthetic properties on labouring women.

Simpson's discovery led to heated international debates about obstetric anaesthetics and analgesics, a group of drugs that included chloroform (toxic to the liver and kidneys and associated with liver cancer),[260] methylene chloride (associated with damage to the eyes, skin, liver, and heart; a potential carcinogen, and, in cases of severe exposure, potentially fatal),[261] carbon tetrachloride (associated with the degeneration of the liver, kidneys, and nervous system),[262] and cocaine (associated with placental abruption, symptoms of toxicity in the newborn – including hyperactivity and seizures, and later central nervous system problems – slower growth rate, and language difficulties):[263] an array of deformities, the multilayered legacies of which would endure for centuries.

At the 1848 American Medical Association Meeting, it was reported that ether and chloroform had been administered to over 2,000 labouring women with 'few, if any, untoward results'. As poet Henry Wadsworth Longfellow's wife, the first American to inhale ether during labour, said, 'I never was better or got through a confinement so comfortably, I feel proud to be the pioneer to less suffering for poor, weak womankind.'[264] Thus misinformed, women started to champion obstetric intervention. The vogue 'took hold quickly'.[265] [266]

There were 'serious' objections.[267,268] In 1848, British gynaecologist Samuel Ashwell wrote that unnecessary birth intervention 'is sure to be followed by injurious and fatal consequences.' The following year, Irish obstetrician William Fetherstone Montgomery lobbied against their use, arguing that a labouring woman should not be kept 'in a state of stupefaction ... with her blood blackened, and her brain poisoned.'[269]

Despite these and other protests, one in 37 deliveries in 1850 at a major Irish maternity hospital involved chloroform;[270] its administration was becoming practice.

British chemist Sheridan Muspratt was among the many to express further misgivings. In 1860, he wrote, 'For the introduction of chloroform as an anaesthetic remedy, mankind is indebted to Dr. SIMPSON of Edinburgh ... Nevertheless, the Editor is of opinion, that it ought to be brought into requisition only in very few instances. Its effect upon unborn generations cannot be anticipated, and he thinks that for *accoucheurs* ... to give chloroform in simple cases, even at the earnest solicitations of patients, is most reprehensible.'[271]

Again, these words had little effect. Chloroform, in all English and German-speaking countries, was involved in 80 to 95 percent of all anaesthesia cases, obstetric and otherwise, between around 1865 and 1920.[272] Rapidly, the field of obstetric anaesthesia expanded.

Deep sedation Twilight Sleep (*Dämmerschlaf*), an amalgam of the opiate narcophine (synthetic morphine) and the amnesiac scopolamine, was first used in an obstetric context in 1902 by German obstetrician Richard von Steinbüchel.[273] [274] In 1906, German obstetrician Karl Gauss published his report on its use in over 600 cases. With fellow obstetrician Bernhardt Kronig, who in 1907–08 published his report of the drug cocktail's use in over 1,500 cases,[275] Gauss further developed Twilight Sleep. Adapted through the decades,[276] it replaced chloroform as the obstetric anaesthetic *du jour* in 1910s Germany.

Chloroform, morphine and scopolamine all penetrate the placental barrier,[277,278,279] but the effects on babies were never the focus.

Administered through needles, Twilight Sleep was billed as erasing all conscious memory of birth. Labouring women, 'having no sense of pain or terror', were said not to resist contractions. In noting that scopolamine stopped mothers doing 'mischief' in their 'semi-voluntary' excitement,[280] obstetricians revealed their proprietorship of the female body: maternal agency was now seen as *interfering with*, rather than directing, the process.

The feminine was remastered as an impediment to successful childbirth, a bad neighbourhood from which babies had to be rescued by the masculine.

American artist Hanna Rion, in researching her 1915 book *The Truth about Twilight Sleep*, was in 'close contact' with the Freiberg maternity hospital in Germany, where over 5,000 mothers, injected with Twilight Sleep, had given birth. Describing labour pain as 'one of the greatest problems of humanity',[281] Rion, in the spirit of triumph, wrote, 'Through twilight sleep a new era has dawned for woman and through her for the whole human race.'[282]

Her prediction would prove disquieting in its accuracy, if not in the sense she intended.

A physician who observed a Twilight Sleep birth marvelled, 'It was as if I had seen the natural action of a woman for the first time.'[283] The new 'natural': a convulsing, straitjacketed, labouring woman blindfolded, shackled and strapped on her back with her legs bound to a frame, intellectually disabled by drugs administered by a male stranger, and observed by emotionally uninvested strangers in an unfamiliar environment.

The mother's supine position and drugged delirium also precluded active birthing, which meant that babies had to be dragged out with forceps. One in four forceps deliveries causes trauma to the mother and child,[284,285] including the occasional severance of the baby's head.[286,287] All serious injury to an infant's forecoming head is 'almost invariably' a result of this delivery method,[288] and traumatic brain injury at birth has been associated with cannabis addiction, serial murders, and suicide, among other issues.[289] As 18th-century Scottish obstetrician William Hunter – the Royal College of Surgeons' Hunterian Museum was named for his younger brother and pupil John[290] – said of forceps, 'where they save one, they murder twenty.'[291]

In using the word 'natural', then, the 1915 physician was, in effect, stating that agency renders women 'unnatural', that it detracts from or obscures the feminine itself, which is at its most authentic when engaged in basic biological functions under the stewardship of the masculine.

Eighty-three years later, Leary made the same statement when he spoke of the feminine being 'neutered' by intellectual assertion. His disempowerment of sexual partners through cannabis and hallucinogens was a way of saying the same thing.

On the basis that the use of Twilight Sleep didn't involve 'constant supervision', British doctors had been using it in hospitals and home birth environments since 1907.[292] At one major Scottish maternity hospital, its use was so normalised as to no longer even be recorded.[293] Correspondingly, a report of Missouri's largest hospital noted that the drug cocktail 'has been used rather freely in the obstetrical service since 1915, and the results obtained under this treatment during this time have been so very encouraging and its popularity has so increased that we are now using it practically as routine.'[294]

A century later, Missouri is one of the top eight American states in terms of serious mental illness[295] and leads the country in terms of unmet mental health needs.[296]

From 1915 onwards, 'very few' labouring women in the US were not administered anaesthetic, and 'practically all' Twilight Sleep mothers were also administered ether or, more commonly, chloroform. The feminine's perception of itself as 'poor, weak womankind' created a demand for intervention, one on which the masculine capitalised.

'There is,' an obstetrics professor acknowledged in 1923, 'an inclination toward giving too much chloroform and by so doing the mother is not only chloroformed to a much deeper degree than the occasion demands, but the foetus is also chloroformed so deeply that it is bound to be born apneic [suffering a temporary cessation of breathing], to become asphyxiated and to require resuscitation.'[297]

This 'inclination' in male obstetricians to administer increasingly dangerous doses of obstetric drugs during delivery was not elaborated upon, but the 'unfortunate' tendency of labouring women to become 'excited' under scopolamine was known to trigger administration of further opiates.

Various drugs were employed 'to combat this state of [maternal] agitation,' and, since 1939, Demerol (pethidine) had been added to prevent the excitement 'quite satisfactorily'. The fact that this 'satisfactory' new analgesic cocktail also had a 'moderately depressive action on the foetal nervous system' and resulted in blue or stupefied infants was seen as 'undesirable' but, in the end, unavoidable.[298]

Obstetric anaesthesia taught women to associate emotional power with a savage decline in gender status. Given this, the feminine had no choice but to consent to its own decapitation. Violent emotions destroy ornamental composure, which is why the suppression of feminine 'hysteria' became a priority for 19th-century doctors. Feminine beauty was predicated on deference, fragility and susceptibility. Drugs were – and continue to be – prescribed to women to prevent the open expression of pain, both emotional and physical, and maternal territoriality.

Even in the rural areas of 1920s Ireland and 1930s New Zealand, labouring mothers were persuaded – or coerced – to submit to injections of Twilight Sleep and other obstetric drugs. A Maori woman remembered, 'I went to the hospital again for five [births] altogether. It was terrible when I first went there … You have to lie on your back. Twilight Sleep or whatever they call it. Chloroform. They put it over here [pointing to her nose] and then they take it away. You don't feel anything and you wake up later. I don't know why they give it to you. But they can still do things to you, I suppose, and you wouldn't be able to stop them … you're just like a cow or something, you know. That's what I felt like.'[299]

The infiltration of the pastoral by the pharmaceutical: in addition to the 'essentials', a standard Irish hospital midwifery bag from the era featured 'a special compartment for a chloroform drop bottle, a mouth gag, tongue forceps, large artery forceps and a Schimmelbusch mask. There was also room for cotton wool and a roll of gauze. Among the tablets were morphine, scopolamine, atropine, strychnine, ergotine, heroin and digitalin.'[300]

In Twilight Sleep threads, women have written of their mothers and grandmothers waking with 'bruises all over' their ankles, legs and wrists where they had been strapped down; of being 'knocked out' against their will; of regaining consciousness 13 hours later; of being handed babies they did not recognise; of babies 'beaten and bruised up' by forceps; of episiotomies 'from here to beyond'; and of the resultant attachment fractures. One wrote, 'I'm still coming to terms with it all. Knowing what I know now about birth, it just makes me so, so sad. While there is no knowing what things would be like if my birth had been different, I really can see in myself today what I could interpret as consequences of my birth (and the 4–6 hour separation from my mother that followed).'[301,302]

Another mother wrote of having grown drowsy after the administration of Twilight Sleep, and '[t]he next thing I knew I was awake, and … I thought to myself, "I wonder how long before I shall begin to have the baby," and while I was still wondering a nurse came in with a pillow, and on the pillow was a baby, and they said I had had it – perhaps I had – but I certainly can never prove it in a courtroom.'[303]

Culturally, Twilight Sleep was the catalyst for a new formula of femininity at its most vulnerable: technically operant – if functioning without agency – within a masculine context, and prevented from developing the memory-based obsessive territoriality that had characterised mother/baby passion throughout history.

Never again would the feminine challenge the Abrahamic god by being perceived as the universal source of love. In the place of this understanding, a model of the ideal feminine as intrinsically deficient, and if the feminine was not deficient, then it would be made so by the masculine: halved like an apple by a blade.

The perception of birth was shifting from that of the ultimate rite of feminine passage to a pathological episode requiring disablement by the masculine. Labouring mothers were, by male obstetricians, infantilised, intimidated and rendered imbecilic.

Motherhood became understood as discrete, a medical episode rather than the strongest of currents determining the flow of all feminine consciousness and evolution.

Women nonetheless continued lobbying for Twilight Sleep's use. Natural childbirth was promoted as status-endangering: 'old-fashioned, ordinary'.[304] Such fear and ignorance in relation to childbirth was not new; in 1591, Scottish gentlewoman Eufame MacAlayne was buried alive for asking her midwife for an analgesic potion.[305] As Dutch-American epidemiologist L.H. Lumey noted, the 'increased demand for hospital confinement was largely due to the interwar propaganda on maternal mortality.'[306]

Much of the propaganda about obstetric drugs – and licit and illicit psychoactive drugs for women – continues to concern liberation or release, but Twilight Sleep offered the feminine not only liberation, but liberation *through the masculine*. Like LSD, obstetric analgesics were discovered, produced and administered by men;

every 'influential individual' associated with their glamourisation was male, and men were the financial beneficiaries.[307]

In the 19th century, Genesis 3:16 ('Unto the woman he said, I will greatly multiply thy sorrow and thy conception; in sorrow thou shalt bring forth children')[308] was cited as an objection to obstetric drugs, aligning as it did the pain of labour with Divine punishment.[309,310]

Ironically, it was through religion that this ancient association – of femininity and pain with weakness and wickedness – became a kind of cultural shorthand: as wickedness was thus innate to the feminine, punishment was appropriate. Obstetricians, then, became understood by women as their *saviours* from the penalisation of pain, and as men who, unlike popes and priests, appeared to believe that women did not deserve to be punished – in short, obstetricians became understood as *men who believed that women were not wicked by definition.*

Obstetric anaesthesia as absolution.

Decades after it was recommended by researchers[311] that morphine and scopolamine be 'avoided at any stage' of labour for their 'very real' association with potentially fatal foetal asphyxia – one study reported that only 63 percent of Twilight Sleep babies 'breathed spontaneously at birth'[312] – the drugs continued to be administered to labouring women internationally,[313] including to Queen Elizabeth II, who in 1960 was administered Twilight Sleep to deliver Prince Andrew.[314]

In 1952, scopolamine was described as 'one of the most common components of combinations of drugs used for relief of pain in labour' and would continue to be used for decades. While Twilight Sleep per se hasn't been administered since the 1970s, the later substitution of Demerol (also known as meperidine or pethidine) for morphine remained 'widely' in use in America,[315] and global rates of birth intervention continue to rise.[316]

American anthropologist Sarah Blaffer Hrdy reported that issues relating to status trump even a child's life. Biological parents are responsible for the largest percentage of infanticides, in which status invariably plays a 'central' role.[317]

Male obstetricians – with the consent of the women they

misinformed – had thus not only appropriated the definitive feminine act through abuse of process, but effected an even more sinister – and ultimately catastrophic – result: the masculine in conjunction with psychoactive drugs became associated with the genesis of humanity itself.

6. FUCKPIG

'Women are rubbish.'
Our Friends in the North, Peter Flannery

Richard Alpert, Leary's close friend, fellow psychologist, and researcher into the effects of LSD – the two were dismissed from Harvard in tandem – shared his fear of mammalian attachment, a distrust they masked with beads, kurtas and beatific smiles. As Baba Ram Dass (his 'spiritual name'), Alpert explained human attachment as a 'clue that there's work to be done' – meaning that territoriality was remastered by him as dysfunctional and primitive, and as requiring the curative attentions of a guru, ordinarily an older man.

Devotion, to Alpert and his millions of followers, was 'the love affair between the Soul and God'[318] – incorporeal, unequal, and unilateral: love experienced at a remove.

The Indian Swami Sivananda, another popular guru, also believed that to cultivate peace 'in the garden of your heart', the 'weeds of lust, hatred, greed, selfishness, and jealousy'[319] – all mammalian characteristics – had to be yanked out, and American Buddhist teacher Jeffrey Miller, under his 'spiritual name' Lama Surya Das, more recently advised readers to '[s]oar in the freedom of desirelessness'.[320] (The paradoxes inherent in these teachings – the desiring of desirelessness, and so on – were not addressed; nor was the destructive suppression of the 'negative' emotions and impulses that, in fact, reveal unpalatable truths.)

Accompanying these 'spiritual' maxims, a circus of fabulous iconographies. Among their wonders, flying monkeys, 10-armed goddesses, skeletal Buddhist demons, and the dazzle of pink and orange silks, all serving the same purpose to the susceptible as rattles do to babies. For the most part, however, the teachings were no more than a rehashing of the same patriarchal beliefs that had poisoned the ideological groundwater for millennia.

Whether achieved through LSD, meditation or sexual indulgence, the severance of awareness from the body and its feelings – rather than from its easy appetites – was, like that of the Abrahamic scriptures, the Psychedelic Revolution's ultimate 'spiritual' goal.

Represented by the feminine, Nature – Maier's mother – was to be transcended.

Contempt for the feminine in the spiritual tradition has always been pronounced. In *The Imitation of Christ*, the most widely-read devotional text other than the Bible, the word 'man' appears over a hundred times; the word 'woman', four. Its author, 15th-century German-Dutch priest Thomas à Kempis, described Nature – to which he exclusively applied feminine pronouns – as 'wily', 'covetous', as drawing 'many to her, whom she oftentimes snareth and deceiveth', as labouring 'for her own profit and advantage', as loving 'idleness', and – with disapproval – as unwilling to 'be kept in subjection.'[321]

American academic Robert Miola hailed the book as a 'spiritual masterpiece'.[322]

The intensity of this cultural shame demanded a poster boy who would deter 'bestial' human behaviours and presentation, and so to the genesis of Satan, 'the beast' – a carnal, hairy, lascivious, malevolent, stinking satyr capable of taking sexually suggestive serpentine form: the humanising of the mammalian self. His domain is Hell, that subterranean realm of fire – heat symbolising emotion ('the heat of the moment', 'crime of passion') – in contrast to the cold, clear, aspirational ether of Heaven.

Conversely, divinities have always been distinguished by their immateriality.

Reflecting the human apprehension to evolve beyond 'beasts of the field',[323] 19th-century German philosopher Nietzsche described man as 'a rope, fastened between animal and Superman – a rope over an abyss. A dangerous going-across, a dangerous wayfaring, a dangerous looking-back, a dangerous shuddering and staying-still.'[324]

Acknowledgement of the mammalian self, then, was not only status-threatening, but life-threatening, for in Abrahamic cultures, animals are beaten, caged, consumed, enslaved, slaughtered.

Man's mastery over wildlife – a metaphor for the transcendence of the animal self – is symbolised by sport-hunting, which is why the aristocracy and royals have always been associated with fox hunts; again, in order to justify rank, dominance of the animal self must be demonstrated. Fur worn frivolously, rather than for pragmatic reasons, by the feminine elite serves the same purpose, as did the Nazi lampshade crafted from Jewish skin and bones.[325] The bloody subtext acts as a warning.

Similarly, the private zoo remains a hallmark of alpha males – among them, late *Playboy* founder Hefner,[326] billionaire heir Rashed Saif Belhasa,[327] and the Sultan of Brunei:[328] emblems of the pleasure taken by the elite in the suffering of the vulnerable.

This approach extends to the feminine. Like Hefner, American businessman Dan Bilzerian[329] and Australian tobacco tycoon Travers Beynon, both burnished, muscular, square-jawed and wealthy men, effectively run zoos of beautiful young women[330] (participation is, of course, voluntary). Beynon courts publicity by walking his wife and other women on leashes. These are not harems, 'sacred' and inviolable places in which essentially invisible women are 'protected', but display cabinets for status objects; the welfare of the women is, in effect, irrelevant outside their aesthetic and sexual market value.[331]

As Beynon, guiding a journalist around his sex dungeon, stressed, 'No boundaries.'[332]

In a 1955 American Lucky Tiger Hair Tonic advertisement, a man with a tiger's head, monocle, and in hunting attire with a rifle, surveys – not unlike Bundy would a few years later – the severed women's heads on the wall, revelling in his status-based sexual wastage.

Their smiles represent consent – the women's, to being 'decapitated' and collected in bulk for the purposes of male gender status, and the man's, to the brutalising, collection and sexualised trivialisation of the feminine: advertising as a codified gender template.

The value of femininity is so low that even in the ostensibly inclusive gay community, 'masc' or 'straight-acting' men are considered to be significantly more desirable than 'fem' men,[333] who continue to be marginalised.[334] Gay men have been found to adopt a 'straight-acting' style on apps if sex, rather than a relationship, is sought.[335]

Even male sex workers who advertise masculine behaviour charge 'significantly' more than their effeminate peers.[336]

American *Lucky Tiger* Hair Tonic advertisement, 1955.

'Anti-effeminacy' is thought to be related to negative feelings about being gay,[337] when it is, in actuality, related to negative feelings about femininity. 'Masc' gay Mark Bittlestone confirmed this, noting that 'in some ways, gay male culture has just sort of drafted a lot of the heteronormative sexual roles, language and bigotry. Life is just a lot harder for fem gays.'[338]

Discrimination is central to all the Abrahamic ideologies, placing them – ironically – at loggerheads with the very anti-discrimination laws created to protect the ideologies.

According to the Bible, the masculine must have 'dominion

over the fish of the sea and over the birds of the heavens and over the livestock and over all the earth and over every creeping thing that creeps on the earth.'[339] The Quran goes a step further, stating that horses, mules and donkeys were created specifically for 'transportation and adornment'[340] – that is, they have no purpose outside that of man. In the Bible, women are said to have been created for the same reason: 'Then the Lord God said, "It is not good that the man should be alone; I will make him a helper fit for him."')[341]

Through these and other determinations of the feminine and the bestial as *adjunctive* to the masculine, the Abrahamic texts are doctrines of rank, both social and in relation to other species. In this separation, the denial of self that is at the core of all human destructiveness.

Overtly mammalian behaviour is still categorised as a *faux pas*, and any 'slippage' – belching, body odour, farting, and so on – is humiliating, the nervous stuff of comedy. In an Abrahamic culture, the worst possible insult is to be accused of being primitive. American director David Lynch's 1980 film *The Elephant Man* remains unforgettable because of the monstrously deformed protagonist's plea (*'I am not an animal!'*). In these words, the desperation we all knew as little children in our efforts to please adults by denying our mammalian impulses: dehumanisation, manifested by cruelty or indifference, is essential.

French novelist Octave Mirbeau depicted this inhumanity in *The Torture Garden* (1899): 'I asked: "What crimes have these creatures committed, to suffer such torment?" She replied carelessly: "I don't know. Nothing, perhaps, or doubtless very little. Petty thefts from shopkeepers, I suppose. *Besides, they are only common people ... wharf-rats ... vagabonds ... paupers!* They don't interest me very much [italics mine]."'[342]

In a patriarchal culture, to be human is to be at war with the animal self.

My Roman Catholic mother, born in northern Italy during World War Two, wept on first seeing me. I looked, she said, 'like a Sicilian' (dark-eyed and dark-haired, hirsute, primitive, lesser). Later, she half-joked that she hadn't even been certain I was hers. Raised in Hitler's Europe, my mother was conditioned to equate fair colouring with the right to exist. It was thus a source of pride to her that she and my brothers had been blond as children. In this aesthetic prejudice, a life-distorting terror; she knew first-hand what could happen to those who looked like 'Sicilians'. When the lanugo (fine foetal hair) on my arms rubbed off, she was finally able to 'recognise' me, however reluctantly, as her own.

In a patriarchal culture, a mother's acceptance can turn on the issue of a newborn's hair.

My late friend Horst Bleicher, a Nazi soldier from an upper-class German family – he was conscripted at 16 – always spoke of his father's vigorous disgust at his mother's devotion to their children; any show of maternal affection or territoriality was derided by him as 'monkey love'. In the envelope of this status-based devaluation, envy – of the emotional scope permitted women, and of his own children. Horst's mother's shows of tenderness only emphasised the rigidity of his father's inner world, triggering unbearable feelings of loss.[343]

Even in the 21st century, the epithets applied to women reveal this Abrahamic bias. A conventionally unattractive woman is disdained as a dog or pig (utilitarian quadrupeds). Women who permit sexual humiliation are fuckpigs (quadrupeds who revel in filth, born to be slaughtered). Throughout the First World, women are still referred to as birds or chicks (less offensive as they are bipedal and can fly and sing). Conversely, a beautiful woman is an 'angel', a 'goddess' or 'madonna', a woman who, through her alignment with divinity, bestows, rather than subtracts, gender status on the man who fucks her.

In the 19th century, privileged men idealised their wives as the 'angel in the house'. This expression – from English poet Coventry Patmore's poem – came to embody the feminine ideal: 'Man must be pleased; but him to please / Is woman's pleasure.'[344]

Between 1995 and 2018, the American lingerie label Victoria's Secret held the world's most watched[345] annual fashion parade, which featured models known as 'Angels'. Equipped with large wings, these Angels certainly intended for Man to be pleased. With an average age of 22, unusually tall, in lingerie and shod in the highest heels, the Angels of Victoria's Secret were always smiling, creating an illusion of indiscriminate acceptance, goodness, and happiness in being lustfully observed in their underwear by unseen men; in a different context, they would have requested restraining orders. Mostly naked, these women were – unlike, say, strippers – sexually inaccessible to their audience; overt reminders of their bestial origins (nipples, body hair, anogenital regions) were never visible. In keeping with the patriarchal mandate, the extremity of their leanness only increased over time, increasing their gender status and furthering their distance from the average woman.[346]

Although angels are not born of woman, they *evolve from the human state* – according to 18th-century Swedish theologian and philosopher Emanuel Swedenborg, they are '*wholly men in form,* having faces, eyes, ears, bodies, arms, hands, and feet ... and in a word lack nothing whatever that belongs to men except that they are not clothed in material bodies [italics mine]'[347] – equipped, in essence, with ornamental phalluses and testicles.

The subtext of Swedenborg's insistence is that the angelic is exclusively masculine and, in effect, an *improvement* on the 'material body' – that is, the body sculpted by the feminine – making it clear that the feminine is not only inferior but continues to be aligned with the bestial: a lower rung on the ladder to spiritual perfection.

Like *Fifty Shades of Grey*, *The Torture Garden* is, rather than an erotic novel, an allegory of the animal self distorted by the unnatural demands of class, with the characters embodying the two principles. As Mirbeau writes, 'Clara releases herself from my clumsy embrace, and in a voice, in which there is anger, irony and also lassitude and enervation: "God! how frightfully boring you are, if you only knew ... and ridiculous, my poor friend! *What a common goat you are!* Leave me alone. In a little while, if you insist, you can *work out your dirty desires on the harlots.* You're really too ridiculous! [italics mine]"'.[348]

The carnal woman, defined by her mammalian functions, presents, and has always been treated, very differently to the elite feminine 'angel'. In *The Dirt*, a biopic of American glam metal band Mötley Crüe, Tommy Lee, the band's merry, accessibly stupid[349] Greek-American drummer, is depicted, drunk and high, as vomiting on a stripper.[350] Supposedly humorous, the scene is, in fact, a reinforcement of the patriarchal behavioural template: the bestial (predominantly sexual) feminine is to be addressed with derision, disgust or disregard by the high-status masculine. The fact that Lee is drunk in the scene neutralises any accusations of misogyny.

In the 21st century, the pornographic vogue of 'ass to mouth', in which the feminine, after being sodomised by the masculine, is expected to orally clean the penis, is an eroticised example of the same impulse. Women, who for centuries have metaphorically eaten shit, are now expected to literally do so, like swine: *fuckpigs*. British musician Viv Albertine wrote of a fling she had after her midlife divorce: 'I got myself tested for everything at a clinic afterwards. On my way out I asked a doctor if it was OK to have a cock in your mouth after it's been up your backside – asking for a friend.'[351]

When a 22-year-old American model alleged her 34-year-old movie star boyfriend suggested having her ribs surgically removed so he could barbecue and eat them in front of her,[352] two politically correct women insisted to me that his desires should be classified as a 'kink' – like countless other abusive acts, the literal preparation and *consumption* of the feminine by the masculine is neutralised through eroticisation.

The feminine, in an Abrahamic culture, cannot be permitted mammalian agency without punishment. As the trailer for the film adaptation of British writer Martin Amis's *London Fields* says of Nicola Six, the novel's calculating, intellectual, sexually confident anti-heroine, 'Everyone wants Nicola Six ... *dead*.'[353] Of course Nicola has to die; her intelligence and erotic mastery make her invulnerable to men, challenging their supremacy.

As mammals are defined by attachment, the masculine, in order to justify its domination, has to cultivate detachment. To achieve this, the masculine has to brutalise, ghettoise or trivialise those defined by mammalian vulnerability – children, the feminine, the 'feminine' masculine – and the matrix of attachment: pregnancy, childbirth and mothering.

Italian poet Filippo Tommaso Marinetti's *Futurist Manifesto* (1909) arguably determined the first half of the 20th century: '*Noi vogliamo glorificare la guerra-sola igiene del mondo - il militarismo, il patriottismo, il gesto distruttore dei libertarî, le belle idee per cui si muore e il disprezzo della donna.*'[354] ('We want to glorify war – the cleansing agent of the world – militarism, patriotism, destructive libertarianism, these beautiful ideas for which we die, and contempt for womanhood.')[355]

Seven decades later, films such as American director Ridley Scott's *Alien* (1979) and its sequels, in which malevolent extraterrestrial life-forms 'burst out' of their human hosts, reinforced these ideas. Protagonist Ellen Ripley embodies the patriarchal ideal (defined musculature, invulnerable, a flair for weaponry). Revealed as a bereaved mother in *Aliens* (1986), she takes a flamethrower to the extraterrestrial queen and her embryos: mother killing mother, a reworking of the Susan Atkins and Sharon Tate story, in which the annihilation of maternal plenitude is spurred by maternal loss.

Alien, American critic David Edelstein wrote, 'remains the key text in the "body horror" subgenre that flowered ... in the seventies.'[356] The franchise's resonance reflected a revulsion that had been building for over a century. This disgust, which extended to birth and the female sexual organs (the film is replete with symbolic 'rampaging gooey vaginas *dentate*'),[357] was Abrahamic.

Eighteenth-century German philosopher Immanuel Kant, a central Enlightenment thinker, believed that the sexual act ('a principle of the degradation of human nature') serves to 'dishonour' mankind by placing it 'on a level with animal nature'.

This apprehension ('danger of equality with the beasts')[358] continues to be realised, notably in a sub-genre of erotic art – Japanese 'tentacle erotica', in which women are pleasured by octopuses[359] (*shokushu goukan* or 'tentacle violation'). The Greek myths also depict Zeus as seducing women in the guise of animals (a bull, an eagle, a swan), and Roman mythology features lascivious satyrs (half man, half goat). Likewise, Dracula, the most sexually engaging monster of the past 200 years, shapeshifts into a dog and a wolf. Logically, then, pregnancy is not merely contextualised by 'degradation' and 'dishonour', but its byproduct.

Two centuries or so later, American feminist academic and lesbian Camille Paglia concurred, describing childbirth, something she had

The infant alien emerging from its host's body in *Alien* (1979).

only ever viewed rather than experienced, as 'barbaric', an 'affront to beauty and form', a 'spectacle' of 'frightful squalor' and 'appalling pain and gore' whose 'ugliness has produced the giant displacement of women's historical status as sex object'.[360]

Twenty years before Paglia, American radical feminist and lesbian Shulamith Firestone, who, like Paglia and Kant, was raised in an Abrahamic household (Orthodox Jewish, Roman Catholic and Pietist Lutheran respectively), and who, like them, would also die biologically childless, also described pregnancy as 'barbaric' and the associated weight gain as disgusting ('What's wrong with that Fat Lady?'). Pregnancy was defined by Firestone as 'the temporary deformation of the body of the individual for the sake of the species'.[361]

Such a jeopardising of feminine gender status clearly required containment.

To this end, Firestone called for 'a revolutionary ecological programme' to 'establish a humane artificial (man-made) balance in place of the natural one, thus also realizing the original goal of empirical science: human mastery of matter.'[362]

Firestone, in her emphasis on the domination of nature, was fundamentally patriarchal. She wanted the protectorates of childhood, the family unit, monogamy, motherhood and procreative sex to be relegated to history, attributing the very desire for pregnancy to the influence of 'cultural superstructures'. Like Leary, she promoted emotion as stifling and superfluous. Defining motherhood as a state of being 'stuck' and reliance on a partner as 'corrupt', she believed that human reproduction should be artificial.

Firestone was also a committed advocate of child-adult sex. 'Relations with children would include as much genital sex as the child was capable of – probably considerably more than we now believe – but because genital sex would no longer be the central focus of the relationship, lack of orgasm would not present a serious problem,' she wrote.

Sex between family members, too, had her vote ('an end to the incest taboo, through abolition of the family, would have profound effects: sexuality would be released from its straitjacket to eroticise our whole culture.') Firestone held that laws against incest were no more than 'sexual repression, demanded of every individual in the interests of family integrity', and the cause of 'individual neurosis' and 'widespread cultural illnesses.'[363]

Feminists, in vivid essays praising Firestone's legacy, fail to mention this emphatic celebration of incest and paedophilia; had she been male, she would not only have been dismissed by the same women on these very grounds, but her legacy would have been cancelled. Even childless[364] American writer Susan Faludi, in her *New Yorker* eulogy (in which Firestone is described as 'thrilling' and 'incandescent'), made no mention of her views on child-adult sex; bizarrely, Faludi closed the essay on a quote about Firestone – a schizophrenic paedophilia apologist who died alone – being a 'model' for Jewish girls 'everywhere'.[365]

Firestone's visions of artificial reproduction in particular continue to be misunderstood as prescient. If anything, her stance would appear to be that of a child sex abuse victim who suffered attachment disruptions at birth (schizophrenia has been aligned with severe early trauma,[366,367] and her position on child-adult sex – in tandem with her aversion to pregnancy – suggests a childhood rape that she was unable to emotionally address).

Half a century later, and ostensibly designed to help support premature life, transhumanist 'biobags' or 'exowombs' – extra-uterine life-support systems – now effectively render mothers obsolete. The question of whether infeasibly premature human infants *should* be kept alive is not addressed; instead, the patriarchal appropriation of feminine territory. 'With appropriate nutritional support, lambs on the system demonstrate normal somatic growth, lung maturation and brain growth and myelination,' one study reported.

Photographs of lamb foetuses[368] seemingly vacuum-packed in plastic were used to illustrate what, in essence, was Firestone's wish for the future: the feminine denied, reduced to the sum of its functions – as it was by the masculine – namely, nurturance, sex, and reproduction.

There was no mention of the feminine's sculptural sovereignty over humanity.

Reproduction, too, had become understood as an essentially robotic process, as American 1940s/1950s movie star Jerry Lewis made clear when he described his understanding of a woman as 'a producing machine that brings babies in the world.'[369]

In the transparent exowomb, the foetus is a spectacle. Were the foetus understood as human, the exowomb could, in Britain and by definition, be a contravention of Article 8 of the Human Rights Act,[370] which recognises privacy as a fundamental entitlement. This lack of privacy, by which pornography is also characterised, is now demanded by the patriarchal, which must have access to all feminine territories in order to control them.

The vagina, for example, is hidden between the thighs, and pubic hair and vulval folds obscure its opening, which, in turn, is hidden by muscle and mucosal tissue: secret. Femininity is defined by its secrets, but there can be no feminine secrets in a patriarchal state. Through the practice of 'gaping', in which feminine cavities are stretched out, pornography asserts visual authority to ensure that *all men have right of access* to women's secrets. Cameras linger over semen left in the rectum, as if it were a flag planted on the lunar surface – visual shorthand for masculine 'ownership' of historically feminine territory – and ejaculate aimed at a woman's face symbolises the obliteration of her identity.

The same principles apply to the exowomb, which permits the masculine to monitor, modify and terminate foetal development, previously exclusively feminine privileges.

Through such technology, the feminine is denied both its identity and territory.

Given that the act of observation has been shown to change matter,[371] what does it mean for gestation to become, as birth and sex have, a performance? Issues of alteration aside, observation is a territorial assertion. *The human eye lays claim.*

In keeping with Firestone's blueprint of patriarchal access to, and segmentation of, the feminine, extra-uterine life-support systems also deprive the foetus of attachment to, and veneration of, the feminine. The exowomb blocks the mammalian privilege of love. Developed within, a foetus can only understand its existence as an end unto itself, disconnected and discrete. The relationship between a foetus and its exowomb is one-way. There can be no tailored emotional or endocrinological exchange. Imprinted on the baby, the understanding that love is, rather than reciprocal, an exercise in infinite yearning, in the fruitless extension of self, unmet and unwanted by its indifferent, mechanical source.

There is also this: the foetus is not the product of, or related to, the

Lamb foetus in biobag. Picture Dr Alan W Flake / Children's Hospital of Philadelphia.

exowomb. There is no mutual developmental relationship between them. The exowomb was created *for* the foetus; it has no purpose in itself. To all intents, the exowomb is dead, incapable of engaging in the immeasurably intricate neurodevelopmental dance of reflected sensitivities. However, it achieves a critical patriarchal purpose: the disabling of the mechanism of love.

As Richard Alpert, in the guise of Baba Ram Dass, counselled those who seek enlightenment, '[T]he first job is to extricate yourself from attachment.'[372]

Our cultural aspirations are symbolised by our architecture – increasingly inorganic, in design, form and texture, and constructed to stand at the greatest possible distance from Maier's feminine. The greater the distance from the earth, the more desirable the property. Heaven, after all, is a celestial realm, an immaterial state involving ascension and populated by great angels impervious to suffering, in contrast to Hell, which is of the earth, subterranean, three-dimensional, and inhabited by the afflicted, deformed and primitive.

In this cultural exodus from our humanity and the shame of its primate origins, the most important figure to oust or eliminate, the one responsible for humanising us through attachment and from whose influence we must thus 'extricate' ourselves in order to become 'enlightened' – literally: unencumbered – the one designed to give birth through her bloody, hairy, sweating, odoriferous genitals, is the mother.

7. THE FEMININE ELITE

'As the model-turned-anaesthesiologist by my bedside explained
the various medications, I cut in to say: "Actually I'm thinking a
natural birth." Whereupon he burst out laughing: "Honey, in L.A.
a natural birth means giving birth without your make-up on."

Celia Walden, *The Telegraph*

In America, the 'Twilight Sleep societies'[373] formed by upper-middle-class women were, in essence, futuristic, paving the way for the maternal technologies that would further erode the cultural centrality of mothers.

Through chloroform, ether, masculine birth intervention and Twilight Sleep, the feminine elite lost its confidence in its capacity to give birth, and in the coming decades, all others would follow. This wasn't just a perceptual fracture, but the ransacking of the deepest feminine sense of accomplishment and meaning. During his tenure as Romanian president,[374] Nicolae Ceaușescu commissioned orphanage signs that underscored the new doctrine of maternal incompetence: 'The State can take better care of your child than you can.'[375]

No longer confident of their ability to nurture their own babies, women *en masse* began to willingly relinquish their maternal power to male 'experts' and, in the coming decades, their babies to the care of strangers.

Globally, the erosion of attachment was accelerating.

A steadfast denial of the mammalian need for attachment – bonding, intimacy, tenderness – has, transhistorically, been the primary marker of the elite. Their fitness for leadership, which rests in codified behaviours demonstrating their greater distance from our animal origins, must be established, even if only through lies. As aristocratic British author Enid Bagnold allegedly said, 'Only negresses have orgasms.'[376]

The unparalleled public impact of Diana, Princess of Wales, for example, was due to the highly unusual combination of her angelic presentation – blue-eyed, fair, smooth-bodied, tall – and her resolute lack of emotional containment. Openly affectionate, Diana challenged the highly restrictive British royal behavioural code, threatening the very premise of the monarchy with her 'animal' displays of anger, jealousy, and maternal passion. As she said, 'I don't go by the rule book. I lead from the heart, not the head.'[377]

Frankness about emotional needs constitutes anarchy in elite circles.

Even in the Republican and Imperial Roman eras, sculptors depicted children as emotionally controlled. This visual code was an extension of the elite's emotional restriction. To the Romans, patriarchal masculinity was an achievement symbolised by the 'mastery' of the face.[378] Over 2,000 years later, this 'mastery' continues to be inflicted on privileged children, who, as adults, no longer understand the face as the intermediary between the inner and outer worlds but as a shield or tool of deception. Such 'mastery' is achieved through the premature separation of the infant from his mother, which results in his 'declining behavioural responsiveness',[379] as evidenced by the blank expressions characteristic of businessmen, criminals, and members of the monarchy. The 'stiff upper lip' must be maintained, lips being a barometer of feeling; authentic feeling entails forfeiture of status.

In saying, 'Prince Philip is the only man in the world who treats the Queen simply as another human being. I think she values that,'[380] Queen Elizabeth II's former private secretary Lord Charteris made the routine dehumanisation of royals clear. Aristocrats and those in royal circles are addressed as patriarchal symbols rather than human beings, and expected to behave accordingly. The emotions that characterise the 'lower' mammals are to be cauterised, disguised, hidden, or managed by substances.

As Patrick Bateman, the financier protagonist of the bestselling novel *American Psycho* (1991), says, 'I had all the characteristics of a human being – flesh, blood, skin, hair – but my depersonalisation was so intense, had gone so deep, that the normal ability to feel compassion had been eradicated, the victim of a slow, purposeful erasure. I was simply imitating reality, a rough resemblance of a human being, with only a dim corner of my mind functioning.'[381]

The American writer Joan Didion, also celebrated for her

patrician froideur, said, 'I don't know what 'fall in love' means. It's not part of my world.' Tracy Daugherty, Didion's American biographer, reported that 'lots of drinking' was not unusual in Didion's marriage to fellow writer John Gregory Dunne. On one occasion, Dunne called his wife from Las Vegas, where he was researching a story. He said that he had a 'date' with a 19-year-old who was 'supposed to suck me and fuck me.' Didion replied, 'It's research ... You're missing the story if you don't meet her.' 'But I don't *want* to fuck her,' he said.[382]

In this vignette, Dunne revealed the disparity in status between him and his wife: Didion, through the cultivated detachment from territorial emotion by which she was characterised, was the less mammalian – that is to say, superior to her openly emotional husband.

British journalist Anna Pasternak wrote of the elite, a circle to which she has always emphasised that she belongs, 'To admit to as pedestrian and visceral an emotion as jealousy would be to acknowledge insecurity, which is considered reprehensible.'[383]

Sophistication, then, is emotional censorship. Urbanity: the investiture of denial.

Children enrolled in privileged boarding schools have been found to be 'more likely than not to turn into adults living private, guarded, strategic lives, exiled from their emotional vitality, and internally dominated by the need to stay in control.' An elite British boarding school alumna recalled that her mother, on seeing her crying before term, instructed her 'not to worry' because she would soon learn to hide her feelings.[384]

Her mother had, of course, also boarded as a child.

Predictably, rates of anxiety, depression and substance abuse are one-and-a-half to two-and-a-half times higher than the national norm among the children of affluent mothers, findings that have been replicated 'over and over again'.[385] Two factors appear to be implicated: excessive pressures to excel and emotional and physical isolation from parents.[386] I will never forget the unnaturally delicate, divorced wife of a German billionaire, herself a child of immense privilege, showing me the ketamine IV bruise on the back of her hand. 'Depression,' she said. 'All my life. The doctors think it's biological.'

The legacy of birth practices in relation to this suffering cannot be overestimated.

paulinaporizkov ☉ · Follow · · ·

paulinaporizkov ☉ We live in unprecedented times. We are going through a national, perhaps global collective depression. Most of the people I know are now on antidepressants. Or at least, seriously considering it. If it wasn't for my own battle of getting OFF antidepressants, I would have started taking them this fall when everything seemed never-ending and utterly bleak. But because of my previous experience (no libido, weight gain, no interest in writing, and the nightmare of getting off the drugs) I have been resisting as long as I could. Do not misunderstand. Antidepressants can save lives. If this is what you need, then- isn't it so wonderful and amazing that a pill

♡ ○ ▽ 🔖

19,916 likes
MARCH 9, 2021

☺ Add a comment...   Post

Manhattan-based former supermodel Paulina Porizkova's post about how 'most' of the people she knows are now on antidepressants.
www.instagram.com/p/CMM1gBCBWfb/ March 9, 2021

Obstetric anaesthesia was, in effect, promoted as *humanising* labouring mothers by distancing them from awareness of the animal suffering that betrayed their origins. Queen Victoria made the need for it clear when she described childbirth as 'a complete violence to all one's feelings of propriety (which God knows receive a shock enough in marriage alone).'[387]

A labouring woman stupefied by anaesthesia may continue avoiding the core truth of her existence, but a woman who births – bleeding, defecating, grunting, stinking, shouting – in full consciousness, must confront the déclassé reality that she is not, and will never, be sufficiently inhuman. The woman who births in full consciousness can only be, as Pasternak ('a writer and member of the famous Pasternak family')[388] put it, 'pedestrian and visceral', the very antithesis of the Elephant Man's statement: she really *is* an animal.

The primary purpose of obstetric drugs, then, is to deliver women not from pain, but shame.

In itself, the administration of obstetric anaesthesia to privileged women served as evidence of their moral superiority.

An activity associated with the working classes, 'labour' – literally: *to work hard, to make great efforts* – remains distasteful to privileged women, who, like Didion, define themselves through studied indifference. From the late-1800s, the feminine elite had become aligned with an exaggerated susceptibility to infirmity,[389] meaning that the drug-induced disablement of privileged women during labour assumed an aristocratic cachet.

Recognising the profits to be made, physicians argued that Twilight Sleep was essential for all 'women of sensitiveness'. These 'mothers of the better class' were, unlike the 'women of no great intelligence' in public hospitals, 'incapable of enduring the pain of delivery'.[390]

The willingness of doctors to administer obstetric anaesthesia was determined by the socioeconomic status of patients, and this trend continued into the 1930s and 1940s.[391]

Lower-class women and 'savages' – women of colour – were said to suffer less during childbirth 'because they are stronger, and have less feeling and apprehension.'[392] In 1937, American physician Roy P. Finney disdained the 'primitive ... squatting on her bed of leaves'; far better the 'mother with no recollection of having become one.'[393]

The subtext was clear: the sense of feminine entitlement can be fatally altered by the 'primitive' – and socially levelling – process of childbirth. It was thus imperative that the feminine elite be separated from the experiences of mammalian fear, pain and passion during childbirth.

In 1927, American novelist Edith Wharton satirised this drug-facilitated dissociation of the mother's awareness from the birth experience, and the resulting objectification of – rather than attachment to – the baby. She wrote, 'Lita drifted into motherhood as lightly and unperceivingly as if the wax doll which suddenly appeared in the cradle at her bedside had been brought there in one of the big bunches of hot-house roses ... "Of course there ought to be no pain ... nothing but Beauty ... It ought to be one of the loveliest, most poetic things in the world to have a baby," Mrs. Manford declared, in that bright efficient voice which made liveliness and poetry sound like the attributes of an advanced industrialism, and babies something to be turned out in series, like Fords.'[394]

The issue of labour pain in relation to feminine privilege was also significant in terms of emotional trauma. Generated within the self, the pain of childbirth carries through deeper, unacknowledged griefs – in the case of the feminine elite, that of sacrificing their femininity.

Privileged women continue the tradition of compensating for their authority through affectations of disablement – from dieting and other disorders to substance abuse, institutionalised detachment from their children, and so on. American novelist Tom Wolfe nailed the phenomenon: 'Social X-rays ... they keep themselves so thin, they look like X-ray pictures ... You can see lamplight through their bones ... while they're chattering about *interiors* and *landscape gardening*.'[395]

This is no trivial matter. In a patriarchal culture, duty of care is determined by class. The lower a mother's socio-economic standing, the more pronounced the medical indifference to her fate and to that of her baby, so the best chances for survival hinge on a higher social status.

With fellow obstetrician Bernhardt Kronig, who in 1907–08 published his report of Twilight Sleep's use in over 1,500 cases,[396] Karl Gauss further developed Twilight Sleep, stressing that the method's success or failure stood by the stringent observation of the memory test: checking patient recall before giving second or third doses.

However, as George Blacker, President of the Obstetrical Section of the British Royal Society of Medicine, wryly noted, this was not the case with all mothers at the Freiburg Clinic. There, Twilight Sleep was administered 'at certain intervals of time without any reference to the state of the patient's memory' to 'those women whom they euphemistically term their "third-class patients".'[397]

The recommended Twilight Sleep protocol was, along with the recommended three-year course, also ignored by American doctors, who were considered 'trained' after observing births at the Freiburg Clinic. Given the American demand for the administration of Twilight Sleep, they then 'cut corners' by giving set, rather than personalised, doses to labouring mothers. Nurses untrained in the technique would watch over the patients until the birth was imminent. No family presence was permitted; these traumatic births were only ever witnessed by medical personnel.[398]

Curated exposure also ensured that privileged women could not be defined or identified by biological function; rather, they were permitted only to distinguish themselves through paternal lineage, demonstrating their submission to the patriarchal by deemphasising or limiting their access to their own feminine capacities.

Obstetric anaesthesia was a wall erected between women and their femininity.

Appropriately, the Twilight Sleep era ushered in the *'garçonne'* vogue for breast-binding. As a June 1925 advertisement for Butterick, the world's oldest sewing pattern company, read, 'Have you a boyish figure? Or have you lost some of your clean cut lines?' The suggestion being that the unstructured feminine body was, in essence, dirty – the opposite of clean – and disordered. In particular, the female breast and everything it represented – comfort, devotion, the mother's tenderness, nurturance – came to be understood as ineffably vulgar, the stuff of 'primitives'.

Large-breasted women continue to be advised to invest in 'at least one'[399] minimiser bra (reducing 'bust size optically by one cup')[400] to deemphasise their femininity. As American supermodel Cindy Crawford noted, 'You start out happy that you have no hips or boobs. All of a sudden you get them, and *it feels sloppy* [italics mine].'

This denial – of feminine luxuriance and flow – is now characteristic of the privileged.

Of a show by French couturier Coco Chanel, a critic wrote, 'The models had the figure of 1930 – no breasts, no waist, no hips.'[401] The preference for the tall, lithe, small-breasted silhouette made the template clear: one of a far darker, life-negating restriction. This pathogenic ideal would be embodied by models, whose '[h]ollow hips, visible ribs and empty stares'[402] have been synonymous with the feminine elite for decades.

'You can never be too rich or too thin,' American-born Wallis, Duchess of Windsor, said.

In a literal sense, the cultivated thinness of the privileged is a metaphor: they are starved of the mother's nurturance on the basis of class. The most influential couturier of the late 20th century, Karl Lagerfeld, had a 'very tough, and very nasty' mother[403] who regularly slammed the piano lid on his fingers as he practised and ridiculed him, 'telling him that his hands were ugly, his nostrils too wide, his hair absurd'.[404] When he later said that he 'admired' pornography and didn't 'like' having sex with people he 'really' loved ('I think this is healthy'),[405] he was, in effect, telling the story of his emotionally isolated infancy, one in which he was made to feel undeserving of passionate attachment by his mother.

Thus conditioned, Lagerfeld, a gay German man forever at war with his weight and vulnerability, later said, 'No one wants to see curvy women.'[406]

American heiress Edie Sedgwick, who, like Leary, was a 1960s American countercultural luminary, was institutionalised at 19 for the eating and related disorders that would characterise her life. 'Her body was threatening to her,'[407] a friend said. This self-alienation was Sedgwick's USP: she embodied the aspirational disordered feminine – a Sleeping Beauty for the late 20th century, drugged and emotionally comatose in her tower of privilege.

'I've got pictures in this album,' American designer Betsey Johnson said of Sedgwick, her first fitting model. 'Here's Edie in the "skeletal" – silver outlining the collar bone, the arm, the pelvis … a kind of bone layout. I mean, that's *timeless.*'[408]

During a day pass from the hospital, Sedgwick fell pregnant to 'a young man from Harvard'. She said, 'I was terrified to tell him that I thought I was pregnant, but I finally did … I could get an abortion without any hassle at all, just on the grounds of a psychiatric case. So that wasn't too good a first experience of love-making. I mean, it kind of screwed up my head … He split, and I didn't see him again until the summer had passed.'[409]

I mean, it kind of screwed up my head.

Sedgwick became a promiscuous, habitual LSD user with a severe drug use disorder. Prescribed Thorazine[410] and subjected to electroconvulsive therapy, she died at 28 from a barbiturate overdose. The coroner concluded that her death was an 'accident/ suicide'.[411]

This aspirational feminine template, involving substance-facilitated indifference to the mammalian (attachment, babies, femininity, vulnerability), is now entrenched. In 2018, American socialite Cat Marnell, infamous on the basis of her wealth and substance use disorder, wrote, 'My *top* concern was still losing weight. I don't think I ate for a month!'[412]

The curves that define femininity remain associated with low gender status because the value attributed to femininity is so low. Fatness is cultural shorthand for low socio-economic standing, which is why it is deplored and why television audiences are mesmerised by its transcendence (*My Big Fat Diet Show, Secret Eaters, I Used to Be Fat*, and so on).

American data scientist Seth Stephens-Davidowitz observed that a significant percentage of men are far more sexually attracted to overweight women but, on the basis of gender status, date slender women. 'Porn featuring overweight women is surprisingly common among men,' he said. 'But the data from dating sites tells us that just about all men try to date skinny women. Many people don't try to date the people they're most attracted to. They try to date the people they think would impress their friends.'[413]

Pregnancy, then, is the ultimate threat to the fragile construct of the feminine elite. Not only a humiliating reminder of its mammalian origins, but – inescapably – of its parity with the underprivileged. American and British historians Leonore Davidoff and Catherine Hall observed the former emphasis in late 18th and early 19th-century documents, in which women, 'particularly when pregnant and thus incontrovertibly sexual beings, were associated with animalistic nature.'[414] Even as far back as the 16th century, male 'clerical moralists' decided that breastfeeding and sex were incompatible, meaning that privileged women 'who persuaded their husbands to allow them to breast feed were exceptional.'[415]

Queen Victoria concurred. When giving birth, she held, a woman is 'like a cow or a dog', going so far as to rebuke her daughters and granddaughters for 'making cows of themselves' while breastfeeding, which she addressed with 'insurmountable disgust'.[416] In the aristocratic tradition, Princess Michael of Kent, Queen Elizabeth II's cousin by marriage and the daughter of SS officer Baron Gunther von Reibnitz,[417] described breastfeeding as a 'dreadful practice' and advised women against it. 'I didn't breastfeed,' she said. 'My nanny said it was disgusting.'[418]

The inferiority of the feminine has always been predicated on its overtly mammalian nature.

8. THE RULES OF DETACHMENT

'Never touch your idols: the gilding will stick to your fingers.'

Madame Bovary, Gustave Flaubert

Initially the hallmark of the maternal elite, the post-birth separation of mother and baby is now standard practice. Associated with a host of issues with significant economic and social repercussions, the isolation of the newborn not only fractured mother/baby attachment, but also the baby's *capacity* for attachment. The impact of this loss on the mother, which was emblematic in terms of character, was recorded by American novelist F. Scott Fitzgerald in *The Great Gatsby* (1925), in which the disengaged upper-class heroine is asked about her child.

"'I suppose she talks, and – eats, and everything.'"

"Oh, yes." She looked at me absently. "Listen, Nick; let me tell you what I said when she was born. Would you like to hear?"

"Very much."

"It'll show you how I've gotten to feel about – things. Well, she was less than an hour old and Tom was God knows where. *I woke up out of the ether with an utterly abandoned feeling, and asked the nurse right away if it was a boy or a girl. She told me it was a girl, and so I turned my head away and wept* [italics mine].'"[419]

Prince Charles, born by caesarean section – which, in 1948, involved the administration of general anaesthesia – would not have seen his mother, Queen Elizabeth II, for a significant period of time after his birth, and was only briefly breastfed as the Queen contracted measles. Often absent for long periods on foreign tours during his childhood, the Queen was later described by her son as 'cold, distant or unavailable.'[420] The Queen's sense of duty to the Commonwealth is cited as the justification for her inaccessibility to her son in his childhood, but it was clear that there had been significant attachment ruptures. Reported to have been birthed under Twilight Sleep herself, the Queen, in describing childbirth, quoted British poet William Wordsworth: 'a sleep and a forgetting'.[421]

The dawn of motherhood was sold to women by men as something better forgotten.

Adult children of mothers who were – through the administration of drugs, isolation at birth, formula feeding, and/or upper-class tradition – unable to attach to their infants, adopted the usual unilateral Abrahamic ideal (man relating to deity) to manage an otherwise unmanageable primal anguish. As British Prime Minister Winston Churchill wrote of his mother, 'She shone for me like the evening star. I loved her dearly – but at a distance,'[422] and Alice, Edie's sister and the eldest of the seven American Sedgwick heirs, described their glamorous, wealthy mother as a 'god' to whom they had 'very little access'.[423]

British heiress Nancy Cunard, the compulsively promiscuous Jazz Era icon, endured a characteristically upper-class infancy and childhood – 'numerous servants, fresh flowers in her room every morning and absentee parents. Often she did not see either of them for months at a time' as her mother 'felt that with her daughter's birth she had done her duty and could carry on with her own life.' She died in her late sixties weighing 29 kilos, a violent alcoholic and incoherent, burning money and arguing that her condition was the result of fascist cruelty.

In some cases, obstetric anaesthesia made it so that motherlove, which has always visibly thinned up the social ladder, never evolved beyond the most cosmetic displays.

British-Zimbabwean novelist and Nobel Laureate Doris Lessing birthed her first two children in the 1940s. Her second child, a girl, was born, drugged, within half an hour ('There had been very little pain before the chloroform').[424] Lessing abandoned both children twice before they turned 10: once when she remarried, and then again when she emigrated to England. Her justification for the abandonment is remarkable for its lack of empathy: 'You have no idea of the awfulness of it, I was going completely mad … I knew I had to leave … It wasn't the children I was leaving.'[425]

But... it was.

Like all novelists, Lessing used her fictional characters to exorcise socially censured feelings – in particular, the antipathy she felt for her own children. One character finds pregnancy tolerable only 'because of the amount of drugs she took', and refers to her baby as a 'monster', a 'little beast', and 'a troll, or a goblin or something', whom 'no one could love'.[426]

For Lessing, there was no unimpeded flow of attachment or pleasure, no evolution through the experience of motherhood. 'There is nothing more boring for an intelligent woman than to spend endless amounts of time with small children,'[427] she wrote.

British novelist Nancy Mitford's The Pursuit of Love (1945) pivots on the same detachment, if with a reversed trajectory. 'The Bolter,' a character based on five-times divorced Lady (Myra) Idina Sackville,[428,429] captured the zeitgeist. In 1919, Sackville had left her two sons, both under six, and her husband to marry her lover and move to Kenya, where she became the 'High Priestess' of Happy Valley; two husbands and 11 years later, she arranged for her five-year-old daughter to be raised by an aunt in England.[430] Likely indirectly administered chloroform, ether or morphine at birth and isolated from her own mother, Sackville, in her youth, mixed in circles in which 'vast amounts of alcohol', cocaine and morphine were abused.[431] To return to that comforting 'haze of drugs and alcohol,'[432] she divested herself of all responsibilities that required sobriety.

As Iris Storm, the wild fictional femme fatale based on Sackville, says, 'You don't know the bodyache for a child, the ache that destroys a body. *I am … she who destroys her body because she must* [italics mine].'[433]

Taken to extremes, this destruction of the physical self became iconic. In part, the continued relevance of American poet Sylvia Plath's work pivots on the resonance of the same detachment.

Almost a month to the day after her first and only novel, The Bell Jar, was published, Plath placed her head in a gas oven and asphyxiated herself. This suicide was not merely in keeping with the punitive aspirational feminine ideal, but its glittering climax. Plath had married Ted Hughes, the future British Poet Laureate, and challenged him, through her work and demands for intimacy, with her desire for reciprocal respect. Hughes responded by asserting his dominance through emotional and physical violence. Manipulating her jealousy, he was unfaithful – Assia Wevill, his married German mistress, became pregnant to him – ostensibly justifying Plath's chilling final act of feminine gender mastery.

Daddy, I have had to kill you.[434]

By marrying and provoking a patriarch like Hughes, Plath engineered a situation in which she could fulfil the cultural mandate. In its way, it was the perfect victory. Insulated from her emotions by the anti-depressants she'd been prescribed by a male doctor, sealing the room so that the gas could not reach her two little children, having written *Ariel*, the posthumously published poetry anthology that secured her place in literary history, and effectively severing her own head in an oven, that symbol of nurturance, Plath executed a peerless act of revenge against the patriarchal without sacrificing any gender status. As it had with Sedgwick, her self-destructiveness amplified, rather than detracted from, her femininity.

> *If I've killed one man, I've killed two –*
> *The vampire who said he was you*
> *And drank my blood for a year,*
> *Seven years, if you want to know.*[435]

Plath wrote these words a month after leaving Hughes, and killed herself a fortnight before the seventh anniversary of their first meeting.[436] Hughes was in the arms of another woman at the time.[437]

Ironically, Plath's adherence to the patriarchal rules of gender secured her against criticism for abandoning her babies in an act of violence so vindictive that it triggered a domino chain of five deaths – the first in 1963, when Wevill terminated her pregnancy out of respect for Plath's suicide; the second and third in 1969, when Wevill gassed herself and Shura, the four-year-old daughter she had to Hughes, with a gas oven (an homage of sorts to Plath); the fourth when Hughes's mother Edith, shocked by the murder-suicide, suffered a thrombosis, lapsing into a coma and dying three days later;[438] and the last in 2009, when Nicholas, the second of Plath's two children by Hughes, hanged himself.[439]

Suicide as serial murder.

In *The Bell Jar*, Plath reveals not only her impaired ability to love, but her troubled relationship with infancy and motherhood, suggesting that her suicide was not only vengeful but evasive. The words 'I love' appear only once in the novel in relation to another person, whereas 'I hate' appears 13 times ('I hated his guts', 'I hated the idea of serving men', and so on); in comparison, the word 'baby' appears 69 times, often in a grotesque, medicalised context and associated with death and torture ('a baby pickled in a laboratory jar', 'big glass bottles full of babies that had died before they were born', 'the baby in the last bottle ... seemed to be looking at me and smiling a little piggy smile').[440]

As she witnesses a hospital birth, *The Bell Jar*'s protagonist Esther Greenwood is told, 'You oughtn't to see this. You'll never want to have a baby if you do. They oughtn't to let women watch. It'll be the end of the human race.' Greenwood is 'struck' by the sight of the 'awful torture table, with these metal stirrups sticking up in mid-air at one end and all sorts of instruments and wires and tubes' at the other. She discovers that the labouring woman, who 'never stopped making this unhuman whooing noise', had, through Twilight Sleep, been made to 'forget she'd had any pain ... the sort of drug a man would invent ... when all the time, in some secret part of her, that long, blind, doorless and windowless corridor of pain was waiting to open up and shut her in again.'[441]

Plath's fascination with disturbing, drug-distorted births is an echo of her own suffering as an infant.[442] Her now-commonplace themes in relation to childbirth – depersonalisation, drug-induced dissociation, medicalisation orchestrated by the masculine, mother/baby separation and the resultant and enduring self-alienation – are unique to the past two or so centuries.

The Bell Jar makes the elisions in her psyche clear. Even when Greenwood attempts suicide, it is by crawling into a 'dark gap' that 'felt thick as velvet' and overdosing on pills secreted in *her mother's drawer*,[443] returning to the disorientating, transformational sphere of drugs and dark uterine space she knew at birth. This was a gossamer fictionalisation of Plath's first serious suicide attempt by overdosing on her mother's sleeping pills and hiding in a crawl space in the basement, behind a pile of firewood. When she awoke, she 'just kept smashing her head against the stone,' wanting only to die.[444]

In the guise of Greenwood, Plath could safely wonder, 'Why was I so unmaternal and apart?'[445]

Higher rates of medicalised birth intervention,[446] lower rates of breastfeeding,[447,448] a propensity to delegate the care of babies and children to staff,[449] and the institutionalisation of children in schools[450] ensure that the 21st-century feminine elite continues to feel 'unmaternal and apart'.

The delegation of mothering among the elite, whether artistic, corporate or in terms of wealth, continues to be encouraged and applauded. Maternal abuse in the guise of detachment and emotional neglect, described by researchers as 'a pervasive public health challenge with serious long-term effects', is the most rapidly increasing and widespread form of child maltreatment today.[451]

For working- or middle-class mothers, the disengagement of the attachment mechanism can result in a species of emotional void in relation to the child. A Reddit member posted, 'Me and my fiancé planned for this baby, she is 3 months old now but she has been nothing but a disappointment since the day she was born. I don't feel depressed ... I just don't enjoy taking care of her ... I don't hate her. I just don't feel any love towards her. I do all the things I'm supposed to – I feed her, I change her, I bath her, I hold her when she cries – she is never neglected, and I don't enjoy a single second of it. Every time she cries I just think I made a horrible mistake by having her. Even when she is happy and being all cute it is boring.'[452]

My mother was the same: a hollowed bone.

In early childhood, I was regularly taken by her with my infant brother to Palm Cove, then little more than a remote road scattered with hippie communes, shacks, and a few motels in far north Queensland, Australia. My father mostly remained in Sydney, working. The influential industrial designer Marc Newson, two years my senior, lived with his young mother, who had been abandoned by his father, up the road; many of his pieces, which now sell for record-breaking millions at auction, look like the jellyfish and shells we used to find washed up on those sands.

I walked alone on those empty beaches, their waters rippling with sharks and stingrays, and, hatless and in nylon shorty shorts, by the sugar cane fields. There, deadly snakes – Black Whips, Death Adders, Eastern Browns, taipans – slip, glistening, in among the greeny-yellow stalks. I remember the slap of my flip-flops (invariably worn on the wrong feet) as they adhered, melting, to the unfinished tarmac, and tripping at any sudden crackling in the bunched-up leaves. If a man, as he drove past, glanced at me over the rolled-down window of his car, I would sing to myself, frightened that I would end up like the girls I heard about on the radio.

My mother was, for the most part, indifferent to my absences.

(Logically, less attached mothers, on the basis of their lesser investment, are willing to take greater risks with their children.)

Half a century or so later, after my brother committed suicide at midnight in a car, I told my mother that I knew she wished that I had died in his place. In reply, only her silence.

The upper classes reframe such detachment as tradition.

Over dinner during their courtship, Elon Musk asked the American author Justine Wilson, who would become his first wife, how many children she wanted. 'One or two,' she replied, 'although if I could afford nannies, I'd like to have four.' Musk, who was raised in privilege, laughed. 'That's the difference between you and me. I just assume that there will be nannies,'[453] he said. Of his five IVF sons to Wilson, he later commented, 'Children are awesome, but I don't see them much. I do [work] email while I'm with my children. And I keep a nanny around – so they don't kill each other.'[454]

Musk's children not only had nannies, but a nanny manager.[455]

British aristocrat Jonathan Gathorne-Hardy asked, 'How was it, that hundreds of thousands of mothers, apparently normal, could simply abandon all loving and disciplining and company of their little children, sometimes almost from birth, to the absolute care of other women, total strangers, nearly always uneducated, about whose characters they must usually have had no real idea at all? It was a practice, as far as I knew, unparalleled on such a vast scale in any other culture which had ever existed.'[456]

That which is never addressed is the sacrifice that these mothers unknowingly make in terms of their own happiness and pleasure.

Among others, the dopaminergic regions – the pleasure centres – of a mother's brain are involved in her optimal response to her baby,[457] meaning that babies are, quite literally, *designed* to make their mothers happy. When this ancient mechanism is impaired, the mother's own pleasure is curtailed. Rather than experiencing passion for her baby, she perceives him as 'boring', rudimentary, discrete, and, on a subconscious level, this understanding becomes the baby's legacy in terms of self-perception: that he is fundamentally undeserving of love.

Engagement with the symphony of labour, the astonishing climax of birth, and tender, sustained postnatal exposure to the infant, was, through masculine birth intervention and obstetric anaesthesia, intercepted in the feminine elite. Thus circumscribed, privileged women – who have always set behavioural fashions for other women – were conditioned to understand sustained intimacy with an infant as primitive, tedious or unnatural. As Queen Victoria said, 'I don't dislike babies, although I think very young ones are rather disgusting.'[458]

These constraints are far from insignificant. It has been shown that even after a year, mothers who were separated from their newborns at birth touched them less than mothers who remained intimate with their babies.[459] Swaddling, the ancient practice of restricting infant movement with fabric, also decreases the mother's responsiveness to her baby; the degree of a mother's emotional involvement will be lessened, as will the sharing of feelings and reciprocity between her and her baby.[460] In the first two hours after birth, breastfeeding and skin-to-skin contact increase a mother's sensitivity to her baby, the baby's self-regulation, and the sharing of feelings and reciprocity between them for up to a year later.

Unless her own infancy was blighted by trauma, routine or otherwise, a woman is revolutionised by the *pleasure* she takes in her baby and in her instinctive maternal competence.

Over the past two or so centuries, the more privileged the woman, the more likely she was to be chemically, and through incremental cultural customs and abuses, detached from the deep joys unique to the feminine and maternal experiences. Her gilding was not permitted to be touched, particularly by her child. The cavernous anxieties these separations created became associated with femininity itself, leading men to reframe the 'theoretical merger of the female nervous and reproductive systems' with dysfunction as a phenomenon 'beyond the regulatory power of the individual will.'[461]

Femininity itself had become the problem, or rather its cultural distortion, so the solution was simple: femininity would have to be phased out.

9. ÜBERMENSCH

> 'Around the hero everything becomes a tragedy.'
>
> *Beyond Good and Evil*, Friedrich Nietzsche

In a 1963 US Navy 'Maternity Care' training film, a male obstetrician pulls an infant from its comatose, mostly obscured, maternal casing. Pale and motionless, the baby could be dead. He remains unresponsive throughout, held upside-down – babies were often gripped by the feet, brandished like prize halibut – and is repeatedly, and roughly, prodded by the masked obstetrician, whose efforts to revive him are unsuccessful. In those days, babies were tested with a finger flick,[462] or held upside-down and slapped on the bottom, at times so violently that their hips were dislocated, to encourage breathing.[463]

There is no tenderness or jubilation at this baby's birth. Instead, only the obstetrician's detachment in the guise of concern. For over two centuries, newborns have been abused, bullied and terrified into understanding that men are in charge.

The US Navy film's male narrator instructs his listeners, 'Notice the appearance and sleepiness of this baby.' (The infant is not sleepy but unconscious and unable to breathe.) 'It takes quite a bit of time for the doctor to arouse him and get him breathing satisfactorily on his own. This occurs more commonly when the mother is unconscious or sleepy from receiving general anaesthesia [which is] necessary for certain types of deliveries.' (Again, the doublespeak: the obstetrician is presented as a hero, saving a baby he stupefied through the life-threatening interventions then justified as 'necessary'.)

Heroes cannot exist without victims, so where there is no victim, one must be manufactured.

The labouring women in this film are forced into helplessness: incapacitated by obstetric drugs, flat on their backs, their faces erased by oxygen masks, their vulvas bald, and with their legs wide apart and strapped to a frame in the lithotomy position.

Their wrists are secured by leather straps to keep their hands 'from *unintentionally infecting* the perineal area [italics mine]'.

Unintentionally infecting: the maternal as pathogenic, unclean.

In the sonorous tone associated with hypnosis, the male narrator continues, patronising his female viewers: 'You will no longer feel the urge to bear down. So, when your doctor tells you to, you'll bear down, *and only then* [italics mine].'[464]

Like most 19th-century doctors, Gauss and Kronig, the developers of Twilight Sleep, perceived mothers as children of sorts who must, at all costs, be prevented from maturing into adults. Labouring women were to be 'protected' from the levelling and maturing experience of pain. Their understanding of the vagina would never evolve – to them, it would forever remain a sheath for the penis, rather than the door to human existence. In order to secure subordination, feminine awareness of the power and potential of its own body was denied.

The feminine head, with full consent, was thus severed.

Within the space of a few generations, the understanding of femininity and motherhood was, by men, almost entirely altered. Women would no longer understand the sculptural impact on the psyche of birth and intimate motherhood. Instead, they were, through obstetric brutality, conditioned to perceive themselves as vessels for the dominant masculine. This was, of course, in keeping with Nietzsche's sentiments ('Let your hope say: "May I bear the Superman!"').[465]

Through obstetric anaesthesia, the masculine assumed power of attorney over human reproduction. The authorship of birth was attributed – with maternal consent and gratitude – to the male physician, with the mother reframed as *his patient*: an envelope of flesh to be delivered of a child.

Selling the process to women was like shooting fish in a bucket.

During an American Gynaecological Society meeting in 1920, and without considering the inhibitory impact on labour of environment, the influential American obstetrician Joseph DeLee described the experience of childbirth, for a woman, as something like 'falling on a pitchfork and driving the handle through her perineum'.[466]

Given 'authoritative' statements of this nature, it's not difficult to see why women began to clamour for obstetric anaesthesia. The drug-facilitated erasure of authority, consciousness, involvement and memory in the labouring feminine soon became pivotal to the maintenance of masculine domination. Even in 2021, British-South African anaesthesiology professor Abdul-Ghaaliq Lalkhen described the labouring mother demanding pain relief as 'reduced' – that is, diminished, made lesser – 'to a feral and illogical spectre as she is consumed with pain.'[467]

Feral, illogical, spectre, consumed – the language of masculine horror in relation to the most powerful physical expression of femininity has become the cultural prism through which childbirth is understood.

Scopolamine, the deliriant in Twilight Sleep, disturbs both memory function[468] and the brain's organisational processes.[469] As George Blacker explained in British medical journal *The Lancet*, the 'abolition of memory' was the aim.[470] To this end, some of the memory tests suggested by Gauss involved flashing the labouring mother a knife and asking if she'd seen it before.[471]

Not a spoon or a coloured card, but a *knife* waved by a masked doctor at a restrained, naked woman in a drugged delirium. *At its most vulnerable, the feminine was threatened by the masculine with a weapon.* Imagine, for a moment, the resulting terror of the women who remained semi-conscious, and the hormonal impact of their terror on the foetus.

If the mother's response to the knife passed muster, the delivery suite was darkened, her ears were plugged with cotton wool, and, at the moment of birth, a towel was placed over her face lest she distract the medical staff with her 'excitement'.[472]

These associations, between childbirth and feminine effacement, and between feminine silencing and violence, would, for the first time, become imprinted on the subconscious in relation to birth, creating, in place of passionate and proud attachment, a terror-based antipathy between mother and child, and between the feminine and its biology.

Given that only 58.9 percent of Twilight Sleep mothers achieved 'complete amnesia',[473] the rest – blinded by bandages, semi-conscious, their breathing stifled, perineal muscles sliced, and with restrictions placed upon their agency that left them bleeding – experienced the panic that called for a deeper drugging.

Physicians, in an attempt to control the feminine, administered layers of drugs that would later be associated with death and deformation. George Blacker, for example, advised that when the baby's head 'is escaping over the perineum', a 'little chloroform'[474] should be administered to the mother in addition to the original Twilight Sleep cocktail, and 'considerable chloroform' was to be administered if she exhibited 'violent states of agitation'.[475]

Through scopolamine, the mother was thus not merely stupefied, but rendered psychotic. An American who gave birth at the age of 19 in 1966 under Twilight Sleep remained traumatised by her partial recall. 'I was in a labour room with eight other women in labour,' she wrote on a forum. 'I was in a stainless steel crib with the sides up – high metal bars. I was thrashing around and screaming uncontrollably. Even as I was screaming, I was thinking that I should not be screaming because I would upset the other labouring women, but I had no control over my actions. I can remember screaming my doctor's name and yelling.'[476]

Memory functions differently when the fear circuitry is triggered. A seahorse-shaped formation at the brain's core, the hippocampus encodes experiences into short-term memories and stores them as long-term memories, but fear subverts its capacity to encrypt and log time-sequencing and contextual information.[477]

What this means is that, in addition to the delirium created by Twilight Sleep, the fear experienced by labouring mothers in semi-consciousness scrambled their ability to create any kind of continuous, coherent narrative. In relation to birth, this was a catastrophe. The terror experienced would not have been recalled in context – resulting from the obstetrician brandishing a knife in order to test memory, say – but as a dog's breakfast of horror: masked man flashing knife, struggling, drugged, unable to move, screaming, searing pain, masked man penetrating the vagina with his hands, a bloodied baby.

This is, of course, in addition to the terror experienced by the drugged foetus in response to the mother's psychosis.

Another American Twilight Sleep mother remembered drifting 'in and out of awareness; I could not control myself in any way – I remember the pain, nurses laughing at me, and horrifying things happening to me. After it was over, I tried to tell my doctor that I could remember a lot of my labour. He just laughed and said that was impossible. I suffered PTSD [Post-Traumatic Stress Disorder]

… night terrors, depression, flashbacks. The worst was that I had no recognition of my baby. Nothing! He was a complete stranger to me.'[478]

Twilight Sleep didn't merely interrupt the narrative of childbirth, but completely changed it. No longer a revolution in a woman's life with everything a revolution entails, birth became a podium for masculine triumphalism. As Abdul-Ghaaliq Lalkhen wrote, 'The rescuer feels guilty if he or she doesn't go to the rescue.'[479] Namely, birth intervention, rather than being for the benefit of the mother and child, has always been primarily driven by the needs of medical professionals.

Through the administration of drugs, obstetricians established themselves as the new deities of childbirth. As American academic David Leeming wrote, when 'gods and humans become involved, the humans always suffer.'[480]

The gender status needs of the obstetricians – to feel like heroes and saviours, embodiments of the Nietzschean *Übermensch* – overrode all other considerations. In every respect, delivery suites were theatres for this ancient patriarchal gender template: the bound, naked feminine, stripped of its identity through the obscuring of the face and often presented in multiples – production-line generic – was, in its entirety, vulnerable to the masked, clothed and dominant singular masculine.

This gender template, further ratified by artists, was not criticised but celebrated.

Male artists routinely stripped their muses of identity – clothing is also part of our cultural identity – in order to define themselves as cultural leaders. In 1947, American photographer Saul Leiter, in a belted mackintosh, included in his self-portrait a young, naked woman identified only as 'Inez',[481] and in 1963, French-American artist Marcel Duchamp, 76, was photographed playing chess in a suit with a naked 20-year-old woman.[482,483]

A different emphasis to the same effect can be found on the back cover of 1968's *The Madcap Laughs*, the first solo album by Syd Barrett. In the shot, he is clothed and addressing the camera, while a naked woman is in the background, looking away.

In all three shots, the women's faces are deliberately obscured, by shadow, hair and angle respectively.

In 2013, the trope was rehashed for the cover of Nick Cave's album *Push the Sky Away*, in which an erect Cave – suited and booted – opens the shutters as his naked wife Susie (hair obscuring her identity, looking down) enters the frame. The power dynamic in the image is unambiguous, and supported by the name of Susie Cave's fashion label, The Vampire's Wife, in which the feminine is, however ironically, identified exclusively in relation to, and as solely remarkable because of, the mythological masculine.

Patriarchal status has always been contingent on the display of property. In the photograph, Cave appears to be expelling his wife from Paradise, or, on a more prosaic level, opening the shutters in order that she can be better seen. In reality, Cave was assisting at her fashion shoot, but the French photographer, Dominique Issermann, captured a dynamic between the couple, one in which Cave – characteristically neutralising the subtext with talk of art and mythology – revelled. 'How lovely the cover is and how beautiful my wife looks – the animal stance, up on her toes, the defensive positioning of her arms, and her face hidden in her hair,' he wrote, adding that it was 'probably' her 'most treasured shot of herself'.[484]

That is to say, Susie Cave's most treasured shot of herself is one in which her face cannot be seen.

In these and other examples, the feminine is depicted as an Abrahamic subset of the masculine: mute, stripped, ornamental, a species of domesticated animal. The pornographic magazines *Playboy* and *Penthouse* took this understanding further, christening the women who modelled for them 'bunnies' and 'pets'. Lack of individuality (through nudity in conjunction with the obscuring of the face or identity) is, in such *mises-en-scène*, essential; any feminine assertion of character would not only detract attention from the masculine, but suggest that the feminine warrants attention beyond its physical self.

Picasso, whose rearrangements of the female face symbolised the same principle, could only have become synonymous with art in a patriarchal century. He perceived women as 'machines for suffering'[485] – a machine being the construct of, and operated by, men, whose job it clearly is to calibrate the degree of pain. To Picasso, sexual penetration was a *coup d'état*, with the feminine cast as excitingly hostile territory.

As he aged and his 'muses' grew younger and more powerless, Picasso increasingly presented the feminine as generic. This was a reflection of waning sexual interest, for he equated charged eroticism with violence, but his gender blueprint never changed: the dominant masculine redefining the vanquished feminine through the progressive processes of penetration, emotional abuse, and visual possession, for which he was rewarded in status by the greater culture. As Picasso told French artist Marie Françoise Gilot, the mother of his youngest two children, 'You imagine people will be interested in *you*? They won't ever, really, just for yourself. Even if you think people like you, it will only be a kind of curiosity they will have about a person whose life has touched mine so intimately. And you'll be left with only the taste of ashes in your mouth.'[486]

The artist, in making victims of his muses, remasters himself as a hero, saving them from their otherwise inconsequential lives.

Painted when he was a small, bald man of 87, Picasso's 1968 erotic etchings feature almost comically vapid young women being penetrated by an artist with a preposterously large penis. In this respect, he was continuing an artistic tradition dating back to Ancient Egypt, one that persisted through the Chinese, Greek, Japanese, Roman and other male-dominated cultures. This weaponisation of the penis – rather than, say, presenting it as what Leeming called 'an instrument of love'[487] – is understood as a visual directive for the male to sexually dominate the female, a directive that has distorted our civilisation for millennia. Also implicit in this exaggeration is an importance – the penis is presented as the mutual focal point: in essence, an idol – validated by its depiction in a significant work of art.

Over the past two centuries, the same principles have been at play in obstetric theatres, where the feminine is disabled before being penetrated by masculine hands or instruments, and symbolically owned: belittled, humiliated, and deprived of her identity as a mother through the isolation of her infant.

At the core of this deprivation, a transference of ownership.

Stripped of all agency and memory in relation to birth, Twilight Sleep mothers had no visceral sense of ownership over their babies. Some have posited that the experience of natural, rather than drug-amplified, labour pain segues into the maternal territoriality that triggers desire to nurture the baby. The Ancient Greek philosopher Aristotle, for example, believed that 'the reason why mothers are more devoted to their children than fathers ... is that they suffer more in giving them birth and are [thus] more certain that they are their own.'[488]

In the American Navy 'Maternity Care' film, one of the mothers tentatively reaches out to her newly-born infant and just as suddenly withdraws her hand. This fleeting sequence illustrates the impaired territoriality by which modern mothers are defined, whereas the nurse's confident appropriation of the baby – deciding the angle at which she holds the baby to its mother, and for how long – tells a story. The infant, in effect, *belongs to the hospital*: an obstetric junta over feminine territory.

Even now, images of babies in hospital still largely feature them in the arms of nurses.

In keeping with this transference of territory, nurseries became a fixture of US hospitals in the early 20th century. The 1943 edition of the American Academy of Paediatrics' *Standards and Recommendations for Hospital Care of Newborn Infants* specified that a 'viewing window should be provided ... so that relatives may see the infants *without coming in contact with them* [italics mine].'[489] American midwife Faith Gibson described nurseries as 'an almost military regime, with limitations on visitors and a host of precautions that made hospital maternity wards user-unfriendly.'[490]

Babies isolated from their mothers in hospital were, in the 1940s, found to exhibit symptoms associated with sensory deprivation. Such babies 'would lie in their cots with averted faces, refusing to take part in the life of their surroundings.'[491] Forty years later, the same syndrome was observed in hospitalised infants. Isolated babies seemed 'hopeless and listless, indifferent to food, immobile, and despairing', 'sad and hopeless', 'dejected' and showing 'a withdrawn affect that is utterly unresponsive to environmental stimuli.'[492]

Conversely, babies who are immediately placed skin-to-skin with their mothers after birth have been shown to make the transition to life *ex utero* with superior glucose, respiratory and temperature stability, optimal brain development, and significantly less crying.[493]

Judging from his year of birth and later bonding impairments, drug abuse and well-documented sexual compulsivity, British Rolling Stones frontman Mick Jagger[494] was likely indirectly administered

Twilight Sleep at birth, as the cocktail remained popular in England until the 1950s.[495] He was also undoubtedly isolated from his mother in a nursery immediately after birth. This theory is also borne out by the song 'Sister Morphine', in which Jagger asks how long he has been lying in an unknown place, where the doctor has no face – that is, he was masked.[496]

Born in 2005, my daughter was not taken from me after birth, but there was a limit to the intimacy the nursing staff were willing to tolerate without attempts at dissuasion. I remember the affable young midwife on duty who, on seeing that I'd taken my newborn into my bed, suddenly observed that the hospital refused to be legally liable for injury.

Legally liable.

I now wonder at the impact of that brief, almost lyrical, burst of alliteration on more susceptible new mothers. With those two words, the midwife altered the tenor of my maternal reverie with *consciousness of my subordination* – to the hospital, to the law, to her – in relation to my baby, establishing my awareness of an unimportance that would, a decade later, reach its zenith in the Family Court. With those two words and a soft smile, she triggered in me an atavistic fear of loss.

Would my baby be taken from me because I loved her too much?

In Bethesda's hospital notes, the midwife wrote: 'Mother wishes to sleep in bed and have baby in bed with her … Mother made aware that it is not hospital policy and that baby is in a bed *with no protection* except for cot sides and could fall out and that no responsibility can be taken by staff. Mother still wished to sleep on bed with baby [italics mine].'

With no protection.

Was I not my baby's source of nurturance, emotional and physical, and bodyguard? What is a mother if not a protector?

The likelihood of my baby being injured during co-sleeping was, in reality, significantly lower than it would have been had I left her in the hospital cot. In the UK, 90 percent more babies die alone in baskets or cots – Sudden Infant Death Syndrome – than they do when they securely, rather than hazardously, co-sleep with their mothers.[497] The midwife's warning, then, was founded not on fact, but her own discomfort at my intimacy with my baby.

I still wonder at the social cost of her aligning mother/baby closeness with potential injury to the infant. As a result of her words, younger or more nervous mothers may have questioned not only their instincts, but also the wisdom of mother/baby intimacy itself.

Billions of women have been duped into surrendering – in the process derealising – their babies on this basis, and even more have been duped into believing that they need drugs at birth.

Midwives, too, can serve the patriarchy.

10. WASTED

'I didn't know how to live without drugs.'
Creation Stories: Riots, Raves and Running a Label, by Alan McGee

The emphasis on the maintenance of masculine status at the expense of the feminine is, in the 1963 US Navy 'Maternity Care' training film, self-evident.[498] To this end, the camera pans over a selection of obstetric anaesthetics and analgesics, some of which are still in use. In order of viewing and to be administered under the guidance of masked obstetricians – Jagger's doctors without faces – they are:

- *Ether*: now obsolete as an anaesthetic, and associated with liver damage, convulsions, impaired immune response and respiratory paralysis;[499,500,501]

- *Morphine sulphate*: the principal alkaloid of opium, and associated with respiratory depression and lowered blood pressure;[502]

- *Trichloroethylene*: a halocarbon used as an industrial solvent, identified as a carcinogen and associated with altered sperm structure, cardiac arrhythmias, cranial nerve dysfunction, foetal toxicity, menstrual disorders, and reduced fertility;[503]

- *Promethazine hydrochloride*: adverse foetal effects have been shown in animal studies although there are, as yet, no corresponding human studies;[504]

- *Lidocaine hydrochloride*: associated with slowed foetal heartrate, low muscle tone and neonatal respiratory depression;[505]

- *Nembutal Sodium*: used for human and animal euthanasia, pentobarbital is a barbiturate associated with adverse effects on foetal brain development and can pass into breastmilk with harmful effects on the nursing baby. Discontinued since 1999, it is, like other barbiturates, high in alkalinity.[506] This is a critically important factor in relation to obstetric anaesthesia.

The most suble changes in amniotic pH – the scale of acidity – can cause significant derangement of the foetal central nervous, cardiovascular and other organ systems, resulting in distress and poor outcome.[507,508,509]

- *Meperidine hydrochloride*: given the rapid placental absorption, the obstetric administration of pethidine has a 'significant' effect on foetal heart rate and, used with other neurodepressants, is associated with profoundly lowered blood pressure, feeding problems, and changes in the brain's electrical activity;[510]

- *Nisentil*: known as prodine, and linked to potentially life-threatening respiratory depression and, even at normal therapeutic doses, with respiratory depression;[511] and

- *Pontocaine hydrochloride*: administered in an anaesthetic capacity, tetracaine hydrochloride is linked to cellular oxygen deprivation – potential outcomes include coma, seizures, and death; babies are more susceptible to these effects, and the risk is increased if combined with some of the aforementioned drugs, such as lidocaine.[512]

Anaesthetic and sedative neurotoxicity in foetuses through the administration of obstetric drugs to the mother has been found to place the foetal brain at 'significant risk for neurodegenerative changes.'[513]

While coloured and working-class women were, for the first quarter of the 20th century, generally spared obstetric anaesthesia, its administration to women of all classes soon became commonplace. Those for whom such drugs had, since the 19th century, been synonymous with birth – namely, the upper classes – had, however, always been distinguished by their emotional remoteness and partiality to psychoactive substances.

British journalist Sean Thomas, a former 'middle-class [heroin] addict', documented his experiences with this 'refined subspecies of addict: the upper-crust junkie.' There is, he wrote of Narcotics Anonymous meetings, 'something disagreeable about spending your afternoons listening to poor little rich girls and boys tell their tragic life stories to one another. You can't help thinking of all the truly deprived addicts, for whom heroin is an analgesic necessity, rather than a giggle gone wrong.'[514]

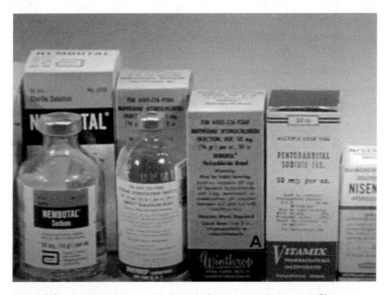

Still from 'Maternity Care', a United States Navy training film, 1963.

In this analysis of dysfunctional aristocrats, Thomas revealed only his own prejudice and status anxiety. A 'giggle gone wrong' minimises the grave emotional and neurodevelopmental abuses of babies born to the elite, a trivialisation that, in its cultural entrenchment, serves not only to compound divisiveness, but ensures the continuation of obstetric abuses that bleed the ruling classes of the empathy and tenderness they are then criticised for lacking. While privilege has always assured individual comfort and status, it was also a guarantee of critical emotional deprivation during infancy and, over the past two centuries in particular, neurodevelopmental damage.

The consequences of both would prove far-reaching.

Prince Charles, born to the 22-year-old Queen Elizabeth by caesarean section in 1948,[515] is likely, in an obstetric capacity, to have been indirectly administered either chloroform or ether[516] in addition to an amalgam of atropine, cyclopropane, thiobarbiturate and tubocurarine.[517] It's also likely that the Prince was stupefied or unconscious at birth, whereupon he would have been separated from his mother for up to two days, perhaps even longer on an intermittent basis, as the Queen recovered from her neurotoxic ordeal.

As it had been with Queen Victoria, the administration of these drugs to royalty was the greatest of endorsements.

The drugs that were indirectly administered to the Prince were commonplace in terms of their obstetric application. In certain circumstances, the use of atropine was, in fact, considered 'almost essential' in tandem with Twilight Sleep.[518]

Atropine, like scopolamine, is an anticholinergic drug. In its capacity as an obstetric anaesthetic, it suppresses the mother's sweat,[519] interrupts active labouring, decreases the production of saliva, is associated with the suppression of foetal breathing, and inhibits the production of breastmilk through the inhibition of oxytocin – a key birth, and the key love, hormone – and growth hormone.[520]

The inhibition of oxytocin is particularly relevant as the hormone contracts the uterus, helping labour progress, and helps with the birthing of the placenta, the minimisation of bleeding, and warms the breast for the baby.

Research has shown that oxytocin- and dopamine-rich pathways in the brain are used to form the 'model motivational system' in mothers, determining their degree of engagement with, and tenor of responses to, their babies.[521,522] Critically, oxytocin 'reduces anxiety, stress and pain in labour and switches on brain pleasure and reward centres, making the new mother relaxed, and happy as she meets her baby for the first time.'[523]

Modern obstetric drugs also reduce the natural flow of the mother's oxytocin.[524]

As with oxytocin, levels of dopamine – the brain's motivational system – have been shown to be decreased by scopolamine,[525,526] meaning that Twilight Sleep mothers felt less, little or no motivation to nurture their babies. In terms of neurodevelopment alone, this was a catastrophe. The more intense the intimacy enjoyed by a mother with her infant, the more refined his oxytocin system. As adults, individuals with well-developed oxytocin systems are confident and trusting in their interactions, attach securely in intimate relationships, and know how to manage their anxiety.[527]

The majority of the post-birth hormonal changes that determine nurturing behaviours in mothers are not inherent, but *driven by interactions with their babies*.[528]

What this means is that Queen Elizabeth took significantly

less pleasure and felt more anxiety and stress in the wake of her first child's birth than she would have otherwise, and felt less of an inclination to nurture him.

The mother's experience of anxiety, depression, or fear, whether in response to past or present stimuli, disrupts the equipoise between emotional regulation and the evolution of maternal empathy and motivation.[529] Agitated mothers fail to love their babies properly. Prince Charles, as a result, would have been anxious, distrustful, lacking in confidence, and characterised by insecure attachments.

Such deficits determine the tenor not only of a single existence, but those of the following generations.

Despite its FDA Pregnancy Category C rating ('Animal reproduction studies have shown an adverse effect on the foetus and there are no adequate and well-controlled studies in humans'),[530] atropine continues to be used in an obstetric context.

Tubocurarine, historically an arrow poison,[531] has been shown to significantly decrease heart rate and mean arterial pressure in foetal lambs.[532] Thiobarbiturates, too, have been shown to constrict airways and 'may have a loose association with clinical bronchospasm', which is why preventative 'large doses' were said to be necessary.[533]

It has been shown that many neurological disorders are the result of environmental hazards in early life.[534] The synthetic opioid pethidine (meperidine), for example, was once one of the most widely-administered obstetric drugs. Dangerous to babies due to its sedative effects, pethidine is associated with apnea (breathing cessation), bradycardia (dangerously slow heart rate), and cyanosis (the blue colouring that results from low oxygen in red blood cells), in addition to being aligned with breastfeeding complications.[535,536] It takes 13 to 23 hours to be expelled from the newborn system, with its toxic metabolite[537] norpethidine, a stimulant and convulsant or seizure-causing drug,[538] still present in the baby's system at 62 hours.[539]

All of this and related information has been available for over a decade, and yet pethidine continues to be administered to labouring mothers.

A decade after the 1963 US Navy 'Maternity Care' film was made, obstetric anaesthesia was used in 95 percent of deliveries in 18 large American teaching hospitals. In Houston alone, women were prescribed an average of 10 drugs during pregnancy and childbirth, and four years later, the number rose to 15.[540]

This pathological tendency to flood the labouring mother's body with neurotoxins continues.

Like the early 20th-century lobbyists for Twilight Sleep, women continue, both in fiction and in person, to advocate the administration of drugs during childbirth because they have been assured by medical professionals that such drugs are both necessary and harmless. In the television adaptation of Canadian novelist Margaret Atwood's 1985 novel *The Handmaid's Tale*, the protagonist Offred says, 'I think I'll just feel safer in a hospital ... I want doctors and nurses and ... lots of drugs.'[541]

British journalist Teresa Fitzherbert's 'debut labour went on for days. Short of smoking the baby out, they used every contraption and drug known to man.'[542] American actor Tina Fey 'very quickly accepted Stadol, which is a narcotic. A lot of women would say it's bad to do that because you are giving your baby a narcotic. But she's fine. She's really, really fine. When I woke up, somehow I was almost completely dilated and the nurses were congratulating me. Then I had an epidural, and I was lucky that it was a good one and effective. I always knew I wanted an epidural. I am not a daredevil. I had lived a drug-free life until that moment. I had never done any recreational drugs, and I felt like I had saved them all up for the moment when that baby was coming.'[543]

I had saved them all up for the moment when that baby was coming.

Stadol (Butorphanol), the drug Fey not only 'very quickly accepted' but effectively promoted to women ('But she's fine. She's really, really fine.') has been linked to low blood pressure and respiratory depression. There are no adequate reports or well-controlled studies of the drug's impact on pregnant women prior to 37 weeks, or on nursing mothers, despite the fact that it passes into breastmilk. And even though Butorphanol crosses the placental barrier, there are, again, 'no adequate reports or well-controlled studies in human foetuses.'[544]

The administration of Butorphanol to labouring women is, in fact, discouraged on the basis of animal studies that have shown it has adverse effects on the foetus and is associated with a higher incidence of stillbirth.[545]

Drugs widely administered to pregnant and labouring women – among others, benzodiazepines, barbiturates, dexmedetomidine, isoflurane, ketamine, nitrous oxide, and propofol[546,547] – are all associated[548,549,550] with 'acute neurodegenerative changes and long-term neurobehavioral changes' in non-human primates. Three hours of exposure to isoflurane, which has been described as the 'most detrimental of all inhaled anesthetics',[551] creates 'widespread neurotoxicity in the developing primate brain.'[552]

Incredibly, the global prevalence of benzodiazepine administration during pregnancy is only increasing.[553]

General anaesthesia administered during critical foetal neurodevelopmental periods can result in 'very long lasting' brain function deficits,[554] and regional anaesthesia (epidurals) has been linked to various neurodevelopmental complications in the foetus. Multiple studies have found that 'a wide range of anaesthetic agents can harm the developing brain.'[555,556]

Drugs earmarked by the US Food and Drug Administration (FDA) as potentially dangerous to babies, young children and pregnant women include desflurane (marketed as Suprane), etomidate (Amidate), halothane, isoflurane (Forane), ketamine (Ketalar), lorazepam (Ativan), methohexital (Brevital), midazolam, pentobarbital (Nembutal), propofol (Diprivan), and sevoflurane (Ultane, Sojourn).[557]

Emerging evidence suggests that children under three who've been exposed to general anaesthesia 'are particularly vulnerable to developing a variety of behavioural impairments', and the longer the exposure, the 'more likely it is that the child will exhibit some form of learning disability later in life.'

As researchers noted, the 'few' studies available align the exposure of babies to anaesthesia to 'significant neurocognitive impairment and a variety of behavioral sequelae' – that is, the behavioural consequences of the impairment.[558] Other animal and human studies have shown links between infant exposure to analgesics and impaired neurodevelopmental outcome.[559,560]

Never have the long-term effects of obstetric and other drugs, both legal and illegal, on pregnant women, neonates and children been conclusively studied.[561,562] Their impact on mother and foetus for the duration of labour, say. Or on newborn status. Or on breastfeeding. Or on child growth and development. Or on mother/baby bonding. Or on immediate and long-term maternal and child mental health.[563,564,565]

The full cultural consequences of two or so centuries of unnecessary birth intervention, on a continuum ranging from the subtlest mental and physiological disturbances to maternal or infant death, remain unknown.

In innumerable cases, the toll has been life-altering. One unwed 16-year-old American mother who was administered Twilight Sleep recalled sitting up and down on the bed until her elbows had sheet rash. 'I was crying and wanted to see my aunt,' she recalled. 'The nurse said if I would stop acting like a baby and stop crying, she would let my aunt come in. I begged my aunt to call the doctor, I couldn't bear any more. My son went to his adoptive home for three weeks. I was then notified he was not adoptable because he was brain damaged and would be retarded. He had forceps scars on his head for many years.'[566]

When I asked a fifty-something American writer notorious for his substance abuse if I could interview his mother about her 1960s birth experiences, he refused, stating that she would be too traumatised after years of wondering whether a concatenation of birth interventions had been responsible for his sister's epilepsy and subsequent death.

On 26 August 2001, the British graphic designer Miranda Snow felt ill. A direct descendant of Queen Victoria's physician John Snow through his brother, she was 39 weeks pregnant with her first viable child. As her husband was away, she took herself to hospital. The night wore on and the doctors grew agitated. 'The baby's heart rate is slowing down,' one said. 'Just to be on the safe side, let's get him out.' An anaesthetist was called to perform an epidural. Snow recalls, 'I got really nervous because he was so incredibly terse. He tried to put this thing in my back and couldn't get it right. So he abandoned it. And that's when the story completely changed.'

Snow was put under general anaesthetic so quickly that they didn't even have time to change her clothes. Like generations of Twilight Sleep and c-section mothers around the world, she awoke to complete disorientation, numbness, and no baby.

'I didn't know what time it was, I didn't know where I was. I didn't have the sense that I'd had a child – I felt *nothing*. It was all so surreal. I'd had such a big tummy, and I was so stretched, and then … there was nothing. White noise. I didn't feel like I was *part* of what was happening, even though I realised that I must be from the way everyone addressed me. Everything felt *completely* wrong – I felt as if I were wandering in the woods, lost.' She pauses. 'I didn't feel like screaming until a lot later.'

When one of the consultants told Snow that it took 10 minutes to get her son to breathe, she remembered reading that a human being can only survive for seven minutes without breathing.

'Later that night, I saw Milo for the first time,' she says. 'I knew that it was my son, but it just felt so alien – I couldn't get near him. He never became conscious. It felt very … it just felt … *sad* … that he was so perfect and yet he was never going to open his eyes. After six days, they gently unclipped all his monitors and his respirator and handed him to me properly for the first time.' Snow begins to cry. 'We were on the 13th floor. I took him to the window. All he'd seen was this ghastly room, and so I showed him London – we could see over the rooftops: this lovely view. He died within minutes because he couldn't breathe on his own.'[567]

Within days of her husband's return, Snow told him, 'If I can't have my son, I don't want you, either.' And with those words, their marriage was 'just … *over.*' Eighteen months later, she lost both breasts. The doctors said it was 'quite common' for major trauma to manifest as cancer.

Snow's sense of dissociation was, because of the obstetric general anaesthesia administered, complete. In the disablement of her consciousness, she was removed from the experience of giving birth and in that, from the recognition on which the maternal revolution pivots.

Her body, however, told a darker story, one of insupportable maternal loss. This created a schism so marked that even now, decades later, she feels a need to distance herself from her femininity: the wound remains associated with sex. The prospect of sexual intimacy unnerves her; she fears it will unlock the truths that her body, like a box, contains. Even the scheduled recognition of her son – not in the sweaty, bloody passion of delivery, but in the context of polite consent to his sterile death – seems removed.

She required medical permission to hold her own infant.

Snow still doesn't know what drugs she was administered, or why her baby died.

Sometimes she wonders whether it was because of something she did or ate.

While obstetricians and other medical professionals have, for many decades, been aware that the drugs they administer may damage foetal and newborn brains, their ratification and administration of drugs during pregnancy and labour has only accelerated.

The World Health Organization's (WHO) observation that the 'increasing medicalisation of normal childbirth processes are undermining a woman's own capability to give birth and negatively impacting her birth experience'[568] has been met with medical indifference: obstetric and other drugs continue to be administered to a 'significant' percentage of women with uncomplicated pregnancies.[569]

In Australia, Europe, and North and South America, a multinational study of 9,459 mothers found that 66.9 percent had used over-the-counter medication during pregnancy, and 68.4 percent and 17 percent had, respectively, taken a minimum of one medication for the treatment of acute or short-term illnesses and chronic or long-term disorders during pregnancy. Housewives, women with a lower educational level, and those who had an unplanned pregnancy – in short, those most vulnerable to medical doublespeak – most often reported using medication during pregnancy for chronic or long-term disorders.[570]

For example, an American study found that 28.2 percent of pregnant women reported chronic pain conditions (neck and/ or back pain, headaches, and so on). In this group, 95.5 percent had been prescribed at least one medication. Acetaminophen, also known as paracetamol and Tylenol,[571] was prescribed to almost half these women despite the fact that, during pregnancy, its use has been associated with 'significantly' higher risks of ADHD, Autism Spectrum Disorder (ASD), and hyperactivity in the child.[572,573]

Interestingly, Abdul-Ghaaliq Lalkhen noted that it's 'common' for chronic pain to begin during pregnancy.[574] While, on a mechanical level, this pain can be attributed to other causes, I believe that pregnancy, in its inescapable and sometimes involuntary femininity – a state that fundamentally patriarchal activists are currently working to deny – confronts women with the deepest pain: the grief resulting from millennia of culturally sanctioned abuses, disregard and oppression.

Findings show that, excluding iron, drugs had been prescribed
for 82% of the women during pregnancy, and the average number
prescribed was 4. Self-medicated drugs were taken by 65% of the
women, and the average number taken was 1.5. The proportion
of mothers taking different categories of drugs ranged from 82%
to 1.2%. The mean duration of drug therapy for the various categories of drugs ranged from 125 to 10 days. Fifty-seven percent
of the women smoked, and only 12% abstained completely from
alcohol.

Of the drugs prescribed for "medical" purposes, analgesics
(especially aspirin) rated twice as high as any other category.
Next came barbiturates, then antacids, diuretics, antiemetics, and
drugs acting on the respiratory system. These were followed by
the combined groups of antibiotics and sulfonamides, tranquilizers
and hypnotics combined, antihistamines, and appetite suppressants.

Excerpt from a 1973 study. Despite the fact that 'very little information
is available about the effects of most drugs on the human foetus', the
authors found that 82 percent of pregnant women had been prescribed
drugs by medical professionals during pregnancy.[1286]

In keeping with an American study that found chronic pain
disorders are 'conspicuously' more prevalent among women,[575]
Lalkhen's clients are predominantly women 'simply because they
live longer than men'.[576] While it may be true that most of Lalkhen's
clients are female and that women live longer than men, I believe
the prevalence of chronic pain among women is due the fact that
it is one of the few culturally permissible expressions of feminine
anguish in a patriarchal culture.

The management of chronic pain during pregnancy is, of
course, under studied.[577]

Correspondingly, there is an urgent need for well-controlled
studies on the use of cannabis, which is increasingly legalised,[578]
during pregnancy. Researchers are calling for evaluations of Δ9-THC
(Δ9-tetrahydrocannabinol, the principal psychoactive component
of cannabis responsible for the 'high' – the Δ is pronounced
'delta') as a developmental neurotoxicant (a substance associated
with adverse impacts on the foetal and infant nervous system and
sense organs).[579] Human and preclinical species data suggests that
prenatal Δ9-THC exposure may lead to 'subtle, persistent changes'
in neurological function and later psychological well-being.[580]

There is no known safe level of cannabis use during pregnancy
or breastfeeding.[581] In America, the Surgeon General has now
issued warnings to pregnant women regarding cannabis use on the

basis of studies showing neurodevelopmental damage in babies.[582]

A significant issue is that the mother's tissues retain Δ9-THC, extending the period of foetal exposure, and even in cases of occasional use of cannabis during pregnancy, exposure persists throughout the term of foetal development.[583,584,585] Rapidly crossing the placental and blood-brain barriers,[586] Δ9-THC accumulates in the foetus, potentially – and permanently – harming its neurodevelopment. In pregnancy, cannabis use is associated with ADHD, memory dysfunctions, miscarriage, and learning disabilities, among other impairments.[587]

Neurodevelopmental damage in babies has, in multiple studies, been shown to result from the mother's cannabis use during pregnancy.[588]

Exposure to Δ9-THC during pregnancy 'can disrupt the complex foetal endogenous cannabinoid signalling system'[589] (biological endocannabinoids – that is, those we produce naturally – are neurotransmitters that are thought to play a role in the regulation of appetite, fertility, foetal development, immunity, mood, pregnancy, and sexual arousal, among other functions).[590,591,592] The fragile foetal brain, exposed to Δ9-THC, responds by increasing its cannabinoid receptors, failing to mature properly[593] and rendering the adult brain more susceptible to addiction.[594] Maternal cannabis use is also linked to acute non-lymphoblastic leukaemia in the child, and teenagers exposed to Δ9-THC in the womb are more vulnerable to nicotine and cannabis addictions, anxiety and depression,[595,596] triggering a cascade of other issues in later life – among them, rapid kidney function decline.[597]

A study of 11,489 children exposed to cannabis prenatally found that, relative to no exposure, they were more likely to have ADHD, social issues and difficulties with attention, body mass index, and sleep, in addition to emotional dysregulation, reduced brain volume and an increase in psychotic behaviours and a proclivity for substance-use disorders.[598,599] Another study associated cannabis use during pregnancy with abnormalities in the child's general development and ADHD, anxiety, depression, hyperactivity, and other mental disorders.[600] The incidence of both autism spectrum disorder diagnosis and low birth weight has also been found to be 50 percent higher in children exposed to cannabis in utero.[601,602]

Despite this, cannabis is the now most commonly used illegal drug during pregnancy.[603] Cannabis use among pregnant women in California between 2009 and 2016, the year the drug was legalised, almost doubled. A fifth of pregnant women under 24 got high: a statistical leap of 69 percent.[604] Given the potency of new cannabis strains, the impact of prenatal use on foetal and infant brains is now a cause for serious concern.

In 1995, the average $\Delta 9$-THC content in cannabis was 4 or so percent; by 2014, it was 12 or so percent: *a 300 percent increase in 19 years.* By 2017, the $\Delta 9$-THC content had increased in potency by 500 percent to 20 percent,[605] with some products potentially containing around 30 percent or higher. Conversely, the CBD (cannabidiol) content associated with various therapeutic benefits has, on average, fallen from approximately 0.28 percent in 2001 to under 0.15 percent in 2014.[606]

The sharp increase in potency is not only commensurate with the inflating market for emotional regulation, but with an equal increase in threat to pregnant women, foetuses and children.

The strongest determinant for maternal cannabis use during pregnancy is cannabis use by the child's biological father.[607] In itself, this tells a story: that the majority of pregnant women who abuse cannabis are patriarchal. Their feelings for their children are, in effect, determined – or permitted – by the father's attitude to their child.[608]

The scarcity of studies analysing the impact of cannabis on both the health and nurturing behaviours of pregnant women and mothers, and on the neurodevelopment of babies and children, has resulted in widespread ignorance. Close to 70 percent of contacted cannabis dispensaries contacted by researchers recommended cannabis products to pregnant women. With no conclusive evidence, 36 percent of these dispensaries assured their pregnant clients that prenatal cannabis is safe. Only a minority suggested further research online or seeking a medical opinion.[609]

These dispensaries also failed to mention that some babies born to cannabis-smoking mothers show altered visual responses, increased tremors and startling, and emit high-pitched cries, suggesting neurological impairment.[610] The process of smoking itself is associated with preterm delivery, and cannabis is associated with a doubling of the risk. Cannabis smoking during pregnancy has also been aligned with over twice the risk of stillbirth.[611]

Like obstetricians and related medical professionals, the owners and employees of these dispensaries – and the companies that manufacture cannabis products without warnings – exploit uneducated, unintelligent and vulnerable mothers and are, through their advice, potentially permanently limiting the potential of babies.

Women who use cannabis during pregnancy have, tellingly, been shown to be significantly more likely to suffer from anxiety, depression and trauma, supporting studies that pregnant women use cannabis to manage stress and other feelings[612] they don't know how to manage.[613] These women are the daughters of mothers who were, in fundamental ways and predominantly because of obstetric practice, unavailable to them in infancy. Confronted by intense feelings such as guilt, helplessness and loneliness, these women become anxious and seek to escape themselves.

They are, quite literally, wasted – by history, by men, and, in the end, by themselves.

Zia McCabe, a mother of one and the keyboard player for American band the Dandy Warhols, is a high-profile advocate of cannabis. On Christmas Eve 2020, she captioned a photograph of musician Willie Nelson, an even higher-profile American cannabis advocate, 'I love him so much #smokeweedeveryday'.[614]

During our interview, McCabe told me that she smoked cannabis 'very moderately' during her pregnancy after deciding that 'the toxins in my body created by stress would be far worse for a growing foetus. So I smoked when I felt I needed to but not recreationally.' Since then, she doesn't 'wake and bake or smoke much during the day' unless she's taking a day off. 'I mostly smoke cannabis to unwind at bedtime. A few big bong rips at night and I'm good.'

Without cannabis, McCabe explained, 'life would be a little less vibrant and a little less funny and falling asleep would take forever and suck. I have a lot on my plate so yeah, there's anxiety mixed in. There's always so much to do that's it's hard to stop thinking. I've got plenty of anxiety to deal with.'[615]

Unmodified, McCabe's emotional landscape would be very different. Falling asleep 'would take forever and suck' because she lacked the capacity to manage the surfeit of anxiety and, perhaps, other feelings she may not acknowledge, understand, or wish to share.

Regular users of cannabis, in comparison to non-users, had worse memory performance and reduced cortical thickness of brain regions such as the fusiform gyrus.[616] The latter is extremely significant in terms of a mother's sensitivity to her baby.[617,618] The fusiform gyrus is not merely critical in terms of facial recognition, but in the *perception of emotion* – that is, in terms of reading the least and most subtle of facial cues that betray feeling, potentially the most important of maternal – and, for that matter, paternal – qualities.

What this means is that regular cannabis users are significantly less sensitive to the needs of their babies, children, and each other because their brains do not function optimally in terms of perception.

A mother's sensitivity to her infant's distress has been found to be a 'better predictor of the child's outcome' than her sensitivity to his affection, curiosity, joy, or other non-distress cues. To successfully manage her baby's distress, however, she must first manage her own in relation to his,[619] rather than, say, feeling so frightened or overwhelmed that she needs to numb herself with substances to cope, in the process decreasing critical sensitivity to her baby.

Forums about cannabis use during pregnancy pivot on the twin issues of anxiety and depression. Repeatedly, stress has been found to be a 'significant' factor in the regular use of cannabis.[620]

'Pregnancy is rough and it just makes the whole process easier,'[621] one user wrote. Others use cannabis to mask anxiety, depression, or 'emotional imbalances, like when I would start crying because I bought the wrong kind of pasta' – not because such responses are abnormal during pregnancy, but because, like McCabe, the women lack the skills to regulate intense emotion or because they are unsupported in their vulnerability.

Strong feelings other than benign contentment, pleasure or sexual arousal are experienced as overwhelming or unpleasant by those who lacked stabilising maternal containment in infancy.

The overriding picture is one of pregnant women foundering under the weight of anxiety, loneliness, marginalisation, poverty, sadness, stress, and entrenched emotional illiteracy. Young mothers have proved particularly susceptible to the punitive cultural ideal. The damage done to mothers is incremental, and has been compounded by each new generation. A significant percentage of young mothers are falling through the cracks – derided or ignored by the wider culture, marked as lesser, and producing troubled children.

Traditionally, single mothers – I am now one – are maligned as the most contemptible of this contemptible group. Addressed through a patriarchal prism, single mothers, rather than being understood as warranting concentrated attention and support, are presented as 'selfish' and as responsible for 'breeding a huge underclass', thus harming their 'fellow human beings'.[622] The role of fathers, family, the community and belief systems in the creation of this 'huge underclass' of course remains unaddressed.

Again, it's those who symbolise attachment, femininity and susceptibility who are demarcated as the enemy.

Pregnant women are, one study reports, 'therapeutic orphans as the majority of therapeutics and biologics were never studied in them during development.'[623] This not only reveals the low cultural value attributed to the feminine and the vulnerable, but the threat to the prevailing ideology therein.

In the 21st century, mothers and babies are the lab rats.

11. ARIADNE'S THREAD

'But what mother ever reads a medical journal?'
The Truth About Twilight Sleep, Hanna Rion

Obstetric anaesthesia was the biggest salvo in the patriarchal war against the 'animal' senses.

A series of directives in chemical form, scopolamine did not stray from the party line. Through its administration, women came to understand childbirth and the mother's passion as infractions warranting containment and punishment. The labouring mother was a Medusa that could not be directly faced, requiring a Perseus to decapitate her, if with drugs in place of a blade – again, that timeless severing of the female head, essential to the consolidation of patriarchal masculinity.

Scopolamine is an anticholinergic, a member of the family of drugs that block acetylcholine, a chemical messenger that, among other functions, plays a critical role in muscular operation and memory function.[624] Acetylcholine also activates the sweat gland, meaning that mothers who were administered scopolamine, whether as a component of Twilight Sleep or other drug cocktails, did not sweat.[625] In this respect, scopolamine became even more attractive to women who sought to distance themselves from their 'primitive' origins.

The drug disabled a gratifying number of status-threatening mammalian feminine functions: attachment, active labouring, and perspiration.

Anticholinergics remain the go-to drugs to manage sweating.[626]

In the context of childbirth, however, maternal sweat is far from a matter of mere indecorousness; it's thought to be the most important factor in the newborn's recognition of, and subsequent responsiveness to, his mother.

In the first hours of life, smell is the means through which we, as babies, map out our existence on this earth.[627,628] The fact that 1 to 2 percent of the human genome is reserved for producing olfactory epithelium receptors[629] – each baby is born with a 'practically unique' set of almost 400[630] – reveals the importance of this under-researched sense, particularly in relation to birth.

Acting as a GPS or 'Ariadne's thread'[631] of sorts for the newborn to localise his mother's life-sustaining breast,[632] her 'unique odour signature'[633] – the scent of her armpits in particular – is a chemical code,[634] the olfactory cue for him to understand her as the source of the life-sustaining love he knew *in utero*.

The more organically stinky the mother during childbirth, the better. Deodorants, scented products, perfume, and all strong-smelling cleaning or antiseptic products should, because of this, never be used in delivery rooms.

In mice, three molecules have been discovered in the immediate post-birth 'olfactory imprinting' window that determines the pup's lifelong intimate and social responses; one is the 'love hormone' oxytocin. The receptor that kicks off this process is only localised for a short period after birth.[635] As the time to 'set' the blueprint is extremely limited, facilitation of the mother's bonding with the pup after birth is critical.

Through such intimacy, the pulses of oxytocin that are released in both human mothers and their babies develop into reflexes. 'After a while just seeing, hearing, or smelling the mother may trigger oxytocin release in the infant in a Pavlovian manner,' a Swedish study reported. Over time, even only the thought of the mother triggers oxytocin in the child.[636]

Released through nursing in mice, oxytocin imprints passionate emotional associations in the pup with the odour memory of the mother.[637] Human babies respond in the same way, meaning that generations were, through scopolamine and similar drugs administered in an obstetric context, *chemically prevented* from associating their mothers with feelings of love, as scopolamine also inhibits the secretion of oxytocin.

A number of the brain areas disabled by scopolamine are those specifically involved in a mother's deep, emotional recognition of her newborn,[638] the same recognition that chemical signalling evolved to facilitate: motherlove.

In short, one of the most widely-administered obstetric drugs in history blocked all the mechanisms of attachment, which is critical to human evolution. Patriarchal trivialisation of attachment or birth issues as 'girly stuff' reflects the ideology's toxic cultural impact.

Love – or its absence – is the greatest sculptural force of the human brain, which is why severely deprived adoptees have 'substantially smaller total brain volumes' – 8.6 percent smaller – than peers who suffered no such deficits. Neurodevelopmental insults of this nature result in lower IQ and attention/hyperactivity disorders, and even with subsequent emotional enrichment, these issues carry into adulthood.[639]

In the ancient world, where the prefrontal cortex was thinner, the 'exposure' of unwanted babies – that is, the abandonment of newborns to the elements – was 'increasingly common' after the fourth century BC; over the course of time, 'exposure' was 'freely and arbitrarily' practised.[640] 'As to the exposure of children,' Aristotle wrote, 'let there be a law that no deformed child shall live.'[641] American historian Cynthia Patterson explained that in Ancient Greece, 'exposure' was not routinely a form of child-murder or malicious infanticide, but a 'limited and specific act affecting not a recognised member of the household ... rather a newborn ... who had as yet no place within the family.'[642]

What this once-common practice makes clear is that an infant was considered to have no right to exist without his mother's recognition – that is, without the endorsement of the mother's territoriality. The price of maternal indifference has, for the infant, always been steep.

Attachment is impossible without identification. The newborn's preference for his mother is dependent on his recognition of her as *distinctive from others*. In turn, this identification is thought to intensify his mother's attraction and responsiveness to him, and, importantly, the delight and pleasure she takes in him.[643] Far from qualities to be eradicated, then, discrimination and territoriality are critical to the survival of our species. Smell identifies our tribe and in that, determines the parameters of our joys and our fears.

An infant's odour signature also acts as a chemical messenger for his mother. Vernix caseosa, the cheesy biofilm on newly born babies, is not uterine seepage to be wiped off after birth, but a substance of near-miraculous properties. It eases the infant's transition from the womb, minimises friction during delivery, acts as an antimicrobial filter against the mother's rich genital bacteria, supplies him with important amino acids when swallowed, assists the adaptation and retains the hydration of his fragile skin, prevents the growth of pathogenic bacteria, acts as an antioxidant and an emollient, and, among other properties, has been shown to heal wounds. It's also thought to contain pheromones that attract the mother's care.[644]

The 20th-century convention of scrubbing babies at birth – another manifestation of the Abrahamic mandate to distance the self from its bestial origins – has been shown, like almost every other medicalised practice in relation to birth – to impair mother/baby attachment. Delaying the washing of a newborn has been shown to increase the mother's inclination to breastfeed.[645] WHO recommends waiting 24 hours,[646] and other organisations have recommended a delay in bathing for 48 hours or more, particularly with premature or c-section babies.[647] The infant's odour signature, then, is a critically important means of the mother's instruction as – outside the cries that are now routinely dismissed as colic or as an irrelevant reflex – he has no other means of communication.

When a newborn is washed soon after birth, his mother, in infinitely subtle ways, reveals less interest in keeping him alive. The chemical directives have been erased.

Motherlove, a complex expression, is conducted by multilayered emotional, hormonal and neurochemical factors.[648] Non-pregnant females in most mammalian species find the potent odour of newborns disgusting, meaning that smell plays a vital role in activating this very specific kind of love. In mammals, the mother's nervous system is profoundly altered by the smell of her newborn. These changes in circuitry heighten her response to her baby and to the memorisation – or internalisation – of him, strengthening her feelings for him, which leads to improved length and quality of his care. A baby thus becomes a powerful stimulus for his mother,[649] his smell a shortcut to her passionate preoccupation.

While smelling infant odours, mothers show significantly increased bilateral prefrontal cortex activity; childless women do not have the same response.[650] The prefrontal cortex, which covers the brain's frontal lobe behind the forehead, is associated with empathy, reasoning, guilt, personality, language, problem-solving, impulse control and related functions, and amounts to almost 13 percent of the brain's volume.[651,652]

Reduced prefrontal cortex volume – and the resulting limitations in interconnectivity with other brain areas – have been noted in suicides,[653] men addicted to cannabis[654] or pornography,[655] and those with substance-use disorders, showing that smooth behavioural and mood regulation is dependent on a well-functioning prefrontal cortex. Significant reductions in prefrontal volume are also characteristic of violent and psychopathic men,[656] and early-onset prefrontal damage is associated with defective or sociopathic social and moral reasoning.[657]

Given that reductions in prefrontal volume are also consistent with Major Depressive Disorder,[658] heavy cannabis use – which, as mentioned, reduces the area's volume, damaging the brain's behavioural 'braking system'[659] – compounds the depression it masks.

Interestingly, 'significant' prefrontal cortex dysfunction has also been found in regular users of major stimulants (such as amphetamine and cocaine), dissociative hallucinogens (such as ketamine and PCP) and polysubstance use,[660] meaning that the Psychedelic Revolution was directed and facilitated by *men with significant prefrontal cortex dysfunction* – that is, men with an impaired ability to control their impulses, to empathise, to feel accountable, or to experience remorse: sociopaths, in other words, or men with sociopathic qualities.

The fact that the human prefrontal cortex has increased six-fold in size over five million years[661] makes it clear that it is qualities such as consideration for others, the capacity for guilt and empathy, and the ability to defer gratification – rather, say, than the primitive Darwinian brutality by which the patriarchal is defined – that are responsible for the evolution of our race and essential to its continued evolution.

As the prefrontal cortex evolves, so do we.

What this means is that the compulsive use of pornography and cannabis in particular – both of which have been shown to erode prefrontal matter – acts as an evolutionary retardant. Far from facilitating the liberation promised by Leary and his Psychedelic Revolutionaries, cannabis and pornography are, in fact, agents of dehumanisation.

The festival of lights in the mother's brain in response to infant odours reveals that tender feeling and affectionate preoccupation is a manifestation of *evolved* humanity in both sexes rather than a 'primitive' behavioural remnant; if anything, the smaller prefrontal cortex of our distant ancestors would tend to indicate that they experienced significantly lesser feeling and consideration for others and, in particular, for their babies, which may explain the extreme violence sanctioned by so many ancient cultures.

What the maternal brain's lightshow in response to infant odours also means is that there is a corresponding mechanism in the baby, who is dependent on this concentrated intimacy and passionate preoccupation. The popular understanding that the needs of babies haven't changed[662] since the Stone Age is untrue; on the basis of accelerated prefrontal cortex sophistication, the needs of infants have *increased* in their complexity.

On this basis alone, surrogacy can be construed as an act of child cruelty.

Maternal sweat is not only the axis of motherlove, but of *all* human love as it also alters the father's biochemistry. Pregnant women develop distinctive and evolving odour signatures not found in non-pregnant, non-lactating women, and these hormonally-charged scents are thought to underpin behavioural changes in fathers.[663] When the mother's sweat function is hijacked by obstetric drugs, these natural masculine behavioural shifts are diluted or sabotaged, a loss that can be said to be reflected in the increasing dissociation of fathers from their babies and the mothers of their children.

Sweat is a language.

Supporting my theory: children have been shown to prefer clothing worn by their own mothers, particularly the parts that were in contact with their armpits.[664] As a young child, I would sift through my parents' laundry basket for my mother's lingerie and, on finding a bra, silk slip, or panties, would press them to my face and breathe in her fragrance. There was nothing sexual about the act. It was, I remember, simply like inhaling peace.

I have no memory of my mother ever holding or comforting me – only of her narrowing glance and the dig of her fingernails in my skin. Sometimes she took my arm in hers as we walked. But by holding her panties to my face, by rubbing my small thumb against the flaking, nacreous print of her sex on those cotton gussets, I was returned to a different mother, an eyeless ocean-mother of salt and tilting waters, to the orientation of my pulse by her unseen heart, to that warm universe of susurration in which I was once suspended like a point of light: my dreaming.

The most intense human connections I have ever known were characterised by smells.

My late ex-fiancé Michael said that after I first left him, he didn't wash the sheets until he could no longer smell me through his own perspiration; in the residue of my sweat, the residue of my love for him. Of course I understood: smelling a beloved's body odour reduces anxiety and increases comfort,[665] which is, in part, why bereavement is so frightening. When a beloved dies, we can no longer be comforted by their odours. We lose our emotional compass. And in those who suffered separation from their mothers at birth or during infancy, such a death resurrects the unmanageable – and seemingly inexplicable – feelings of anxiety, despair, terror and worthlessness they experienced as little babies.

Michael's tenuous sense of belonging to the world was characteristic of those who experience profound obstetric intoxication at birth. His substance use disorder finished him: he fatally overdosed in 1995, seeking comfort in cocaine after a transatlantic argument in which I had – deliberately, in anger, and for the first time – emptied my voice of love.

I still remember the sandalwood scent of his skin, and his lips smeared with my menstrual blood as he rose, like Orpheus from the underworld, between my thighs to kiss my mouth. Redolent of iron, those kisses forged a bond.

Like mother/infant recognition, deep sexual and romantic attraction pivots on subconscious responses to odour. We are 'instinctively' attracted to those with dissimilar MCH (major histocompatibility complex) genes, which carry information about genetic relatedness. Pheromones, chemosignals and the neurochemical pathways created by historical associations also trigger feelings of love and desire by releasing dopamine, oxytocin and testosterone.[666]

The capacity for profound love is created by the original stinking, sweaty, tender merger of odours and touch at birth. Sexual love, an experience described by French historian Robert Muchembled as 'olfactory ecstasy', is an echo of this union.[667] It is only through the original merging that a sense of interconnectedness is created, not only between mother and child, but between mother, child and the greater web of love that extends as far back as human consciousness. Babies permitted to seamlessly merge with their mothers become, in a sense, one with the world itself. This was Maier's vision.

Removal of the olfactory bulb (the neural structure responsible for the sense of smell) can result in severely agitated depression.[668] In 1992 and heavily inebriated, Australian rock star Michael Hutchence was assaulted in Copenhagen. He fractured his skull, in the process losing his sense of smell and taste: anosmia and ageusia. 'I can't smell my woman,' he told a friend. 'Her hair, her beautiful skin, her scent.'[669] A sensualist, Hutchence despaired. He felt, he said, as if he were 'floating in space'.

Five years later, he hanged himself.[670]

The waning of the sense of smell is, in older adults, a strong biomarker of death within five years,[671] although whether the olfactory degeneration is symptomatic of other dysfunction or whether it simply erodes the will to live is unknown.

Hutchence's equation of anosmia with 'floating in space' makes it clear that the human sense of smell is, in essence, a geolocation device directing us to emotional and physical nurturance, and also that odours anchor us to three-dimensional contexts, bestowing a sense of connection, of reality – the bridging with, or intersection of, the self and the environment that determined its design. The depression resulting from the loss is a response to alienation.

Through the act of smelling, we are, on a nonverbal level, *realised* – that is, made real – to ourselves and others. In an essay, American producer and stroke victim Elizabeth Zierah wrote, 'As the scentless and flavourless days passed, I felt trapped inside my own head, a kind of bodily claustrophobia, disassociated. It was as though I were watching a movie of my own life.'[672]

I remember my disorientation when Bethesda, then two, came to me after playing dress up, her scalp redolent only of a wig's nylon filaments. Pressing my nose to the crown of her head, I became frantic. *She no longer smelled like my child.* I immediately put her in the bath, scrubbing her hair until the alien smell could no longer be detected.

In retrospect, I find it interesting that I felt no anxiety when

Bethesda wore a mask – that is, when I could not see her face – but was terrified by the absence of her smell. I felt like British novelist Neil Gaiman's character Coraline, confronted by her alien 'Other Mother' with black buttons for eyes. My panic was the precursor to rejection.

Stripped of her odours, Bethesda no longer seemed mine.

Mammalian animal mothers with anosmia have no maternal feeling for their newborns; no nesting behaviour takes place, and most of them eat their babies.[673] Anosmia caused by the depletion of the hormone noradrenaline within the main olfactory bulb results in the majority of these animals cannibalising their babies.[674]

What this suggests is that the newborn's smell determines the degree of tender early maternal preoccupation. The more secure this preoccupation and the more intricately it is interwoven with pleasure, the more passionate – and indelible, and significant – the mother's sense of territoriality.

This territoriality is not the one-way 'investment of the self into an object'[675] – that of a fetishist into a sex doll, say – but an exhilarating, protective, and reciprocal devotion. Tender maternal ownership determines the normal infant's development and immunises him against emotional – and, to an extent, physiological – dysfunction.

Immediately after Bethesda's birth, I lay awake all night with her in my arms, repeatedly pressing my nose to the crown of her unwashed head. The scent was like nothing I'd ever before experienced – to call it an intoxicant would be inadequate; its power over me remains unrivalled. (During pregnancy, I had a similar response to her father's scrotum: the smell was so comforting to me that I could have lain between his thighs for hours.) As I'd read that mammals lick their newborns to stimulate circulation and consolidate bonding, I smelled and licked my baby's round, blinking face in the half-light of the maternity ward.

I may have been instinctively compensating for the obstetric anaesthesia that had stupefied us both, I don't know.

Semi-conscious or unconscious during delivery, Twilight Sleep mothers had no such opportunity, and, given the restrictive cultural gender template within which they operated, would not have wanted it. Scopolamine – like many other obstetric drugs, a lactation inhibitor[676] – also derails the powerful natural maternal impulse to breastfeed immediately after birth.

During the critical post-birth window, babies establish an understanding of the world, presented to them in the form of the mother's largesse, as meeting their every need with love.

Obstetric anaesthesia changed this understanding.

This thwarting of a baby's every instinct in the wake of birth – to be breastfed, coddled, proximal to his mother and, by her, passionately loved – is, in terms of infant brain development, both calamitous and far-reaching. As these episodes were, because of obstetric practice, invariably repeated, a sense of frustration and worthlessness became the infant's lifelong emotional baseline.

To adults who were denied maternal passion in infancy, no amount of love will ever be sufficient because *they lack the neurodevelopment to feel emotionally sated*. Such babies learn that that love is a sustained exercise in frustration and pain, and their feelings of love are thus triggered by frustration and pain. Isolation is presented to them as the fundamental truth of human existence, and their attunement of their senses – life instructions in themselves – are junked.

Such babies also learn to understand the feminine as unresponsive and unstable, unable to be trusted. Inculcated in them, an aversion – in some cases only partial – to femininity and all that femininity entails, and one that is only (superficially) resolved in adulthood through identification with the Abrahamic concept of masculinity.

12. THE CUTTING EDGE

'But it was the image of the swan, and the man's longing to hear his own blood gush, which haunted Lisa for weeks, as a compulsive daylight nightmare. She would stop dead in the street – her head spinning with the thought of the sleeping swan, the falling blade.'

The White Hotel, D.M. Thomas

The volume of general anaesthesia during caesarean deliveries is decreasing, but is still prevalent enough to be disturbing. In 2018, 31.9 percent of all US deliveries were caesareans.[677] In 2007, 30.9 percent of all Australian births were caesareans.[678] In 2016, 28.2 percent of all Canadian births were caesareans – an increase of 50.8 percent in 20 years.[679] In the Caribbean, 40.5 percent of births are caesareans.[680] In China, Egypt, parts of South America and south-eastern Europe, the caesarean rate has increased to – or is above – 50 percent of all births.[681] In Brazil, 80–90 percent of private births are caesareans.[682]

Described as 'alarming', this epidemic – unrelated to evidence-based medicine[683] – is being driven by elective c-sections.[684]

Twenty-first-century women are, as their grandmothers and great-grandmothers were before them, intimidated or persuaded by medical professionals into making this choice. The major driver behind the disastrous global surge of c-sections and obstetric drugs is profit.[685] Even in 1920, this association was made obvious in a Scottish doctor's poem for the centenary celebrations of the Royal Medico-Chirurgical Society of Glasgow:

> *Then anaesthetics' soothing power*
> *Had not become our common dower,*
> *Nor did they golden guerdons reap*
> *By recommending Twilight Sleep.*[686]

'Guerdons' are, of course, rewards.

The same association was made in a 1925 issue of *The British Journal of Anaesthesia*:

'Is your daddy in?' A visitor asks the little girl who answers the door.
'No,' she says, 'he is out giving an anaesthetic.'
Surprised, the visitor says, 'An anaesthetic. That is a big word. What does it mean?'
The little girl replies, 'Five guineas.'[687]

From 1967 to 1986, there was a 116 percent increase in the number of anaesthesiologists,[688] a leap not unrelated to a staggering increase in obstetric intervention. Between 2004 and 2014, the field grew by almost 20 percent – in contrast to the 3 percent growth of other medical sectors – and salaries rose by 1.21 percent per year, the greatest hike in the medical sector during that period. In 2014, anaesthesiologists earned more than surgeons: a median of US $246,650.[689]

Ironically, the current shortage of anaesthesiologists is attributed to the explosion in chronic diseases which are, as studies show, *created* by the administration of obstetric anaesthetics.[690] What this means is that anaesthesiologists are, through the injudicious application of their skills, blighting the lives of generations – in the process, expanding the demand for their services.

A multiplicity of surgical procedures performed on wealthier patients is, in the medical field, associated with professional advancement – as one authority reported, 'Physicians who generate better paying patients are always in demand by a hospital administrator.'[691]

Given that in 2018, over 98 percent of US births took place in hospitals[692] and one in four births are caesarean sections,[693] it's clear that a significant percentage, if not the majority, of pregnant women are subjected to varying degrees of pressure from medical professionals – solely on the basis of profit – to capitulate to obstetric intervention.

Fifty thousand of these women and/or their babies will, in the process, be injured, some permanently. Since 2000, the rate of injury has increased by 75 percent, and that of post-delivery complications by 50 percent.[694]

The primary risk involved in a caesarean is major haemorrhage. In 2005, the prevalence in Scotland alone was 4.4 women per 1,000, and the majority were shown to have had a previous caesarean.[695]

Globally, there were 8.7 million obstetrical cases of major haemorrhage and 83,000 deaths in 2015.[696] Outstanding claims against the British NHS in 2000 amounted to £39 billion; 70 percent of the funds expended related to obstetrics and gynaecology.[697] In the US, researchers found 'overwhelming evidence that part of the recent rise in the caesarean section rate in this country is the result of the medical-legal environment.'[698]

The pressures are also social. I remember an Australian curator urging me to have a caesarean lest I become incontinent. She said that her obstetrician had assured her that the female body, which is designed to reproduce, is devastated by reproduction. As I discussed her advice with a group of women, one suggested that it sounded as if I was 'too posh to push', showing that the relationship between obstetric intervention and feminine status remains definitive.

In 2001, 21 percent of 150,139 British births were caesareans, an increase of 17 percent since the early 1960s. While the Royal College of Anaesthetists recommends that fewer than five percent of elective c-sections be performed under general anaesthesia, published audits reveal that *nine to 23 percent are performed on unconscious mothers*. And despite the suggestion that only 15 percent of emergency c-sections warranted general anaesthesia,[699] 41 percent are performed on unconscious mothers.[700] As 13 percent of British births are elective c-sections and 16 percent are classified as emergency c-sections,[701] that means that over 9,300 unconscious British women are delivered of infants stupefied by drugs each year.

As Anne Sexton wrote, ostensibly about her suicide attempt, in the poem, 'The Double Image': 'I pretended I was dead/until the white men pumped the poison out.'[702]

Neurodevelopmental events in the foetal and infant brain are 'easily perturbed by environmental and pharmacological influences,' yet most research focuses on the teratogenic – that is, on dramatic foetal abnormality – and measurable newborn status[703] rather than on subtler, long-term manifestations of drug-facilitated dysfunction. No test exists to clearly separate the impact of obstetric drugs on mother and infant during labour and delivery.[704] Instead, mothers are assured – and without conclusive evidence[705] – that, as American anaesthesiology professors Jill M. Mhyre and Brian T. Bateman stated in an editorial for *Anaesthesiology*, the American Society of Anaesthesiologists' journal, in 2015, 'Anaesthesia and analgesia for childbirth have become remarkably safe.'[706]

In keeping with the medical profession's disregard for mothers and infants, researchers found that 52 percent of c-section mothers had 'at least' 10 unused opioid tablets in their possession two weeks after hospital discharge. The amounts prescribed had no correlation with body mass index, current or past drug abuse, the mother's age, smoking status, or other factors. Opioids are prescribed in excess after caesarean delivery,[707] making it far less likely that the mothers would feel like nursing their babies, and potentially endangering the health, neurodevelopment and lives of their babies. Maternal opioid use during breastfeeding is, after all, associated with infant central nervous system depression, drowsiness or sedation, and death,[708,709] as newborns are especially sensitive to even the most minuscule dosages of narcotic analgesics.[710]

Far from being maternal 'choices' with no real repercussions for the infant, vaginal births and the breastfeeding they facilitate have a 'substantial' impact on the child's lifelong health through the establishment of the infant's gut microbiota – a complex ecosystem of millions of microbes associated with the development of the human immune system.[711]

Unimpeded childbirth also safeguards the mother. Breastfeeding is associated with a 10 percent lower risk of cardiovascular disease for the mother in later life – the longer the mother breastfeeds, the greater her protection[712] – and the lower her likelihood of developing endometrial and ovarian cancers,[713] – in addition to significantly lessening the incidence of breast cancer[714] and type-2 diabetes.[715]

For every 12 months a mother breastfeeds, her risk of cancer decreases.

Were all First World mothers to breastfeed, the cumulative incidence of breast cancer would be reduced by more than 50 percent. Similarly, were breastfeeding to become a universal, extended practice supported by the community, the result could be a spectacular 66 percent reduction in breast cancer incidence.[716]

If these estimates are correct, it can be said that routine obstetric practice and aggressive infant formula advertising were, and continue to be, in effect responsible for over half the breast cancers in the world.

The safeguarding of the human organism is inherent in its

design-based function.

Vaginal births, for example, have been found to transmit multiple strains of the mother's microbes necessary to establish a diverse infant gut microbial community,[717] a transfer that doesn't take place during c-section deliveries, which are associated with increased risk of metabolic disorders.[718] The hospital itself interferes with protective gut flora colonisation in the baby. New findings highlight the 'critical role' of the birth environment in the establishment of gut microbiota, identifying intestinal colonisation with opportunistic pathogens as 'a previously underappreciated risk factor in hospital births.'[719]

First identified in 1963, autoimmune diseases are characterised 'by the failure of an organism to tolerate its own cells and tissues,'[720] a metaphor for the mother's rejection of her infant by refusing – generally in compliance with a patriarchal context – to bestow lifelong protection on him through her breastmilk. Early exposure through nursing and vaginal delivery to the 'right' microbes lessens the likelihood of a baby developing allergies, asthma, diabetes,[721] multiple sclerosis, psoriasis and other chronic or life-threatening conditions from the 80-plus autoimmune disease family in later life.[722]

In alignment with these findings: the dramatic increase in the global prevalence of autoimmune dysfunction.

On the WHO map showing the proportion of babies who remain breastfed at around 12 months, the UK, along with Saudi Arabia, is the worst in the world with close to zero percent.[723] Concomitantly, there has, over five years, been a 72 percent increase in the number of English children admitted to hospital with anaphylaxis, and over the same period, related child admissions in London rose by 167 percent.[724]

These statistics reflect a broader trend. The First World has experienced 'an explosion' of food allergies – for example, six to eight percent of British children have a food allergy.[725] Between 2008 and 2018 in England and Wales, the number of asthma fatalities increased by 32.7 percent,[726] and, again in the UK, 3.7 million people have been diagnosed as having diabetes, a doubling of cases over a 20-year period.[727]

Children's chronic allergies entail substantial social cost:[728] anxiety, compromised lives, lost wages, medical costs, missed schooling, and fatalities. The most rapid increases in allergy rates are taking place in countries of increasing affluence and, as I have shown, the birth intervention that accompanies it. Globally, some 250 million people now have food allergies.[729]

I am one of them.

Similar increases in these pathologies can be found throughout the West. The National Institutes of Health reports that 14.7 to 23.5 million Americans – over seven percent of the population – have been diagnosed with an autoimmune disease, and, 'for reasons unknown', the incidence continues to worsen.[730] After cancer and cardiovascular disease, autoimmune illnesses are the third most common category of disease in the United States.[731] Throughout central Europe and North America, rates of diabetes are rising.[732]

It is not known why 78 percent of Americans with autoimmune diseases are female.[733]

In Britain, the direct and indirect burden on the NHS for just three autoimmune conditions – rheumatoid arthritis, multiple sclerosis and type-1 diabetes – is over £13 billion per year. Some 400,000 British people live with rheumatoid arthritis alone. The incidence of autoimmune diseases is rising by between 3 and 9 percent each year.[734]

I believe unnecessary obstetric anaesthesia and intervention during birth to be the factors responsible for our 'rapidly rising' global rates of autoimmune disease.[735]

Similarly: in reducing working connectivity between several brain areas, scopolamine is a 'pharmacological model of Alzheimer's Disease' – that is, Alzheimer's in chemical form.[736] Given that depletions in the cholinergic neurotransmitter system have been implicated in Alzheimer's-type dementia,[737] it seems only logical that the obstetric administration of, historically, scopolamine and other obstetric anticholinergic drugs, may be the primary 'pathogenic mechanism' responsible for the staggering global increase in dementia. In 2006, 26.6 million people were diagnosed with Alzheimer's; its prevalence is expected to quadruple by 2050.[738] Between 1990 and 2016, the global incidence rose by 117 percent.[739]

At birth, a newborn's oxytocin levels are, and remain, higher than his mother's,[740] meaning that a baby's love for his mother is greater than that of even the most devoted mother for her infant. Oxytocin levels have also been shown to be twice as high in babies born vaginally as those born by c-section, and the same hormonal dynamic applies to mothers.[741] What this means is that babies born vaginally love their mothers significantly more intensely than their c-section peers, and the converse also applies.

It can thus be said that women who elect to have c-section deliveries trade a lifetime of love for expedience.

In the guise of convenience and liberation, routine caesarean births and the obstetric drugs they make necessary continue to impair our cultural capacity for attachment. Like Leary, his Psychedelic Revolutionaries and the obstetricians who orchestrated their births, the architects and major beneficiaries of this disablement remain the patriarchy.

13. THE BLUEPRINT FOR HUMANITY

'They are stupid, they are beasts, they are meat, they are death.'

The Diary of Vaslav Nijinsky, Vaslav Nijinsky

In 1903, British writer and father-of-four H.G. Wells described the human newborn as 'no more than an animal. Indeed, it is among the lowest and most helpless of all animals, a mere vegetative lump; assimilation incarnate – wailing. It is for the first day in its life deaf, it squints blindly at the world, its limbs are beyond its control, its hands clutch drowningly at anything.'[742]

Among the lowest and most helpless of all animals.

Half a century or so later, French philosopher Simone de Beauvoir joined this chorus of dismissal for the feminine and its territory. To her, newborns were not vegetative, but bestial: less than human. No more than a vessel for a 'small, prattling soul,'[743] the newborn was described by her as living a life 'as mysterious as that of an animal, as turbulent and disorderly as natural forces'.[744] Men, on the other hand, were aligned by her with heroes and demigods.[745] De Beauvoir, who, in her private life, was a take of sorts[746] on the disgraced British socialite Ghislaine Maxwell[747] in her emotional and sexual exploitation of young women, essentially regarded infants as human facsimiles.

This perspective, far from being exclusive to 20th-century feminism, dates back millennia. To the Greek philosopher Plutarch, a newborn 'is more like a plant than an animal,'[748] and to Aristotle, 'The transition from not being to being is effected through the intermediate state, and sleep would appear to be by its nature a state of this sort, being as it were a borderland between living and not living: a person who is asleep would appear to be neither completely non-existent nor completely existent.'[749] Two thousand years later, Queen Victoria said that she felt no tenderness for any of her nine children until they *became* human, and dismissed all newborns on the basis of their 'animal existence'. An 'ugly baby',

Queen Victoria added, is 'a very nasty object'.[750]

The understanding of newborns as essentially inhuman not only made it possible for infants to be abused and murdered with impunity for thousands of years, but also made the delegation of mothering to indifferent menial workers seem appropriate.

It also trivialised mothers and motherhood. If an infant is no more than an animal or vegetable, then the mother's passion can only be a byproduct of her primitive nature. This perspective has always served the obstetricians and medical industry. 'I know of many instances of cruelty, stupidity and harm done to mothers by obstetricians who are callous or completely indifferent to the welfare of their patients,' an unnamed maternity nurse revealed in 1958, 'Obstetricians today are businessmen who run baby factories.'[751]

In this increasingly casual disparagement of the newborn and his fascinating, intricately calibrated vulnerabilities, the erasure – and it is gradual – of humanity itself.

American actress Angelina Jolie reflected our prevailing patriarchal values when she said of her first biological child, 'A newborn really is this ...yes, a blob!'[752] Similarly, a parenting magazine article read: 'If we're all being honest, newborns are so boring it hurts... newborns just aren't that exciting. Their daily schedule looks a little like this: eat, sleep, poop, repeat. They can't communicate (except through crying) or move.'[753]

Newborns are perceived as 'boring' and essentially worthless because they cannot reason or control their faculties, and also on the basis of their sensitivity and vulnerability. The ability to reason without passion – historically understood as a masculine province, and the basis of our legal system – is our defining indicator of human value, and conscious memory is the axis of reason. On the basis of their incapacity to construct a narrative of early events, foetuses and newborns are assumed to be incapable of remembering and are thus dismissed as lacking intrinsic worth; the only value they have is that attributed *to* them.

It was only in the last stages of pregnancy and in the immediate wake of childbirth that I learned that the foetus and newborn is far from a blank slate.

Giving birth to Bethesda, I sustained second-degree internal tearing. As I was being sutured, she was taken from me and placed in another's arms. Her agitation was violent, and she began to cry. Without knowing that singing is 'non-pharmacological emotion regulation intervention'[754] – a form of pain management now highly recommended to all parents, carers and medical personnel – I began to sing to her from across the delivery suite. I had no conscious memory of my father soothing me as a newborn by singing, but the association had been triggered. During pregnancy, I sang Woody Guthrie's *Who's My Pretty Baby?* to my abdomen each night, alight with love.

At the sound of my voice, Bethesda immediately stopped crying. It was as if she had been shot. Eyes wide, even in her drugged state, Bethesda was transfixed by *recognition*: this, then, was the song she'd heard on the other side of the membrane. Associations were visibly taking place. I laughed at her comical response and, again, she started at the sound – aligning my face with her internal experience of my laughter.

A newborn's field of vision is thought to be 8 to 10 inches from his face, but Bethesda's gaze, however unsteadily, was fixed on me; perhaps she'd merely identified the location of the laughter, or perhaps I was a blur, but there was no error in her focus. The fact that her identification of me had, as conclusively as a tap, stopped her tears, is evidence that a newborn's tears are not meaningless but an expression of grief *at separation from the mother*.

This demonstrates that babies are hardwired for intimacy, and that the mother's separation disrupts the critical continuum of attachment.[755,756,757,758]

Bethesda's focus was uniquely charged; she didn't react in this manner to any other noises in the room. The midwives' coos and general theatre clatter caused her to fret and mewl, but her reactions to my voice were uniquely powerful. My baby had carried the memory of my laughter, Woody Guthrie's song, and my voice through with her *from the womb*, and all three had an incomparably soothing effect on her.

At the last ultrasound, performed two or so weeks earlier, the technician had marvelled, 'Will you look at that – she's playing with the umbilical cord!' The wonder I experienced in that moment was a form of incandescence. Bethesda, all squashed up in her uterine universe, was, with her tiny hands, gently and repeatedly batting her umbilical cord from side to side as if it were a skipping rope between her knees. This was no accident; the careful placement of her hands and her calibrated gestures showed an understanding that if she batted the cord, it would swing back. She was literally *whiling away time*, entertaining herself with the only toy at hand.

How long had Bethesda been playing games? Were there others? Had she sought this game out, manipulating the umbilical cord into position, or was the choice spontaneous?

All this was in contrast to the idea that a newborn, on the basis of cortical immaturity, is a being who remembers and understands nothing: a person only within the context of the mother's acknowledgment, blank, a species of human cabbage. This issue of infant memory is, however, not merely a matter of value, but pivotal to our civilisation.

To understand why, the nature of memory itself has to be considered.

Human memory takes two forms, nondeclarative and declarative – that which 18th-century German philosopher Friedrich Schelling called 'an unconscious, dark principle and a conscious principle'[759] and Sigmund Freud, the Austrian founder of psychoanalysis, referred to as the id and the ego.

Declarative memory is conscious – recollections able to be contextualised, elaborated on, verbalised and utilised to construct reason: in essence, textual. Sociopaths work with declarative memory, as do fraudsters.

Declarative memory pivots on spin; nondeclarative memory is honest.

An animal, sensory language – auditory, gustatory, olfactory, textural, visual – nondeclarative memory is conveyed impressionistically through behaviour, feeling, imagery, and instinct. Nondeclarative memory is unconscious, wordless, the realm of metaphor. This is why art, cuisine, the environment and music are fundamental to human equilibrium – the senses tell our nondeclarative secrets and our nondeclarative stories, hence the cultural constraints. Addiction, anxiety, depression, chronic pain, digestive issues, disordered emotions, violence and other issues are also all nondeclarative expressions, which is why our prisons, psychiatric hospitals, rehabilitation centres, and similar institutions are populated by adult victims of early trauma.

Visual recognition memory – the 'robust form of memory'

evident from early infancy – is, it has been discovered, 'surprisingly resistant to decay and interference'.[760] Therefore, when an adult is triggered by colouring, features, gestures, or smells that are similar to those of his mother at birth and during infancy, he will be flooded by the same feelings he experienced for his mother at those times.

Ted Bundy, for example, felt compelled to murder women around the age his mother was when she birthed him (22), and who shared her colouring, eye-brow ratio, and/or facial proportions. Charles Manson, too, targeted girls around his mother's age when she gave birth to him (15) and who shared her glittering sexual avidity and susceptibility to boundary violation.

The newborn memory is something like the 19th-century ambrotype process, in which a wet glass plate is exposed in the camera, except the newborn records an image in conjunction with the corresponding feeling. Recorded at birth and during infancy, this series of images and feelings becomes in itself a narrative: the attachment template or the blueprint for the child's capacity for intimacy.

Imagine, then, the impact of a mother disordered by scopolamine or similarly disabling drugs on her child at birth. Life-altering horror aside, the infant's expectations – for instinct and design are forms of expectation – *are not met*, creating a nondeclarative understanding of fundamental wrongness: either he is wrong or the world is wrong, an understanding that transforms into a generational legacy of addiction, anger, depression, disordered emotion, and emotional detachment, particularly in relation to the feminine.

American cultural critic Marrit Ingman, who 'went crazy' after the birth of her son, failed to link her own traumatic experience of birth and infancy to her own troubled experience of being birthed and mothered. Instead, she expressed a wish to be 'like those other "stupid" women' – one of whom was her own mother, 'who birthed in twilight sleep and fed both her babies formula without a second thought.'[761]

In the place of the exultant mother whose rich smells and voice a newborn identifies as the continuum of love – a warm mother vivid in her greed to coddle and nurse him – there was, for much of the 20th century, one of three options: a groaning, mindless monster; a blurred facsimile of a mother; or a bleeding body on a slab.

Mother: a humanoid thing blinded by bandages, nurturing breasts hidden, limbs restrained, tongue lolling from its slack mouth, and with no recognisable sweat signature.

Unrelated, unreceptive.

The cover of Marilyn Manson's 2003 album *The Golden Age of Grotesque*, showing his blurred face with red eye sockets and what could be needle teeth or strands of saliva from his open mouth, is, I believe, a nondeclarative memory of profound drug-facilitated birth trauma. Manson said that his 'mentally ill' mother had issues with drugs, maternal attachment, and psychosis during his childhood,[762] and that her own mother had been a 'pill-popper'.[763]

In adulthood, Manson's 'horrific' abuse of women[764] and the sadistic pleasure he took in mocking the vulnerable suggest the same thing.

Unconscious of the deeper resonance of his words, Manson wrote, 'Hospitals and bad experiences with women, sexuality and private parts were completely familiar to me.' In a self-consciously histrionic poem ('Hotel Hallucinogen'), he continued the theme: 'It is a baby's cry of his mother's treason./The screaming fear of abandonment.../The weeping of an abandoned infant.'[765]

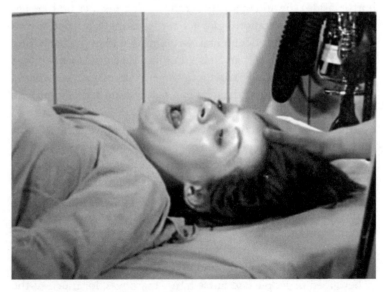

A mother typically stupefied by drugs just after giving birth. Still from 'Maternity Care', a United States Navy training film, 1963.

At birth, generations of babies for almost two centuries have had no option but to address the maternal as absent, abused, disordered, indifferent, monstrous, terrifying, ugly, unresponsive, and untrustworthy. Flea, the Australian-American bassist for the band Red Hot Chili Peppers and a recovering disordered polysubstance user, recalled in his autobiography *Acid for the Children*, 'Not for many years did I begin to reckon with the void left by the lack of my mother's affection; to be brave enough to consciously feel and see this subtle and invisible fear, which had been influencing my movements until it was rooted out.'[766]

The void to which Flea refers was captured by Norwegian Expressionist Edvard Munch in 'Der Schrei der Natur' ('The Scream of Nature') – more commonly known as 'The Scream'

Edvard Munch's 'The Scream of Nature', 1893.

– a painting that came to symbolise the anxiety of the human condition in the 20th century. Munch's schizophrenic sister Laura was institutionalised at the foot of the hill depicted in the painting, not far from the local slaughterhouse.

Landscape as metaphor: the animal self, incarcerated, brutalised and extinguished by Abrahamic men.

Munch wrote, 'Suddenly the sky became blood – and I felt the breath of sadness I stopped – leaned against the fence – deathly tired / Clouds over the fjørd dripped reeking blood / My friends went on but I just stood trembling with an open wound in my breast I heard a huge extraordinary scream pass through nature.'[767]

This scream belonged to Munch's newborn self, alienated from Nature – his mother – by the usual fusion of patriarchal ideologies: his aristocratic, deeply religious, emotionally disordered doctor-father dominated the family. In the wake of his mother's death, the five-year-old Munch[768] was taken to the house of friends. Above their sofa, a painting 'of a deer being torn to pieces and devoured by wolves.'[769] The resonance of this image – a nondeclarative patriarchal behavioural template in itself – coloured Munch's entire life.

Alienation from the animal – or nondeclarative – self would become the hallmark of humanity.

14. WORLD WAR Z

> 'When one thinks of the Mummy an image comes to mind
> of a bandaged monster sent out to do the evil bidding
> of a sinister high priest.'
> Brian Senn and John Johnson

At some point around 1863, American and European doctors started wearing masks in surgical theatres. By 1923, two-thirds were masked.[770] For the first time, the first face an infant saw was not that of his mother, but that of a masked man: unfamiliar and unreadable, a 'sinister high priest' of sorts.

The first sighting of any face is of inestimable importance in terms of the human psyche as it is a baby's introduction to ex-uterine humanity and to depth perception, and the impact, in however many ways, changes the course of history.

In 1903, Hungarian-British Baroness Orczy's play *The Scarlet Pimpernel* introduced the concept of a masked hero,[771] and Zorro made his debut in 1919.[772] Countless other masked heroes would follow – most recently, Batman, Deadpool, Iron Man, and Spiderman. There are others. While masks had always played a role in celebratory, criminal, erotic, militaristic, punitive or shamanic contexts, the alignment of a mask with heroics was new.

I believe that the spectacular resonance of the masked superhero in the 20th and 21st century is attributable to nondeclarative memories of an empathetic – rather than incapable or indifferent – masked obstetrician at birth.

Conversely, in conjunction with birth trauma, blades, forceps, obstetric anaesthesia and the scissors used to slice the umbilical cord, the masked masculine becomes a thing of terror, associated with confusion, pain, suffering, and violence towards the vulnerable, which explains the global resonance of masked – and generally knife-wielding – gore/horror/slasher villains such as Bane from the *Batman* franchise, Hannibal Lecter from *The Silence of the Lambs*, and Michael Myers from the *Hallowe'en* franchise.

Even in 1970, only 7 percent of obstetricians were female,[773] meaning that an image of the masculine was, and continues to be, imprinted on the infant at birth as not only dominant, but, because of the mask, as *fundamentally unknowable*. When a sex is introduced as withholding facial communication cues, the infant can only register the understanding that the masculine principle is one of denial, with the concealed mouth symbolising muting; fittingly, the phrase 'strong, silent type' was first used in 1905.[774] The iconic 'masculine' characters played by 20th-century American actors John Wayne and Clint Eastwood typified this ideal.

If male, the infant will, to a degree, attempt to replicate these behaviours in later life.

I also believe that the reason that many or most female drug users are more likely to associate drug use with an intimate partner, while men are more likely to associate drug use with male friends,[775] is because they were indirectly administered potent drugs *in utero* and were delivered, in effect stoned, by a man.

The infant brain is hardwired for facial recognition. A baby has an 'attentional bias' towards the face,[776] meaning that the identification of human faces, and the experience of looking at them, is critical to his neurodevelopment. By four months, an infant can visually process a face almost as efficiently as an adult.[777] Masks serve only to create and intensify stress in the baby, who, to feel safe, heavily relies on facial cues to regulate his emotional responses and to alert him to potentially dangerous situations. If the facial cues are limited, the baby feels anxious and uncertain about the safety of his environment.[778]

I am not the only one to wonder at the life-impact of universal face-masking during the Covid-19 crisis of 2020/21 on babies, who, as a result of this widespread denial of facial exposure, touch and communication, will experience unusually high levels of anxiety in addition to having 'under-stimulated synaptic connections',[779] impaired attachment skills and pattern-learning, and lower emotional, social and sensual literacy. There will be ellipses in the development of the fusiform gyrus, that part of the brain involved in facial and linguistic recognition, memory, the perception of emotion, and multisensory integration.[780,781] It's highly likely that this generation will have an autistic sheen.

The visual aspect of birth practices, then, is much more than significant.

A 'largely cinematic fabrication,'[782] the trope of the shambling, bandaged mummy is considered to have been inspired by archaeologist Howard Carter's discovery of Eighteenth Dynasty Pharoah Tutankhamun's tomb in 1922, but the first mummies in popular fiction were female.[783] In the Victorian and Edwardian eras, writers such as Englishman H. Rider Haggard and Irish *Dracula* author Bram Stoker depicted mummies as powerful undead beauties who vengefully attempted to seduce upright male archaeologists for disturbing their afterlives.

While Carter's discovery may well have been the trigger for this cinematic genre, its emotional resonance – and later critical disparagement – had other sources.

In *The Jewel of the Seven Stars* (1903), Stoker's mummy lay 'dormant', 'swathed and coffined and left as dead.' The father could never forget that the child's birth 'had cost her mother's life.' Stoker writes of the 'grave silent men [who] carried the white still figure, which looked like an ivory statue when through our moving the sheet fell back ... We placed it on the couch ... where the blaze of the electric lights shone.'[784]

Stoker's protagonist sees 'the still white shrouded figure on the couch,' and hears the infantile 'piteous mewing' that 'was the only sound in the room.' The 'Nurses ... kept watch ... All night the patient remained in his trance ... Every breath of the Nurse or the rustle of her dress; every soft pat of slippered feet ... every moment of watching life, seemed to be a new impetus to guardianship.'[785] When the mummy's wrappings are 'torn away and the body of the queen' was revealed, she is 'reborn as a woman'.[786]

Stoker's description was, of course, that of a modern delivery theatre, and of a child born to a woman rendered unconscious by chloroform or ether.

Like Stoker, Rider Haggard envisioned his mummy as a queen. Her titles include 'Royal Wife, Royal Mother, Lady of the Two Lands, Palm-branch of Love, Beautiful-exceedingly.' (Rider Haggard's mother was, like his fictional queen, a 'lady of two lands'. Born in Bombay, India, she was a poet and a woman of piety – a 'palm branch of love'.) His protagonist is struck by 'a woman's little hand, most delicately shaped. It was withered and paper-white, but the contours still remained; the long fingers were perfect, and the almond-shaped nails had been stained with henna.' (Again, his mother's culture.) '[Smith's] heart swelled within him, for here was the hand of that royal lady of his dreams. Indeed, he did more than look; he kissed it, and as his lips touched the holy relic'.[787]

The name of Rider Haggard's queen? 'Ma-Mee' – that is to say, *Mummy*.[788]

In the wake of Twilight Sleep, the 'singularly iconic figure' of the undead mummy metamorphosed from an attractively incapacitated feminine dominant to a 'monstrous, shambling, bandage-swathed creature that has been revived'.[789]

Photographs of mothers incapacitated by scopolamine show essentially mummified women – heads and hands padded and bandaged, strapped to beds, their parted legs bound in the air to frames in the lithotomy position. Labouring American women were blinded by gauze pinned by adhesive strips and deafened by cotton wads soaked with olive oil.[790]

'I've seen [mothers] with no skin on their wrists from fighting the straps,' an American nurse wrote in 1958. 'I can surely testify to

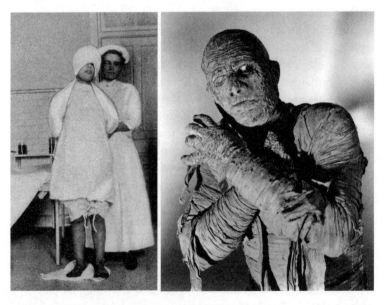

Left: Twilight Sleep mother with obstetric nurse.
Right: American actor Lon Chaney in *The Mummy's Ghost* (1944), made after the first generation of Twilight Sleep infants had come of age.

real cruelty in the delivery room.'[791]

Another nurse reported in the same year, 'At one hospital I know it is common practice to take the mother right into the delivery room as soon as she is 'prepared'. Often she is strapped in the lithotomy position, with knees pulled far apart, for as long as eight hours. [One] obstetrician informed the nurses on duty that he was going to a dinner and that they should slow up things. The young mother was taken into the delivery room and strapped down hand and foot with her legs tied together.'[792]

As Plath's and other reports show, Twilight Sleep births were literally a form of torture that could not in their entirety be consciously recalled. Instead, mothers and babies would tell their horror stories in nondeclarative form – through anxiety, aversions, depression, detachment, disgust, nightmares, self-loathing, and sexual or substance-use disorders.

The bandaged, moaning or screaming grotesque of horror films, then, was not, as has been posited, 'a metaphor of colonial relations', but a literal representation of the violent scopolamine or drug-disabled 'mummy' during birth from the perspective of the infant.

As scopolamine-induced obstetric deliriums were phased out in favour of new obstetric drug cocktails, the mummy was replaced in the public imagination by the insensate zombie, a technically dead cannibalistic monster or human facsimile. *The zombie's reproductive organ is its mouth* – the living are transformed into the living dead by its bite.

Parallels to the *vagina dentata*, the 'toothed vagina' of folklore, are straightforward.

In *World War Z: An Oral History of the Zombie War*, American author Max Brooks writes that while 'many may protest the scientific accuracy of the word *zombie*, they will be hard-pressed to discover a more globally accepted term for *the creatures that almost caused our extinction. Zombie* remains a devastating word, *unrivalled in its power to conjure up so many memories or emotions … many of those memories may no longer exist, trapped in bodies and spirits too damaged or infirm.'* Of one character, he adds, 'every time we would be close enough *to hear him whimper softly for his mother* [italics mine].'[793]

The zombie: the adult's nondeclarative memory of a mother disordered by drugs, both before and in the immediate wake of birth.

Even the characteristic noises associated with zombies – the distorted growls, grunts, screams and screeches[794] – are those that would be *heard from within* a drugged mother by her drugged foetus.

Ketamine, one of the most 'widely'[795] used obstetric drugs, causes auditory and visual disturbances;[796] a 'k-hole' is the 'sub-anaesthetic state'[797] in which ketamine users experience dissociation. British electronic duo The Chemical Brothers released *Lost in the K-Hole* in 1997, after the first generations given ketamine in an obstetric context[798] had come of age. Despite ketamine's association with bladder damage and incontinence,[799] it's now a standard party drug, and commonly used to facilitate chemsex.

There is a paucity of studies investigating the wellbeing of mothers and babies after the obstetric administration of ketamine.[800] Correspondingly, there are no adequate and well-controlled studies on the impact of being born to an unconscious or a violent, drugged, and semi-conscious woman.

Gay American serial killer Jeffrey Dahmer tried to keep victims alive by 'inducing a zombie-like state',[801] the same state induced in labouring mothers by scopolamine (the drug is said to be part of the compound administered by Haitian voodoo sorcerers to 'zombify' victims).[802] The fact that Dahmer was aroused by sexual activity with a 'zombie' is the most telling detail; I believe that he was, through a grotesque prism of neurodevelopmental damage, simply attempting to remaster an unmanageably traumatic birth through his murders. A habitué of gay bathhouses, Dahmer would invite a man to his private room, offer him a spiked drink, and wait. It has been theorised that he 'wanted to gaze upon, and touch, a body which did not resist his attentions … like the game of "playing dead".'[803]

'Playing dead': a labouring mother rendered immobile by general anaesthesia or related obstetric drugs.

Gay British serial killer Dennis Nilsen was also sexually aroused by the dead. Nilsen remarked that he experienced 'a feeling of oneness' with the corpses of his victims. Dahmer echoed his sentiments, stating that he yearned to be 'at one' with another.[804]

'To be at one': the adult desire to return to the foetal state.

During his first interview at the William S. Hall Psychiatric Institute, serial killer Larry Gene Bell, who enjoyed sexual activity with corpses and was later diagnosed as a sadistic sexual deviant, said that his mother was dead. Ostensibly, this was a lie, but within the framework I have presented, Bell was telling his neonatal truth: he was born to a mother who was, to all intents and purposes, 'dead'.

Like Nilsen, Bell's aim was to be at 'one' with his victims. He said of one, 'Shari is now a part of me – physically, mentally, emotionally, and spiritually. Our souls are now one … Remember, we are one soul now. When located, you locate both of us together. We are one.' His words – nondeclarative memories of severe birth trauma – were interpreted by professionals as 'grandiosity'.

Jeffrey Dahmer, Dennis Nilsen and Bell were 'insane' only insofar as they were failed by the obstetricians who delivered them, and, in Dahmer's case, by the doctor who fed his pregnant mother drugs (Nilsen's and Bell's mother may have had the same experience, I do not know). Clearly, there was severe birth trauma. Clearly, there was drug-related neurodevelopmental insult *in utero* and at birth, possibly aligned with later brain damage. The fact that Dahmer lay with corpses for hours, 'hugging them, cherishing them',[805] is evidence that his relational blueprint – the one set at birth – was, like Nilsen's, unilateral. These were men who had no primal understanding of reciprocal love.

Necrophilia: the sexualised desire to return to the warm internal responsiveness of a mother who was, at birth, cold and unresponsive, in order to 'reset'.

The life-deforming anguish and horror of the drugged infant birthed to a drugged mother has, to the best of my knowledge, never been adequately addressed.

Twilight Sleep mothers who could not afford private rooms were delivered of their babies with two, sometimes eight, other women labouring under the drug cocktail in 'labour cribs'.[806,807] As an American woman who gave birth in 1971 posted on a forum, 'I remember very clearly hearing a woman screaming her lungs out during my first time and I asked the nurse if she should check on her. To this day I remember her response, "Oh don't worry about her, she's asleep."'[808] The babies of such women were born into a senseless, sometimes psychotic, maternal cacophony, with the stench of antiseptic and unfamiliar amniotic fluids, waste and blood everywhere.[809]

This, then, is what a male physician in 1915 described as 'natural'.

And this is where the fabric of our culture began to unravel.

For billions of people over the past two centuries, the deepest, most intimate, individualising and passionate of human experiences was not only rendered emotionally sterile, but the stuff of nightmares. Through obstetric doping and medicalised masculine appropriation, birth was industrialised: scripted and brightly lit, associated with a cast of strangers, drugs, gender-based discrimination, genital focus and standardisation of the feminine – as it happens, just like pornography.

Thus depersonalised, birth was redefined as a forum for the abuse of the feminine by the masculine for profit and consolidation of the patriarchal ideology – again, just like pornography.

Obscenity, then, is a facile label for pornography, our most accurate cultural mirror held to the inhumane treatment of women and babies during childbirth. A form of nondeclarative memory for a mass trauma unrivalled in the history of our species, pornography becomes a compulsion for those under the same pressure that causes others to take drugs: that of stifling the anguish and panic caused by the absence of passionate maternal territoriality at birth. The more monstrous the pornography, the deeper – and more deeply buried – the devastation.

Without understanding why, Sigmund Freud, the Austrian founder of psychoanalysis, wrote that it's 'beyond doubt' that cruelty and sexual impulse are 'most intimately connected'. In *Three Essays on the Theory of Sexuality*, the treatment of mothers at birth is not addressed, and birth is mentioned only once.[810]

This blindness to the relationship between birth and sexuality preferences is universal.

In 2011, American media, culture and communication professor Roger Friedland wrote that a friend's attractive, sexually active, college-aged son had never encountered female pubic hair.[811] From an evolutionary perspective, the culturally sanctioned erasure of female pubic hair – a source of public debate – appears counterintuitive, as pubic hair traps important, sexually arousing olfactory messages and reduces 'mechanical friction during sexual intercourse' in addition to protecting the vagina 'from parasites or other pathogens'.

Described by researchers as a 'puzzle',[812] this pornographic vogue has been variously attributed to a cultural emphasis on 'heightened sexuality', the facilitation of genital visibility onscreen, paedophiliac urges, and to the retaliatory patriarchal infantilisation of women.[813]

This is not why female pubic hair disappeared from mainstream pornography.

Female pubic hair began to be depilated in the 1940s,[814] around the time that babies born to women whose pubic hair was shaved in preparation for birth began coming of age. As one study reported, 'By the 1920s, obstetrics had refigured the perineum as pathological, and the practice of pubic shaving [in preparation for birth] became widespread.'[815]

Obstetric shaving and swabbing of the vulva remained standard practice in the First World until the 1980s, ostensibly because in the event of perineal tearing, it reduces infection.[816] It has, in fact, been shown that the very opposite is true: the tiny abrasions and lacerations created by shaving act as 'vectors' for infection.[817] The discrediting of the 'infection' theory has not affected the routine nature of the obstetric practice in certain countries,[818] demonstrating that shaving and swabbing are, like so many other current obstetric practices, unrelated to hygiene. The aim is to

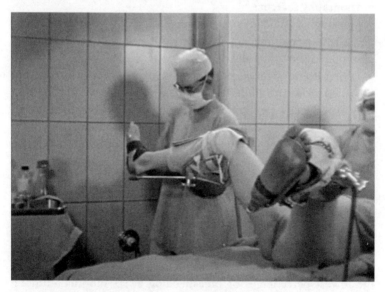

A labouring mother in the lithotomy position, one of the most common positions featured in BDSM pornography. Still from 'Maternity Care', a United States Navy training film, 1963.

dehumanise the mother.

Female hair, with what Robert Muchembled described as 'all its erotic, visual and olfactory messages', has always been subject to patriarchal taboos.[819]

The reason billions of men are now aroused by depilated vulvas is not because they are paedophiles, but because they seek to replicate the circumstances of their births.

Cleverly repackaged as liberating for the feminine, the obstetric drug- and practice-facilitated disconnection of breastfeeding from childbirth has had an equally destructive impact on attachment, sexuality and mental health.

The world's biggest pornography site found that the American state with the fewest breast-related pornography searches is Mississippi,[820] which, along with Alabama, has the lowest percentage of breastfeeding at six months. (Alabama and Mississippi, as it happens, are also the most fervently Abrahamic, or religious, of American states.)[821] Three of the states featuring the highest percentages of breastfeeding at six months[822] – Minnesota, Oregon and Washington – show the highest numbers of breast-related pornography searches.[823]

Through its fundamental disparagement of the feminine and its denial of our mammalian origins, patriarchal religions are, as I will continue to show, literally destroying our planet.

What these figures also show is that babies who are not breastfed grow into adults *who fail to see the point of the female breast*: they experience no excitement on seeing or imagining breasts, and have no primal sense of connection with the feminine. In effect, bottle-feeding is rendering the female breast superfluous from an evolutionary perspective: not only eroding attachment and tender mutuality between the sexes, but further denying the intelligence of feminine design and accelerating the denial of femininity itself.

The new adult feminine: physically hairless, breastless, and detached from her young – in herself, purposeless. A proto-human or unfinished model, available for modification by the masculine.

This is not a frivolous analysis. The same American states with the lowest percentages of breastfeeding at six months – among them, Mississippi, Alabama, Louisiana, and Arkansas[824] – are also those that feature the highest rates of adult depression.[825] These are four of the core Confederate states – areas historically known for their Abrahamic reviling of affectionate, sensual black culture and for their religious denial of our mammalian origins. Arkansas and Mississippi have the second and third highest concentration of hate groups in America.[826]

It can thus be concluded that hate and depression are byproducts of obstetric practice and the dehumanising patriarchal ideologies that created it.

After two centuries of obstetric drugs, babies have, *en masse*, had their humanity diluted – they have been essentially masked and emotionally muted, no longer fully capable of the emotional and sexual intimacies characteristic of the species: increasingly humanoid rather than human.

The first hours of *ex utero* existence, then, are not merely imprinted on the newborn memory, but determine the sexual and emotional parameters of his entire life.

Birth is where we learn to be human.

15. RUBBER SOUL

> 'Pygmalion gazed, inflamed
> with love and admiration for the form,
> in semblance of a woman, he had carved.'
>
> *Pygmalion and the Statue*, Ovid

At the age of 19 or so, I was befriended by a publicist who called herself Nancy Kulp after the closeted American character actress who, as it happens, also died of cancer. I remember watching in wonder as Nancy, a fetishist, changed into perilously high patent leather heels and tailored monochrome latex skirt suits in drunk butterfly hues – violet and primrose, petrochemical blues – for nights out. The relationship between the constraints presented by her small, dank, rented flat and the brilliance of her plumage may have been causal, I don't know.

Through Nancy and her close friend, who modelled herself on the 1950s American bondage pin-up Bettie Page, I was introduced to the London fetish nightclub scene. Intrigued by the aesthetic rather than the practice, I superficially familiarised myself with the rubber underground, now so popular that monthly Torture Garden events there can attract thousands.[827] I revelled in the theatre of it – the art, the sartorial drama, the stylised containment of sexuality – going so far as to pose in designer latex for the cover of an industry magazine.

While I loved the inaccessibility of wearing a latex dress, and had always savoured the smell of my erasers at primary school – I remember inhaling, with an unusual degree of relish, their textural scents in class – my interest in rubber was otherwise purely aesthetic.

I very briefly dated a man, a serious fetishist, whom I met through work. I would model (long, modestly cut) latex dresses and shoes for him – he never reacted in an inappropriate manner – but I remember noting the slant and intensity of his focus: *his interest in me was limited to my ability or willingness to animate the rubber*. He confessed that all he really needed to climax was a high-heeled patent leather shoe. Sexually, this man was aroused not by an emotional connection or by female flesh, but by its casing of inanimate material – namely, rubber.

The feminine, in his erotic prism, was a *subsidiary* of rubber.

In 1974 and to widespread outrage, British designer Vivienne Westwood OBE, in conjunction with her then-partner, the British impresario and Sex Pistols manager Malcolm McLaren, opened the King's Road boutique SEX, which sold her punked-up designer rubber and BDSM-inspired clothing. Featuring a heart-shaped apron and a balcony corset exposing the nipples – the same irresistible illusion of the mother's availability that characterised the 1960s hippie festivals – Westwood's 'Rubber Maid's Dress' encapsulated the infant's feminine ideal: defined by service, fetishised, and symbolising motherlove.[828]

From left: Steve Jones of the Sex Pistols, unknown, writer Alan Jones, Chrissie Hynde of the Pretenders, punk icon Jordan, and designer Vivienne Westwood in Westwood's King's Road boutique SEX.

Westwood's rationalisation for her designs was that used by Barrett, Leary and other Psychedelic Revolutionaries to justify their substance abuse and promiscuity: 'rebellion.'[829] Her designs, in conjunction with German photographer Helmut Newton's fetish-inspired portraiture, inspired some of the world's greatest couturiers – among them, Azzedine Alaïa, Dolce e Gabbana, Jean-Paul Gaultier, Thierry Mugler, Jil Sander, and Versace Couture – to incorporate rubber and fetish iconography into their designs, serving to reframe the sartorial hallmark of marginalisation as elite sexual refinement.

In the 21st century, black rubber or latex clothing is a primary signifier of the emotionally dispossessed.

Hollie Pryce-Jones, a British tattooist with a split tongue – now an illegal procedure in America, England and Wales and which presents a serious risk of haemorrhaging, infection and nerve damage[830] – posted a lockdown photograph eroticising her marginalisation. In it, she poses in improbably high black platform stilettoes, black latex leggings, long black latex gloves, and a pale

'Ripped my stocking because I'm a useless monster that doesn't deserve nice things.' @erotic.funeral, Instagram, September 11, 2020 www.instagram.com/p/CFAjPSxl8rp/).

latex humanoid mask with a black latex hood, its face anonymised by white eyes. Her t-shirt underscores the nondeclarative narrative of birth trauma: 'Mother of Sorrow.'[831]

In other posts, Pryce-Jones describes herself as a 'monster' and a 'piece of trash'[832] with a 'constant feeling of dread'.[833] Throughout her account, the usual homage to Marilyn Manson and the porn aesthetic: *fin de siècle* decadence.

American superstar Madonna joined the chorus on her 2015 album *Rebel Heart*, singing about latex lingerie and leather whips.[834]

Tim Brough, the American editor of *Rubber Rebel* and *Vulcan America* magazines, regularly received letters from men confused about their passion for rubber. Some had grown up wrapping their mothers' dishwashing gloves around their penises, while others had masturbated in the garage to the smell of the inner tubes of tyres.

'For many of us,' Brough wrote, 'it wasn't a learned behaviour.' There was, he added, 'just something about the old gasmask in the attic … that triggered an unexplainable segment of the brain, the one that sends cascades of hormones to the appropriate reactive body zone. But why? How does something as simple as a photo of men in diving suits trigger such an intensely private erotic response for so many people?'[835]

In 2018, a British 60-something rubber fetishist expressed the same perplexity: 'It all began when I was about 13 and had a swim cap; I was mesmerised by the smooth feel of the rubber, the sounds it made, and the smell. I don't know what made me associate rubber with sex but I began masturbating with it.'[836]

First reported in the 19th century and almost 'nonexistent in traditional societies',[837] fetishism involves the investment of a highly specific inanimate object – sometimes a non-genital body part, such as feet – with erotic feeling. For over a century, psychiatrists have struggled to explain its aetiology ('No cause for fetishistic disorder has been conclusively established').[838] Such paraphilias (once known as 'sexual perversions') are thought to originate in 'childhood or early adolescence, and perhaps become better defined as an individual enters adulthood.'[839]

One certainty: true 'rubberists', rather than those who parade rubber attire as a statement of 'edge' or 'rebellion', score high on introversion scales,[840] suggesting that they are unusually vulnerable with an element of disengagement.

This disengagement is the axis of American artist Robert Mapplethorpe's 1978 photograph 'Joe Rubberman',[841] in which a man, encapsulated in a black rubber catsuit of sorts with gloves, booties and hood, lies supine against a plastic backdrop:[842] vacuum-packed humanity.

Mapplethorpe rose to prominence in the 1970s through photographs recording the sexual practices and tribal fetish regalia of New York City's gay subculture – involving blood, latex, leather, rubber, and urine – through a prism of 'sumptuous classicism'[843] (graded monochrome, sculptural poses). The aesthetics, however, were only ever a decoy. Mapplethorpe's narrative was one of fatal loneliness, of the organic isolated within a staged, brightly lit, and inorganic context.

Even the overt sexual acts Mapplethorpe depicted are portraits of alienation.

The preferred framework for explaining rubber fetishism is the symbolic or compensatory, with overcomplicated theories explaining it as the 'devaluation of the human love object',[844] an attempt to 'destroy reality',[845] a 'problem of desire',[846] the 'model of all psychic conflict' (Freud),[847] or, ludicrously, as the 'destruction of the paternal universe'.[848] Italian philosopher and psychoanalyst Massimo Recalcati went so far as to write that 'Fetishistic desire is, as such, deaf to love,' and that fetishism, 'like violence visited upon another', is 'one of the male ways of exorcising the uncontrollable anarchy of woman.'[849]

But what if fetishism is none of these things? What if sexual deviation plays no part in it? What if, in certain contexts, fetishism is the only normal – or possible - 'lovemap'?

The first rubber clothing factory was established in England in 1820. In 1824, Americans were experimenting to see how liquid rubber latex could be applied to protective clothing and other direct uses. Issues with the preservation and supply of uncoagulated latex meant that these experiments could not be resumed for years.

In the US, the first rubber company began producing waterproofed cloth and clothing in 1833. That same year, over

71 million yards of rubberised fabrics, over 178 million feet of rubber hose, over four million square feet of rubber flooring, over 12 million pairs of rubber gloves, and over six and a half million fountain syringes, a significant proportion of which were used in a medical capacity, were produced.[850]

In 1849, two years after pioneering the use of obstetric drugs, James Young Simpson designed the first obstetric vacuum extractor – the 'Air Tractor',[851] a large metal syringe connected to a rubber cup, which, a century later, became the rubber-capped plunger-like ventouse: during difficult births, both were attached to the infant's head in order to help pull him out.

The 'Kelly pad' or 'Kelly's pad', a rolled rubber sheet designed by the influential American gynaecology professor Howard Kelly to carry childbirth discharges away from the labouring mother, was invented in 1887,[852,853] and rubber gloves were introduced into the context of obstetrics in 1889.[854]

All Twilight Sleep and delivery suites were equipped with rubber mats,[855] but the use of latex and rubber was not restricted to maternity hospitals and clinics. At the turn of the 20th century, when half or so of all American babies were still being delivered at home by midwives or family physicians, one practitioner wrote that 'Rubber gloves, a Kelly pad, surgical gowns and cap, antiseptics and good soap, are always to be found in my obstetric bag.'[856] Another, who practised in rural areas, reported always using rubber gloves and 'a Kelly pad or rubber sheeting'.

Within a decade or so, rubber was part of 'standard' obstetric practice.[857]

Babies were, and continue to be, delivered by the latex- or rubber-gloved hands of obstetricians and midwives, who once wore rubber aprons and sometimes rubber masks,[858] onto rubber or rubberised sheeting or a sponge-rubber mattress. Rubberised scales are used to weigh them, rubber adhesive is used in c-sections, and babies are now wrenched from the vaginal canal by rubber-coated forceps – the 'soft' forceps now recommended for such deliveries.[859]

Breast pumps were made of rubber,[860] flavouring the mother's nipples. In maternity wards, mother and child slept apart on 'thick red rubber mackintosh sheets'[861] disguised by hospital bedlinen. Premature babies were fed through rubber gastrostomy tubes[862] or 'belcroy feeders', slender tubes with a thick, odoriferous rubber bulb at one end and a teat at the other, meaning that, as with their bottle-fed peers, all their food would have tasted overwhelmingly of rubber. Neonatal Intensive Care Unit (NICU) endotracheal tubes were also originally made of rubber.[863] Maternal douches had rubber tubing[864] and catheters inserted into mothers after birth were made from rubber.[865]

Even now, rubber is the 'most rapidly growing choice' of NICU flooring.[866]

Rubber was, and remains, one of the dominant flavours, scents, sounds and textures in the newborn's universe. As a result, rubber was, and continues to be, synonymous with comfort, love, and nurturance for the overwhelming majority of First World – and, in particular, for privileged – babies.

To the premature baby in particular, latex, plastic, silicone and rubber were, and continue to be, significantly more consistent than any maternal flavour, odour, sound, or texture. In conjunction with culturally-facilitated mother/baby alienation, this repeated and intimate exposure to these materials at the most fragile of neurodevelopmental – and most critical of olfactory – junctures logically segues into fetishism.

The phenomenon known as 'imprinting' is the process by which birds and mammals become fixated on that which they see and smell during and immediately after birth. Environmental stimuli not only create neural circuits and sensory maps in the brain, but help determine behaviour and perception in later life.[867] If maternal odours shape later sexual preferences,[868] it only makes sense that other odours experienced in the critical birth and immediate post-birth timeframe do too.

In reply to Tim Brough's question: consider masked, gowned, gloved male obstetricians redolent of rubber and fishy vaginal fluids, and then consider masked men in diving suits smelling of the sea.

Rubber fetishism is a byproduct of modern obstetric practice, meaning that those who ostracised fetishists as perverts were effectively punishing them for a deviation that their ideology had created.

By 1922, 73 percent of the world's total rubber consumption was American. The principal consumers of rubber in 1934 in order of size were the US, the UK, Japan and Germany.[869] These four countries are now among the top seven with the highest population of 'rubberists', as rubber fetishists are known, England and Germany being the top two respectively.

Given the historically higher rates of birth intervention among the privileged, it's unsurprising that British fetish impresario Tim Woodward estimates that 45 percent of latex/rubber fetishists are upper class, 45 percent are middle class, and only 10 percent are working class.[870]

The boom in latex couture during the 1980s and 1990s, then, was unrelated to rebellion or sexual refinement – it was simply a reflection of the increasingly inhuman environment First World newborns experienced in birth and early infancy. Marketed to the most privileged of women – those most likely to have endured obstetric intervention at birth – latex couture also served to make them more sexually appealing to men who had suffered the same or similar birth trauma, men who would feel disturbed if confronted by the fleshy, passionate, territorial, unstructured feminine they had not experienced at birth.

The name of Europe's biggest fetish club, the Torture Garden,[871] named for Octave Mirbeau's novel, has intense resonance for those whose mothers were abused at birth ('garden' being a popular colloquial term for the vulva).

A vulva brutalised by modern obstetric practice: the Torture Garden.

Rubber fetishism, then, is 'nonexistent in traditional societies' and did not exist prior to the industrialised 19th century because rubber had no role in childbirth and childrearing before that time. The average baby was delivered by women and then nurtured and regulated by the intimacy of skin-to-skin contact with his mother, who was not only capable of, but motivated to initiate, breastfeeding. No inanimate proxies were necessary. Correspondingly, there was no association between doctors, nurses, and sex prior to this era either.

Colloquially known as 'rubbers', rubber condoms were first manufactured in 1855,[872] a contraceptive milestone made possible by American inventor Charles Goodyear's 1939 discovery of rubber vulcanisation (a range of irreversible processes that increase flexure without cracking and longevity).[873] In 1920, the first latex condoms were produced.[874,875]

The relationship between birth, sex, and rubber, and, in the case of condoms and other products, between birth, sex, and latex, was not merely pragmatic, but served to further distance human beings from each other and from the mammalian sensitivity to – and concomitant bonding facilitation of – skin-to-skin contact.

Detachment became the defining principle of 20th-century birth, motherhood, and sex.

Baby bottles once had thick, rubbery teats. I have an oddly distinct memory of the stiff ochre-coloured rubber nipple on my brother's graduated glass bottle, and the way it changed colour and cracked over time.

In 1845, the 'India rubber' artificial nipple, an 'Instrument for Protecting Sore Nipples' was patented in New York by Elijah Pratt;[876] in the early 1900s, this artificial nipple was adapted for use with baby bottles. Christian Meinecke, who patented the first baby pacifier in 1900, named it the 'Baby Comforter'[877] – a role that had, up until then, been played by women. A New Jersey pharmacist, he may have been asked by women for help with their infant's babbling or distress. As the developmental importance of a baby's babbling or cries was not yet known – babbling is a critical stage of language development[878] and a critical means of both communicating and strengthening mother/baby intimacy – Meinecke, recognising a new market, designed an easily manufactured maternal replacement that would make billions of dollars for its male producers.

Extended infant and child suckling other than during breastfeeding has been linked to corrupted speech development in young children[879] and with reduced breastfeeding duration.[880] Early weaning has been associated with ruptures in proper oral motor development, which may cause, among other issues, difficulties with breathing, speaking and swallowing.[881,882]

The tongue, too, is developed by breastfeeding, facilitating eloquence.[883] Breastfed babies have superior speech-processing abilities to their bottle-fed peers.[884,885,886,887] The issue of retarding or delaying a child's verbal literacy is not trivial. Children with language disorder have more behavioural, emotional, and social problems than their peers, and fall below academic expectations,[888] which leads, in turn, to multilayered adult dysfunction.

Unsurprisingly, none of this is mentioned in advertisements for infant formula.

Speech, language and communication needs are now the most common class of needs at British schools, with 22 percent of Special Educational Needs (SEN) students, the number of whom has increased for the third consecutive year, requiring assistance in the area.[889] Overall, the prevalence of language disorder of unknown origin – that is, unrelated to an existing medical diagnosis or intellectual disability – among British children is 7.58 percent. In SEN school children under the age of four, 59 percent suffer from a language disorder;[890] the fact that this drops to 8.5 percent by the age of 15 suggests that a significant number of infants and young children are being silenced by pacifiers (also known as 'dummies') and other means.

In Sweden, researchers who observed a 'recess' in children's expected verbal development over the summer holidays concluded, having taken variances into account, that 'structural language promoting activities' – otherwise known as engaged, age-appropriate conversations, reading and games – are 'carried out to a much lesser degree' by parents and caregivers.[891]

Around the world, parent-child love is weakening.

The prevalence of speech sound disorder among young American children is now 8 to 9 percent. Approximately 5 percent, by the first grade, show noticeable speech disorders – again, the majority of which have no known cause.[892] Between 1963 and 1979, there was a 50+ point decline in mean verbal scores for the SAT college admission exams.[893,894] The economic impact of such communication disorders is significant, both in terms of cost and labour losses, and amounts to 2.5 to 3 percent of the Gross National Product in the US alone.

In 1900, four-fifths of the US labour force depended upon manual skills to survive; by 2000, 62 percent of the same labour force was white collar – that is, working with language – and the remaining 37 percent of blue collar workers and farmers depended on communication.[895] In short, survival of the 'fittest' no longer depends on the greatest capacity for three-dimensional force, meaning that formula and pacifiers, particularly for disadvantaged children, significantly lower the likelihood of success in later life.

The use of a pacifier is now a socio-economic marker: the mothers most likely to silence their children with pacifiers have greater financial difficulties, lower levels of education, live in council housing, or are younger.[896] Variables explaining the maternal reliance on pacifiers (and infant formula) can, for the most part, ultimately be laid at the stoop of medical professionals, whose increasing tendency to prescribe legal drugs to pregnant lower-class women – and to administer obstetric drugs to the same demographic – has created generations of addicted, depressed, distractible, or indifferent women with an impaired capacity for mothering.

Whatever the motivation, mothers, in silencing their babies with rubber and then latex pacifiers and bottle-feeding, have not only incrementally eroded the mother/baby bond, but taught their babies to associate consistency, love, and nurturance with an interchangeable – and disposable – inanimate object made of rubber. Because of this, pacifiers are now classed as *attachment objects*,[897] insentient items invested with the mother's power to comfort.

Through the use of pacifiers and through other maternal delegations, mothers have contributed to their own increasing obsolescence.

'Dear Baby,' reads a satire aimed at new parents, 'Do you feel that no one understands the relationship you have with your dummy? Don't worry. A lot of babies feel this way. We're here *to help you get the comfort you need, from the dummy you love* [italics mine].'[898]

A baby's relationship with his pacifier is, however, unilateral, the same one-way passion a rubberist experiences for rubber. In this, pacifiers not only reduce the infant's emotional intelligence, but also his ability to recognise the developmental need for submission to the mother. Increases in breastfeeding duration have been attributed to reductions in pacifier use.[899] In the place of this acknowledgement of the mother's nurturing power and of its fundamental relationship to emotional regulation, only contempt. Through distancing tools such as the pacifier, babies are wrongly taught to understand that, with the help of an inanimate object, they can regulate their own emotions.

The maternal comes to be seen as superfluous, an outmoded indulgence.

Materialism, then, is a perversion of the infant's attachment instinct.

In the 21st century, the Pirelli Tyres calendar, first issued in 1964, continues the increasingly popular association between rubber, disposability, patriarchal masculinity and sex (almost 80 percent of the world's rubber is bookmarked by the car industry).[900] The gold standard in elite erotica, 'The Cal', as it is known, features the world's most celebrated beauties photographed by the world's most celebrated photographers.[901] The 2015 calendar's iconic shot – American model Gigi Hadid, thighs apart, in a sculpted, strapless black rubber bodysuit – was styled by *Vogue Paris* editor Carine Roitfeld and taken by American Steven Meisel.[902]

Addressed outside the prism of contemporary erotica, the image could be a stylised representation of a woman on an obstetric table, preparing to give birth. Nature in high contrast to the manufactured: a portrait of sexualised isolation and the containment of femininity.

Even outside the erotic, art is often a means of communicating birth trauma. British designer Gareth Wrighton's 'Self Portrait as a Cherry Pie',[903] for example, clearly alludes to birth.

Mapplethorpe's photographs found an audience because they resonated with viewers traumatised by 20th-century birth practices. That disquieting intrusion of a finger in a genital cavity;[904] a head emerging from draped white fabric as if from sheeted thighs;[905] the figure in latex able to breathe only through a tube.[906] The detached classicism, too, echoes the disengagement the profoundly sensitive Mapplethorpe experienced at birth. 'White Gauze' (1984),[907] for example, depicts two figures effaced – and suffocated in their embrace – by bandages, like mummies; or, perhaps, like a man bound to the nondeclarative memory of a mother rendered unrecognisable – and terrifying – by anaesthesia and surgical drapes.

Beneath the gauze, his mouth is open in an attempt to breathe.

Fetishism, then, is a nondeclarative narrative – a means of sharing pain, of being *heard*.

The dominant theme in the work of Mapplethorpe is the organic isolated within a staged, brightly lit, inorganic context, its characteristic monochrome suggesting that the true story, the original *inciting incident*, took place in the distant past – in 1946, say, when the artist was born in a New York hospital.

Even the overt sexual acts Mapplethorpe documented are representations. The naked man suspended upside-down by another man[908] (as naked babies were once routinely held in attempts to

Compare a patient prepared for Twilight Sleep with Robert
Mapplethorpe's photograph 'White Gauze' (www.nationalgalleries.
org/art-and-artists/130230/white-gauze)

revive them from their drugged stupor); the greased male anus
penetrated by two male hands[909] (as the vulva was penetrated by
male obstetricians during delivery); and his self-portrait, on a gauze-
sheeted platform, with a long whip coiling from his partitioned,
ravaged anus[910] (an umbilical cord pulsing from a partitioned,
ravaged vulva on a sheeted surgical table): sexualised symbols of
birth trauma and its related alienation.

Why else would the word 'mancunt' be gay slang for an effeminate
gay male's 'well used' anus?

Similarly, Mapplethorpe's portraits of fisting,[911] the sexualised act
of inserting a fist into the vagina or anus, are also a nondeclarative
replay of an unusually aggressive birth. The patriarchal made
manifest in the obstetric theatre.

Fisting, then, can be understood as a direct byproduct of
Leviticus.*

---

* In encouraging murderous violence against homosexuals Leviticus created shame
and self-loationg in gay men. In addition, the depiction of birthing women as 'unclean' effectively encouraged violence or contempt towards labouring women, resulting in punitive birth practices. Leviticus 13:21: 'If a man also lie with mankind
as he lieth with a woman, both of them have committed an abomination. They shall
surely be put to death: their blood shall be upon them.'

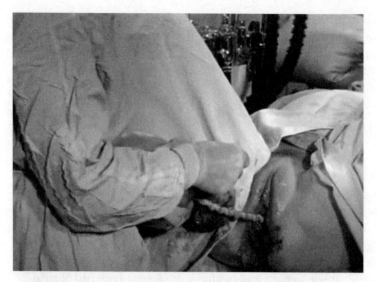

Compare this still of an umbilical cord in the 1963 US Navy
'Maternity Care' film to Robert Mapplethorpe's 'Self Portrait
with Whip' (www.getty.edu/art/collection/object/109FW8).
The umbilical texture of the whip is telling, as is the organic tissue
(leather) and the 'partitioning' of the chaps. Mapplethorpe used sex
to tell his narrative of severe birth trauma.

Human sexuality is a witness statement, and what we
understand as paraphilias or 'sexual deviation' are the literal acting-
out of trauma. The more compulsive, disengaged or violent the
sex, the more traumatised the individual.

In relation to Mapplethorpe's oeuvre, both artistic and erotic,
the fetishisation of rubber was only one of his innumerable
references to a trauma he would never consciously recall.

When a mother, because of abusive birth practices, unrelated suffering, or other reasons, is unavailable to her infant in her entirety,
he can only love the inorganic fragments – among them, latex or
rubber – that return him to the matrix of his consciousness. For
this reason, these fragments must be presented in a humanoid
form: a rubber mother.

While pygmalionism – sexual responsiveness towards an inanimate object, particularly of one's own making – is an ancient

concept, the industrial capacity for mass-produced rubber simulations of femininity did not exist until the 19th century, and even then, prudery scuppered their manufacture. It wasn't until the 1970s, when Westwood made fetishism hip, that the first crude latex, silicone, and inflatable vinyl sex dolls hit the market.[912]

The 1973 Roxy Music song, 'In Every Dream Home a Heartache', is Bryan Ferry's lovesong to an inflatable sex doll, whom he refers to as the 'perfect' partner.[913]

Men who develop feelings for these 'synthetic humans' are known as 'iDollators', and are not unlike Dahmer and Nilsen in terms of their limitation. Some live with their sex dolls as partners, styling and dressing them, taking them out in wheelchairs and in company, and generally relating to them emotionally as a newborn would to an unconscious or uninterested mother. On removing his doll from her crate, one recalled, 'I just held her in my arms for a while. It felt so right and natural... It seemed perfectly normal for me to treat something that resembles an organic woman the same way I'd treat an actual organic woman.'

A mother stupefied by anaesthesia: *something that resembles an organic woman.*

This man concluded that relating to 'an organic woman doesn't seem worth it to me.'[914]

Reciprocity, by those who, as newborns and during early infancy, had emotionally or physically restricted access to their mothers, is experienced in adulthood as destabilising, exhausting, and unmanageably intense. Even my 'rubber goddess' friend Nancy was known for 'losing the plot'[915] when intimacy became sexual; she preferred the prophylactic of yearning.

Betrayals and conflicts cannot be metabolised by such people as the necessary foundation – namely, a solid sense of self – was never established. Love, to them, is one-sided, which is why they prefer masturbation, prostitution, sex dolls, stalking and unrequited love.

The only passion that feels safe for adults who endured separation from their mothers at birth is unilateral.

Babies are also *emotionally* silenced by pacifiers. Through the pacifier, babies are conditioned to understand communication, enthusiasm, and the expression of emotion as undesirable to their mothers. Pacifiers also teach them that distress is resolved through inanimate objects. Is it surprising, then, that so many men consider 'organic women' to not be 'worth it'? The 'partner' of another sex doll, a married father, explained his passion for it: 'She never betrays, not after only money. I'm tired of modern rational humans. They are heartless.'[916]

The doll's literal heartlessness was of no interest; this man had retreated into a fantasy of perpetual maternal accessibility in the only emotionally resonant form for him, that of silicone.

Texturally, sex dolls – adult *attachment objects* – would have a powerful emotional resonance with those who, during infancy, were, for long periods, exposed to silicone in particular in the form of bottle teats, feeding tubes, pacifiers, and so on. This exposure would, of course, have to exist in tandem with other factors: the absence of tender, territorial maternal investment, say, or severe and sustained abuse or neglect, such as that resulting from mental illness or substance abuse.

The cultural impact of sexualised attachment objects, however, is problematic.

Anatomically correct 'partial sex dolls' include sex doll heads (the life-sized head of a sex doll on a steel stand) for fellatio, and headless, armless and legless sex doll torsos (equipped with metal spines to create a more human-like resistance) for vaginal and anal sex. Hundreds of thousands, perhaps millions, of men are now learning, like Ted Bundy, to associate sexual pleasure with headless, inert feminine bodies and severed female heads.

In this seemingly harmless activity, not only the rehearsed reduction of the feminine to a set of cavities, but the reinforcement

Left: Generic rubber pacifier. *Right:* Generic dildo gag for sex play.

of the idea that the female head (representing independent thought and feeling) and limbs (representing agency) are unrelated to – and perhaps even subtract from – feminine sexual appeal to the masculine.

Sex dolls, like pornography and prostitution, are both reflections and reinforcements of the patriarchal ideology. Importantly, sex dolls reinforce the idea that the masculine is not only dominant, but the *only permissible voice* in any dyad. They teach that the feminine exists exclusively within the context of the masculine, and that its animation – its *life span* – is dependent on the masculine, as Bundy, in his career as a killer, also made clear.

Objects of comfort to men conditioned at birth to associate intimacy with latex, rubber or silicone, partial sex dolls are also tools that effectively reinforce the idea of sex as unilateral: something done *by* a man *to* an inert object, not unlike an obstetrician delivering the infant of a woman drugged into lifelessness or submission.

I still wonder if the blueprint for Nancy Kulp's lymphoma, along with that of her rubber fetish, was established at birth.

16. BREATHLESS

'To die for want of love is dreadful. Suffocation of the soul!'

Les Misérables, Victor Hugo

The global prevalence of rape and sexual assault aside (both have always been disproportionately associated with the feminine and sexual minorities),[917] girls and women now understand being choked (asphyxiophilia or 'breathplay'), restrained, slapped, spat upon, verbally abused, urinated on and, in some cases, *cut* ('bloodplay') as erotic.

In itself, the use of the suffix 'play' is a clever rebranding of illegal, sadistic, and potentially fatal or injurious activities. Thirteen percent of sexually active American girls aged 14 to 18 have endured nonconsensual choking, and a quarter or so of American women have experienced fear during sex (the partner, rather than asking, simply began to strangle them during sex).[918]

A 14-year-old friend of my daughter's, on discovering that I was writing about sexualised choking, casually told me that out of her three closest female friends, two 'play-choked' themselves while masturbating. On the understanding that strangulation is now part of sex, adolescent girls now practice varying degrees of auto-erotic asphyxia, unaware that 'breathplay' is responsible for 250 to 1,000 American deaths per year.[919]

Swedish pornography director Erika Lust observed that pornography is now dominated by choking and strangulation scenes. 'Face slapping, choking, gagging and spitting has become the alpha and omega of any porn scene and not within a BDSM context,' she told a newspaper. 'These are presented as standard ways to have sex.'[920] In 2016, 28 percent of pornographic scenes ('increasingly an unavoidable source of sexual education') depicted choking, and 41 percent depicted slapping;[921] on the basis of desensitisation, these numbers would have since escalated.

The practice has been normalised by the media. 'If blindfolds and role play have veered into vanilla territory for you and your partner, there are still plenty of sex moves that are considered extra freaky. Like choking,' American *Women's Health* magazine advised readers (over a million of them aged 18 to 24) in 2016.[922] 'As a result [of allowing a sexual partner to choke you], you feel you have an erotic power over him. And your dopamine receptors are firing on all cylinders.'[923]

Clearly not wishing to come over all Karen, the magazine failed to mention that the cumulative toll of regular 'breathplay' is brain damage.[924] Other dangers include airway obstruction, the aspiration of vomit, blood vessel and cervical spine damage, cumulative brain damage, larynx fracture, stroke, seizures and windpipe rupture.

Sexually choked without complaint at the time, some victims are later found dead.[925]

American psychology professor Debby Herbenick is one of many who would 'love to know why choking has become a thing. And it is a thing, especially among young adults.'[926]

Researchers have been mystified by the 21st-century vogue for sexualised choking, attributing feminine compliance with choking and the desire to be choked during sex to the conditioning agent of pornography; in turn, the pornographic vogue for choking has been attributed to a desensitised market and the usual degradation of the feminine.

But what if sexualised choking is not, as one group of researchers described it, a masochistic 'disease'? What if the threat of death in elective strangulation – 'breathplay' – is simply a reenactment of the threat of death in elective medicalised birth?

And which, I ask, is the greater perversion?

In contrast to scheduled births, spontaneous birth is triggered by the foetus. Through a series of rhythmic hormonal secretions, the foetus signals to his mother that his lungs have sufficiently matured, kickstarting labour.[927,928] This hormonal surge is, however, determined by the mother's serenity: the rate of pre-term (before 28 to 37 weeks) deliveries in women who do not have socioeconomic or physical risk factors is 3 to 4 percent, whereas in those at risk, the rate jumps to 5 to 18 percent.[929] Far from a process the mother merely endures or hosts, then, labour is an intricate series of *interactions* between a mother and her baby,[930] a conversation rather than a foetal monologue.

Given the normalisation of forced birth in the 21st century, it seems logical to assume that this mass expulsion from the womb of drugged babies with lungs that do not function at optimum is the variable responsible for the recent,[931] unexplained global 'epidemic'[932] of asthma and other sensitivities.[933] Globally, a quarter of a million people now die prematurely each year from asthma alone.[934]

Induced births – including caesareans – entail the infant being born *before he is ready*: while he may be capable of breathing, he is not yet ready to breathe. The psychobiological shock of induction, and its impact on the foetus, is something that is not taken into account by obstetricians. Despite the permanent nature of the repercussions on the infant, the only consideration in elective induction is the mother's choice, as if the foetus were impervious, inhuman or insensate.

The elective c-section is yet another means of imprinting on the infant that his health – his very *design* – is secondary to considerations of maternal gender status.

At birth, a significant number of infants now routinely experience 'air hunger' or dyspnea ('breathing discomfort') as a result of misinformed maternal choices. A 'significant' percentage of babies delivered by caesarean section, for example, suffer respiratory distress, a failed transition to air. As a result, these babies require additional treatments such as ECMO (extracorporeal membrane oxygenation), inhaled nitric oxide, surfactant, or ventilation, creating a host of new issues,[935] not all of them yet understood.

Doctors continue the tradition of administering, and being remunerated for administering, pregnant and labouring women drugs they have for decades been aware are potentially dangerous – even fatal – for babies. As American obstetrician William P. Sadler said in a 1937 address, 'We all know the deleterious effect upon the foetus, when morphia alone, morphine and scopolamine, heroin and pantopon [opium alkaloids hydrochlorides] are administered within two to four hours of its birth. Many of these babies are apneic [unable to breathe], while a smaller number are so deeply asphyxiated that resuscitation is exceedingly difficult and in some instances impossible.'[936]

Respiratory difficulty entails breathlessness that segues into panic – as an asthmatic, I am not unfamiliar with the sensation

– but a newborn cannot fight for long, so quickly passes out. This association of breathlessness, terror, and unconsciousness with the feminine at its most vulnerable – has changed the way we function.

As I mentioned, my brother, at the age of 32, asphyxiated himself. To more effectively suffocate himself, he pulled a black garbage bag over his head and torso and tied his hands to the steering wheel after releasing the helium tank valve in the back seat: an almost perfect reenactment of the trauma he had experienced at birth. My brother could have chosen to die in any number of ways, but because he was shoved back into the vaginal canal as he was crowning by an obstetric nurse, hypoxia, for him, had primal resonance – breathlessness in a dark, narrow space was not only familiar, but *comforting* to him. In the vaginal canal, his tiny hands were crushed up against his chest in the same crossed position as they were, full-sized and at the time of death, against the steering wheel.

I believe that a significant percentage, if not most or all, of those who commit suicide by asphyxiation or hanging, were victims of respiratory distress at birth.

Similarly, a teenage girl who asks to be choked during sex is simply fulfilling the blueprint given to her, however inadvertently, by her mother at birth.

Love as air hunger.

Love as fear.

Love as the threat of death.

American musician Thea Taylor, as carolesdaughter, captured the terror of the drugged infant in her song, 'My Mother Wants Me Dead', writing that drugs were disorientating her, persuading her that her mother wished only to murder her.[937]

The increasing prevalence of both premature birth[938] and the administration of obstetric drugs[939,940] – all associated with the newborn's respiratory distress[941] – corresponds precisely with the increasing prevalence of sexualised choking.

For example, fentanyl, a synthetic opioid 'widely used'[942] during delivery, has been variously described as 'safe for both you and your baby',[943] able to be used 'safely',[944] and as 'safe for newborn infants' in 'modest' doses.[945] Fentanyl is, in fact, known to be associated with infant respiratory distress, 'even in low concentrations'.[946]

A five-year study showed that *59 percent* of newborns whose mothers were given fentanyl during labour needed resuscitation,[947] and yet it continues to be recommended by medical professionals and midwives. Even the association of hypoxia (oxygen deprivation) at birth with schizophrenia[948] has failed to dent fentanyl's popularity.

Like c-sections, fentanyl is also one of the 'main determinants of bottle feeding' – that is, its obstetric application *impedes* breastfeeding.[949] In this respect, the drug, along with others administered during labour, *literally creates a market for infant formula*.

It's now not only considered 'normal' for a foetus to be stupefied at birth by drugs that in marginally bigger doses would be lethal, but *desirable*. Similarly, it's now considered 'normal' for a foetus to be forced into the world before he is developmentally ready. In the 21st century, it's considered 'normal' for a newborn to be unable to breathe without assistance because of the drugs with which he was, through his mother, poisoned.

'Normal', for the 21st-century newborn, involves being denied the comfort and immune protection of his mother's breast after the routinely severe trauma of birth and respiratory distress; being fed manufactured powder associated with the gravest of long-term complications for his health, community, family, and for his country's economic burden; being taught to understand love as an unmanageably frustrating, interiorised, one-way experience; and being silenced with a silicone gag if he expresses fear or pain.

As English philosopher and the founder of utilitarianism Jeremy Bentham asked in 1789, 'The question is not, Can they *reason*? nor, Can they *talk*? but, Can they *suffer*?'.[950]

Were vulnerable adults to be treated in this fashion, their abusers would be imprisoned. Were laboratory mammals to be treated in this manner, the products resulting from their testing would be boycotted on the basis of animal cruelty. But because the protective maternal instinct of the average woman has, for almost two centuries, been incrementally impaired by abusive obstetric practices, she is no longer even conscious of the harms she does herself and her child at this most vulnerable of junctures, or of the resulting life-altering emotional losses they will both permanently bear.

The developmental harming of a child is now presented to mothers as an *option*.

Asphyxiation was ranked first in relation to uncontrollability and second only to rape in terms of distress in a list of 46 different methods of torture.[951] Breathlessness has been described as 'an intensely traumatic event' and as 'a multidimensional symptom with a sensory and an affective component,' and creates anxiety, depression, fear, and PTSD, which may, in part, be why rates of anxiety and depression spiked during the Covid-19 pandemic.[952]

Imagine, then, the experience of a drugged newborn, dragged or ejected before he is ready from the warmth and familiarity of his regulated uterine universe into one of panicky breathlessness. Unlike an adult, an infant has no sense of agency, meaning that his experience of helplessness and terror is global. Gasping in his desperation to breathe – to *survive* – he rapidly becomes exhausted and surrenders to unconsciousness.[953]

Defeat, then, is his first experience of the world.

The adaptation of the newborn with respiratory distress to the environment that dictated his design has failed. If he survives, his mother's behaviour during his first hours and weeks of life will determine whether this defeat will be compounded into endogenous depression or whether it will be transmuted by the triumph of her love.

The trauma, however, will remain with him forever, as will the imprint of air hunger and the understanding of life as too difficult, and all will manifest variously in adulthood.

For example, panic disorder, which has an 'unknown aetiology [cause]', is characterised by chest tightness, fear of losing control, the conviction that one is dying, palpitations, shortness of breath, dizziness, and other symptoms,[954] all of which are shared by respiratory distress.

The smoking of cannabis and/or tobacco is another popular means of telling the same story. While rates of tobacco smoking have declined due to the well-publicised toll on health and the resultant behavioural restrictions, a billion people around the world continue to smoke,[955] and the links between the two substances are strong. In a study of over 1,000 people who reported cannabis use over the past year, those who reported use of high-potency cannabis were more than three times as likely to be dependent on tobacco.[956]

Global cannabis consumption has increased by over 60 percent

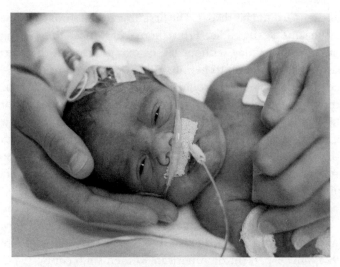

Compare an infant in Neonatal Intensive Care Unit with Robert Mapplethorpe's photograph 'Scott (Jockstrap)', 1978 (www.artsy. net/artwork/robert-mapplethorpe-scott-jockstrap)

over the past decade, with 192 million people smoking it in 2017: 2.5 percent of the world's population.[957] The most rapid growth in cannabis abuse since the 1960s has been in Australia, North America and Western Europe,[958] the same First World continents where the administration of obstetric drugs has also escalated, supporting the idea of a connection.

Rates of vaping, too, are skyrocketing internationally, with 41 million people now regularly smoking e-cigarettes.[959]

As medical historian Professor Allan M. Brandt reported, 'It has been conservatively estimated that 100 million people around the world died from tobacco-related diseases in the twentieth century … In this century … the death toll is predicted to be one billion.'[960]

In limiting the flow of oxygen to the bloodstream, smoking is an elective form of breathlessness. The panic addicts experience when they cannot smoke – I have known smokers to frantically light cigarettes or joints in airport toilets before catching a flight – reveals a deep attachment to the experience of breathlessness, to the mimicry of respiratory distress.

British actor Russell Brand, who regularly smoked heroin in airport toilets, was born with his umbilical cord – he refers to it as a 'noose' – around his throat. The first time Brand smoked cannabis, he 'became a drug addict. From then on, I smoked draw [slang for cannabis] every day without fail or exception until the narcotic baton was passed on to heroin. Whenever I went to school – or, indeed, anywhere – I would have a joint first.' Graduating to smoking heroin was straightforward ('I'd burn it and then inhale the vapour *and hold my breath until there wasn't a single bit left*'). Brand also described 'the terror' of performing on a first night as 'almost transcendental. Euphoric fear, so vertiginous, awesome and profound that *I felt it could only be a prelude to death* [italics mine].'[961]

Not unlike being born with a 'noose' around the neck, then.

Women adopted cigarettes *en masse*[962] around the time the first generations that had been anaesthetised at birth came of age. In 1924, only 5 percent of American women smoked; by 1948, the figure had risen to 40 percent.[963] Cigarettes were associated with liberty – not because of advertising, but because they comforted, through the experience of breathlessness, those who had suffered respiratory distress at birth. Margaret Atwood, for example, showed her age by using cigarettes as symbols of freedom for her female characters. Offred, the protagonist of her novel *The Handmaid's Tale*, says, 'I looked at the cigarette with longing. For me, like liquor and coffee, cigarettes are forbidden.'[964]

Cigarettes, e-cigarettes, joints and spliffs serve as adult pacifiers, satisfying two crucial needs of the adult victim of infant respiratory distress: breathlessness and the objectification of comfort. Why else would breathlessness, a state that the body is programmed to respond to with panic, be associated with consolation, independence, or sexual sophistication?

Breathlessness is also a core symptom of Generalised Anxiety Disorder (GAD), the most prevalent psychiatric disorder.[965] In 2015, WHO found that 3.6 percent of the global population was estimated to have an anxiety disorder.[966] In keeping with my theory, GAD is 'especially common and impairing in high-income countries'. Wealthier countries – again, those in which the administration of obstetric drugs to labouring mothers is now routine – repeatedly show higher rates of psychopathology.[967]

Adults who have suffered acute respiratory distress report a 'high prevalence, persistence, and co-occurrence of depression, anxiety, and PTSD symptoms'.[968] The same trauma, experienced at birth, would not only be global in its intensity on the basis of cortical immaturity, but *terrifying* – in conjunction with the mother's insensitivity or separation, the matrix of GAD.

As bassist Flea wrote, 'All my life I've gone through periods of horrific anxiety: a tightness in my stomach that creeps up and squeezes my brain in an icy grip. My mind relentlessly whirring, I can't eat or sleep, and I stare into a seemingly infinite void of despair, a bottomless pit of fear.'[969]

American writer Daniel Smith describes his anxiety with a similar emphasis, as a thought that escapes, 'sparking down the spine and rooting out into the body in the form of breathlessness, clamminess, fatigue, palpitations, and *a terrible sense that the world in which I find myself is at once holographically unsubstantial and grotesquely threatening* [italics mine].'[970]

That which Flea and Smith describe is typical of those with an anxiety disorder: an automatic cascade of *inappropriately extreme physiological responses* in response to even the most benign threat. The automatic nature of their physical reactions suggests that the original threat took place before declarative memory kicked in: *their bodies are telling a story their memories cannot access*. Smith's words – 'the world in which I find myself' – are particularly telling. These are the words of an adult who, as an embattled and exhausted infant, found himself unable to breathe and was, as a result, enveloped by terror in this, his 'grotesquely threatening' new world. The fact that this new world also appeared 'holographically insubstantial' suggests visual hallucinations created by the administration of obstetric opiates – morphine, say.

Excluding the GADs resulting from declarative trauma and obvious injury, what if a significant percentage, if not most, anxiety disorders are the result of birth trauma – in particular, of neonatal respiratory distress? What if the breathlessness and panic characteristic of anxiety are – like rubber fetishism; like Mapplethorpe's art – nondeclarative narratives of the same trauma triggered by stress?

Critically, what if the 'resurfacing' of birth trauma is homeostatic in essence, a story told *to be heard* and not ignored as it was at birth, so that emotional stability may be restored to the psyche? How would such an understanding change the way we treat those who suffer from anxiety and depression? How would it change the way we treat all mental illness?

I was, perhaps, 11 when I first saw hardcore BDSM pornography. In combination with black latex, the emphasis on air restriction struck me even then: the ball-gags, the breather tube gags, the inflatable ball hoods, the inflatable butterfly gags, the masking tape over the mouth, and so on. I failed to understand how this experience of being *muted* – of fighting for air – could be construed as exciting. Even now, the thought of air hunger frightens me. Fear, for me, has never been aligned with pleasure, not even peripherally. But for those who are aroused by the restriction of air – Mapplethorpe's 'Joe, N.Y.C',[971] say – such fear is *soothing*, familiar, it has a tranquillising effect.

BDSM in particular, with its air restriction, costuming, focus on hygiene, genital partitioning, gloves, infliction of pain, inflexible sexual scripts, medical equipment, and textural focus, resonates with those who were traumatised at birth and/or during infancy.

A murderer's *choice* to fatally strangle – rather than, say, poison, shoot, or stab – a victim may, in part, be a projection of, or revenge for, respiratory trauma experienced at birth. Strangulation has been described as 'particularly gendered' and shown to affect 10 times as many women as men,[972] supporting my theory of revenge. Before choking his partner, one man asked her, 'Do you know what it's like to drown?',[973] the wording suggesting that his action was vindictive rather than punitive, an effort to show her *what his mother had made him experience*.

Ian Brady, who, with accomplice Myra Hindley, killed five children aged between 10 and 17, was born at the Rottenrow Maternity Hospital in 1938 to an unmarried tearoom waitress from a Glasgow slum.[974] As the 1937 Maternity Services (Scotland) Act made provision for anaesthesia – generally associated with upper middle- and upper-class women – to be available to every labouring woman when necessary,[975] it's likely that his mother was administered chloroform or other drugs during labour.

Either way, Brady certainly didn't experience an abundance of oxytocin at birth or during infancy. To the 10-year-old victim who piteously begged, 'I have got to go because I am going out with my Mama. Please, please help me,' he flatly replied, 'If you don't keep that hand down, *I will slit your neck* [italics mine].'[976]

My belief that Brady, who chain-smoked strong, untipped French cigarettes (Gauloises)[977] and who, as a result, died of severe chronic obstructive pulmonary disease,[978] suffered respiratory distress during birth is also supported by his fetish for strangulation.

Brady, who fatally strangled four of his known victims and slashed the throats of two, also used the threat of strangulation to heighten their terror. In the recording of her murder, his 10-year-old victim cried, 'I cannot breathe!'[979] And, when confronted by a colleague, Brady 'grabbed him by the throat and dug his fingers into the man's carotid artery.'[980] Hindley, Brady's girlfriend and accomplice, reported that he regularly strangled her ('I used to ask him why he kept strangling me so much, so many times – this was before the offences took place – and he told me he was "practicing"').[981]

The theme of 'air hunger' is always significant.

Brady told the story of his birth trauma through murder as Mapplethorpe told his through art: his every victim was, as he had been, a child who struggled in terror, gasping for air. Like all other murderers, Brady *used his victims to tell a story that he was unable to articulate because no one had ever really listened.*

Dahmer was also partial to strangling his victims, if after drugging them with 'sleeping pills' – in his case Halcion, the same drug given to me as a child. During her pregnancy, Dahmer's nauseated mother was injected with an unnamed drug[982] that may have been Bendectin (doxylamine, dicyclomine, pyridoxine), which was widely administered to nauseated pregnant women at the time. Bendectin was discontinued in 1983 on the basis of its association with a smorgasbord of infant abnormalities.[983] In keeping with my theory, Dahmer, from birth to four months, required 'correctional casts' on his legs.[984]

The hallmarks of an abusive hospital birth are evident in a television interview with Dahmer: the characteristic detachment, depersonalisation, sexual arousal at the prospect of domination, substance abuse, and the persistent theme of air hunger. Like Dennis Nilsen, who also strangled his victims, Dahmer was a heavy smoker.[985]

Is claustrophobia the byproduct of foetal trauma experienced while trapped, drugged, in the vagina? First coined in 1879, three or so decades after the advent of obstetric anaesthesia, the word itself means 'morbid fear of being shut up in a confined space'.[986] Imagine the foetal experience of being stuck in a restrictive muscular tube and fighting to access oxygen while hallucinating. I believe that the later experiences which psychiatrists understand as the genesis of claustrophobia are no more than triggers, resurrecting the most primal of terrors: dying in the process of being born.

My guess would be that a significant percentage of those attracted to scuba diving, with its gloves, immersion in salt water, monitors, regulators, rubber, and oxygen tanks, also experienced respiratory trauma at birth, especially those drawn to the characteristically dark, narrow, dangerous spaces of caving. The potential for narcosis, a condition that, in many respects, mirrors smoking cannabis in its symptomology – difficulty concentrating, euphoria, reduced muscle function, others – is part of the attraction.

A number of these symptoms are also those of respiratory distress.

American biologist and Nobel laureate Gerald M. Edelman believed that serious threat is the origin of awareness in animal evolution. His theory was that it was through feeling threatened that we first individuated[987] – in becoming aware of a threat, we become aware of our existence as *separate* to that of the threat. If Edelman's theory is applied to the context of birth, it means that any threat at birth – that of air hunger, say – imposes a dangerously premature awareness of separateness on the newborn. I use the word 'dangerous' because an infant is not neurodevelopmentally ready to separate from his mother, meaning that his only possible response to the individuation in the circumstances is an incapacitating panic.

To fully grasp the extent and peerless importance of the sensory intelligence, sensitivity and vulnerability of the newborn is to change not only our understanding of birth, but of humanity itself.

17. BLACK SUN

'There has been something worm-eaten in you since your birth.'
Ghosts, Henrik Ibsen

British serial killer Ian Brady chose his victims very carefully. He never murdered neglected children: his victims were the kind of children who wore party dresses and visited their grandparents, children sculpted by gentle reciprocity. An unclaimed, unseen child would have reflected his own fathomless pain – as a boy, he wept on seeing an injured, bedraggled carthorse, 'its great liquid eyes rolling in terror' as it was about to be killed[988] – but there was, for him, no resonance in the happy, well-fed children he murdered.

By revealing to Brady that *their mothers would miss them*, his victims sealed their fates.

On the night of Brady's birth, there was a 'cold, sharp frost'. That January, Glasgow was buffeted by winds, and there was snow. The temperatures were low – two degrees on certain days; the heating in the tenement in which he lived with his unmarried mother would have been minimal. As a newborn, he was left alone almost every day for the first three months of his life while his mother worked. Alone, cold, dehydrated, foetid, denied the love, comfort, interaction and visual stimulation critical to neurodevelopment, grieving, hungry, squirming in his own claggy waste, his anogenital region burning with nappy rash, and unable to even roll over, Brady had only the echo of his breath for company.

He would have stopped crying soon enough; tears are a form of communication, and no one was listening. Adults who have difficulty crying or showing vulnerability – the emotionally contained, the *reserved*, and those who 'act out' by using substances or sex in place of simply sharing grief – were, as babies, ignored or neglected when distressed.

Such an ordeal experienced during the most sensitive of neurodevelopmental stages can only produce a cruel, impervious, and profoundly disordered adult with no understanding of emotional or sensual pleasure. As newborns have no capacity to understand temporary absence, the mother's separation is experienced as a 'sense of collapse, fear of death, and irreversible loss'[989] – blind *terror* – and strongly associated with later depression, psychosis, and other disorders.[990,991]

The repetition of such early attachment disruptions is now recognised as instrumental in the genesis of psychopaths.[992]

Hunger experienced at such a vulnerable age is particularly ruinous, and Brady's was multilayered – not only in terms of nutrition, but also neurodevelopment, precluding the emotional literacy and regulation by which functionality is defined.

Newborns who are not fed every two or so hours are at risk of dehydration, hypoglycaemia (low blood sugar), and other issues. Glucose deficits disrupt cerebral function; in a newborn, the result is irreversible brain injury. Other signs of low blood sugar – and Brady undoubtedly endured them all – include apnoea (stopping breathing, another means through which he may have known respiratory distress), hypothermia (low body temperature), lethargy, and loss of interest in feeding (reflecting the defeat, depression, disconnection, and ultimate sense of deadness by which he was defined).[993]

A cold, stilled, thin, wan infant in the shadows, all eyes.

Inadequate nutrition in four- and five-day-old babies has resulted in extensive damage to the occipital, both parietal, and temporal lobes.[994] In relation to Brady, temporal lobe damage is of particular interest. Among other functions, the region regulates bonding and emotional stability, sexual desire, the ability to identify the emotions of others, and the integration of emotion with perception.[995] For example, those with functional occipital, parietal and temporal lobes would, on witnessing a 10-year-old girl's distress, react accordingly rather than, say, rape, torture and murder her. Functional people would, in fact, go out of their way to *prevent* distress in a 10-year-old girl rather than cause it, and the idea of revelling in a child's pain would not only be incomprehensible to them but abhorrent.

Injury to the temporal lobes is associated with major depression (as winter, the season in which Brady was born, approached, he always 'felt empty and deeply depressed,' slowly becoming 'forgetful to the degree that some days, even a whole week, would be a complete blank').[996] Similarly, removal of the lobes reduces anxiety and fear,[997] meaning that damage to the area would be associated with abnormal fear responses. As Brady, who was known for his indifference to death, wrote, 'Fear evaporates in the absence of hope.'[998]

Psychopathy is now attributed to the same incapacity to experience 'anticipatory fear'[999] (the behaviour-modifying evaluation of a situation and calculation of potential risks); in psychopaths, the fear-circuitry simply isn't activated.[1000] Damage to the same region of the brain results in a failure 'to make normal use of information' when confronted by emotion,[1001] and has been found in a notable percentage of sexual sadists.[1002] Related damage has also been linked to a predisposition to paedophilia and what we understand as sexual deviation[1003] – Brady had both – suggesting that, like Mapplethorpe's art, it's associated with infant trauma.

Imagine, then, the injury resulting from *three months* of sporadically underfeeding a newborn.

Brady could not have been breastfed – even if his inexperienced, shamed, stressed, overburdened, and unsupported mother had been willing, her milk would have dried up during her long absences – so what was already a paucity of oxytocin would have dwindled to negligible quantities. The capacity for attachment, empathy and kindness is determined by oxytocin flowing from consistent, reciprocal, tender parental-infant engagement,[1004] something that the infant Brady never experienced. By the end of those three months, his increasingly detached and overburdened mother had placed an advertisement for his adoption in a local shop window.[1005]

Such early deprivation, and Brady's was extreme, has been shown to be related to changes in adult brain structure, however enriching the intervening emotional environment.[1006]

Brady's agony at the abuses he had endured metastasised into a hatred of mothers who emotionally 'claimed' their babies. He wanted their lives to be parenthesised by unrelieved unilateral suffering, like his. His blindness to the anguish and terror of his victims reflected his mother's blindness to his own; he had no capacity for empathy because empathy is *the legacy of love* and not innate. Like Bundy, Brady was corroded by envy – he could not bear to witness the tender territoriality that brought his pain into relief.

Institutionalised after prison in a high-security psychiatric hospital, Brady held a series of hunger strikes over 17 years.[1007] 'I frequently experienced the *black light* when I was starving,' he later recalled. '[I]n the total darkness of my cell, I would see the aura of the *black light* outlining my physical frame, which was becoming more skeletal by the day.'[1008] The fact that Brady, who had highly restricted access to his feelings, repeatedly *elected* to re-experience starvation in adulthood is telling. Through the language of hunger, he told his story of profound infant trauma in an attempt to be *understood*, but again, no one was listening.

Brady's hunger strikes were, as usual, wrongly interpreted as a 'symbol of his need to control'.[1009] Instead of addressing the inclusive language of *action* – which reveals the source of all dysfunctional behaviour – patriarchal psychiatrists relied on explanations that justified their governing ideology.

In starving himself, Brady was returning to his experience of 'mother' – or her absence.

Even in sharing his vision of the 'black light' – significantly, Brady wanted the phrase to be the title of his autobiography – he was again *calling attention* to the genesis of his sociopathy. In actuality, he was, through his 'black light' memories, drawing attention to the anxiety- and hunger-fuelled hallucinatory psychosis of his early infancy. The truth of Brady's life was further obscured with the usual Abrahamic judgement in the guise of medical opinion. Even now, he continues to be referred to as 'evil',[1010] a 'monster',[1011] and 'the most hated man in Britain',[1012] rather than as the victim of neurodevelopmental abuses so obscene that he was incapable of functioning as a normal member of a community. The birth abuses, hunger, isolation and fatal absence of love in his earliest infancy remained unaddressed.

Brady showed no remorse as he was never shown remorse. Babies are our mirrors.

To my knowledge, his suffering as an infant has never before been addressed because babies, for the most part, continue to be perceived not as human, but in terms of their human *potential*, meaning that their suffering is irrelevant. As Brady demonstrated, however, the happiness of babies is the bedrock on which a culture is built.

There are 17 hours of night in the average January day in Glasgow; for much of his early infancy, the newborn Brady would have lain face-up in darkness. The shadowed ceiling at which he stared must have seemed like a lunar landscape: it was more mother to him than his own. Its blankness would be reflected in his adult 'poker face', the hallmark of those ignored by their mothers at birth. Brady remained 'obsessed by bleak, open spaces,'[1013] repeatedly returning, if only symbolically, to source. The disposal of his victims' bodies on the moors was a metaphor for his own spiritual burial in that cold, dark, and, from his perspective, near-featureless room.

The instinct for death is a reflection of emotional silence or severe trauma in infancy.

With tragic insight, Brady wrote of 'strange chords in the human heart, which will lie dormant through years of depravity and wickedness, but which will vibrate at last to some slight circumstance apparently trivial in itself, but connected by some undefined and indistinct association, *with past days that can never be recalled, and with bitter recollections from which the most degraded creature in existence cannot escape* [italics mine].'[1014]

Such admissions were rationed: Brady typically took refuge behind provocative intellectualisation, ensuring his isolation – he could not tolerate love – by describing himself at a tribunal as a 'comparatively petty criminal' and his murders as 'recreational', attributing them to his desire for 'existential experience'.[1015]

The resonance of existentialism[1016] for Brady was revealing.

Founded by 19th-century Danish philosopher Søren Kierkegaard, existentialism, the patriarchal philosophy founded on the idea that the only meaning of the universe is that which is attributed to it, failed to resonate with the public until the early 20th century, when the first generations of babies born to anaesthetised mothers had come of age. Jean-Paul Sartre, the founder of French existentialism, encapsulated the philosophy in his novel *Nausea*: 'Every existing thing is born without reason, prolongs itself out of weakness and dies by chance.'[1017]

French existentialist and Nobel laureate Albert Camus' 1942 novel *L'Étranger* (*The Stranger*), a core existentialist text widely recognised as a masterpiece, could have been a fictionalised version of Brady's life. It begins with the words, *'Aujourd'hui, maman est morte. Ou peut-être hier, je ne sais pas.'* (Today Mother died. Or it may have been yesterday, I don't know.')[1018] Here, the protagonist Meursault's emotional paucity is laid bare; he is so 'cool', so fundamentally detached, that he appears indifferent to the death of his own mother.

Like Brady's, Meursault's indifference is, however, superficial; there are 40 instances of the word 'mother' – and many further references – in the spartan novel, which both begins and finishes within the context of her death. Meursault finds certain memories of the funeral, which takes place on a 'blazing hot afternoon', impossible to dislodge – in particular, that of the man whose eyes were 'streaming with tears, of exhaustion or distress, or both together. But... they couldn't flow down.' Seemingly without motive, Meursault later murders a man identified only as 'the Arab'. As Meursault explains, 'The heat was beginning to scorch my cheeks; beads of sweat were gathering in my eyebrows. It was just the same sort of heat as at my mother's funeral.'[1019]

On a day 'so stiflingly hot' that 'big flies were buzzing round and settling on my cheeks', Meursault is interviewed about the murder at the magistrate's office. The hearing, too, is held on a 'stiflingly hot' day. Echoing the newborn Brady's experience, Meursault says of his cell, 'I'd been staring at those walls for months; there was nobody, nothing in the world, I knew better than I knew them.' He imagines his lover's 'sun-gold' face on them. The novel ends with his acceptance of 'the benign indifference of the universe' as he awaits execution.[1020]

Like Brady's psychiatrists, the critics misunderstood everything.

L'Étranger, a book that sold well over 10 million copies in France alone,[1021] has been described as 'gripping and puzzling', as a 'colonial allegory, an existential prayer book, an indictment of conventional morality.'[1022] The novel was none of these things. Its continuing resonance is based on its allegorical value as the story of a man who, maddened by his emotional disablement, no longer wishes to live.

It's only fitting that Camus, a classic patriarchal male (football, promiscuity,[1023] and so on), wrote the most elegant 20th-century literary indictment of patriarchal masculinity.

The central symbol in *L'Étranger* is the sun, which symbolises the emotion that Meursault *cannot access*. The old man whose tears 'couldn't flow down' cannot be forgotten by Meursault because he represents his own inability to grieve. In place of experiencing strong emotion, Meursault externalises it – the stronger and more destabilising his suppressed emotion, the stronger and more destabilising the heat and light. The popularity of this metaphor among patriarchal writers could be due to the newborn's forced ejection from the warm maternal universe to the cooler – even cold – terrestrial atmosphere.

Almost half a century later, Martin Amis, in the bestselling novel *London Fields*, employed the same symbolic framework. Guy, Nicola Six's married suitor, 'steered his stare into the sun of her face'; earlier, he wonders if he can find a specialist who can 'surgically remove' the memory of her face ('this image, like the sun's imprint, but never fading'). The sun, he then realises, 'does many things but it's far too busy to flatter the human being with its light.' Throughout Amis's patriarchal allegory, the sun is aligned with both love and death; this was clearly Amis's experience of his mother – and her absence – in his infancy. When Guy goes outside with his child, 'the sun was right there at the end of the street like a nuclear detonation.'[1024]

Russian novelist Leo Tolstoy, in *Anna Karenina*, also aligns the sun with true love. On seeing his beloved Kitty, the character Levin 'stepped down, avoiding any long look at her as one avoids long looks at the sun, but seeing her as one sees the sun, without looking.'[1025] Another of Amis's influences, Russian-American novelist Vladimir Nabokov, describes, in the first person, his character Lolita, of the eponymous novel, as the 'light' of his life, and also of his 'dissolv[ing] in the sun' – that is, dissolving in love – in her presence.[1026]

Logically, then, Brady's 'black light' – that of an eclipsed or black sun – was a visual symbol of the understanding that to an infant, maternal absence, or the presence of the malevolent maternal, results in death.

The 'Black Sun', which, since the 1950s, has been a 'central motif of esoteric neo-Nazism'[1027] – and of patriarchal Satanism, whose devotees associate it with a 'Dark God'[1028] – is the anti-sun: if the Sun is life-giving, then the Black Sun is life-negating, a black hole, the annihilation of self. (Predictably, Marilyn Manson engaged with

Satanism,[1029] as did Susan Atkins and Dahmer.)[1030,1031]

Adults deprived of sufficiently sustained maternal intimacy in infancy are at once fatally compelled and threatened by love. To the deprived newborn, love and yearning for the mother becomes synonymous with the terror of extinction contained in her absence or malevolence. As Amis wrote, 'the sun was now taking life away, the life-taker, the carcinogenic sun.' And even Nicola Six describes herself as '[a] black hole. Nothing can escape from me.'[1032]

Camus' spin was a little different. To him, death was the preferable *option* to love. In *L'Étranger*, when Meursault's detached mother ('for years she's never had a word to say to me') is being buried, the undertaker's man says, 'The sun's pretty bad today, ain't it?', and in the lead-up to the murder, Meursault, each time he feels a 'hot blast' of sunlight, 'grit[s] his teeth' and 'clenche[s] his fists, marshalling 'every nerve to fend off the sun and the dark befuddlement it was pouring into me.' In the end, he chooses death over the acknowledgment of status-threatening emotional vulnerability that crying would involve: '[M]y jaws set hard. I wasn't going to be beaten.'[1033]

To the patriarchal male 'unseen' by his mother, death is always more attractive than the 'dark befuddlement' of emotion. As Meursault's prosecutor says, 'We cannot blame a man for lacking what it was never in his power to acquire.'[1034]

The same could be said in defence of Brady, Bundy, Leary, and those like them.

Sweat, in *L'Étranger*, symbolises *the stress of feeling that cannot, and must not, be declared*, the intense labour involved in remaining emotionally 'cool', which is also why it has become cinematographic code for all patriarchal masculinity in film – Marlon Brando sweating through his t-shirt in *A Streetcar Named Desire*, Bruce Lee heavily sweating in *Enter the Dragon*, Sylvester Stallone glittering with sweat in *Rambo*, and so on. Other than in the patriarchal contexts of fitness and pornography, the onscreen feminine is defined by an *absence* of sweat.

Sweat, a nondeclarative language, is now considered as indecorous as the feeling it represents.

'The Arab' needs no name as he represents the emotional shadow-self Meursault must murder; Meursault's feelings about his mother and her death are beginning to break through, to destabilise his patriarchal impassivity, and must thus be extinguished. Names, too, are declarative, whereas 'the Arab' symbolises the nondeclarative, the primitive, the mammalian, the emotional. Meursault, even after the Arab is dead, fires 'four shots more into the inert body',[1035] an act of emphasis: to the patriarchal, *all evidence of the 'dark' animal self must be eradicated.*

Describing Meursault as 'the only Christ we deserve',[1036] Camus was only superficially controversial; in choosing death at the hands of men over his feeling (mammalian) self and rejecting (mammalian) attachment to the feminine, Meursault *is* a Christ-like figure. Christ, too, chose death at the hands of men over his mammalian self, rejecting attachment to the feminine – his mother, and Mary Magdalene – in favour of his incorporeal father.

However movingly contextualised – Christ dying for our sins and so on – biblical lore recommends extinction, to the masculine, as preferable to being vulnerable to the feminine.

In *L'Étranger*, there is only one mention of Meursault's father, whom Meursault experiences only *declaratively*: 'I never set eyes on him. Perhaps the only things I really knew about him were what Mother had told me.' This was also Christ's experience of his father (God), and that of Brady, Bundy, and of Leary after the age of 13. It's only when the chaplain who visits Meursault before his execution addresses him as 'my son' that Meursault is no longer able to contain his anguish: 'I don't know how it was, but *something seemed to break inside me,* and I started yelling at the top of my voice [italics mine].'[1037]

The chaplain's assertion of *territoriality* ('my son') *releases Meursault to feel.* Through this assertion, Meursault is able to drop the charade of indifference and, 'in a sort of ecstasy of joy and rage,' 'hurl insults', coming to the recognition that '[n]othing, nothing had the least importance'. The 'benign indifference' with which his mother, once his 'universe', addressed him can no longer be borne, and Meursault – unseen, unknown, unloved – walks into death.[1038]

As I wrote, the price of maternal indifference has, for the infant, always been steep.

Those who feel unseen and unclaimed at birth and in early infancy are 'dead' to themselves. The mother is the gateway into self-acceptance; through her passion, she validates her baby's existence, investing it with significance. Only those who have not experienced maternal validation at birth question their meaning; those whose mothers exerted tender territoriality over them instinctively understand their existence as precious, as part of the evolutionary continuum. Through love, they are contextualised.

Like the adult who endured respiratory distress at birth and feels compelled to 'reenact' his breathlessness, the unseen and unclaimed 'reenact' their invalidation by, and 'invisibility' to, their mothers, obliterating the self literally or symbolically. Meursault chose literal death; Brady chose to 'die' to the world; and Leary and his Psychedelic Revolutionaries obliterated their true selves with substances.

Mothers are the architects of emotional identity.

The critical deprivation of maternal passion at birth and in early infancy manifests in adulthood as the courting of death through dangerous activities and habits reframed, so as not to upset others, as 'fun'; as risk (through criminality, military service, police work, security work, and so on); and as suicide attempts or completed suicide.

Mother/baby deprivation: the genesis of the 'strong, silent' type linked to suicide.[1039]

British Formula One champion James Hunt, in a conversation with another driver, made his conscious courtship of annihilation clear: 'Racing drivers never talk among themselves about death, but … *chances were pretty high that we'd both get killed* [italics mine].' Predictably, the patriarchal Hunt was also a binge-drinker, a heavy cannabis and tobacco smoker, a regular drug abuser, depressive, promiscuous (when married, 'his desire for other women was insatiable and uncontrollable'), an inveterate risk-taker, and known for recoiling from emotional and physical intimacy.[1040]

In tandem with his dislike of being touched, Hunt's 'coldness' and substance abuse strongly suggest a deeply traumatic, drug-disordered birth. An international sporting hero, he died of a cardiac arrest at the age of 45.

Just as overeating, substance-use disorders and risk-taking are maladaptive efforts to avoid, control, or regulate intense emotional pain,[1041] *so are violence and murder*. Culturally, the only reason we tolerate the former is because they are self-inflicted, rather than an encroachment on another's property like the latter, but the motivation is the same. For the neurodevelopmentally abused, art and violence can feel like the only means available of expressing rage at early injustices that no one ever stopped or, in later life, attempted to understand.

During the Second World War, the *SS-Totenkopfverbände* was the ultimate agency of terror. While masculine status, in a patriarchal culture, is always enhanced by the indirect pursuit of death, the *SS-Totenkopfverbände*, the Nazi paramilitary *Schutzstaffel* branch responsible for orchestrating the 'Final Solution' (Jewish genocide), aligned the *direct* pursuit of death with alpha masculinity. The skull and crossbones (*Totenkopf*) badges that identified them were not symbolic warning shots but a mandate: the mid-20th-century German masculine, brutalised at birth and throughout infancy, embodied the very principle of annihilation.

Like Brady and Bundy, the *SS-Totenkopfverbände* was not indiscriminate in its choice of victims. The right to exist was determined by the most ancient of patriarchal prejudices. They humiliated, terrorised, tortured and murdered only those they

French World War Two anti-Semitic poster dehumanising Jews as vermin and as a 'scourge' to humanity greater than cancer, syphilis and tuberculosis.

considered *Untermenschen* ('subhumans'). Animal imagery, as various academics have observed, played an integral role in this classification. Jews were referred to as bacteria, leeches, lice, rats – as sources of contagion requiring extermination. The same class-based dehumanisation was normalised in late 20th-century Australia when I was growing up, with Southern and Mittel-Europeans, Jews and so on being scorned as 'wogs' (germs) and accused of 'preciousness' if they objected.

Like the Africans persecuted in the patriarchal American South, the Jews and Mittel-Europeans share a tradition of intensely emotional familial closeness. Throughout the 20th century, the fastidious, traditionally nurturing behaviours of Italian and Jewish mothers in particular were a comic staple throughout the First World – affectionate, focused, protective motherhood was derided, pathologised and trivialised: denunciation in the guise of a joke. Thus weaponised, this humour was also a means of lessening the threatening feminine sovereignty over the masculine. Just as it had with Brady's victims, motherlove has always guaranteed persecution by the deprived, envious patriarchal.

World War Two was a war on the feminine.

Predictably, the history of modern German birth and

A 'humorously' dehumanising Australian certificate created for Italian men to accept their status as vermin. This is not an historical document, but was disseminated in 2017.

contraception practices is notable for its harshness. The average birth was addressed as a species of evacuation, and often took place in the toilet. Newborns were considered to be soulless until the age of six weeks, meaning they could be legally murdered – 'smashing their heads' was not uncommon. Mothers who killed their newborns were notably 'full of indifference, coldness and callousness [and gave] the impression of a general impoverishment of feeling'. In the late 19th century, German infant mortality ranged from 21 percent in Prussia to *58 percent* in Bavaria. Breastfeeding was unpopular for centuries, and tight swaddling for up to nine months was commonplace.[1042]

In 1864, British journalist Henry Mayhew reported that in Germany, 'babies are loathsome, foetid things – rank with the sour black pap or goat's milk upon which they have been fed, and offensive to the last degree with the excreta that are kept bound up within their swaddling clothes for *twelve hours* at a time. Then the heads of the poor things are never washed, and are like the rind of Stilton cheese.' Mayhew never witnessed one of these babies laughing.[1043]

Not unlike Brady, then, who once felt like 'the most degraded creature in existence'.

Johanna Haarer, Nazi Germany's most popular childcare author and a physician – her book, *The German Mother and Her First Child*, sold over 1.2 million copies – advised mothers to isolate their babies for 24 hours after birth. The theme of separation – of detachment – dominated her work. 'The child is to be fed, bathed, and dried off; apart from that left completely alone,' she wrote. 'It is best if the child is in his own room, where he can be left alone.' If an infant cried, she advised, 'Whatever you do, do not pick the child up from his bed, carry him around, cradle him, stroke him, hold him on your lap, or even nurse him').[1044]

The relationship between the dehumanisation of babies and the desire for death, whether symbolic or actual, is causal. When a mother fails, through drug- or trauma-induced incapacity, to 'ignite' her newborn, darkness will characterise his life: she is, in effect, his Black Sun, her love eclipsed. When dehumanisation at birth is culturally imposed, the culture will, in itself, begin to implode – by destroying the very planet that sustains it, say.

At the beginning of the Weimar Republic (1918–1933), abortion, which was illegal, had, for many women, become the primary method of birth control.[1045] While access to safe, legal terminations is essential for reasons I will address in a later book, abortion – a procedure which, in 2014, concluded one in five American pregnancies[1046] – is far from the anodyne experience certain feminist factions promote it as being. Recent studies on its repercussions fail to focus on the resulting subtle psychological distortions for women. Other than the obvious risks involved in illegal abortions, the cultural repercussions of Weimar Germany's abortion rates were to prove significant.

By giving birth in toilets and 'smashing' the heads of unwanted newborns, German mothers of the 19th and 20th century were also proving that they were fit to live in a patriarchal culture. It could be argued that economically secure 21st-century women in steady relationships who elect to have abortions on the basis of career are doing the same. And why wouldn't they, in a culture in which femininity is synonymous with the bestial, the infantile, and the expendable? Why would they jeopardise the income that ensures their safety and status and that of those they love?

At 28, Brady's mother would have been aware of the dangers of leaving a fragile baby alone for hours. She could have called on a local church or charity that helped vulnerable families, but she did nothing. However ostensibly dutiful she may have been, it's clear that whether on a declarative or nondeclarative level, she had hoped that her baby would die; Brady's existence, after all, secured her impoverishment and lifelong shame.

Like the exposure of unwanted babies in Ancient Greece and the indifferent starvation of German newborns in the late 19th century, neglect is also a passive form of birth control. This phenomenon is not exclusive to the era. In 2021, 19-year-old British mother Verphy Kudi was arrested after leaving her 20-month-old daughter to starve to death; Kudi had abandoned her baby in order to party for six days in three other cities. The child, who was left with no food or water, is, in a photograph, shown with large frightened eyes and baring her bottom teeth as her mother, an aspiring model, incongruously smiles.[1047] Like Brady's mother, Kudi clearly wanted her unwanted baby to die.

When, as a man, Brady wrote of the 'callous power and indifference'[1048] of the moors, he was, in reality, referring to his mother. To Brady and the Nazis, the urge to exterminate the vulnerable was a matrilineal legacy.

18. UNSEEN

'I am nothing but a scream in the night
to which no one responds.'

The Enduring Kiss, Massimo Recalcati

In the 1963 US Navy 'Maternity Care' film, one of the two women who have just given birth is struggling to smile through the pall of anaesthesia. Her eyes momentarily cross, each closing at different times, and her tongue lolls and then folds over, thickened, in her mouth before she is able to control it. The effect is of a woman so drunk that she can barely speak.

It is in this condition that the mother is introduced to her drugged newborn by a nurse, who lowers the baby, facing the ceiling, to her shoulder. The infant's movements are asynchronous to her mother's because babies are regulated only by sustained skin-to-skin contact with the mother. Biting her lip, the mother tentatively extends the back of a hand to touch her child, but quickly pulls it back. There is no sense of territoriality; the infant has been washed of all maternal odour signatures. It is at this point that the nurse pulls the baby away to take her to the nursery.

The extent of this newborn's exposure to her mother at birth is 20 or so seconds.

This was the first experience of billions of First World babies of their mothers for decades; at worst, the mothers – or their babies – experienced respiratory distress, were stupefied, unconscious, or in a delirium. The babies of such women can resort to compensatory narcissism in adulthood to survive the foundational agony of this primal separation. As Narcissus, the mythological hunter of Greek mythology, lamented of his unattainable reflection – that is, the unattainable mother at birth – 'I am enchanted and I see, but I cannot reach what I see and what enchants me... and it increases my pain the more, that no wide sea separates us, no road, no mountains, no walls with locked doors.'[1049]

Instead of coming into being through gazing into his mother's face, instead of being informed of his meaning through the act of being *seen* by her, instead of being welcomed – at a pace respectful of his fragility – to the ex-uterine universe by the face and breasts and arms of his uterine universe, the newborn has, for almost two centuries, been poked and pulled and slapped and scrubbed and swaddled by masked strangers, isolated in a plastic crib where he would lie, drugged and dysregulated by the cries of unseen infants, smelling disinfectant and starch, and left for hours or days to stare, like Ian Brady, at the walls and ceiling instead of communicating, with all his senses, with his mother.

This is why landscapes of disquieting alienation and sometimes terror, in the form of late 19th, 20th, and 21st-century science fiction narratives, swept the world.

British rock star David Bowie's 1969 song 'Space Oddity', released one month before Sharon Tate was stabbed to death by Susan Atkins, reached number one on the British charts because the alienation and nostalgia it depicted was, at the time, an almost universal experience at birth – alienation and the overwhelming desire to return 'inside', expressed in language showing his deference to an infinitely greater power.[1050]

With similar impact, in the 'baffling' ending[1051,1052] of the Academy Award-winning landmark work of sci-fi existentialism[1053] *2001: A Space Odyssey* (1968), the protagonist, astronaut David Bowman, is shown as an old man in bed, isolated in a spacious room, and at the foot of his bed, a forbidding entity: a featureless, tall, black, rectangular monolith.

As Bowman slowly reaches out to it – with the same gesture depicted in 16th-century Italian artist Michelangelo's biblical fresco of Adam touching God with a finger[1054] – he suddenly transforms into a foetus within a luminous orb. American director Stanley Kubrick explained that Bowman was 'taken in by god-like entities... They put him in what I suppose you could describe as a human zoo to study him, and his whole life passes from that point on in that room. And he has no sense of time.'[1055]

Infancy is characterised by the unawareness of time, and the 'human zoo' was a nursery.

In the novel on which the film was based, the monoliths are luminescent, transparent crystal blocks or tablets,[1056] but this had no resonance for Kubrick, so he changed the monoliths to conform to his own nondeclarative memories and therein, the scene's unforgettably dreamlike power.

The scene,[1057] then, is a witness statement. Appropriately, the walls and sheets in the scene are 'misty' green – as Canadian curator of physical sciences and medicine David Pantalony wrote: 'Green used to be the colour of medicine... a major symbol of the modern hospital, advocated by hospital administrators and architects, and would remain a staple of the medical experience well into the 1970s.'[1058] The very particular shade of 'misty' green featured in *2001: A Space Odyssey* was, in fact, the standardised American hospital hue, which also applied to hospital bedlinen and equipment.

Tiled with luminous white squares, the scene's set suggests the flooring and the calming, similarly misty, recessed lighting of a hospital. Bowman – bald, wizened, and supine in a loose white nightshirt – could be a newborn in a crib; the size of the room reflects the same grandeur perceived by a tiny infant in his high-ceilinged early 20th-century hospital surroundings. But it is the scene's divergence from Michelangelo's fresco that makes it iconic: where the biblical fresco symbolises what could be described as an antiquated reciprocity – life-giving *contact* between Adam and God – Kubrick's isolated astronaut attempts to connect with an inscrutable, unrelated, unresponsive black entity.

This one-way attempt to love has been the experience of most, if not almost all, babies at birth for almost two centuries, which is why the film resonated – and continues to resonate – with millions.

In 1928, Kubrick was born in Manhattan's Second Avenue Lying-In Hospital, the same maternity hospital[1059] – now a block of luxury apartments – where his father had studied obstetrics.[1060] Considered high even for the era, the ceilings there were 17.5 feet.[1061] The 1902 hospital was built in the Renaissance Revival style[1062] and featured recessed lighting, and curved junctions in the ceilings, walls, and upper corners of doors and windows.[1063] While the décor in the suites was aseptic modernist, the building's theme was classical.

In the closing scene of *2001: A Space Odyssey*, the high-ceilinged room in which Bowman lies is decorated in the Renaissance Revival style, ornamented with Renaissance paintings,[1064] and features recessed lighting and curved junctions in the ceilings, door frames and walls. The black entity at the foot of the bed is not, as has been posited, a 'monolith without an explanation',[1065] but a 'snapshot'

Left: Second Avenue Lying-In Hospital window around the time Kubrick was born. *Right:* Closing scene from *2001: A Space Odyssey*. The 'monolith' is his newborn memory of the Lying-In Hospital window blind.

infant memory of one of the hospital's long rectangular windows, which, around the time Kubrick was born, were shaded with long, dark blinds.[1066]

In all respects, including that of dimension in relation to a newborn, *2001: A Space Odyssey*'s 'monoliths', then, are no more than a little baby's visual 'imprint' of his environment contextualised by his feelings at the time. Even the monolith's strong contrast to its surroundings – a kind of framing – was only a memory of sunlight escaping the blind's edges.

Other scenes from the film can be traced back to the Lying-In Hospital. Machines that gauge, among other things, cardiovascular and metabolic function, and the contrast between small, primitive hominids (babies and toddlers) and human adults in protective attire (medical staff) – in particular, the smiling stewardess in white with white bulbous headwear and white outfit (a nurse in a bulbous 1920s white scrub cap and white outfit). The nurse at Kubrick's birth may also have worn a nursing pin on her gown, a detail depicted in the film as an airline emblem.

Left: Obstetrics nurse, 1920s. *Right:* Stewardess from *2001: A Space Odyssey.*

In the film, astronauts sleep in crib-like pods proximal to machines. The 'red eye' of the sinister computer HAL was the industrial steel lamp hanging over the obstetric table: a threatening eye, seen from below through maternal blood and 'controlled' by a male voice (the obstetrician's).

The widening gyre, the film's dominant motif, is the birth channel (for example, the tense scene in which Bowman is filmed – helpless, flailing – in the air lock bathed in red light before being ejected into an alien atmosphere). There is also this: in the film, the masculine is looked *at*, whereas the feminine *is* the environment. The angle at which Bowman is filmed for much of the film – slightly from below – is the same angle at which an obstetrician would first be seen by a newborn; my guess is that like Bowman, the obstetrician at Kubrick's birth had pale eyes.

The blinds, windows, and so on of the Lying-In Hospital could not have been seen by Kubrick during a later visit as its last patient was discharged in 1932, the year the building was vacated and its staff absorbed by New York Hospital.[1067] Kubrick would have been

Left: Birthing room with classic rubber 'Kelly pad' and overhead industrial lamps in the Lying-In Hospital. *Right:* The 'eye' of the computer HAL in 2001 – in reality, Kubrick's memory of one of the overhead industrial lamps seen from below at birth.

three, perhaps four, at the time. Similarly, post-birth visits to the hospital would not have exposed him to the industrial lamps in the obstetric theatre, particularly from the vantage point of a freshly delivered infant.

What this shows is that the emotional/visual recall of human newborns is close to perfect.

To Kubrick, the drawn black blind also functioned as a symbol of everything he was, by 20th-century obstetric practice, denied – mainly, the opportunity to bask in the sunlight Amis, Camus and others instinctively understood as love. *Kubrick's monoliths are versions of the black or eclipsed sun.* Of Mother, gone. They are forbidding because without Mother, there is, for the newborn, only the threat of blackness (hunger, unconsciousness, death), as the newly-born Ian Brady understood.

On the stone spandrels of the Lying-In Hospital's façade and

Left: Room in the Lying-In Hospital. *Right:* The airlock from *2001: A Space Odyssey.*

portico, there remain unusual bas-relief sculptures of infants suspended in orbs.[1068] While it's thought that newborn sight is limited to 10 or so inches from the face, it's obvious that Kubrick registered, if imperfectly, one of the orbs as he was carried out; he would have been in a carrycot at the time, looking up at the portico and façade. Sunlight had clearly struck the orb, which is why in the film, the orb is luminous. As Kubrick was born in midsummer, this is likely.

The ending of *2001: A Space Odyssey* reveals two truths that have the potential to revolutionise both our understanding of infancy and the way in which babies are treated. Current belief dictates that newborns have no conception of objects as separate from themselves, and that they have no *expectations of continuity.* In fact, having emerged from a warm, breathing, sentient universe, the newborn – only logically – *expects his new environment to be conscious,* which is why the infant Kubrick attempted to communicate with a black window blind. (Separated from his mother, why *wouldn't* a newborn try to interact with the nearest humanoid object?)

Kubrick's use, in relation to the monolith, of the same gestures

Left: One of the unusual 'orbs' from the Lying-In Hospital façade.
Right: The 'orb' from *2001: A Space Odyssey*.

associated by Michelangelo with life – in the fresco, 'birth' is effectively defined as the twinned acts of being 'seen' and touched by God – also indicates that to all babies, *God is a woman*.

In an Abrahamic culture, however, God may only be depicted as a man for fear of reprisals in the form of marginalisation, ridicule or violence.

Bowman's expectation – in the form of his lifted hand – that the monolith/window blind will respond to him is also significant because it reveals that an infant *needs* his first environment to be conscious. As if seeking to resume a telephone call that has dropped out, the newborn seeks to reestablish the connection that was severed with his umbilical cord: the biochemical 'conversation' with his maternal environment *must continue in order to sustain his narrative of self and belonging.* Any divergence from this evolutionary mandate is catastrophic.

The trauma of the newborn's expulsion from his maternal environment is inestimable, and yet remains unaddressed.

Helplessness, shock, and the disorientating lack of any reference point, compounded by derangement resulting from powerful obstetric drugs and separation from the only universe the newborn has ever known, make the sensitivity of his mother's immediate post-birth response pivotal. The 'lying-in'[1069] period – those 40 days in which the mother and baby bond in peace – is critical, allowing for tender, restorative preoccupation from the maternal 'god' from whose Eden-like garden the newborn was expelled ('garden' being, as I have pointed out, slang for the vulva), and for the mother's adjustment on all levels, including that of her emotional transformation into a mother.

2001: A Space Odyssey is a narrative of the isolation and trauma – and resulting lifelong sense of alienation – that 'unseen' newborns have, *en masse* and for over a century, endured.

Birth is the first 'seeing', the first slow, deep, mutual, ex-uterine exchange of information.

The newborn's preference for a mutual, rather than unilateral, gaze[1070] shows that *babies are designed for reciprocity*. Adults rarely gaze at each other for more than 10 seconds without being spurred into action – fighting or having sex – but mothers and babies can lock into a gaze for over 30 seconds.[1071] The newborn's unique sensitivity to this communication indicates that the principle of reciprocity is of a critical foundational importance to humanity. Given that babies whose mothers gaze at them show enhanced neural processing,[1072] giving them inestimable advantages in adulthood, babies who are separated from their mothers, ignored, or, like Brady, isolated for long periods after birth, are at a fatal developmental disadvantage.

Francis Bacon, the gay Anglo-Irish figurative painter known for his agonised biomorphs and passion for violent sex, was born to a privileged family in a 'lying-in' hospital favoured by the wealthy. His young mother, too 'distracted by hunting and the social whirl' to raise her sons, clearly suffered attachment ruptures at their birth. Raised by a nanny, the asthmatic Bacon later recalled his childhood as 'something very heavy, very cold, like a block of ice'.[1073]

These are the words of a man who, as an infant, was left alone for long periods, possibly under a weighty blanket, in a cold room.

Bacon's most revealing work in this respect was 'Second Version of Painting 1946' (1971), in which a discrete male figure with a distorted face sits between the thighs of an amputated, decapitated, genderless carcass, his umbrella opened beneath its ribs. The suit, boots and open umbrella symbolise Bacon's individuation *from birth* from his mother. Her absent head and his obscured face represent his being 'unrecognised' and 'unseen' by her at birth, possibly as a result of her drugged stupefaction or unconsciousness. The crucifixion-like posture reveals Bacon's nondeclarative understanding of his mother as a victim of the Abrahamic ideology, and her amputated legs represent what Bacon perceived as her lack of agency at birth.

Arguably the most disturbing aspect of this painting is the contrast between the sexes. The 'feminine' is depicted as bestial, butchered, helpless, a carcass, whereas the masculine is impervious, obscured (by cultural and gender identity in the guise of clothing), protected (umbrellas represent safety, which is why they are used in insurance advertising campaigns) and fundamentally self-contained.

This and a number of Bacon's other works – in particular, 'Crucifixion' (1965) and the middle panel of 'Three Studies for a Crucifixion' (1962) – are nondeclarative memories of his traumatic birth, and his screaming biomorphs – male genitals – are statements of uniquely masculine suffering. Predictably, the latter were dismissed by patriarchal critics as 'funny' and 'goofy'.[1074]

A mother's passionate 'seeing' of her infant at birth, then, is not only altering but instructional: she is teaching him about the congruence of feeling and facial expression. Those 'seen' at birth and during infancy become emotionally transparent – their emotions are visible in their eyes and faces. Unclouded by early trauma, the adults these babies become are also direct in the expression of their needs. As their mothers recognised their expressed needs and met them, they are able to show their needs without fear. When a baby's expressed needs are, for whatever reason, repeatedly unmet, the baby learns to associate the expression of need with the pain of it being unmet. To avoid suffering, he learns to hide the unmet needs from his own consciousness: Brady's empty face, masking a pandemonium of pain, rage and terror, say.

Dahmer, too, had an impassive, almost casual, delivery when discussing his murders.[1075]

A mother's charged 'seeing' of her baby at birth and during infancy is not merely pleasing in its impact; it literally alters him on a quantum level. *Maternal attention sculpts the infant.* Understood as 'a meaningless side effect of brain mechanisms',[1076] this directed consciousness – the act of seeing – physically changes matter,[1077] as I wrote in relation to the exo-womb. Medical insistence on 'rest' for a mother in the wake of birth thus intercepts this crucial expansion on the deepest level of being *for both mother and infant.*

In being seen, we become aware that we exist.

I remember this dynamic with an intimate partner at whom I would find myself involuntarily staring. The phenomenon was mutual; we would sit gazing at each other, inexplicably enraptured, until others, discomfited, felt compelled to alert us to the existence of the world. Having never before experienced the consuming hunger to stare into another's eyes – to *flow* into another – we were bewildered; on being 'awoken' from one of these trances by a friend, my partner turned, shocking him with the words, 'Time to cut my wrists.'

Having endured sustained birth trauma and multiple fraught long-term separations from his narcissistic mother in infancy, he was characterised by violently disorganised attachment patterns he justified, like Leary and the Psychedelic Revolutionaries, with various philosophies. As with Meursault, death seemed preferable – or easier – to him than love.

To an extent, I was the same.

German musician Nico, with American band the Velvet Underground, also sang of being a mirror, reflecting the reality of the beloved to show that they are 'home'.[1078]

Facial decoding – the understanding that the face reflects internal states or thoughts – is imperative to both human development[1079] and the evolution of empathy, strongly suggesting that narcissists and psychopaths were deprived of this form of sustained maternal contact during early infancy. Bottle-feeding, too, makes it easier to ignore the infant, as there is no direct biochemical reciprocity involved, whereas breastfeeding *demands* attention; it's impossible to ignore being suckled, and the baby will, through proprietary pats on the breast, ensure that this is so.

Because of this, breastfeeding makes mother/baby eye-contact far more likely.[1080] During breastfeeding, a mother looks into her baby's eyes 70 percent of the time,[1081] suggesting that the increase in disorders such as psychopathy[1082] is related to bottle-feeding.

Blind children are at a particular disadvantage in this respect. The conjunction of – or causal relationship between – visual impairment and developmental disorders has long been established. Blindness in itself has been said to entail 'considerable implications for a child's development and learning'.[1083] While blind children can feel and hear and smell and taste, the accelerated neurodevelopment triggered by reciprocal gazing and other forms of visual stimulation cannot take place.

A significant correlation has been found between autism and congenital infant blindness. Some 30 percent of completely blind children are autistic.[1084] Autism is understood as a pervasive developmental disorder ('a primary deficit in the foetus or infant begins a cascade of secondary developmental failures'), but the primary deficit has yet to be identified. If a blind infant's mother relates to him through intense sensual intelligence then his development may be close to normal, but if she doesn't, then he is 'very likely' to develop autism.

In California, there was a 1,148 percent increase in the number of autistic people between 1987 and 2007, a leap that cannot be justified by diagnostic criteria changes, immigration, the inclusion of milder cases, or misclassification,[1085] suggesting that intense mother/baby eye contact is close to extinction. Hospitals facilitate this by equipping private and public maternity suites with televisions, and by encouraging mothers to disengage from their babies by separating them, taking multiple visitors, and so on.

In children institutionalised at birth, there is also an unusually high incidence of autism – in Romanian babies born with normal sight who were neglected in cribs during infancy,[1086] for example. Autism is also prevalent in babies with cranial nerve palsy, which leads to the paralysis of eye muscles. These three different categories of children – the congenitally blind, those with cranial nerve palsy, and those institutionalised at birth, 'share one common deficit: they are all unable to track a caregiver's face.' Given that mother/baby eye-contact begins at birth, it's thought that a deficit in eye-contact may begin at the same time.[1087]

The more intense the eye-contact between a mother and her infant, the more she will pay attention to him, and the more attention she pays him, the greater the permanent baseline increases of oxytocin and vasopressin, the hormones associated with loving pair-bonding. Logically, deficits in oxytocin and vasopressin are created by non-maternal care of, and the use of computers, iPads, smartphones and televisions by, young children. Even the American Academy of Paediatricians Committee on Public Education stipulated that babies under two not view screens. [1088]

Among other causes, then, autism is strongly associated with the absence or deficit of mother/baby eye-contact.[1089] Diagnosed with Asperger's in 2019, I remember my mother's evasiveness when, as a child, I repeatedly sought to meet her gaze. That space in me remains silent. When my daughter was five, I telephoned my mother and, in a measured tone, asked her to please stop pretending that she had ever loved me. *I was there*, I said; *I remember everything.*

'I just didn't feel it,' she replied.

Jeffrey Dahmer, German Peter Kürten, Dennis Nilsen, 'Yorkshire Ripper' Peter Sutcliffe and other serial killers shared one or more traditionally masculine manifestations of autism: a fascination with machinery, incomprehension of attachment, marked social difficulties, monochromatic processing, monotonous delivery, ritualistic behaviours, pronounced pedantry and factual recall, and sexual dysfunction.[1090]

'Unseeing' is not, of course, entirely dependent on obstetric practice – agitated, disordered and unsupported mothers throughout history have psychologically fractured their babies – but obstetric drugs and mother/baby separation disrupts sculptural mutuality *en masse*.

The unilateral focus of being 'unseen' stunts the baby's capacity for love, which is, quite literally, determined by reciprocity. In the absence of being 'seen' at birth and during early infancy, the infant inwardly closes in upon himself, like an anemone. This drama is played out in *2001: A Space Odyssey* when, confronted by the monolith's threatening unresponsiveness, Bowman spontaneously transforms into a foetus. Misinterpreted as a 'rebirth',[1091] it is, in fact, a *regression*: 'rejected' by the monolith, the astronaut reverts to a foetal state. The uterine was the only world in which his sensitivity was – if only by pulse and fluid – justified by the perpetual responsiveness of its warm sensual intelligence.

In this allegory, wisdom: a child met with maternal unresponsiveness cannot evolve.

The mother's face is the sun that bestows life-sustaining light – in the form of love and attention – upon her infant. In effect, this means that patriarchal birth practices – among them, the administration of obstetric drugs and separation of mothers from their babies – have, since the mid-19th century, severely depleted the global supply of love and its byproducts, compassion and happiness.

A direct byproduct of modern obstetric practice, mother/baby detachment has created an increasingly unmanageable epidemic of disorders. Ranked by WHO as the single largest contributor to disability, depression is of particular concern. Over 300 million people – 4.4 percent of the world's population – are estimated to suffer from depression, and the incidence rose by *18.4 percent* between 2005 and 2015.[1092] Among 15- to 44-year-olds, suicide remains one of the three leading causes of death internationally,[1093] and globally, there are now close to 800,000 suicides each year.[1094]

Through birth trauma, mother/baby separation, obstetric drugs, and the use of infant formula, the establishment of the infant's delicate intestinal flora is also disrupted, further reducing his future capacity for joy. The human gut, increasingly known as 'the second brain', houses 95 percent of the body's serotonin,[1095] the mood-stabilising hormone associated with happiness.

Despite this, we continue to celebrate the demotion of motherlove and to implement birth strategies and government policies that make it difficult, if not impossible, for mothers to deeply 'see' and securely establish tender territoriality over their babies in a serene environment. As German writer Daniela Krien wrote of mother/child separation, 'And in this distance the warmth faded.'[1096]

Researchers have, over the past century, observed a 'significant' increase in narcissism, even only between 1982 and 2009.[1097] The widespread absence of sustained exposure to the joyous maternal 'sun' at birth for over a century has resulted in the insatiable need for its substitution; as a result, our world is now one of approving faces, beaming out from billboards, the internet, social media, and television. The very name 'Facebook' – a global community of faces – shows this insatiable need for the mother's approval.

Without access to approving faces, the human spirit falters and, eventually, fades. This is why the character played by American actor Tom Hanks in the 2000 survival drama *Castaway* paints a smiling face ('Wilson') in his bloody handprint on a volleyball; the sole survivor of an aircraft accident, he needs the likeness of a smile to remain sane.

We seek to be *accepted* by the reflexively approving faces of others, and by the responses to images of our own reflexively approving faces. This global explosion of narcissism, a one-way attention feedback loop, is symptomatic of the mass denial of motherlove to babies at birth and during infancy. Without being deeply 'seen' by the sun of our mothers, we remain unfinished, as if part of our psyche were left in shadow.

Being 'seen' is a very different experience to the recognition on which territoriality hinges. Rather than being identified as belonging to others, to be deeply 'seen' is to be *known* and in that, to feel both knowable and worth knowing. This is not an exercise in semantics. The newborn who has been 'seen' will grow into an emotionally accessible adult who will never wonder at his emotional responses, or at his value to others. In that first, deep 'seeing' by his mother, he is contained: being *known*, to him, will always feel safe. Emotional vulnerability will never be experienced by him as a threat – the very opposite: intimacy will be his goal, not something to be feared.

This is the same ancient 'knowing' that was once synonymous with sexual intimacy, the same deep 'seeing' as the quantum-altering gaze of lovers – that visual synchrony – that triggers the release of oxytocin:[1098] a mutual invitation to the vulnerability that patriarchal birth practices have, for billions of people, associated with abandonment, trauma and the terror of annihilation.

As a result of this mass obstetric disruption of mother/baby attachment, sex is now widely perceived as recreational or as a form of stress relief – fundamentally flippant, limited in its resonance: an interlude or reflex of sorts. The understanding of sex as the most profound stillness and communion is no longer commonplace. Attached sexual expression is now seen as 'an evolutionary hang-up',[1099] an impediment to individual 'freedom'.

Pornography, in this respect, is yet another barrier to evolution. Viewers have the same relationship with pornography as Bowman has with the monolith: unilateral, devoid of the evolutionary properties of mutual observation – in terms of the quantum, a dead end.

When used by couples, pornography stops them from *changing* each other. The locus of their arousal is not each other, but the pornography. There is no sustained investment of consciousness in each other, only carnal choreography. The unparalleled creative power of the sexual act is reduced to kinetic mimicry. An eroticised version of the pacifier, pornography is a means of isolating and silencing its emotionally hungry viewers, of training them to associate pornography with relief from the very isolation it reinforces.

Pornography leaves users only with a nondeclarative sense of frustration and futility on the basis of its reinforcement of disconnection. Like the mother separated from her baby at birth – whether through the administration of drugs, emotional dysfunction or physical isolation – the pornographic object of desire is, by definition, *inaccessible*, literally (on a screen) or emotionally (prostitution). The use of pornography thus reinforces the user's sense *of being unloved and unseen, as most people now feel unloved and unseen*.

Through pornography, sex is thus less threatening to those who were 'unseen' at birth.

The first 'seeing' is a vaccine against a fear of intimacy. It is mutual by definition as the mother, too, is deeply seen – in some cases, for the first time. The newborn's gaze, artless in its profundity, is not just receptivity but intimacy in its purest form. As American psychiatry professor Stephen W. Porges observed, the 'face-heart connection' is fundamental to human happiness, which is why 'the neural regulation of the striated muscles of our face and head are neurophysiologically linked to the neural regulation of our heart.'[1100]

Throughout the 20th century, the administration of Twilight Sleep – and, later, general anaesthesia and powerful obstetric anaesthetics – made this mutual initiation impossible, creating generations of people who felt indecipherable and in that, alienated even from themselves. Twilight Sleep not only obstructed the deep 'seeing' essential to self-acceptance, but replaced it with terror – in particular, the blinding of the mother with bandages or towels, which also rendered her faceless to her baby and in that, effectively dead.

As the intersection of the internal and external worlds, the face, when obscured, is, even on a nondeclarative level, understood as symbolising death. The shroud is a sealing-off of vision and air flow. Belgian surrealist René Magritte, whose mother committed suicide, was known for his depictions of sheeted faces, as was Mapplethorpe; even British writer J.K. Rowling's malevolent Dementors in the Harry Potter books are shrouded. To be faceless is to be generic, without identity, unable to convey meaning: the borders to the inner world are closed. As the widespread resonance of American artist Andy Warhol's soup can portraits shows, this sense of homogenisation had become a global issue.

In Australia, the idiom 'off your face' means to be incapacitated by substances – spectacularly drugged or drunk, semi-conscious or inert. The implication is that in such a state one is, in effect, faceless: unidentifiable. This relationship between identity and substances is important. The fact that drugs temporarily blunt or erase consciousness of the self makes it clear that the intoxicated foetus and newborn no longer has an integrated experience of being.

Even before the baby has breathed oxygen, a life-distorting detachment is imposed.

French cultural theorist Marion Zilio believes that the narcissistic 'narcosis' characteristic of the late 20th and early 21st century originates, in part, from photography and the way it has shifted the face's context from the biological to the technological. This technogenesis – the cross-pollination of the face and technology – is now so commonplace as to be unremarkable. The human face, far from being the calling card of our personality, has come to be more of a work of art or modified technical object, a mask. In the assertion of this fictionalised identity, conclusive obscurity. Zilio posits that far from an enshrinement of the self, Instagram, Snapchat, and similar apps are an index of humanity's erosion.[1101] But the matrix of mass 'defacialisation', in which faces are 'devoured, masked, erased' and ultimately rendered faceless ('exteriority without interiority'),[1102] is, in fact, birth.

As Michael Dransfield wrote in his poem 'Heroin Wednesday':

I'd thought
that eyes were windows, mirrors.
They are holes in a life.[1103]

Inert and insensitive, a hole – the infinitely sensitive, receptive vagina is now known by the same dehumanising colloquialism – has no capacity to enfold or to convey empathy and passion. To an infant, the eyes of a depressed or heavily drugged mother are holes – lightless channels – and, by definition, hollow. Dransfield's poems are characterised by the same emptiness, that sense of anguish and futility experienced by an infant who, in his oceanic fragility, has been confronted only by an eclipsed sun; the same denial of love experienced by Narcissus, by the baby in the 1963 US Navy 'Maternity Care' film, and by the astronaut in *2001: A Space Odyssey*.

Depression is impossible when one is deeply seen.

III

RETURN OF THE QUEEN

'Thus a doctrine of subordination based upon medical evidence was entirely consonant with the central theological tenets of women's inferiority.'

Gender, Sex and Subordination in England, 1500 to 1800, Anthony Fletcher

19. FUCKED UP

'All cruelty springs from weakness.'

Seneca

When Queen Elizabeth II quoted William Wordsworth in relation to childbirth, describing it as 'a sleep and a forgetting', she was placing a darker, more disturbing emphasis on the 18th-century English poet's words: the Queen was not alluding to the dreamlike and ephemeral nature of infancy, but – radically – to the chemical hijacking of the feminine by the masculine.

This association of childbirth with unconsciousness was, and continues to be, understood as modern. In itself, this newness was compelling, making it seem that birth – a primitive process – was, through obstetric intervention and the obstetric administration of anaesthesia, somehow elevated, *made less bestial*, and in that, rendered appropriate for the feminine elite.

Intervention is, by definition, a *distancing* between the feminine and its mammalian origins. If the feminine must capitulate to its animal nature, let it at least be made unaware of its debasement. The vagina and the vulva, through this divorce from their functional reality – that is, from pain, the authorship of birth, and the accompanying amplification of feminine power – would thus be primarily understood as masculine sexual territory.

To justify the mass doping of the feminine at its most vulnerable, the lie must be maintained that the feminine is incapable, both physiologically and psychologically, of metabolising the pain for which it was designed. The understanding was, and remains, that the feminine is so weak that it cannot not even bear the *memory* of pain, and thus must be protected from its very nature – from agency – in order to preserve the illusion of its superiority over the animal. To achieve this, the head – or consciousness – must be severed.

Up until the 1960s, any woman in the First World could,

without a second opinion, be lobotomised on her father's or husband's request. Like American Pulitzer Prize-winning playwright Tennessee Williams's sister Rose, American President John F. Kennedy's 23-year-old sister Rosemary was intellectually and physically disabled by the procedure; his sister, Eunice Shriver, set up the Special Olympics in Rosemary's honour.

At birth, Rosemary Kennedy had, like my late brother, been shoved back up into the vaginal canal by a nurse as the obstetrician was not yet available. The resulting loss of oxygen for the newborn, in some cases, results in neurodevelopmental disaster. As biographer Kate Clifford Larson explained in relation to Kennedy, 'Fees derived from supplying health services to Boston's social and economic elite provided a steady, and hefty, income in the days before medical insurance. If the doctor missed the birth, he could not charge what was an exorbitant fee for prenatal care and delivery.'[1104]

In short, Rosemary Kennedy was ultimately rendered imbecilic and incontinent so a doctor could make USD125.

While my brother was neither imbecilic nor incontinent, he was put at the same risk for the same reason. Like her 21-year-old boyfriend, Sex Pistols bassist Sid Vicious, American 'groupie' Nancy Spungen was a casualty of the same obstetric brutality.

Nancy's mother, Deborah Spungen, fell pregnant as a 20-year-old college student in 1958. The contractions began five weeks before the baby was due. When, in hospital, Spungen told a nurse that she was in pain, she was sedated and 'in a twilight state almost immediately'. She awoke hours later, nauseated and in pronounced pain, whereupon she was again injected and 'went under'. At some point in the very early morning, Spungen was given 'a needle in the spine', and after that, remembered nothing.[1105]

Unconscious throughout the birth, Spungen was awoken by a man 'pounding' on her breast and yelling that she had a daughter. She slipped back into unconsciousness. Later, she was again awoken by her obstetrician, who asked if she intended to nurse as the baby had to be put on a 'schedule'. Spungen, her mouth dry, was so drugged that she barely made sense. Laughing at her incomprehension, the doctor instructed her to go back to sleep.[1106]

Waking at some point during the day, Spungen remained groggy. When she asked to see her baby, the obstetrician replied that Nancy had, like Bethesda, been born cyanotic and jaundiced, and, like Russell Brand, with the umbilical cord around her neck. As a result, he said, Nancy had to be given a heart stimulant. Spungen wondered whether her child was going to die 'and nobody was telling me so as not to upset me. Maybe she wasn't supposed to exist. Maybe she didn't exist. I didn't know. I still hadn't been allowed to see her.'[1107]

Spungen, who had yet to nurse, see or touch her child, was then told that the baby's blood had to be 'changed'. The following day, she was, for the first time, asked for permission in relation to treatment. Spungen was taken to the nursery for the first time. As her tightly swaddled baby was unwrapped, Spungen saw the gauze taped to her tiny heels. A 'lot' of blood tests had been taken, the nurse explained.[1108]

That night, doctors, laughing, told Spungen that her baby had screamed and kicked so much during the transfusion that she had to be 'tied down'. Spungen asked to see Nancy, who, 'yellow' and naked but for a patch over her navel, was enclosed in an isolette, 'screaming hysterically' and 'thrashing about angrily'. She watched, stunned, as Nancy, limbs flailing, 'kicked at the nurse with her tiny feet and screamed. Her minute fists began to beat on her own face.' The doctor assured Spungen that babies don't 'feel any physical pain.'[1109] (This lie was not unique to the 1950s; I was told the same thing by a hospital doctor in 2006 when Bethesda screamed as they struggled – and failed – to spike her for a drip.)

On her return home, Nancy would not stop screaming. Told by a paediatrician that her milk was insufficient – I have spoken to countless mothers who were told the same lie by doctors – Spungen began using formula; when that didn't work, she was instructed to feed her newborn solids. Nancy continued to scream. Spungen, by now as traumatised as her baby, consulted a new paediatrician, who told her that she was 'spoiling' Nancy ('You're conditioning her to believe that all she has to do in order to get food and love is to cry. She does it to get your attention, and you reward her by giving it to her... Ignore her. Let her cry herself out').[1110]

At the age of three months, Nancy was given her first dose of phenobarbital, which, as the prescription stipulated, had to be given to her with an eyedropper every four hours. The screaming didn't stop. Frightened, Spungen again consulted the paediatrician, who increased the phenobarbital dosage, and then again as Nancy's behaviour worsened. Like the drugged mother in the 1963 US Navy film, one of Nancy's eyes began to cross, and she found it difficult to keep her tongue in her mouth. Like Dahmer's, Nancy's legs were not developing properly; splints had to be ordered.[1111]

Phenobarbital was only the first of a long chain of pharmaceuticals Nancy was, in her infancy, prescribed by obstetricians and paediatricians.

When, years later, Spungen saw the multiple heroin track marks on Nancy's body, she remembered the repeated injections she had suffered as a newborn.[1112]

As Michael Dransfield, also forever trapped in the anguish of a traumatic infancy, wrote:

> tomorrow came a mirage packed in hypodermic
> the city we lived in then was not of your making[1113]

When, at the age of 14 and believing she was pregnant, Nancy attempted to perform an abortion on herself with a wire coat hanger, she haemorrhaged and perforated her uterus. 'By the time you get this,' Nancy wrote in a note to a boyfriend, 'we'll be on windowpane acid [gelatine squares of LSD] and fucking our brains out.' Sex, Deborah Spungen said, meant 'nothing' to her daughter, who later became a sex worker. Diagnosed as schizophrenic, Nancy was stabbed to death at the age of 20. Sid Vicious, who had been introduced to heroin by his heroin-addicted mother, was charged with her murder.[1114]

From disparagement to neurodevelopmental insult, the catalogue of abuses to which Deborah and Nancy Spungen were subjected in the name of obstetric care is, in the end, obscene. I will address a single aspect: the phenobarbital Nancy was, throughout her infancy, administered.

Incredibly, phenobarbital continues to be administered to babies in conjunction with dicyclomine for *crying* ('colic').[1115] Dicyclomine, which has been linked to psychosis and respiratory collapse in babies, continues to be administered to pregnant women.[1116]

Still the most 'widely used' anticonvulsant for newborns,[1117] phenobarbital, like other barbiturates, enhances GABA activity.[1118,1119] GABA (gamma-aminobutyric acid, or γ-aminobutyric acid), which is involved in the regulation of anxiety and the growth of both embryonic and the brain's stem cells, is the mature central nervous system's main inhibitory neurotransmitter – that is to say, a chemical messenger principally designed to stop neurons from becoming 'overexcited'. Serotonin serves the same purpose. Benzodiazepines – Librium, Valium, and so on – intensify the impact of GABA neurotransmitters, creating a sense of regulation and serenity.[1120]

Given that observable neurobehavioural characteristics in adulthood are determined in part by GABA-A receptors in early life,[1121] and the impact of GABA-acting drugs during pregnancy – in particular, on the construction of the brain – have been said to lead to 'a cascade of pathogenic consequences',[1122] it's clear that the long-term effects of phenobarbital regularly administered during infancy would be severe. In tandem with heavy obstetric anaesthesia and unknown trauma at birth, 24-hour separation from the mother during the first days of life and the trauma of being tied down, multiple blood tests and procedures without the mother's comfort – that is to say, the *regulation* of love – the consequences would be unmanageable.

Critically, GABA activation – through phenobarbital, say – is thought to suppress dopamine,[1123] the chemical messenger associated with action, appetite and pleasure, which is why researchers link it to substance-use disorders.[1124]

The capacity to increase dopamine levels has been described as 'a defining commonality of addictive drugs'.[1125] As one study found, *all currently used general anaesthetic agents have either NMDA receptor-blocking or GABA-A receptor-enhancing properties*. It's now routine in obstetric or paediatric medicine to combine agents from these two classes to anaesthetise mothers and children,[1126] meaning that dopamine deficiency is now near-universal in the First World.

What this suggests is that 'widely used' obstetric and infant drugs such as phenobarbital dysregulate the infant's dopaminergic (dopamine-activating) system, *permanently reducing his potential for pleasure* and creating an imbalance he later seeks to redress through dopaminergic compulsions – substance-use disorders involving drugs such as cannabis,[1127] heroin,[1128] or LSD, say.[1129] Or sexual addiction. And, while the *nature* of pornography[1130] is determined by the culturally sanctioned birth abuses of mothers and babies, the *impact* of pornography is determined by the *susceptibility* created by drugs given to mothers and children.

As a result of the administration of obstetric drugs, we now have a longstanding and ever-increasing *global shortage of dopamine*.

Symptoms of low dopamine include depression, concentration and motivation issues, and an inability to naturally experience deep joy and pleasure:[1131] in short, a pervasive, life-altering unhappiness and the sense of being uninvested in the moment. This ties into the epidemic of human misery that is currently bankrolling the pharmaceutical houses. Globally, 264 million people of all ages have been diagnosed with depression.[1132] The true number – masked by denial, lack of awareness, physical illness, or substance use – is inestimable. Reflected in rates of drug addiction, our insatiable, compensatory hunger for dopamine has always been preventable, but the role of dopamine in human evolution has, predictably, received 'little theoretical attention'.[1133]

Not unlike the impact of obstetric practice on women and children, then.

In 2019, actor Seth Rogen and rapper Snoop Dogg, American cannabis-smoking 'heavyweights', agreed to an interview[1134] that was, in effect, a comfortingly 'relatable' admission of dopamine deficiency aimed at an audience characterised by dopamine deficiency.

'This motherfucker knows how to make a joint that looks like a cross,' Dogg said of Rogen.

'Yes, it's true,' Rogen agreed.

'Oh, he's a *bad* motherfucker. When he pulled that cross out, I was like: *GOD!*' Dogg joked. 'LET THERE BE LIGHT! [underline mine]'

Dogg, in his use of the Genesis quote, was being playful, but he was also just telling the truth. Emotionally, cannabis 'lets in the light' for heavy users. Like pornography – which, predictably, Dogg[1135] and Rogen[1136] also heavily use – cannabis 'tops up' dopamine levels, creating the illusion of emotional regulation. Far from 'cool', the health-threatening 'aberrant pleasure-seeking behaviour'[1137] that was promoted by Leary and his similarly disabled ideological descendants has always, in reality, been no more than a prosthetic: compensatory, an attempt to balance the neurological deficits created by brutal patriarchal birth practices.

This is why otherwise 'rational' people become evangelical in their defence of drugs and pornography. The more aggressive and illogical the defence, the deeper the terror of the emotional flat-lining experienced without the dopaminergic 'high'. Whether that 'high' is at the expense of other lives or in itself life-threatening is irrelevant; for those whose neurodevelopment was impaired at birth and in infancy, life without a 'high' feels like death.

As Michael Dransfield, in 'Still life with hypodermic', wrote,

> *insufficient eats you out*
> *you start to*
> *fall over*
> *until eventually*
> *you can't get up.*[1138]

A 2020/21 study of over 33,000 American university students found that over 50 percent screened positive for anxiety and/or depression, and 83 percent reported that their mental health had interfered with their performance.[1139] Due to the routine administration of obstetric drugs and other obstetric abuses, this is what life feels like for an increasing number of people.

We have reached a point in history where intellectual incapacitation feels like wholeness, and where forgetting trumps remembering. What amounts to a plague of mental illness is now addressed as 'normal'[1140] rather than as an indication that there is something terrifyingly wrong with our culture. The fact that we no longer understand mental illness as a *message* – that is, as a nondeclarative communication of an imbalance that requires rectification – not only demonstrates the degree of our emotional illiteracy, but our failure to understand the principle of balance as the axis of all existence.

What this also means is that the medical profession, in tandem with the pharmaceutical industry, is, in effect, responsible for creating the current global market for drugs and pornography and the inestimable suffering involved in their manufacture, distribution and use.

Dopamine abnormalities are also implicated in schizophrenia, the prevalence of which is on the rise in the developed world[1141,1142] – in

1990, there were 13.1 million cases of schizophrenia internationally; in 2016, this figure had risen to 20.9 million[1143] – and GABAergic dysfunction is associated with bipolar disorder.[1144]

American musician Jimi Hendrix, who died at 27 after inhaling his own vomit while intoxicated on barbiturates, was known for 'very sudden, extreme mood swings' that are characteristic of bipolar disorder. Born in 1942[1145] in what was then known as King County Hospital in Seattle, Hendrix – like Rolling Stones founder Brian Jones, who also died as a result of barbiturates intoxication at the age of 27 – was likely to have been administered increasingly fashionable barbiturates through his mother at birth.

Again, the neonatal impact of these drugs was well-known to obstetricians.

As American obstetrician William P. Sadler noted in an address, from 1932 onwards, the obstetric administration of 'various barbituric acid derivatives such as sodium amytal, Nembutal, Ortal, Allonal, Seconal and others' had become 'widespread' and were, in 'many' cases, administered in unnecessarily 'large' doses with 'deleterious effect upon the babies as shown' and 'restraint' becoming necessary for the mother, placing pressure on her heart.[1146] In combination with the auditory and hormonal chaos caused by the labouring mother's drugged panic, her increases in heartrate, characteristic of high anxiety, were a message to her foetus that they were *both* in danger, amplifying his terror at birth.

In the gatefold sleeve of *The Madcap Laughs*, Syd Barrett is shown repeated, in the fashion of a Hindu god, unto infinity in a celestial cloudscape; in the central image, his head is contained in a television screen. Seemingly incongruously, the top left-hand corner of the image features a newborn's face turning away from a masculine hand administering an unknown substance. This image is a narrative Barrett did not, on a declarative level, understand.

Similarly, lawyer John F. Kennedy Jnr, son of the American president, endured significant birth trauma with the usual bonding and neurodevelopmental aftermath. Held upside-down at birth, Kennedy Jnr, disabled by the same obstetric drugs that had disabled his mother, was slapped by the anaesthesiologist in an effort to revive him. Kennedy Jnr turned blue and had to be intubated. The anaesthesiologist then inadvertently knocked the tube out, whereupon it was reinserted and air was breathed into Kennedy Jnr's lungs by a second-year resident.[1147]

Kennedy Jnr's 'reserved' mother Jackie spent 12 days in hospital after her second caesarean.[1148] In keeping with tradition, her baby wasn't breastfed and his care was mostly delegated.[1149] Impulsiveness, a biographer reported, soon became 'a serious problem.' Kennedy Jnr was 'restless, had a low threshold for boredom, and could not sit still for any length of time. Disruptive in school, he did poorly.' Diagnosed with ADHD and dyslexia, he remained on Ritalin 'for much of his life'.[1150] At 17, he first took LSD and continued to do so 'to blow off steam', almost until his death in a small aircraft crash 20 years later.[1151]

American singer Whitney Houston, who drowned in the bath high on benzodiazepines (prescribed for anxiety), cannabis, cocaine and other drugs at the age of 48 in 2012,[1152] was born to an unconscious mother in 1963. As her mother Cissy Houston wrote, 'This was a big baby, and the delivery wasn't easy. After hours of pain, the doctors gave me an anaesthetic to knock me out.' When Cissy finally came to, her disorientation was such that she refused to believe she had given birth.[1153]

Given that this was an adult female's response to obstetric drugs, imagine, then, the degree of disorientation and neurodevelopmental havoc in the newborn.

Three years after Houston's death, her 22-year-old daughter Bobbi Kristina Brown also died after being found unresponsive in a bath, high on benzodiazepines, cannabis, morphine and other drugs.[1154] Shaped by a patriarchal culture, Houston, like her mother, had no confidence in her ability to give birth. Convinced that she 'couldn't take any kind of physical pain', she elected to have a caesarean, and so, like *her* mother, Bobbi Kristina Brown was born high on drugs. A photograph of her birth shows a sea of surgical scrubs and masks.[1155]

American singer Miley Cyrus, who struggled for years with substance-use disorders and was frequently photographed wearing latex and plastic,[1156] was born 'quite a few' weeks prematurely; there were unspecified 'complications' that required 'extra care' from the 'medical team' and eight days of hospitalisation,[1157] making it clear that intervention was extensive. Cyrus said of her mother, '[F]or all the weed that I don't smoke, my mom has managed to take over the kush[1158] throne.'[1159]

Again, it's likely that Cyrus's mother was also born high on drugs, creating a generational legacy of substance-use disorders.

Seventy-seven years before Cyrus's birth, Alice Delano de Forest, Edie Sedgwick's mother, was administered obstetric anaesthesia during delivery, had an allergic reaction, and almost died.[1160] Given the era, barbiturates were likely to have been included in the drug cocktail. Sedgwick, then, was born into obstetric chaos, hallucinating and invariably suffering respiratory distress, and, on the basis of hospital policy, immediately separated from her unconscious mother. In effect, Sedgwick's suicide from a barbiturate overdose 28 years later was the closing of a circle:

For drugs thou art and unto drugs shalt thou return.

The relationship between obstetric drugs and sometimes ultimately fatal intoxication in adulthood is not accidental. Through amniotic fluid, the foetus develops a taste for the foods his mother prefers; this transmission is thought to assist the transition to nursing and, after weaning, to solids.[1161] The same transmission of preference applies to substances,[1162] meaning that a pregnant woman who drinks or uses drugs passes the preference to her foetus.

Logically, this principle applies to the placental transference of obstetric drugs.

British writer Michele Kirsch, whose life and capacity for motherhood has been marred by anxiety and substance-use disorder, was born to a mother administered Twilight Sleep, making it likely that Kirsch had to be resuscitated – or, at the least, endured respiratory distress – at birth ('I came into this world when my mother was out of it, so to speak').[1163] In adulthood, 'out of it' became the asthmatic Kirsch's default setting. Of her long-term addiction to benzodiazepines, she wrote, 'When you are so consumed with free-floating anxiety, there is very little sense of proper danger... The panic attacks got worse and I would wake up to swallow a mouthful of drugs, would take them throughout the day and go to sleep with them at night.'[1164]

American actress Carrie Fisher, whose adulthood was marred by anxiety, bipolar disorder, and substance-use disorders, was also indirectly administered Twilight Sleep at birth ('my mother was unconscious'). Fisher was later treated with ECT; elective brain damage seemed easier than metabolising her incomprehension at her self-destructive dopaminergic impulses. Describing herself as an 'eager-for-the-altered-state person', Fisher smoked 'like it was food'[1165] – which, to her, it was; denied motherlove and mother's milk at birth, she was taught to align comfort with anxiety, breathlessness, and chemically-distorted perception.

Ottessa Moshfegh's heiress protagonist of the bestselling *My Year of Rest and Relaxation* draws unnerving parallels between birth, drugs and dysfunction: 'When I needed more pills, I ventured out... three blocks away. That was always a painful passage. Walking up First Avenue, everything made me cringe. *I was like a baby being born, the air hurt, the light hurt, the details of the world seemed garish and hostile* [italics mine].'[1166]

As Dransfield wrote in 'Overdose', more birth memory than poem:

> *lassitude that comes of*
> *prior opiates and robs my veins*
> *of meaningful blood, or poisons*
> *with perilous narcotics.*[1167]

PCP – the street drug known as 'angel dust' (phencyclidine or phenylcyclohexyl piperidine) – was also first used as an obstetric anaesthetic in the 1950s.[1168] In 1962, a British doctor complained that PCP was, 'unfortunately, in imminent danger of death from neglect.' He added: 'Fortunately or unfortunately, in most patients between the ages of six and sixty years it causes a catatonic stupor with bizarre hallucinations which may be remembered after the effects of the drug have worn off.' Given this, 'smaller doses are used for children.'[1169]

The same year, a British anaesthetic registrar wrote that he doubted PCP had any 'adverse effect on the baby when used for obstetric cases, even if it did pass the placental barrier,' adding, 'One doubts if the drug passes across the placenta to the baby.' He then refers to the 'catatonic trance', 'vacant blank stare', and four-hour hallucinations of mothers in the context of childbirth as if they were not only normal, but *appropriate*.

This doctor then mentioned other drugs that were indirectly administered to a mother in conjunction with PCP to a particular infant: cyclopropane (caustic to the eyes, now linked with disorientation and alterations in cognitive function)[1170] and suxamethonium (now associated with an 'immediate rise' in potassium levels, putting the newborn at risk of fatal arrhythmia).[1171] [1172] The result? A 'failed forceps' baby, delivered dead.[1173]

PCP has since been described by researchers as 'a dangerous and unpredictable drug' which 'acutely' and 'readily' crosses the placental barrier. Administered to pregnant mice, PCP was, in foetal tissue, found in 10-fold higher concentrations than it was in the the mother's blood.[1174]

The 'recreational' use of PCP began as the first generation of PCP babies came of age.[1175] Between 1978 and 1980, PCP abuse was associated with over 80 percent of overdose cases seen at only one major American hospital.[1176] To give an idea of the impact on a single life: a regular PCP user gave birth to an infant who behaved abnormally, had 'an unusual appearance', and later, developed spastic quadriparesis – all consistent with the reported impact of PCP.[1177] Unsurprisingly, the estimated number of PCP-related emergency hospital visits between 2005 and 2011 increased by over 400 percent (from 14,825 to 75,538 visits).[1178]

Billions of lives, blighted or destroyed, for 'protection' from a few hours of labour pain.

Trillions of dollars were made by hospitals from this slow-release carnage.

If our birth experience involved the administration of powerful psychoactive pharmaceuticals to, and separation from, our mothers, then the ingestion of powerful psychoactive pharmaceuticals and emotional detachment in adulthood will not only feel familiar, but *safe*. The association of powerful psychoactive pharmaceuticals with nurturance – through their transference in the manner of nutrients through the placenta – bypasses all declarative awareness of the dangers they pose. Even considerations of a child's wellbeing will fall by the wayside. Like Kirsch's being 'out of it', the experience of *not caring* will become the adult's default 'setting', and Wordsworth's 'forgetting' – that is, the erasure of the self through drugs – will feel like coming home.

20. INCOMPLETE INTIMACY

'Do not complain. Work harder. Spend more time alone.'

Blue Nights, Joan Didion

A rarely mentioned fact is that morphine and scopolamine, the twin engines of Twilight Sleep, are not merely amnesiacs and anaesthetics but *hallucinogens*. Derived from belladonna (nightshade), scopolamine is, as I have mentioned, known as the 'zombie drug' – as it subtracts awareness from action, its administration to unsuspecting victims is now associated with crimes in Third World countries. It was noted that the 'most intriguing phenomenon [is] the submissive and obedient behaviour of the victim,'[1179] casting a new light on its administration to labouring mothers.

The Psychedelic Revolutionaries of the 1960s, then, were not glamorous ideological freedom fighters 'expanding human consciousness', but adult victims of the obstetric administration of hallucinogens *seeking comfort* in the same way the barbiturate addicts of the 1950s and 1960s[1180,1181] – adult victims of the barbiturates *their* mothers had been administered during pregnancy and labour – sought comfort from prescription pills.

Twilight Sleep and its later, equally hallucinogenic, obstetric adaptations *lay the groundwork for a mass psychedelic movement,* just as the continued administration of obstetric hallucinogens is creating a new, multi-billion-dollar market for legal hallucinogens[1182] through microdosing.

Imagine, for a moment, the experience of a foetus who, up until the toxic drugs administered to his mother pass his blood/brain barrier, experienced only comfort, ease, intimacy and protection. Imagine the violence of the anaesthesia's impact, and the shock, which, in addition to that of birth, could only result in the terror of annihilation. The experience would be something like the climactic tableaux depicted in German director Roland Emmerich's international blockbuster disaster movies, those witness statements of intense foetal agitation.

Imagine, too, the stunning transformation of the maternal environment into a field of poisons, of distorted perceptions, of disorienting sudden shifts in maternal rhythms – blood flow, breathing, cardiac – and unnatural pressure.

In place of flow, psychosis. In place of love, horror.

The foetal experience of a drugged birth is unrivalled as a torture, medieval in its brutality.

Like Mapplethorpe's art and Brady's murders, the liquid light shows characteristic of psychedelia, those strangely-hued mineral oils through alcohol that are often twinned with loud rock music, document part of the neonatal experience – in this case, the auditory and visual hallucinations drugged babies experienced during and after birth.

Timothy Leary's doctrine of altered consciousness only found a cultural foothold because it offered the generations born *tripping* a means of self-soothing denied by drug laws. Promoted as 'countercultural', the directive 'turn on, tune in, drop out' was, in fact, a repackaged reinforcement of the same old 'square' legacy: the abuse and denial of the feminine, the censorship of emotion, the insistence on conformity, and the use of propaganda and violence – in this case, neurochemical – to disable agency.

Innovation played no part in Leary's philosophy. An entire philosophy of life was constructed to justify his generation's return to the anonymised, emotionally disordered, isolated, internalised, pharmaceutically-dictated distortions they knew at birth.

For the most part, pharmaceuticals are solutions to problems created by their manufacturers.

Scottish music entrepreneur Alan McGee, who recalled his mother describing his 1960 hospital birth in Glasgow as 'terrible', started using drugs 'on an industrial scale at 22, 23,' but had used since his teens. 'Until I got into Ecstasy, though, I never really enjoyed drugs; I just did them because everyone else was doing them. Why did I love Ecstasy? It made me feel centred. Feeling destabilised was kind of how I always felt, but Ecstasy made me feel *complete*. I never felt complete before, probably not, no. No idea why.'[1183]

Freud, too, failed to make the connection, understanding 'intoxicating substances' as a finger in the dyke of human suffering, a means of 'slip[ping] away from the oppression of reality' to take 'refuge in a world of their own where painful feelings do not enter'.[1184]

The subtext of Freud's words is that reality is the enemy of happiness, which is why pleasure can only be found in an escape from reality. Substance abuse was thus presented by him as a good thing, a means of 'warding off' misery, rather than as associated with decay and delusion and an obstacle to human contentment and evolution.

We repeatedly 'return' in any number of ways to the terrain of our births not only as a means of self-soothing, but of *self-protection*. Maier's mother: the enfolding, nurturing, protective world of our nondeclarative hearts. Like homing pigeons, we are programmed to follow the psychobiological equivalent of 'infrasounds' (sounds below our range of hearing) in order to map our return to physical – and, in adulthood, psychological – safety.

Feeling unsafe is, for human beings, significantly more than unpleasant: feeling unsafe has been shown to be one of the primary sources of mental and physical illness.[1185]

Untroubled, a mother is not merely Firestone's person-with-a-womb or, as American actor Spencer Pratt memorably dismissed his mother-in-law, 'just [a] vagina',[1186] but *home*, and there is no issue of greater importance in terms of human civilisation on this planet.

The 'home' central to an infant's sense of belonging is his *primal territory*, a territory which he later will, if securely bonded, defend with his life if only because its attack will be perceived as an attempt to destabilise the self. As American adoptee Dave Brown wrote, '*Hiraeth* is a Welsh word for homesickness, nostalgia, longing for a place that never was. For many adoptees, we are never really at home anywhere... Maybe the place I was trying to get back to never existed.'[1187]

The home for which he pined was the primal territory of his mother.

Like the Fates of Greek mythology, obstetric practices determine, for the generations they deliver, birth circumstances, emotional and sexual latitude, cultural strengths and vulnerabilities, and, in many cases, the means of death.

Advances in our study of neurodevelopment make it clear that morality, as we understand it, is little more than a fiction composed to support the prevailing ideology. 'Evil' and 'immorality' – cruelty, deception, murder, emotional perversion, violence, and so on – are, in fact, no more than the logical outputs of impaired neurodevelopment and trauma. What this means is that a significant proportion of the wrongdoing in our culture can be laid at the stoop of medical and obstetric practice.

Dysfunctional behaviour is always a trail of breadcrumbs leading us to a problem that requires a solution.

The impact of obstetric drugs on the human race cannot be overemphasised. Globally, 500,000 deaths result from illegal drug use, and over 70 percent of these deaths are opioid-related. In 2018, some 58 million people around the world were known to use illegal opioids; the unknown number would be significantly higher. Between 2010 and 2018, the number of fatal opioid overdoses in America increased by 120 percent. Fentanyl and other drugs used in an obstetric context were involved in two-thirds of these deaths;[1188] in 2018, there were over 31,335 deaths involving fentanyl and other synthetic narcotics alone.[1189]

'I've heard of an anaesthetic they give to people for endoscopies,' says the thin, depressed, elite addict of Ottessa Moshfegh's *My Year of Rest and Relaxation*. 'Something that keeps you awake during the procedure, but you can't remember anything afterward. Something like that would be good. I have a lot of *anxiety*.'[1190]

A baptised Mormon who also felt like she 'never belonged', Thea Taylor of band carolesdaughter began using drugs at the age of 11 and was first admitted to rehab at 13. She said, 'I tried [drugs] and thought, *That's what I've been looking for my whole life* [italics mine].'[1191]

Despite the popular Mormon belief that obstetric anaesthesia obscures the revelatory nature of labour pain, the usual triumvirate – an Abrahamic cultural background, the sense of alienation, and a substance-use disorder – strongly suggests that Taylor and her mother were victims of obstetric anaesthesia and were, because of hospital policy or cultural mores, separated from each other at birth and during Taylor's infancy. In the entire video for her song 'Please Put Me in a Medically Induced Coma', Taylor sings in a straitjacket from a hospital bed while attached to multiple intravenous drips of her desire to be spared undrugged consciousness.[1192]

During the 2020 Covid crisis, there were, in America, over 81,000 overdose deaths, the highest number ever recorded. In pharmacological terms, the primary driver has again been identified as synthetic opioids – primarily fentanyl, the involvement of which, in a fatal overdose capacity, further increased by 38.4 percent. Fatal overdoses of psychostimulants such as methamphetamine also increased, if by 3.6 percent less.[1193]

The same hallucinations caused by obstetric drugs are also a common side effect of methamphetamine use.[1194]

In many, if not most, of these casualties, the Covid crisis would have triggered unmanageable nondeclarative memories of abandonment, terror and worthlessness that called for self-comforting with the same drugs they had been indirectly given at birth.

The growing global appetite for hallucinogens, opiates and sedatives, then – between 2015 and 2018, the US usage rate of hallucinogens alone increased by over 50 percent – isn't due to the desperation to *escape* 'depression, anxiety and general stress over the state of the world,'[1195] but to *return* in times of stress to the feelings associated with 'mother' and the first moments of consciousness outside the womb, as Houston, Kennedy, Kirsch, the Psychedelic Revolutionaries, Spungen, and countless others have shown.

Internationally, the epidemic of substance abuse – over 35.6 million people[1196] – has literally been *created* by obstetric practice.

As Maier's mother is incapacitated, so is all the world.

Because of this, the US Drug Enforcement Administration (DEA) is a spectacular waste of public funds. Without a market – without the *susceptibility* created by obstetric abuse – there would be no trafficking. If we continue to allow the abuse of mothers and babies, we are not only ensuring that the prevalence of substance-use disorders will become unmanageable, but we are literally *creating the market* for the 'criminals' we then trace and imprison at implausible costs to the community.

Logically, the money spent running the DEA and bodies created to combat drug trafficking would be better spent on researching the long-term emotional, neurodevelopmental and physiological impact of obstetric abuse and drugs on women and children, and on how to manage the resultant social catastrophes: the violence resulting from hospital-birth-related attachment ruptures and neurodevelopmental damage, say. In the US alone, the societal costs of incarceration are $1.2 trillion per year.[1197] Even if the cost of imprisonment were excluded, the US 'aggregate burden of incarceration' would still trump $500 billion, most of it borne by communities.[1198]

Incomprehensibly, the idea that pharmaceuticals have *determined* the tenor of the 20th and 21st century has never before been considered. Through the administration of obstetric drugs and the normalisation of the denigration of the feminine, humanity has come to understand itself as fundamentally inadequate: incorrectly designed, insufficiently stimulating, unacceptably vulnerable, unworthy of devotion.

To be human now is to require pharmaceutical or surgical modification.

Conditioned, for the most part, to isolate from attachment and to associate birth – and sex – with inhuman properties and inhumane practices, we can no longer be classified as fully human in the sense of being emotionally and physiologically actualised.

The success of the Terminator, the cyborg protagonist of the billion-dollar movie franchise,[1199] reflects this sense of being incompletely human. A cyborg (the neologism for 'cybernetic organism') is part organic, part manufactured: the 'man-machine', which, in his 1983 film *Videodrome*, American director David Cronenberg referred to as 'the new flesh'. The term 'cyborg' was coined in a 1960 symposium address in which drugs and surgical procedures designed by men were cited as means of 'enhancing' human performance,[1200] as if to meet standards set at inhuman – and inhumane – levels.

There are, in the human cortical sheet, some one million billion connections. Potential combinations of these connections would run to 'the order of ten followed by millions of zeros'.[1201] Given this, imagine the impact of obstetric drugs administered at generic dosages during the most fragile of neurodevelopmental phases.

The incomparable intelligence and sensitivity of feminine design, poisoned and skewed. Normalised, the distortion of the most important human relationship in terms of determining the cultural tone: that of a mother and her baby.

For almost two centuries, the principle of *division* has been routinely established at birth. Both mother and infant are denied love, disconnected from the intelligence of process, and rendered oblivious to the meaning of pain in relation to emotional evolution.

The territoriality through which humaneness evolves is intercepted – in its place, a detachment that has, to varying degrees, marred all our lives and the planet that nurtures our civilisation. Attachment not only shapes life but sustains it. During the 2020 global lockdown, for example, hospitalised Covid victims permitted to engage with their families were found to be 30 percent less likely to suffer from delirium.[1202]

While there is 'robust evidence' that living alone, loneliness, and social isolation have 'a significant and equal effect on the risk of premature death, one that was equal to or exceeded the effect of other well-accepted risk factors such as obesity',[1203] the issue of *susceptibility* resulting from mother/baby separation at birth has not been studied. My guess is that it's the adults who, as babies, endured the indirect administration of obstetric drugs and separation from their mothers, were the ones who were most deeply traumatised by Covid-related anxiety, breathlessness, and isolation in adulthood.

Babies separated from their mothers at birth will not have the nondeclarative skills to build and sustain intimate relationships in adulthood unless they seek cognitive behaviour therapy; emotional and physical isolation will otherwise always feel far more 'normal' – that is, *familiar* – to them. In this respect, social media serves an inestimably important cultural purpose: it provides the illusion or rudiments of intimacy to those with an impaired capacity to connect. The intimacy offered by social media, unrelated as it is to physical proximity, is curated, declarative, rationed, and sanitised by policy, like a modern mother's exposure to her newly-born baby in hospital.

I also believe that the separation of mother and child at birth and during infancy is the fountainhead of chronic loneliness in adulthood.

When separated from his mother, the activity of a two-day-old infant's autonomic nervous system, which governs digestion, heart rate, respiration, and so on, jumps by *176 percent*.[1204] This neurobiological 'alarm system' makes it clear that far from being a matter of cultural or maternal preference, mother/baby proximity is the very foundation of adult equanimity.

Newborns are literally *designed* to remain close to their mother, and any divergence from this evolutionary mandate impairs their neurodevelopment. The now almost universal infant experience of separation from the mother explains why *an accelerated autonomic nervous system is the new normal*. Acceleration has become the hallmark of the past century and a half in particular – as it happens, the same period in which the administration of obstetric anaesthesia became routine. As André Gorz, the Franco-Austrian philosopher who committed suicide with his wife after her terminal diagnosis, wrote, 'I once more feel a gnawing emptiness in the hollow of my chest that is only filled when your body is pressed next to mine.'[1205]

Incomplete intimacy is now the governing principle of our lives. By definition, pornography, social media, and all psychoactive substances only offer incomplete intimacy. To the damaged, this incompleteness is comforting, unthreatening. The completeness of intimacy with a baby is disturbing for a mother impaired by her own early experiences of obstetric abuse. It's equally disturbing for a male victim of obstetric abuse to care for a partner who passionately nurtures a baby, even if that baby is his own, which is why in America, seven million men are 'absent' fathers to all of their minor children,[1206] and why one in five British fathers no longer has any contact with his children.[1207]

In America, half the population of marriageable age remains unmarried.[1208] Internationally, the number of adults who live alone has doubled in the past half-century.[1209] In Britain, 8.2 million people were living alone in 2019, a 'statistically significant increase' of 20 percent in as many years.[1210] The trend for living alone began as the first victims of obstetric drugs came of age, and accelerated around 1950,[1211] when the Twilight Sleep generation matured; prior to that, the rate was nominal – in pre-industrial communities, around 5 percent.[1212]

Throughout the 20th and 21st century, obstetric practice has routinely interfered with the psychobiological 'infrasounds' necessary for human beings to feel *safe* throughout their lives. 'Home', for a disturbingly high percentage of the population, is understood not as the feminine or maternal passion and nurturance but as the drugs they were administered at birth or drugs that produce the same feelings, and with the same attendant fear, frustration, and isolation. Detachment from the self and others is the new baseline of comfort.

Complete intimacy, to those who were denied it at birth and during infancy, is experienced as intrusive, overwhelming, and, in cases of complete emotional shutdown, 'boring', and there is no more complete an intimacy than that offered by a baby.

To those who knew only cruelty and isolation at birth, such intimacy can only be experienced as threatening, which is why the patriarchal – women included – dismiss babies, emotion, and intimacy as trivial or uninteresting. Leary, for example, had no stomach for attachment, and regularly exposed his children to heavy substance abuse, adult sexuality, and disordered adult behaviour. His daughter Susan, then 13, looked up from her homework one evening, asked what he wanted for Christmas and told him that she loved him. Terror 'convulsed' Leary, who was, of course, tripping at the time. Here was a 'puppet doll teenager', a 'marionette stranger from assembly line America' playing the 'father-daughter game' with her 'shallow, superficial, stereotyped, meaningless exchange'.[1213]

At the age of 42 and after years of abuse at the hands of her father, Susan hanged herself in her cell after being sentenced to a mental hospital for the criminally insane.[1214]

The capacity for intimacy essential to optimal infant neurodevelopment has, over almost two centuries of abusive birth practices, fractured. This is why a disturbing proportion of parents no longer know how to enjoy sustained closeness with a child without drinking, drug-taking, or resorting to an array of inanimate objects to distract themselves (from confronting needs they don't know how to meet) or to distract – popularly reframed as 'to entertain' – their child (from expressing needs they don't know how to meet).

In 2008, a fatally isolated 27-year-old American man punched his 17-month-old daughter to death after she pulled on his Xbox cords, causing his Xbox to fall – he'd been playing videogames for six hours straight as his partner, who had a history of neglecting the baby, slept.[1215] The case made global news not because of its brutality – there are countless more vicious cases of child abuse – but because of the resonant disparity between action and reaction.

In the 21st century, a little child's mute entreaty for undistracted parental attention can amount to a death sentence.

The problem with isolation is that it contradicts our attachment-centred mammalian design, meaning that the only possible response is the deep discontent that, ironically, warrants self-comforting through substance use or other dysfunctional dopaminergic practices.

I understood none of this until I gave birth to my daughter.

21. THE POISONED APPLE

'I lie on my side as the soft-spoken anesthesiologist administers
the drug. I am swept into a lullaby tasting of lemons and sugar,
smelling of lavender and almond oil, sounding of flutes, and
feeling like the silk that is spun on the moon.'

Guarding the Moon: A Mother's First Year, Francesca Lia Block

My baby was born blue and motionless. She didn't even look real.
'Is it dead?' I asked, blurred by morphine.

This was my first response to my only child. Beyond the apathy,
nothing. In that moment, it may even have been all right if the
blue unmoving thing were, in fact, dead. I was naked, listing like a
sloop and on all fours. I didn't feel like a mother. I didn't even feel
human. I'm not sure I knew who I was anymore, not really, or what
I was supposed to feel. Thick felted tongue, that yolk-slow rolling
of my eyes: a routinely dissociated drug-comedown. I'd lost a cup
and a half of blood internally through tearing. The IV had come
loose, and splashed my face with blood. I was a zombie: drugged
and swaying, staring through my dying baby at nothing.

'Oxygen!' one of the midwives, somewhere behind me, said.

Bethesda's Apgar score was 4 out of 10: 'moderately abnormal',
and on the cusp of grave difficulties.[1216] As I said, she was cyanotic
and not breathing. The umbilical cord was not involved. Hospital
notes state that at one minute after birth, she was unresponsive
and her muscle tone was poor. Intermittent Positive Pressure
Respiration (IPPR) was required. Had it been any worse, she
would have needed endotracheal intubation – commonplace in
severe cases of Covid-19 – in addition to the IPPR bag and mask.
'Emergency 33 called to assist neonatal resuscitation,' the midwife
wrote. Bethesda's breathing was established within two seconds. At
five minutes, her Apgar score had climbed to nine.

My child belonged to me, then, not to history.

At no point during my antenatal classes or during the delivery itself was I informed that neonatal respiratory distress is a long-known byproduct of obstetric anaesthesia,[1217] and nor was I warned that as a result of obstetric anaesthesia, my baby could have died at birth.

I was told nothing. Because I was in a major teaching hospital, I assumed that I was safe.

During an examination after my waters broke, I was found to have Streptococcus B (Group B Strep, or GBS) – harmless bacteria, present in two to four women in 10. In rare cases, it can be dangerous to a newborn.[1218] Because of this, I was administered ampicillin, an antibiotic, as a preventative measure during labour for my full-term, uninduced baby.

I wasn't told that in the UK, only 0.2 per 1,000 of all full-term babies contract GBS, and that premature babies comprise 83 percent of the deaths.[1219] I also wasn't told that antibiotics delay the development of protective intestinal bacteria, and that disturbances in early microbial gut colonisation are associated with chronic diseases in adulthood (inflammatory bowel disease, obesity, colon cancer, and so on).[1220]

Culture-proven infections account for only 5 percent of global antibiotic use.[1221] Hospital-based over-use is, in part, responsible for the increasing bacterial resistance to antibiotics,[1222] which kills over 23,000 Americans each year.[1223] In the US, half of all low-risk, full-term babies are exposed to antibiotics.[1224] Dutch researchers noted that of 'all disrupting factors, early antibiotic exposure is considered to have the greatest impact on the gut microbiome in infants, leading to a disturbed microbiome still months and sometimes years after antibiotic treatment.' In turn, the loss of important bacteria and reduced bacterial diversity can lead to pathogen growth, changes in metabolic processes, and an impaired immune system. And, even if the gut regains its diversity, the bacterial composition may be permanently altered.[1225]

My hospital records show that I had a 'long discussion' with a midwife about GBS after the contractions kicked in, but do not mention that she did not tell me about the potential long-term impact of antibiotics on my baby. The midwife emphasised the rare, potential dangers of GBS rather than the routine dangers of the prophylactic drug.

Having planned a natural birth in the hospital birth centre, I capitulated, frightened by the amalgam of her smile and those fleeting mentions of infant death.

Synthetic oxytocin, the drug 'most commonly linked to preventable adverse effects in childbirth', is recommended only in the event of risk to a mother's or baby's life,[1226] but I was given the drug because I wanted a shorter labour.

A sense of control over my femininity was, for me, critical. I refused to be a beast in the thrall of its instincts or a primitive, squatting. At three or so in the morning, my waters had broken, but I had no interest in further vulnerability. It was time to resume authority over my body. A girlfriend, one of the senior partners at a law firm, had, with a knowing look and before I went to hospital, advised me to 'take all the drugs you can get'.

Leary's prescription for liberation.

I wasn't told that synthetic oxytocin causes jaundice in newborns,[1227,1228] reduces oxygen supply to the foetal brain,[1229] and is associated with low Apgar scores.[1230] The first is no small matter; if the level of bilirubin, which measures bile in blood, climbs too high, neurological damage – cerebral palsy, convulsions, deafness, mental retardation, and other issues – can occur.[1231] In addition, far from triggering the profound mother/baby attachment associated with natural oxytocin, synthetic oxytocin administered to a mother during the peripartum period (before, during and immediately after birth) is associated with a higher risk of her being diagnosed with postpartum depression or anxiety disorders – 36 percent higher in women with a history of depression or anxiety, and 32 percent in women with no such history.[1232]

Oddly, the website for the British National Institute for Health and Care Excellence (known by its attractively anodyne acronym, NICE), an organisation that 'improves health and social care through evidence-based guidance' for British government bodies and general practitioners, fails to mention the well-established connection between jaundice and synthetic oxytocin. Instead, NICE associates jaundice with breastfeeding[1233] without mentioning that breastfeeding, in fact, clears bilirubin from the intestines more efficiently, which is why frequent breastfeeding is recommended for jaundiced babies.[1234]

NICE then states that a newborn is more likely to develop 'significant' jaundice if the mother *intends* to 'breastfeed exclusively',[1235] although how maternal feeding intent impacts on neonatal bilirubin levels is not explained.

Bethesda was born jaundiced; I never knew why. Because her bilirubin levels were so high, we were kept in hospital, meaning that she and her father were denied the most critical of bonding opportunities. There was, of course, no provision for partners in the maternity ward.

I wasn't told that the administration of synthetic oxytocin is also linked to uterine hyperstimulation, a serious complication that can impair blood flow to the placenta, resulting in foetal brain damage, eye problems, heart damage, heart rate abnormalities, and respiratory distress, among other serious and potentially life-threatening complications.[1236,1237]

What I was told at hospital antenatal classes was this: that synthetic oxytocin accelerates both the birth process and the intensity and timing of contractions. Amused, I thought, *I'm not afraid of a little pain. Big deal.* The midwives, however, failed to clarify the *degree* of the pain's acceleration; at one point, it felt as if a jackhammer were being driven, at full force, into my pelvis. As New Zealand researcher Sarah J. Buckley wrote, 'Women who are administered synthetic oxytocin also commonly receive epidurals to counter the increased pain, and women with an epidural often require synthetic oxytocin, because epidurals reduce the natural release of oxytocin.'[1238]

The unnatural length and power of these jackhammer contractions reduced Bethesda's supply of blood and oxygen, increasing the risk for hypoxia (low oxygen), which, in terms of neurodevelopment, is a potential catastrophe.[1239] I will never forget my own agonised breathlessness as Bethesda, with a tiny foot, used one of my ribs as leverage to escape the pressure of a uterus unnaturally contracted by synthetic oxytocin.[1240]

When, in response, I grunted, 'Fuck!', the young midwife scowled: 'Language!' Unable to access sufficient oxygen and hallucinating, Bethesda was terrified, fighting to leave what had, for nine months, been her untroubled garden.

Through my choices – through my false consent – I had *doubled* my baby's chances of suffering respiratory distress at birth.

I wasn't told that the administration of synthetic oxytocin to the mother is associated with psychomotor issues in the child.

Variables had no impact in the studies: the resulting delays on fine and gross motor development were clear.[1241,1242] In 2014,[1243] 'a higher propensity in anaesthetic-exposed children to develop motor deficits' was discovered, although there were no significant effects on cognitive or linguistic capacity.[1244]

Bethesda's unusual recall and use of complex words by the age of two – she spoke her first word at five or so months – caused me to have her tested by a developmental psychologist, who found that in terms of emotional and intellectual ability, she was in the 99th percentile; in terms of motor development, however, she was in the 16th percentile: borderline low average, almost a year behind her peers. Her coordination was so poor – she also had issues with perspective – that her ballet teacher asked me to remove her from the class as her inability to follow complex physical instruction was too distracting.

I did not know that natural oxytocin floods the undrugged brain's fluid during labour, combating anxiety and stress and lowering the awareness of pain. Unlike natural oxytocin, synthetic oxytocin fails to penetrate the mother's blood-brain barrier.[1245] This means that there is no 'cushioning' of pain awareness, amplifying the mother's stress. Stress, of course, slows and stops effective labouring. During labour, mental stress experienced by mothers has been found to dominate the physical,[1246] meaning that, in terms of ensuring a safe delivery with the best results for mother and baby, the mother's feelings – her desires, her fears – need to be addressed not only in the lead-up to birth, but throughout her pregnancy.

At no point did it occur to me that women are *designed* to cope with the pain of childbirth.[1247] Oxytocin is naturally released in peak quantities during labour to buoy mothers through delivery. Its release can be triggered by the partner's tender stimulation of the clitoris and nipples,[1248] or by massage-like stroking in the lead-up to, and during, birth.[1249] The repeated massaging of a pregnant woman over a fortnight before birth increases her pain threshold through the intricate interplay between her oxytocin system and opioid neurons.[1250] Beta-endorphins, triggered by her comfort, also play a pivotal role in reducing pain awareness.

A 2020 12-country study concluded that documented variations in synthetic oxytocin dosages are 'inexplicable'. It's 'crucial that the appropriate minimum infusion regimen is administered because synthetic oxytocin is a potentially harmful medication with serious consequences for women and babies when inappropriately used.'[1251] Despite this and other similarly grave findings, a study from Denmark, where *31 percent of labouring women* are given synthetic oxytocin, concluded that no revision of the guidelines is warranted.[1252]

I also wasn't told that obstetric drugs significantly hamper the production of analgesic and bonding hormones, in the process dulling – or eradicating – the delirium of postpartum ecstasy,[1253] and with that, mother/child attachment. None of this information was given to me, or any other woman I knew who gave birth in a hospital. We were processed like livestock. Our babies were all born with dulled eyes – some jaundiced, others fatigued or feeding poorly, listless, stoned. Some screamed, further distancing their distanced mothers.

When the young midwife told me that I was only one centimetre dilated after 10 or so hours of gruelling labour – nowhere close to giving birth – I gasped that I could not go on. The effort it took to stem the swell of panic at her words was significant. Terror coursed, liquid fire, through my veins. This pain transcended my understanding of what it was to hurt: it had become sinister. Like those waves known to surfers as 'bombs', it would, I feared, bury me.

I sensed, and feared, the impending transformation.

This time, there was no going back.

Recognising that my strength was failing, I rose: I had no option but to fight what I understood as mutiny, as gendered oppression. I remember the conviction that I had to fight without identifying an opponent – blind fear, pitted against pain, landing punches. There would be no surrender. Birth, to me, was a battle against biology, not a process of expansion or an unfolding. To me, pain had only ever been evidence of weakness. The worst insult my father could level at someone was that they were 'weak'. As a result, I became a girl who would not weep after that apple was hurled, at full force, at my diaphragm. Yielding was the stuff of women – evidence of subordination, pathetic.

Beneath the pain created by my demand for expedience, the vulnerability I'd warred all my life to disguise.

I thought, *Fuck that.*

Nine months of gestation, in the balance. Nine months of love. Not one person told me the odds. I gambled my baby's life for gender status.

All I wanted was control.

A woman's experience of labour pain is determined by her spin. Women who understand labour pain as contextual – that is, as *purposeful* – associate it, as a successful graduate does her years of study, with ultimate triumph, whereas women like me – anxious, highly controlled, distrustful of vulnerability – associate it with threat, meaning that we feel in need of external assistance during labour.[1254] This is the difference between the matriarchal feminine (women who feel whole and equal to the masculine) and the patriarchal feminine (women who see themselves as adjuncts to the masculine, incomplete by definition and thus requiring masculine intervention to cope).

I demanded an epidural.

What I did not know was that the degree of labour pain is now á *la carte*. Universally, the decision to be administered obstetric drugs is now understood as 'women's choice'.[1255] It is never mentioned that this 'choice' is based on fear, misinformation, patriarchal conditioning, and veiled medical coercion. The 'choice' to be injected with drugs associated with permanent emotional and physiological repercussions for babies and with fractured mother/baby attachment is as false as the choice to be murdered.

Like murder, the routine administration of neurotoxic drugs during delivery should be a crime, consent notwithstanding.

Of the 17 million women who birthed a child at a US hospital between 2009 and 2015, 68 percent of those with a normal body mass index were administered an epidural; the percentage jumped to 76 in heavier women.[1256] What this means is that for almost three-quarters of American women, childbirth is synonymous not with revelation, but with terror; that childbirth is perceived as a medical procedure; associated with financial incentive; and that the labouring mother, rather than feeling like a creative force – the embodiment of Maier's mother – is a species of capsule from which an infant must be excised as expediently as possible in a hospital by a medical professional.

American anaesthesiologist Donald Caton reported that the majority of women now liken childbirth to dental surgery, reasoning, "'I have local anaesthesia when I go to the dentist's office, I'm certainly going to have it when I have my child." So most of them do.'[1257]

Throughout the developed world, birth is now perceived as an ordeal without meaning, a species of nightmare necessitating stupefaction or unconsciousness to endure: a *bad trip*.

My own bad trip is contained in a section of my hospital records entitled ANAESTHETIC PROCEDURES (OBSTETRICS). The anaesthetist's handwriting is almost illegible – an electrocardiogram reading. This lack of attention reveals his indifference, as he was in no hurry at the time: I remember him, as if in an absurdist drama, flirting with the student midwife as I lowed in pain. Bored, he asked me to sit up and lean forward so he could inject me. The drugs he administered only worked for a brief period of time. I required multiple top-ups and even then, experienced every shard of pain; the only part of my body he succeeded in anaesthetising was my diaphragm, meaning that when I was ordered to *push*, I no longer understood how.

By 6.25pm, 'distressed and uncooperative', I refused another top-up. Who knows what the impact would have been on my daughter. The midwives had no idea how to calm me; all they knew how to do, in terms of managing the distress that changed my baby's brain, was offer me more drugs. I was, one of them wrote, 'not cooperating, demanding "it over"'.

Not cooperating, demanding it over.

This was their perception of a first-time mother who had been labouring for over 12 hours, whose pain had been freakishly amplified by synthetic oxytocin, and who had been inexpertly anaesthetised.

Despite an epidural and two top-ups, I could, as they refused to believe but later discovered, both feel the pain of my increasingly intolerable contractions and use my legs ('You just *think* you can,' one said before I flipped over onto my knees to birth my baby squatting rather than working against gravity on my back).

You just think you can.

Birth intervention is not an isolated action but an avalanche: once it begins, it doesn't stop.

The use of Panadeine, an opioid (500mg paracetamol, 8mg codeine phosphate hydrate), is not recommended for children who, like my daughter, had breathing problems at birth. Nor is it recommended for breastfeeding mothers as the drug is transferred through breastmilk and – I quote from the manufacturer's leaflet – 'may harm your baby.'[1258]

The US FDA has gone so far as to issue a 'strengthened warning to mothers (among other warnings) that breastfeeding is not recommended during treatment with codeine... due to the risk of serious adverse reactions in breastfed babies such as excess sleepiness, difficulty breastfeeding, and serious breathing problems that may result in death.'[1259] Despite this, I was liberally administered Panadeine as a result of the pain caused by the post-birth catheter necessitated by the epidural.

The other poisons and dosages that were given me and, indirectly, to my baby, were:

> 11.50am 0.50% Ropivacaine and 150mcg fentanyl - 20ml
> 12.55pm 0.25% Bupivacaine - 5mls
> 13.50pm 0.50% Ropivacaine - 5mls
> 13.58pm 0.25% Ropivacaine - 5mls
> 14.30pm 0.20% Ropivacaine and 50mcg fentanyl - 10mls
> 16.35pm 0.25% Bupivacaine - 5mls

Like the anonymous American mother who dropped acid 250 times during her pregnancy,[1260] I don't know why I didn't consider the impact of this landslide of drugs on my foetus. I don't know how the obvious dangers escaped me. The prospect of injecting heroin while pregnant would have filled me with revulsion – throughout my pregnancy, I refused painkillers on that very basis, and even recoiled from eating *crisps* because of the additives – and yet, in a frenzy of terror during labour – in retrospect, a frenzy of terror over an *idea* of what I should be – I demanded to be injected with over 50ml of drugs so toxic that, in marginally different doses, they would have killed us.

All I wanted was control.

I have written about some of the known effects of fentanyl administered at birth.

Ropivacaine (also known as Naropin) was first released for use in

1996.[1261] Its manufacturer's leaflet acknowledges that newborns are 'more susceptible' to the drug, and that it's 'not known' whether it has any effect on pregnancy or is passed on through breastmilk.[1262] Despite the fact that even the manufacturer acknowledges that no, they have no idea what Ropivacaine might do to my foetus on a temporary or permanent basis, 25ml or more of the diluted drug was administered to me – and, indirectly, to my foetus – by an obstetric professional.

One to 10 in every 10,000 women to whom Ropivacaine is administered suffer 'sudden life-threatening allergic reactions' such as anaphylactic shock; others go into cardiac arrest, or suffer arrthymias (uneven heartbeat) or nerve damage. One to 10 in every 1,000 women to whom Ropivacaine is administered suffer anxiety, fainting, or experience difficulty breathing.[1263]

Again, I was told none of these things.

No mother I have ever met could name the drugs she was administered at birth.

Bupivacaine (also known as Vivacaine; with epinephrine, Marcaine and Sensorcaine; and with lidocaine, Duocaine) was synthesised in 1957 and released in 1965, the year of my birth.[1264] Of all the anaesthetics, it's the most cardiotoxic – that is, a drug that has a poisonous or deleterious impact on the heart.[1265] It's also neurotoxic. The effects of bupivacaine on newborns have been called 'significant and consistent.' In a 1981 study – *available to anaesthetists for almost a quarter of a century prior to Bethesda's birth* – it was shown that immediately after delivery, babies 'with greater exposure to bupivacaine in utero were more likely to be cyanotic and unresponsive to their surroundings.'[1266]

Just as my daughter was, in matter of fact.

After bupivacaine, alertness and visual acuity in the infant is impaired throughout the first day of life and the following six weeks[1267] – again, just like my daughter. I remember wondering why her eyes lacked the brightness and expressiveness of the newborns in the natural birth books I had studied, and noting that she always looked glazed.

A cold drink or even the briefest swim in cold water still turns Bethesda's lips dark blue. I still experience peripheral panic every time it happens, unable to bear the thought that I have, through my own susceptibility to an ancient ideology, permanently hurt my child. It's difficult to even consider it: *my baby, my baby*. Cyanosis is caused by low blood oxygen (poor circulation). The potential ramifications of this debility, caused by my own choices, fill me with anguish, guilt, shame, rage and an impotence that I am still at a loss to metabolise, because it is, of course, the byproduct of a damaged heart.

Out of fear, I elected to have my spine injected with 10ml of a diluted known cardiotoxin that, like 'almost all' anaesthetic drugs, 'easily' crosses the placenta.[1268]

Out of fear, I elected to risk my newborn being born blue, and unbreathing.

Out of fear, I permanently damaged my daughter's heart.

This, as Bethesda's records state, is what is now understood as a 'normal' vaginal delivery. In short, it's now 'normal' for a mother to choose to permanently injure her baby.

At some point during the following weeks Bethesda's heart began to hammer so violently that I thought it would burst from her little chest. Terrified, I held her close to my breasts because I didn't know what else to do. I don't know what I would have done had I lost her. In the wake of my brother's suicide, I know one thing: I would not have survived.

I should have sued the living shit out of that anaesthetist.

In the First World, obstetric drugs are now widely – and seemingly exclusively – addressed within the context of the mother's choice, rather than as Ground Zero for neurodevelopmental and other dysfunction. As the influential, award-winning American professor of obstetrics Howard Minkoff wrote, in relation to the administration of obstetric anaesthesia, 'the choices made by mothers are almost always in the interests of the foetus.'[1269]

But I was not Maier's mother. I was the witch in *Snow White* and this was the apple I gave my daughter. This is the apple most mothers have offered their babies for almost two centuries.

22. RETURN TO THE GARDEN

> 'Art is the child of nature in whom we trace
> the features of the mother's face.'
> Henry Wadsworth Longfellow

The drugs associated with chemsex and clubbing – fentanyl, ketamine, and so on – are those injected into labouring mothers. Billions of human beings have, for decades, mated under the influence of the same drugs – or drugs which trigger similar effects to those – that are or were indirectly administered to them through their mothers, grandmothers, great-grandmothers and great-great-grandmothers, and in environments reminiscent of hospitalised births.

Nightclubs, for example, which feature the amplified musical repetition of the same words – trance is known for this – like the grunted sounds and words of a woman giving birth; the booming, driving, repetitive rhythms characteristic of a drugged maternal heart; the same confusion, hallucinatory auditory and lighting effects; and the same chemical intoxication known to the foetus and newborn during a routine delivery.

Hospital births, music festivals, nightclubs and rock concerts also share, among these other features, the same lack of intimacy, sensory overload, and obscuring or overriding of identity.

Human mating rituals are now, for the most part, at odds with the natural, unhurried rhythms and tender intimacies that characterise an untroubled birth.

Sex, then, is our means of revisiting our experience of birth.

On a nondeclarative level, we 'return' to source through sex in order to comfort and restore ourselves, to edit a narrative that may no longer make sense, to regulate ourselves emotionally, to spiritually 'reboot', and to reconnect with love, even if we only ever knew that love through blood pressure, heartbeat and tissue.

When the patriarchal, male or female, speak of 'wanting a fuck', what they are saying is that they are in need of comforting, regulation, and attachment, in however cursory or symbolic a form, as the intense stress of denying their mammalian humanity is beginning to destabilise them. This is why Leary and his cohorts advocated 'free love', and why soldiers – those of notably brutal regimes in particular – set up rape camps: through sex, however cruel or violent, they regulate themselves emotionally to a degree within the narrow parameters of the only gender model they are permitted.

In the same spirit, when British musician Kate Bush sang of leaving the 'party' (adulthood) to go 'under the ivy' (ivy being a symbol for pubic hair) and 'under the leaves' (leaves representing labia) to return to the 'garden' (mother), she was not singing of sex, as she has said she was, but about returning to the matrix of her consciousness: away from the celebration, beneath the ivy in the garden.[1270]

It's only by returning to an environment – or feeling – similar to that which we experienced at birth that we are able to 'reorient' ourselves emotionally.

The incorporation of celibacy in religions such as Catholicism can thus be said to be a means of destabilising followers, who must, in order to establish obedience, be deprived access to all other sources of comfort. Every embracing, emotional, and sensual – that is, nondeclarative – expression of attachment to the feminine must be overwritten by the declarative, divisive strictures of the great patriarchal ideologies, most of which are justified through inarguable and intricately imagineered alignments with divinity.

This is why evangelical Christians must insist on Creation – that myth of humanity springing, fully formed, from God-the-Father – just as millennia ago, Athena/Minerva was believed by the Greeks and Romans to have sprung, fully-formed, from the brow of her father, Zeus/Jupiter. In both patriarchal mythologies, the masculine is imbued with the powers by which femininity is defined: those of reproduction. As 1 Corinthians 11:8 instructs,

For man did not come from woman, but woman from man.

The ultimate authority of the universe, that of creation, has, for most of history, been hijacked by the masculine from the feminine in the same way that in the 20th century, Jewish property was appropriated by the Nazis: without apology, consent, or reparation.

This *coup d'état*, however, was insufficient. The feminine was redefined as a subsidiary of the masculine, designated as the wellspring of masculine pleasure and succour – a *resource*. Nietzsche was unambiguous: 'Man shall be trained for war, and woman for the recreation of the warrior: all else is folly... A plaything let woman be.'[1271]

Throughout the past 100 or so years in particular, the feminine has been the primary source of pleasure for the masculine – this is, of course, the basis of pornography – which is why Freud understood what he called the 'pleasure principle' as dominant and responsible for drawing up the 'programme of life's purpose.' The drive for pleasure, he believed, is 'in conflict with the whole world' as 'the whole constitution of things runs counter to it'. Happiness, he continued, is narrow, 'by its very nature' transitory.[1272]

Freud also asserted that sexual desire is driven by the urge for pleasure, which leads to happiness, however brief: 'What we call happiness in the strictest sense comes from the (preferably sudden) satisfaction of needs which have been dammed up to a high degree, and it is from its nature only possible as an episodic phenomenon. When any situation that is desired by the pleasure principle is prolonged, it only produces a feeling of mild contentment. We are so made that we can derive intense enjoyment only from a contrast.'[1273]

In essence, Freud defined happiness and pleasure as *relief* – a release from pressure – not understanding that the 'satisfaction of needs' to which he referred related to the *acknowledgment of the mammalian, or nondeclarative, self*, which, in a patriarchal culture, can only ever be 'brief'. Happiness, to Freud, was thus a byproduct of misery rather than a feeling in itself – in effect, he believed a degree of misery to be the point of departure or human condition.

But what if genuine happiness is complete unto itself? What if all pleasure – what if happiness in general – is the result of *integration*, that junction at which design and function are aligned?

What if all human misery derives from the misalignment of form and function?

Disability, for example, is strongly associated with depression.[1274] [1275,1276] The greater the intellectual disability, the more pronounced the depression.[1277] Anxiety and depression are also common consequences of caring for a disabled child,[1278] and, among the disabled elderly, the prevalence of depression is twice that of their able peers: 26–44 percent.[1279]

At the core of this depression, the disjunction of form and function.

The human body is designed to work in a certain way: brains calculate, eyes see, legs walk. When function diverges from form – when, say, a leg that is designed to walk cannot walk – the result is depression and frustration, unhappiness. In itself, this reveals that the entire forward momentum of humanity is not driven by Freud's 'pleasure principle', but *the principle of integration*: the intersection of design and function.

Eunice Shriver, in setting up the Special Olympics out of love for her lobotomised sister Rosemary, was unsurpassably humane in her adaptation of this principle. She amended the concept of function to incorporate disability, in the process expanding our understanding of what it is to be human (pleasingly, some paralympians are now outperforming able-bodied peers).[1280] Through her 'primitive' love for her sister, Shriver changed the world.

Design dictates purpose and fulfillment of that purpose justifies design, creating a sense of being apt, of belonging, of being *part* of the world: and this is happiness.

Being fully human is the greatest of vocations.

The rewards of this design-fulfillment are nondeclarative, and come in endocrinological envelopes: dopamine, endorphins, oxytocin, serotonin.[1281] Natural, sustained, uncomplicated pleasure is the indicator light flashing that we have *fulfilled our design*, not a drive but a *signal* confirming the correctness of our direction.

For example, the joy experienced in loving a baby tells us that we are correct in loving little children, for it is in loving little children that we heal the world, and the deep satisfaction in using our talents, whatever they may be, to help others serves the same purpose. Contextual pleasure – that is, as part of a continuum rather than discrete or artificially induced – acts as our compass throughout life.

This is why punishment must, by definition, involve denial of design-fulfillment. Imprisonment is a punishment only because it restricts *function*: the leg cannot freely walk, the eye cannot freely see. In *The Handmaid's Tale*, fertile women in an Abrahamic dystopia are enslaved as sexual 'handmaids' by infertile wives; if these handmaids in any way rebel, their eyes or hands are removed (rebellious pregnant handmaids are merely chained to a bed under permanent supervision). Punishment is defined by *the imposition of parameters on human expression*, whereas freedom, as we understand it, entails the fulfilment of our design.

The narrowing of the human behavioural prescription is thus essential to the patriarchal as it justifies the brutality that acts as a pressure valve to those denied design-fulfilment. It is through such restrictions that the patriarchal divide and conquer, and feel righteous in punishing the very dysfunction they create. As Nietzsche understood, there can be no hero without a foe. For example, the governments who, through their economic emphasis and the laws that enshrine it, encourage obstetric abuse are also the same bodies who criminalise the behavioural dysfunction that the obstetric abuse creates. And, given that obstetric drugs permanently limit maternal and infant function, they are, perhaps, the ultimate in patriarchal punishments: the death of love.

As Michael Dransfield wrote,

> '*something is wrong which must be sensed
> rather than observed.*'[1282]

The human body's form and responses are instructions, not impediments. We need to learn to listen to its instructions, not muffle or silence them with drugs.

No child should feel as unloved as I felt by my mother. No mother should be so mistreated that she cannot love her own child.

My father, too, was unloved by his mother, a legacy that ultimately resulted in my sexual abuse and then my brother's death.

Clearly, our understanding of birth – of the entire obstetric industry – needs to be revolutionised. The design of maternity wards must change, as must the way they are run. NICUs in particular need to start working with mothers, infusing humidicribs with maternal odours, enabling constant maternal touch, and ensuring the intense involvement of mothers and fathers in the care of their babies.

Mothers are the authors of birth and of their children, not obstetrical subsidiaries.

For almost two centuries, psychoactive drugs have been our primary tool of detachment. Drugged at birth, we learn to drug ourselves and others. Abused at birth, we learn to abuse ourselves and others. Born to abused mothers, we learn to abuse the feminine. Isolated at birth, we fail to develop the skills of intimacy. Modern obstetric practices have taught us that to be human is to be abused, abusive, drugged and separate.

The routine administration of drugs to labouring and pregnant women cannot continue.

Routine obstetric anaesthesia should be banned internationally. Instead, families need to be taught, long before any birth, how to manage the mother's fear – of pain, of suffering, of change – not merely on a biological level, but on an emotional level. The terror of losing control, of being 'primitive', of losing gender status, must be addressed, both on a personal and cultural level. Mothers need to be held, physically and psychologically, in preparation for birth. They need to be encouraged to express their fears of vulnerability and made to feel safe. The hiring of a doula – or even finding online doula accounts on social media – should be encouraged. Information is key.

All parents need to be comprehensively educated about the long-term dangers of bottle-feeding and other aspects of birth and infant care. They also need to be supplied with accessibly written information about behaviours that impair not only their baby's optimal neurodevelopment, but their own capacities for contentment. All children must be comprehensively educated about birth, childcare, intimacy skills and neurodevelopment in high school. Boys in particular must be nurtured and supported in order to erode a socially destructive behavioural template that was set thousands of years ago.

Over one in 10 babies are born prematurely each year, and the rate is rising. If a mother is emotionally stressed, labour can be prematurely triggered. Preterm birth complications are the leading cause of death for children under five.[1283] Maternal *feeling*, rather than routine biochemical impulses, conducts the hormonal symphony of birth. What this means is that the health of our civilisation pivots on the regulation of maternal emotion.

In its entirety, the way we understand birth must change.

In its entirety, the way we understand mothers and children

must change.

In its entirety, the way we understand men and women must change.

The patriarchal underpinnings of our civilisation must be overturned.

Mothers and babies are the litmus paper of cultural health, which is why infancy and the feminine are the fronts on which this ancient war has been fought. Men have been separated from their women, women have been separated from their babies, babies have been separated from the only sources of love by and for whom they were created, and all have been separated from the fulfillment of their intricate, attachment-based design.

This is how patriarchs divide and conquer.

The reason we have, for centuries, abandoned, drugged, hurt, ignored, isolated, and silenced babies – and the reason we think nothing of delegating their care to strangers – is because they are embodiments of the reviled nondeclarative self. Babies remind us of everything we associate with inferiority: they are emotional, inarticulate, needy, out of control, vulnerable, weak. Little children represent the deepest truths of the nondeclarative heart, and for this reason alone, must by all of us be honoured, loved, and treasured, particularly during birth and infancy.

Babies and newborns in particular, beings whose feelings and sensory perceptions will determine the future cultural capacity for happiness, are to be revered.

There is no man or woman alive whose life has not been distorted by abusive obstetric practices, whether directly or indirectly. The woman raped by a man whose mother never attached to him. The child forced to live in poverty because her father died at 40 of diabetes. The gay man whose promiscuous drug-addicted partner unknowingly infects him with HIV. The woman who wonders why she has never experienced passionate feelings for another. The man who dies prematurely of COPD after a lifelong cannabis addiction.

Or my brother, an infant shoved back into the vagina at birth by a nurse for obstetric convenience, who, under duress as an adult, replicated the pulse-points of his birth experience by pulling a black bag over his head and suffocating himself with helium.[1284]

Generations who have suffered and who continue to suffer, each with its own unique pattern of loss.

In adulthood, the suffering of babies becomes a geophysical force. Close to two centuries of obstetric abuse has manifested as an historically unprecedented manufactured mass that exceeds the total weight of all life on Earth: the depositing of 2,500 gigatonnes of emissions and wastes resulting from compensatory materialism.

Of these outflows and wastes, 28 percent occurred between 2002 and 2015.[1285]

It's no longer enough to deal with symptoms such as anxiety, depression, substance-use disorders or suicide; it's time for us, as a civilisation, to address the cause of our dysfunction and to return to the garden, to Maier's feminine, and to that apple which we have, for over 2,000 years, associated with pain and punishment rather than awe.

If, as a civilisation, we do not change, humanity will be leached from us in increments. Our descendants will not know what it is to be happy, experience ecstasy, or how to soothe themselves and others without substances. A sense of alienation and anxiety will be the norm. They will never know tender erotic passion. Devotion will make no sense to them. They will not understand other creatures as having their own integrity because the very concept of integrity – of wholeness – will be alien. Out of indifference, they will trash the planet. They will die prematurely. Their babies will be understood solely in terms of future economic potential rather than as the living principle of union.

Without a global shift, love, to our descendants, will be a dead language.

It is only the restoration of attachment, reinforced on every level of our culture, to each other and to the planet that determined our design, that we will heal our civilisation. The global burden of disease, of emotional suffering, of pollution – all can be reversed, but only if we prioritise design-fulfilment: the core human need for secure, tender attachment.

The adversarial model of interaction belongs to a world *that no longer exists*.

Our ancient behavioural templates are no longer required. It's time to rewrite the human narrative – to expand and unite, rather than degrade and divide. The creative supremacy of the feminine must not only be recognised, but restored on every level, including the incorporation of the feminine principle into all areas of human existence. To evolve, masculinity must be redefined as expressive and inclusive, able to attach in intimate parity rather than only on the basis of domination – and exploitation – of the vulnerable.

Human beings are webs of information: fragile, interconnected, luminous. We are distinguished by our sensitivity, which is why I know that we can – and will – change.

ACKNOWLEDGMENTS

For their unfailing kindness, generosity and emotional sustenance, I owe an inestimable debt of gratitude to Bethesda's devoted godparents, my friend of almost 40 years Mick Mercer and his wife Lynda Barrett-Mercer, and to Deirdre Henshaw, whose great heart is the shore to which I always return. Bethesda and I would have been lost – and, quite literally, homeless – without all three, and this book would never have existed.

I don't know how to thank Caroline Overington, Steve Romei, and Michelle Gunn, my editors at *The Weekend Australian*, for everything they have done. Thanks must also go to Eleanor Mills and Krissi Murisson, then editor and deputy of *The Sunday Times Magazine*, for encouraging my intentions and my work, to Victoria Harper of *The Telegraph*, and, of course, to Geordie Greig and Oliver Thring of *The Daily Mail*.

Matt Freud, old friend, thank you.

Chris Humphries, my always friend.

Derek Ridgers and darling Quentin Bacon: thank you for your infinite generosity and for your genius.

I am so grateful to Dan Hunnable and to Marty Chandler, who both guided me through the PTSD with which I was diagnosed after years of divorce-related legal discord.

Samuel Winstanley, thank you for carrying all our books – thousands of them – up all those stairs that night when Bethesda and I could literally no longer manage.

My friends of over 35 years, writers Ben Marshall and Mat Snow, and Britpop titan Alan McGee, have always made me laugh and feel loved – no small matter in complex times.

Over 30 years ago, I met a British QC whose friendship I treasure, and he has had my back ever since. My nameless friend, your brilliance, implausible generosity of spirit, pitiless honesty and savage strength kept me kicking against the pricks, and for that, I will always be grateful.

In 2019, I was introduced to Martin 'Youth' Glover of Killing Joke, who inspired me in a way neither of us could ever have predicted.

Infinite thanks must go to Martin Wagner and his wife and fellow director, Maria Pinter, at Pinter & Martin. Your faith in my work changed the entire course of my life.

My deepest debt of gratitude must, however, go to beloved Bethesda, who complained on a near-daily basis of having lost her mother to an impenetrable forest of birth books. When, in a frenzy of excitement, I showed her my discoveries about *2001: A Space Odyssey*, she glanced over and said, 'Yeah, I guess they're kind of similar.'

Finally, to the memory of my other great teachers, Alan Leslie Pilkington and Natalina Mistroni. You remain my guiding stars and I still miss you both, every single day.

Antonella

CREDITS

The reference to Joan Didion on page 97 is an abridged version of a quote from 'Joan Didion: LSD, Coca-Cola and Ice-Cream', my review of her anthology *Let Me Tell You What I Mean*, which was published in *The Weekend Australian* on 2 April 2021.

The reference to Michael Hutchence on page 145 is an abridged version of a paragraph from 'Led by the Nose', my review of Robert Muchembled's *Smells: A Cultural History of Odours in Modern Times*, which was published in The Weekend Australian on 5 September 2020.

The reference to Marion Zilio's work on page 233 is an abridged version of a paragraph from 'Selfie-Image', my review of Marion Zilio's *Face World: The Face in the Twenty-First Century*, which was published in *The Weekend Australian* on 13 June 2020.

Throughout the text, I've quoted from the following songs and works:
'Mother's Day,' by Dorianne Laux, from *The Book of Men*, W.W. Norton, 2011, pp5, quoted with permission; *Reality Isn't What It Used to Be: Theatrical Politics, Ready-to-Wear Religion, Global Myths, Primitive Chic, and Other Wonders of the Postmodern World*, by Walter Truett Anderson, Harper & Row, 1990, pp44; *Global Drug Survey 2020: Psychedelics under supervision*, by Professor Adam R. Winstock, Consultant Psychiatrist and Director GDS (www.globaldrugsurvey.com/gds-2020/gds-2020-psychedelics-under-supervision); *The Collected Poems of W.B. Yeats*, by William Butler Years, Wordsworth Editions, 2000 (originally published in 1920), pp179; *Slouching Towards Bethlehem*, by Joan Didion, Fourth Estate, 2017 (originally published in 1968), pp101; *Leonard Cohen, Untold Stories: The Early Years*, by Michael Posner, Simon and Schuster, 2020, pp392; 'The State of Zombie Literature: An Autopsy,' by Terrence Rafferty, *The New York Times*, 5 August 2011 (www.nytimes.com/2011/08/07/books/review/the-state-of-zombie-literature-an-autopsy.html). Accessed February 27, 2021; *Letters Written by the Earl of Chesterfield to His Son*, J.B. Lippincott and Company, 1872, pp193; *Our Friends in the North*, by Peter Flannery, BBC2, 1996; 'Meghan will have the best birthing team LaLaLand has to offer,' by Celia Walden, *The Telegraph*, February 14, 2021 (www.telegraph.co.uk/royal-family/2021/02/14/meghan-will-have-best-birthing-team-lalaland-has-offer). Accessed February 27, 2021; *Madame Bovary*, by Gustave Flaubert, Penguin, 2003; *Beyond Good and Evil*, by Friedrich Nietzsche, introduction by Christopher Janaway, Capstone, 2020 (originally published in 1886), pp87; *Creation Stories: Riots, Raves and Running a Label*, by Alan McGee, Sidgwick and Jackson, 2013, pp186–187, quoted with permission; *The Truth about Twilight Sleep*, by Hanna Rion, McBride, Nast and Co., 1915,

foreword; *The White Hotel*, by D.M. Thomas, Phoenix, 2012 (originally published in 1981), pp178; *The Diary of Vaslav Nijinsky*, by Waslaw Nijinsky, edited by Romola Nijinsky, University of Illinois Press, 2006 (originally published in 1936); *The Mummy on Screen: Orientalism and Monstrosity in Horror Cinema*, by Basil Glynn, Bloomsbury, 2019, pp6; 'Pygmalion and the Statue,' *Ovid's Metamorphoses – Volume 2*, Cornhill Publishing, 1953, pp474; *Les Misérables*, Victor Hugo, translated by Christine Donougher, Penguin, 2013 (originally published in 1862), pp838; *Ghosts*, by Henrik Ibsen, Nick Hern Books, 2013 (originally staged in 1882); *The Enduring Kiss: Seven Short Lessons on Love*, by Massimo Recalcati, translated by Alice Kilgarriff, Polity Press, 2021, pp74; *Gender, Sex and Subordination in England, 1500 to 1800*, by Anthony Fletcher, Yale University Press, 1999, p61; *Critical Thinking Unleashed*, by Elliot D. Cohen, Rowman & Littlefield, 2009, pp125; *Blue Nights*, by Joan Didion, Fourth Estate, 2011, p107; and *Guarding the Moon: A Mother's First Year*, Francesca Lia Block, HarperCollins, 2008, pp4.

Picture credits:

Page 2: Derek Ridgers; Page 52: Ewbank's/Bournemouth News/Shutterstock; Page 68: FabioConcetta/ Dreamstime.com; Page 85: Alamy Images/Retro AdArchives; Page 90: Alamy Images/ TCD/Prod.DB; Page 94: Dr Alan W Flake/ Children's Hospital of Philadelphia; Page 161: Nasjonalmuseet for kunst, arkitektur og design, The Fine Art Collections/ Høstland, Børre; Page 166 (left) and 186: A psychological study of 'Twilight sleep' made by the Giessen method by Elisabeth Ross Shaw by Van Hoosen, Bertha, 1863/ Bookplateleaf 0003 Call number 006379506/External-identifier:oclc:record:1084956196/MARCXML/Digitizing sponsor Open Knowledge Commons Contributor Francis A. Countway Library of Medicine; Page 167 (right) Universal/Kobal/Shutterstock; Page 175: David Dagley/Shutterstock; Page 186: Dreamtime; Page 197: Shutterstock; Page 213: United States Holocaust Memorial Museum Collection, Gift of Rudy Appel/ Museum/https://collections.ushmm.org/search/catalog/irn482; Page 214: diploma-degree.com; Page 220 (left): Library of Congress, Prints & Photographs Division, [reproduction number, masterpnp-ggbain-01300-01362u]; (right) MGM/Stanley Kubrick Productions/Kobal/Shutter stock; Page 221 (left): Topical Press Agency/Getty Images/ Hulton Archive; (right): MGM/Stanley Kubrick Productions/Kobal/Shutterstock; Page 222 (left): The Society of the Lying-in Hospital of the City of New York annual report 1912/Wellcome Trust Collection; (right): MGM/Stanley Kubrick Productions/Kobal/Shutterstock; Page 223 (left): The Society of the Lying-in Hospital of the City of New York annual report 1912/ Wellcome Trust Collection; (right): Moviestore/Shutterstock; Page 224 (left): unknown; (right) MGM/Stanley Kubrick Productions/Kobal/Shutterstock.

REFERENCES

1   Catalogue description: *Medical Journal of the Mary, Female Convict Ship from 12 April to 3 November 1823*, Reference: ADM 101/51/3 Description: 'Medical journal of the Mary, female convict ship from 12 April to 3 November 1823 by Harman Cochrane, surgeon and superintendent, during which time the said ship was employed on a voyage to Van Dieman's Land and New South Wales', Date: 1823, Held by: The National Archives, Kew. Accessed February 28, 2020.

2   'Daddy,' by Sylvia Plath, *Collected Poems*, HarperCollins, 2008, pp222.

3   *The Letters of Sylvia Plath Volume II: 1953-63*, edited by Peter K. Steinberg and Karen V. Kukil, Faber, 2018.

4   'Sylvia Plath poem written two weeks before she died reveals 'disturbed' state of mind,' by Alice Philipson, *The Telegraph*, April 30, 2013 (www.telegraph.co.uk/culture/books/10028478/Sylvia-Plath-poem-written-two-weeks-before-she-died-reveals-disturbed-state-of-mind.html). Accessed February 28, 2021.

5   'Ted Bundy's lawyer: Bundy killed more than 100 women – and a man,' by Lucinda Beaman, *The Times*, May 25, 2012 (www.thetimes.co.uk/article/ted-bundy-killed-at-least-100-women-and-one-man-6ssqrzmclmg). Accessed February 28, 2021.

6   'The Meaning of Beheading,' by Theodore Dalrymple, *Commentary*, The Manhattan Institute, October 24, 2005 (www.manhattan-institute.org/html/meaning-beheading-2029.html). Accessed February 28, 2021.

7   *The Ancient Celts*, by Barry Cunliffe, Oxford University Press, 2018, pp309.

8   *Rethinking Serial Murder, Spree Killing, and Atrocities: Beyond the Usual Distinctions*, by Robert Shanafelt and Nathan W. Pino, Routledge, 2014, p62.

9   '"Hitchhiker Murderer" who was Never Caught,' by Greg Stolz, *The Courier-Mail*, October 28, 2014 (www.couriermail.com.au/news/special-features/in-depth/hitchhiker-murderer-who-was-never-caught/news-story/1125e21ce121d40b7ed9454d943891ab). Accessed February 28, 2021.

10 'Case 56: Anita Cobby' (www.casefilepodcast.com/case-56-anita-cobby) Accessed on February 9, 2020.

11 '"The most savage, fiendish murder ever known' How the Anita Cobby murder by five petty criminals changed Australia and turned the killers into the nation's most reviled people,' by Candace Sutton, *The Australian*, February 23, 2019 (www.news-mail.com.au/news/the-most-savage-fiendish-murder-ever-known/3655120). Accessed February 28, 2021.

12 'Grimes: Live from the Future,' by Brian Hiatt, *Rolling Stone*, March 5, 2020 (www.rollingstone.com/music/music-features/grimes-rolling-stone-digital-cover-960843). Accessed March 5, 2020.

13 *Bit of A Blur: The Autobiography*, by Alex James, Little Brown, 2007, pp227–228.

14 *Fleabag: The Scriptures*, by Phoebe Waller Bridge, Ballantine, 2019, pp8–9.

15 'Nick Cave says he wouldn't have survived heroin addiction without Narcotics Anonymous: 'Go to a fucking meeting,'' by Nick Reilly, *NME*, October 15, 2020 (www.nme.com/news/music/nick-cave-says-he-wouldnt-have-survived-heroin-addiction-without-narcotics-anonymous-go-to-a-fucking-meeting-2785978). Accessed February 12, 2021.

16 *The Nick Cave Interview (Excerpts from Lunch of Blood – Book 1)*, by Antonella Gambotto-Burke, Broken Ankle Digital, 2014.

17 'Nick Cave's Son Arthur Took LSD before Cliff Fall, Inquest Told,' *BBC News*, November 10, 2015 (www.bbc.co.uk/news/uk-england-sussex-34779370). Accessed February 12, 2021.

18 '"Nick Cave announces death of son, Jethro, aged 30," by Mark Savage, BBC News, May 5, 2022 (www.bbc.co.uk/news/entertainment-arts-61383411). Accessed May 5, 2022.

19 'The Monarch of Middlebrow,' by Anwen Crawford, *Overland*, 197, Summer 2009 (overland.org.au/previous-issues/issue-197/feature-anwyn-crawford/). Accessed May 11, 2020.

20 'Bad Seed Rising,' by Bill Black, *Sounds*, May 25, 1985, pp14.

21 'Cave Man Boogie,' by Mick Mercer, Letters, *Sounds*, June 8, 1985, pp24.

22 Reply to 'Cave Man Boogie,' Letters, *Sounds*, June 8, 1985, pp24.

23 'Scum,' *King Ink*, by Nick Cave, Black Spring Press, 1988, inside cover.

24 *Bad Seed: The Biography of Nick Cave*, by Ian Johnston, Little Brown, 2014, pp168, 196.

25 'Halcion Sleeping Pill Banned by Britain; Risks Seen,' by William Tuohy and Marlene Cimons,

The Los Angeles Times, October 3, 1991 (www.latimes.com/archives/la-xpm-1991-10-03-mn-4409-story.html). Accessed February 12, 2021.

26 *Darkness Visible: A Memoir of Madness*, by William Styron, Vintage, 1992 (first published 1990), pp49, 46.

27 *The Handmaid's Tale*, by Margaret Atwood, Vintage, 1996 (originally published in 1985), pp132.

28 *Stairway to Heaven*, by Led Zeppelin (words and music by Jimmy Page and Robert Plant, Island/Atlantic, 1971)

29 'An Advert Won't Stop My Middle-Class Friends from Taking Cocaine,' by Anonymous, *The Times*, March 4, 2021 (www.thetimes.co.uk/article/an-advert-wont-stop-my-middle-class-friends-from-taking-cocaine-g3x6spjsf). Accessed March 5, 2021.

30 'Over 30 Million Psychedelic Users in the United States,' by Teri S. Krebs and Pål-Ørjan Johansen, *F1000Research*, 2(98), March 2013, doi:10.12688/f1000research.2-98.v1.

31 *Psychedelic Drugs Market, By Drugs (LSD, Ecstasy, Phencyclidine, GHB, Ketamine, Ayahuasca, Psilocybin), Route of Administration (Oral, Injectable, Inhalation), Distribution Channel, End-Users, Application and Geography - Global Forecast to 2026*, Research and Markets, December 2020 (www.researchandmarkets.com/reports/5240207/psychedelic-drugs-market-by-drugs-lsd-ecstasy). Accessed March 20, 2021.

32 'First-of-Its Kind Psychedelic Research Centre Debuts at Johns Hopkins,' Brainwise Physician Update, Winter 2020 (www.hopkinsmedicine.org/news/articles/first-of-its-kind-psychedelic-research-center-debuts-at-johns-hopkins). Accessed March 20, 2021.

33 'Imperial Launches World's First Centre for Psychedelics Research,' by Ryan O'Hare, *Imperial College News*, April 26, 2019 (www.imperial.ac.uk/news/190994/imperial-launches-worlds-first-centre-psychedelics). Accessed March 20, 2021.

34 Imperial College of London Centre for Psychedelic Research, 2021 (www.imperial.ac.uk/psychedelic-research-centre). Accessed March 20, 2021.

35 'Global Drug Survey 2020,' by A.R. Winstock, C. Timmerman, E. Davies, L.J. Maier, A. Zhuparris, J.A. Ferris, M.J. Barratt, and K.P.C. Kuypers, *Global Drug Survey 2020 Psychedelics Key Findings Report* (www.globaldrugsurvey.com/wp-content/uploads/2021/03/GDS2020-Psychedelics-report.pdf). Accessed March 6, 2021.

36 'Psychedelics and Personality,' by Marc Aixalà, Rafael G. dos Santos, Jaime E.C. Hallak, and José Carlos Bouso, *ACS Chemical Neuroscience*, 9(10), June 2018, pp2304–2306.

37 'Global Drug Survey 2020,' by A.R. Winstock, C. Timmerman, E. Davies, L.J. Maier, A. Zhuparris, J.A. Ferris, M.J. Barratt, and K.P.C. Kuypers, *Global Drug Survey 2020 Psychedelics Key Findings Report* (www.globaldrugsurvey.com/wp-content/uploads/2021/03/GDS2020-Psychedelics-report.pdf). Accessed March 6, 2021.

38 'An Advert Won't Stop My Middle-Class Friends from Taking Cocaine,' by Anonymous, *The Times*, March 4, 2021 (www.thetimes.co.uk/article/an-advert-wont-stop-my-middle-class-friends-from-taking-cocaine-g3x6spjsf). Accessed March 6, 2021.

39 'Changes in Dispositional Empathy in American College Students Over Time: A Meta-Analysis,' by Sara H. Konrath, Edward H. O'Brien, and Courtney Hsing, *Personality and Social Psychology Review*, 15(2), April 2011, pp180 – 198.

40 *The Narcissism Epidemic: Living in the Age of Entitlement*, by Jean M. Twenge and W. Keith Campbell, Atria, 2009.

41 'Compassion Fade: Affect and Charity Are Greatest for a Single Child in Need,' by Daniel Västfjäll, Paul Slovic, Marcus Mayorga, and Ellen Peters, *PLoS ONE*, June 2014 (doi.org/10.1371/journal.pone.0100115). Accessed March 8, 2021.

42 'Multiple Sexual Partnerships and Associated Factors among Young Psychoactive-Substance-Users in Informal Settlements in Kampala, Uganda,' by Tonny Ssekamatte, M. Tetui, S.P. Kibira, J.B. Isunju, Richard Mugambe, E. Nabiwemba, Solomon Tsebeni Wafula, E. Buregyeya, and J. Bukenya, *PLoS ONE*, 15(10), October 2020, p.e0239323.

43 'Predictors and Consequences of Sexual 'Hookups' Among College Students: A Short-Term Prospective Study,' by Robyn L. Fielder and Michael P. Carey, *Archives of Sexual Behaviour*, 39, October 2010, pp1105–1119.

44 'The Relationship Between Multiple Sex Partners and Anxiety, Depression, and Substance Dependence Disorders: A Cohort Study,' by Sandhya Ramrakha, Charlotte Paul, Melanie L. Bell, Nigel Dickson, Terrie E. Moffitt, and Avshalom Caspi, *Archives of Sexual Behaviour*, 42(5), July 2013, pp863–872.

45 'Predictors and Consequences of Sexual 'Hookups' Among College Students: A Short-Term Prospective Study,' by Robyn L. Fielder and Michael P. Carey, *Archives of Sexual Behaviour*, 39, October 2010, pp1105–1119.

46 'Sexual Uses of Alcohol and Drugs and the Associated Health Risks: A Cross-Sectional Study of Young People in Nine European Cities,' by Mark A. Bellis, Karen Hughes, Amador Calafat, Montse Juan, Anna Ramon, José A. Rodriguez, Fernando Mendes, Susanne Schnitzer, and Penny Phillips-Howard, *BMC Public Health*, 8(155), May 2008, pp155.

47 'Do What U Want', by Lady Gaga (words and music by Stefani Germanotta, William Grigahcine, Etienne Sami, Steve Guess, Robert Kelly, and Paul Blair, copyright 2013 Universal Music – Z Songs, Universal Music Corporation, BMG Gold Songs, Get Familiar Music Llc, Etrange Fruit, Maxwell And Carter Publishing, PW Arrangements, Maxwell And Carter Publishing Llc., Grigahcine).

48 'Die Antwoord get down and dirty on new song "Bum Bum",' by Selim Bulut, *Dazed*, May 17, 2016 (www.dazeddigital.com/music/article/31150/1/die-antwoord-get-down-and-dirty-on-new-song-bum-bum). Accessed April 7, 2021.

49 'Bum Bum', by Die Antwoord (words and music Anri du Toit, Justin Jose De Nobrega, and Watkin Tudor Jones, copyright 2016 Kobalt Music Publishing Ltd.).

50 Telephone interview with Mark Bittlestone, June 10, 2021.

51 'Depression: Fact Sheet,' World Health Organization, January 2020 (www.who.int/newsroom/fact-sheets/detail/depression). Accessed March 7, 2021.

52 *Timothy Leary (1920-1996): The Effects of Psychotropic Drugs*, Department of Psychology, Harvard University, 2020 (psychology.fas.harvard.edu/people/timothy-leary). Accessed June 10, 2020.

53 *The Politics of Ecstasy*, by Timothy Leary, Ronin Publishing, 1980, pp38–39.

54 *The Politics of Ecstasy*, by Timothy Leary, Ronin Publishing, 1980, pp38–39.

55 'Acid Redux: The Life and High Times of Timothy Leary,' by Louis Menand, *The New Yorker*, June 19, 2006 (www.newyorker.com/magazine/2006/06/26/acid-redux). Accessed April 20, 2020.

56 'Timothy Leary: The Playboy Interview (Singles Classic) (50 Years of the Playboy Interview)', *Playboy*, 2012.

57 'The Science of the Psychedelic Renaissance,' by Emily Witt, *The New Yorker*, May 29, 2018 (www.newyorker.com/books/under-review/the-science-of-the-psychedelic-renaissance). Accessed April 19, 2020.

58 'Allen Ginsberg Remembers Mama,' by Elenore Lester, *The New York Times*, February 6, 1972, pp180–184.

59 'The Dreams of Allen Ginsberg,' by Mark Ford, *New York Review of Books*, September 27, 2007.

60 'The Scary Days when Thousands were Lobotomized on Long Island,' by Ward Harkavy, *Village Voice*, October 26, 1999 (www.villagevoice.com/1999/10/26/the-scary-days-when-thousands-were-lobotomized-on-long-island). Accessed April 19, 2020.

61 *The Essential Ginsberg* (Penguin Modern Classics), by Allen Ginsberg, edited by Michael Schumacher, Penguin (Kindle Edition), 2015.

62 'Ginsberg in Hospital,' by Janet Hadda, *American Imago*, 65(2), Summer 2008, pp229–259.

63 *Aldous Huxley: An English Intellectual*, by Nicholas Murray, Abacus, 2003, pp14–21, 30–31.

64 *The Doors of Perception: And Heaven and Hell*, by Aldous Huxley, Vintage Classics, 2004 (first published in 1954), pp19.

65 *The Doors of Perception: And Heaven and Hell*, by Aldous Huxley, Vintage Classics, 2004 (first published in 1954), pp3.

66 *Aldous Huxley: An English Intellectual*, by Nicholas Murray, Abacus, 2003, pp16.

67 *The Burning Wheel*, by Aldous Huxley, B.H. Blackwell, 1916.

68 *When The Going Gets Weird: The Twisted Life and Times of Hunter S. Thompson*, by Peter O. Whitmer, Hyperion, 1993, pp5.

69 *Fear and Loathing at Rolling Stone*, by Hunter S. Thompson, Penguin Modern Classics, pp90, 316, 365.

70 *Fear and Loathing at Rolling Stone*, by Hunter S. Thompson, Penguin Modern Classics, pp492.

71 *When The Going Gets Weird: The Twisted Life and Times of Hunter S. Thompson*, by Peter O. Whitmer, Hyperion, 1993, pp38.

72 *When The Going Gets Weird: The Twisted Life and Times of Hunter S. Thompson*, by Peter O. Whitmer, Hyperion, 1993, pp41.

73   *When The Going Gets Weird: The Twisted Life and Times of Hunter S. Thompson*, by Peter O. Whitmer, Hyperion, 1993, pp216.

74   Foreword by Tom Robbins, *The Politics of Ecstasy*, by Timothy Leary, Ronin Publishing, 1980, pp1.

75   *The Politics of Ecstasy*, by Timothy Leary, Ronin Publishing, 1980, pp5.

76   *How Was It For You? Women, Sex, Love and Power in the 1960s*, by Virginia Nicholson, Viking, 2019, pp217.

77   *High Priest*, by Timothy Leary, Ronin, 1968, pp301.

78   *The Delicious Grace of Moving One's Hand*, by Timothy Leary, Thunder's Mouth Press, 1998, pp119.

79   *Timothy Leary: The Playboy Interview (Singles Classic) (50 Years of the Playboy Interview)*, Playboy, 2012.

80   *The Delicious Grace of Moving One's Hand*, by Timothy Leary, Thunder's Mouth Press, 1998, pp29.

81   *Timothy Leary: A Biography*, by Robert Greenfield, Harcourt, 2006, pp9–13.

82   *The Delicious Grace of Moving One's Hand*, by Timothy Leary, Thunder's Mouth Press, 1998, pp29.

83   *Timothy Leary: A Biography*, by Robert Greenfield, Harcourt, 2006, pp11.

84   *Timothy Leary: A Biography*, by Robert Greenfield, Harcourt, 2006, pp133.

85   *High Priest*, by Timothy Leary, Ronin, 1968, pv.

86   *Flashbacks*, by Timothy Leary, G.P. Putnam's Sons, 1983, pp207.

87   *Flashbacks*, by Timothy Leary, G.P. Putnam's Sons, 1983, pp83.

88   *Flashbacks*, by Timothy Leary, G.P. Putnam's Sons, 1983, pp110.

89   *Timothy Leary: A Biography*, by Robert Greenfield, Harcourt, 2006, pp13.

90   *Flashbacks*, by Timothy Leary, G.P. Putnam's Sons, 1983, pp145.

91   *Flashbacks*, by Timothy Leary, G.P. Putnam's Sons, 1983, pp229.

92   *Flashbacks*, by Timothy Leary, G.P. Putnam's Sons, 1983, pp9.

93   *Flashbacks*, by Timothy Leary, G.P. Putnam's Sons, 1983, pp11.

94   *The Delicious Grace of Moving One's Hand*, by Timothy Leary, Thunder's Mouth Press, 1998, pp120–121, 144.

95   *Flashbacks*, by Timothy Leary, G.P. Putnam's Sons, 1983, pp177.

96   *Timothy Leary: A Biography*, by Robert Greenfield, Harcourt, 2006, pp96.

97   *Timothy Leary: A Biography*, by Robert Greenfield, Harcourt, 2006, pp232.

98   *Flashbacks*, by Timothy Leary, G.P. Putnam's Sons, 1983, pp223.

99   *Hashish Smuggling and Passport Fraud: 'the Brotherhood of Eternal Love'*, Hearing Before the Subcommittee to Investigative the Administration of the Internal Security Act and Other Internal Security Laws of the Committee on the Judiciary United States Senate, Ninety-Third Congress, First Session, October 3, 1973, US Government Printing Office, Washington, pp48.

100 'Higher Than the Sun,' by Primal Scream (words and music by Bobby Gillespie, Colin Andrew Innes and Robert Clearie Young, © Complete Music Ltd, 1991).

101 *The Delicious Grace of Moving One's Hand*, by Timothy Leary, Thunder's Mouth Press, 1998, pp212.

102 *Nobody Loves You 'til Somebody Loves You – The Timothy Leary Wedding – Featuring Monti Rock III*, Youtube, footage by cinematographer Nicholas Proferes for D.A. Pennebakker of Timothy Leary's December 1964 wedding to Nena von Schlebrügge, uploaded July 8, 2015 (www.youtube.com/watch?v=f40oDGhESHs). Accessed June 11, 2020.

103 *Alien Chic: Posthumanism and the Other Within*, by Neil Badmington, Routledge, 2004, pp3.

104 *U.S. Public Health Service Syphilis Study at Tuskegee*, Centres for Disease Control and Prevention, March 2, 2020 (www.cdc.gov/tuskegee/timeline.htm). Accessed June 22, 2020.

105 'The Wages of Sin: How the Discovery of Penicillin Reshaped Modern Sexuality,' by Andrew M. Francis, *Archives of Sexual Behaviour*, 42, October 5, 2012, pp5–13.

106 'Hugh Hefner Sells LA property as Financial Crisis hits Playboy,' *The Telegraph*, August 11, 2009 (www.telegraph.co.uk/finance/recession/6007514/Hugh-Hefner-sells-LA-property-as-financial-crisis-hits-Playboy.html). Accessed June 22, 2020.

107 'What has America been Singing About? Trends in Themes in the U.S. Top-40 Songs: 1960–2010,' by Peter G. Christenson, Silvia de Haan-Rietdijk, Donald F. Roberts, and Tom

F.M. ter Bogt, *The Psychology of Music*, 47(2), January 23, 2018.

108 'History of the Discovery and Clinical Introduction of Chlorpromazine,' by Francisco López-Muñoz, Cecilio Alamo, Eduardo Cuenca, Winston W. Shen, Patrick Clervoy, and Gabriel Rubio, *Annals of Clinical Psychiatry*, July– September 2005, 17(3), pp113–135.

109 'Katharine Dexter McCormick (1875–1967),' *American Experience*, PBS, WGBH Educational Foundation, 2020 (www.pbs.org/wgbh/americanexperience/features/pill-katharine-dexter-mccormick-1875-1967). Accessed August 8, 2020.

110 'Enovid: The First Hormonal Birth Control Pill,' *The Embryo Project Encyclopaedia*, January 20, 2009 (embryo.asu.edu/pages/enovid-first-hormonal-birth-control-pill). Accessed June 22, 2020.

111 'Oral Contraceptive Pill: the Birth Control Pill was the First Medication Approved for Long-Term Use by Healthy People and the First 99% Effective Way to Prevent Conception,' Case Western Reserve University, Cleveland, Ohio, 2010 (case.edu/affil/skuyhistcontraception/online-2012/pill.html). Accessed August 9, 2020.

112 *The Politics of Ecstasy*, by Timothy Leary, Ronin Publishing, 1980, pp135.

113 'Are Amusement Parks Dangerous?' Wilson, Kehoe, Winingham Law, 2021 (www.wkw.com/premises-liability/faqs/are-amusement-parks-dangerous). Accessed March 20, 2021.

114 *The Politics of Ecstasy*, by Timothy Leary, Ronin, 1980, pp131.

115 *The Psychedelic Experience: A Manual Based on the Tibetan Book of the Dead*, by Timothy Leary, Ralph Metzner and Richard Alpert, Kindle edition, 2021 (first published in 1964).

116 *The Delicious Grace of Moving One's Hand*, by Timothy Leary, Thunder's Mouth Press, 1998, pp31.

117 'Timothy Leary: The Playboy Interview (Singles Classic) (50 Years of the Playboy Interview)', *Playboy*, 2012.

118 'This Will Change Your Mind About Psychedelic Drugs,' by Mandy Oaklander, *Time*, May 16, 2018 (time.com/5278036/michael-pollan-psychedelic-drugs). Accessed March 21, 2021.

119 'Dransfield, Michael John (1948–1973),' by Patricia Dobrez, *Australian Dictionary of Biography*, Vol. 14, Melbourne University Press, 1996 (adb.anu.edu.au/biography/dransfield-michael-john-10049). Accessed June 9, 2020.

120 'Island,' by Michael Dransfield, *Collected Poems*, Australian Poetry Library (www.poetrylibrary.edu.au/poets/dransfield-michael/poems/island-0712126). Accessed March 2, 2021.

121 *Jugband Blues*, by Pink Floyd (words and music by Syd Barrett, EMI/Columbia/Tower, 1968).

122 *Vegetable Man* by Pink Floyd (words and music Syd Barrett, 1967).

123 *Syd Barrett: A Very Irregular Head*, by Rob Chapman, Faber and Faber, 2010, pp343–344.

124 *Syd Barrett: A Very Irregular Head*, by Rob Chapman, Faber and Faber, 2010, pp31.

125 'The Elitist Allure of Joan Didion,' by Meghan Daum, *The Atlantic*, September 2015 (www.theatlantic.com/magazine/archive/2015/09/the-elitist-allure-of-joan-didion/399320). Accessed April 11, 2021.

126 *Syd Barrett: A Very Irregular Head*, by Rob Chapman, Faber and Faber, 2010, pp394.

127 'Can Someone Help Me?' by Irmani, Hallucinogen Persisting Perception Disorder (HPPD) Support Forum, February 17, 2021 (www.hppdonline.com/topic/8746-can-someone-help-me-/?tab=comments#comment-44077). Accessed April 2, 2021.

128 *Owsley and Me: My LSD Family*, by Rhoney Gissen Stanley, Monkfish, 2013, Kindle edition.

129 *The Electric Kool-Aid Acid Test*, by Tom Wolfe, Picador, 2008 (first published in 1968), pp247.

130 'Owsley Stanley: the King of LSD', by Robert Greenfield, *Rolling Stone*, July 12, 2007 (www.rollingstone.com/music/music-news/owsley-stanley-the-king-of-lsd-82181). Accessed August 10, 2020.

131 *Owsley and Me: My LSD Family*, by Rhoney Gissen Stanley, Monkfish, 2013, Kindle edition.

132 *Owsley and Me: My LSD Family*, by Rhoney Gissen Stanley, Monkfish, 2013, Kindle edition.

133 'LSD Psychosis or LSD-Induced Schizophrenia? A Multimethod Inquiry,' by Michael M. Vardy and Stanley R. Kay, *Archives of General Psychiatry*, 40(8), August 1983, pp877–883.

134 *Bear: The Life and Times of Augustus Owsley Stanley III*, by Robert Greenfield, Thomas Dunne Books, 2016, pp15–21.

135 *Hans Bellmer: Photographs*, by Hans Bellmer, Krannert Art Museum, University of Illinois, 1991, pp42.

136 *Second Treatise on Government and A Letter Concerning Toleration*, by John Locke, edited by Mark Goldie, Oxford World's Classics, 2016 (originally published in 1690), pp15.

137 'The Female Body as a Source of Horror and Insight in Post-Ashokan Indian Buddhism,' by Elizabeth Wilson, *Religious Reflections on the Human Body*, edited by Jane Marie Law, Indiana University Press, 1995, pp80.

138 *The Psychedelic Experience: A Manual Based on the Tibetan Book of the Dead*, by Timothy Leary, Ralph Metzner and Richard Alpert, Kindle edition, 2021 (first published in 1964).

139 Telephone interview with Ben Marshall, May 11, 2020.

140 *The Psychedelic Experience: A Manual Based on the Tibetan Book of the Dead*, by Timothy Leary, Ralph Metzner and Richard Alpert, Kindle edition, 2021 (first published in 1964).

141 'The British Women's Liberation Movement in the 1970s: Redefining the Personal and the Political,' by Florence Binard, *Revue Française de Civilisation Britannique*, XXII- Hors série, December 30, 2017.

142 *Spare Rib: Violence against Women*, by Aimee Treasure, The British Library (www.bl.uk/spare-rib/articles/violence-against-women). Accessed June 26, 2020.

143 *Syd Barrett: A Very Irregular Head*, by Rob Chapman, Faber and Faber, 2010, pp275–276.

144 'Under My Thumb,' by the Rolling Stones (words and music by Keith Richards and Mick Jagger, lyrics © Abkco Music Inc., 1966)

145 *He Hit Me (And It Felt like a Kiss)*, by the Crystals (words and music by Gerry Goffin and Carole King, 1962).

146 *Run for Your Life*, by the Beatles (words and music by John Lennon and Paul McCartney, Sony/ATV Music Publishing 1965).

147 *Hey Joe*, by Jimi Hendrix (words and music Public Domain first pressing; Dino Valenti aka Chet Powers second and third pressings; Billy Roberts copyrighted, Polydor 1966).

148 *Soul on Ice*, by Eldridge Cleaver, Delta, 1968, pp28.

149 *Soul on Ice*, by Eldridge Cleaver, Delta, 1968, pp29.

150 'Black and Free,' by Jonathan Steele, *The Guardian*, February 7, 1969, pp7.

151 *The Sixties*, by Jenny Diski, Profile Books, 2010, pp53.

152 *Last Girl Standing*, by Trina Robbins, Fantagraphics, 2017, pp49.

153 *Hippie Chick: Coming of Age in the '60s*, by Ilene English, She Writes Press, 2019, pp63.

154 'Suddenly That Summer,' by Sheila Weller, *Vanity Fair*, July 2012 (www.vanityfair.com/culture/2012/07/lsd-drugs-summer-of-love-sixties). Accessed August 12, 2020.

155 *Timothy Leary, the Madness of the Sixties, and Me*, by Charles W. Slack, Peter H. Wyden, 1974, pp18.

156 'A Robert McGinnis Original Painting of the Poster for You Only Live Twice,' Bonhams, May 14, 2019 (www.bonhams.com/auctions/25491/lot/85). Accessed April 15, 2021.

157 *Parachutes and Kisses*, by Erica Jong, Penguin, 2006 (first published in 1984), pp94.

158 *Fear of Flying*, by Erica Jong, Vintage, 1994 (first published in 1973), pp11–12.

159 *The Psychedelic Sixties: A Social History of the United States, 1960–1969*, by Richard T. Stanley, iUniverse, 2013, pp110.

160 *Slouching Towards Bethlehem*, by Joan Didion, Fourth Estate, 2017 (first published in 1968), pp101.

161 *The Gates of Janus: Serial Killing and its Analysis by the Moors Murderer Ian Brady*, by Ian Brady, Feral House, 2015, pp309.

162 *The Long, Hard Road out of Hell*, by Marilyn Manson with Neil Strauss, Plexus, 2009 (first published in 1998), pp229–232.

163 'Wild Sex, Drugs, and 'Naked Girls': Insider Blows Lid on VIP Parties,' by Antonella Gambot-to-Burke, *The Weekend Australian*, October 9, 2020 (www.theaustralian.com.au/arts/review/wild-sex-drugs-and-naked-girls-insider-blows-lid-on-vip-parties/news-story/168e60eb2ed4c-6035cd2e66187e99fb0). Accessed February 28, 2021.

164 Telephone interview with award-winning producer who wished to remain anonymous, October 31, 2020.

165 'Sexual Harassment and Violence at Australian Music Festivals: Reporting Practices and Experiences of Festival Attendees,' by Bianca Fileborn, Phillip Wadds, and Stephen Tomsen, *Journal of Criminology*, 53(2), February 2020, pp194– 212.

166 'Hiding in Plain Sight,' *Camille*, by Scarlett Sabet, 2019.

167 'The 10 Wildest Led Zeppelin Legends, Fact-Checked: Jimmy Page Dated a 14-year-old Girl While He Was in Led Zeppelin,' By Andy Greene, *Rolling Stone*, October 16, 2019 (www.rollingstone.com/music/music-lists/the-10-wildest-led-zeppelin-legends-fact-checked-153103

). Accessed September 12, 2020.

168 *When Giants Walked the Earth: 50 years of Led Zeppelin*, by Mick Wall, Orion, 2008, pp181.

169 'Jimmy Page: The Rolling Stone Interview,' by David Fricke, *Rolling Stone*, December 6, 2012 (www.rollingstone.com/feature/jimmy-page-the-rolling-stone-interview-101221/). Accessed September 12, 2020.

170 'The Effects of Δ9-Tetrahydrocannabinol on the Dopamine System,' by Michael A. P. Bloomfield, Abhishekh H. Ashok, Nora D. Volkow, and Oliver D Howes, *Nature*, 539(7629), November 17, 2016, pp369–377.

171 'How to Bio-Hack Your Brain to Have Sex without Getting Emotionally Attached,' by Sirin Kale, *Vice*, August 25, 2016 (www.vice.com/en/article/59mmzq/how-to-bio-hack-your-brain-to-have-sex-without-getting-emotionally-attached). Accessed December 15, 2020.

172 *Timothy Leary, the Madness of the Sixties, and Me*, by Charles W. Slack, Peter H. Wyden, 1974, pp20.

173 'Women and Drugs: Drug Use, Drug Supply and Their Consequences – World Drug Report 2018', United Nations Office on Drugs and Crime (www.unodc.org/wdr2018/prelaunch/WDR18_Booklet_5_WOMEN.pdf). Accessed July 4, 2020.

174 Madonna Instagram, April 24, 2021 (www.instagram.com/p/COEMFHXheSx). Accessed April 25, 2021.

175 'Madonna reveals she quit drugs for good because they used to "destroy" her for "days and days",' by Rebecca Pocklington, *The Mirror*, January 28, 2015 (www.mirror.co.uk/3am/celebrity-news/madonna-reveals-quit-drugs-good-5060060). Accessed April 25, 2021.

176 "She'd turned her life around': The tragedy and torment of Paula Yates who could have been saved before fatal heroin overdose,' by Grant Rollings and Chris White, *The Sun*, September 16, 2020 (www.thesun.co.uk/tvandshowbiz/12689966/paula-yates-overdose-accident). Accessed April 25, 2021.

177 'Sex, drugs and rock'n'roll stars: the lethal cocktail that ended in tragedy,' by Vikram Dodd, *The Guardian*, September 18, 2000 (www.theguardian.com/media/2000/sep/18/broadcasting.uknews2). Accessed April 25, 2021.

178 'TV star killed by heroin 'binge',' by Tania Branigan, *The Guardian*, November 9, 2000 (www.theguardian.com/uk/2000/nov/09/drugsandalcohol.taniabranigan). Accessed April 25, 2021.

179 'Peaches Geldof: Writer and TV presenter dies aged 25,' *BBC News*, April 2014 (www.bbc.co.uk/news/uk-26931337). Accessed April 25, 2021.

180 'STR8 PPL R THE CUTEST,' Mark Bittlestone, July 6, 2021 (www.instagram.com/p/CQ_XYHQi5r-). Accessed July 6, 2021.

181 *A History of My Brief Body*, by Billy-Rae Belcourt, University of Queensland Press, 2021, pp61.

182 *A History of My Brief Body*, by Billy-Rae Belcourt, University of Queensland Press, 2021, pp92.

183 *A History of My Brief Body*, by Billy-Rae Belcourt, University of Queensland Press, 2021, pp34.

184 *A History of My Brief Body*, by Billy-Rae Belcourt, University of Queensland Press, 2021, pp75.

185 'I Think I'm Finally over Meaningless Sex,' by Annie Lord, *Vogue*, September 11, 2020 (www.vogue.co.uk/arts-and-lifestyle/article/meaningless-sex). Accessed March 24, 2021.

186 *Drug-facilitated, Incapacitated, and Forcible Rape: A National Study*, by Dean G. Kilpatrick, Heidi S. Resnick, Kenneth J. Ruggiero, Lauren M. Conoscenti, and Jenna McCauley, July 2007, pp3–4 (www.ncjrs.gov/pdffiles1/nij/grants/219181.pdf). Accessed August 12, 2020.

187 *Syd Barrett: A Very Irregular Head*, by Rob Chapman, Faber and Faber, 2010, pp275 - 276.

188 *The Delicious Grace of Moving One's Hand*, by Timothy Leary, Thunder's Mouth Press, 1998, pp212.

189 *Timothy Leary, the Madness of the Sixties, and Me*, by Charles W. Slack, Peter H. Wyden, 1974, pp36, 44.

190 *Timothy Leary, the Madness of the Sixties, and Me*, by Charles W. Slack, Peter H. Wyden, 1974, pp44, 48, 53.

191 'Psychedelic Birth: Bodies, Boundaries and the Perception of Pain in the 1970s,' by Wendy Kline, *Gender and History*, 32(1), March 2020, pp70–85.

192 *Daughters of Aquarius: Women of the Sixties Counterculture*, by Grechen Lemke-Santangelo, University Press of Kansas, 2009, pp181.

193 *The Delicious Grace of Moving One's Hand*, by Timothy Leary, Thunder's Mouth Press, 1998, pp212, 125-126.

194 *The Delicious Grace of Moving One's Hand*, by Timothy Leary, Thunder's Mouth Press, 1998, pp66, 122.

195 *The Delicious Grace of Moving One's Hand*, by Timothy Leary, Thunder's Mouth Press, 1998, pp66, 122.

196 'Pornography as Trafficking,' by Catharine A. MacKinnon, *Michigan Journal of International Law*, 26(4), 2005 (repository.law.umich.edu/mjil/vol26/iss4/1). Accessed November 12, 2020.

197 'Diverse Sexual Behaviours and Pornography Use: Findings From a Nationally Representative Probability Survey of Americans Aged 18 to 60 Years,' by Debby Herbenick, Tsung-Chieh Fu, Paul Wright, Bryant Paul, Ronna Gradus, Jill Bauer, and Rashida Jones, *The Journal of Sexual Medicine*, 17(4), April 2020, pp623–633.

198 'German Heterosexual Women's Pornography Consumption and Sexual Behaviour,' by Chyng Feng Sun, Paul Wright, and Nicola Steffen, *Sexualisation, Media and Society*, 3(1), January-March 2017, pp1–2.

199 *Tropic of Cancer*, by Henry Miller, Penguin Modern Classics, 2015 (first published in 1934), pp92.

200 *The Devil at Large: Erica Jong on Henry Miller*, by Erica Jong, Grove Press, 1994.

201 'Don't Cancel Philip Roth,' by Joel Diggory, *The Spectator*, March 22, 2021 (www.spectator.co.uk/article/don-t-cancel-philip-roth). Accessed March 29, 2021.

202 *Portnoy's Complaint*, by Philip Roth, Vintage International, 1994 (first published in 1967), pp116.

203 *Ted Bundy: Conversations with a Killer*, by Stephen G. Michaud and Hugh Aynesworth, Mirror Books, 2019 (originally published in 2000), pp80.

204 'Feds Looking at Alleged Payments Rep. Matt Gaetz Made to Women and Online Solicitation: Sources,' by Alexander Mallin, Mike Levine, John Santucci, Katherine Faulders, and Will Steakin, ABC News, April 2, 2021 (abcnews.go.com/Politics/feds-alleged-payments-rep-matt-gaetz-made-women/story?id=76827846). Accessed April 2, 2021.

205 'Roast: "It's Team-Work",' by David Hills, *The Observer*, March 14, 2004 (www.theguardian.com/football/2004/mar/14/newsstory). Accessed April 2, 2021.

206 'Butch Please: Butch With a Side of Misogyny,' by Kate, *Autostraddle*, April 26, 2013 (www.autostraddle.com/butch-please-butch-with-a-side-of-misogyny-174442). Accessed April 2, 2021.

207 *The Last Living Slut*, by Roxana Shirazi, HarperCollins, 2010, pp290.

208 *I'm with the Band: Confessions of a Groupie*, by Pamela des Barres, Chicago Review Press, pp201.

209 *I'm with the Band: Confessions of a Groupie*, by Pamela des Barres, Chicago Review Press, pp157.

210 *Advanced Sex Tips for Girls*, by Cynthia Heimel, Simon and Schuster, 2002, pp103.

211 *Advanced Sex Tips for Girls*, by Cynthia Heimel, Simon and Schuster, 2002, pp103.

212 *Helter Skelter – the True Story of the Manson Murders*, by Vincent Bugliosi and Curt Gentry, W.W. Norton and Company, 2002 (first published in 1974), pp251, 316–318, 366, 416, 442,

213 *Manson*, by Jeff Guinn, Simon and Schuster, 2014, pp16–20.

214 'Charles Manson: The Incredible Story of the Most Dangerous Man Alive,' by David Felton and David Dalton, *Rolling Stone*, June 25, 1970 (www.rollingstone.com/culture/culture-news/charles-manson-the-incredible-story-of-the-most-dangerous-man-alive-85235). Accessed August 15, 2020.

215 'Linda Kasabian Describes Sex Orgy, Manson's Power,' by Mary Neiswender, *Long Beach Press-Telegram*, July 28, 1970 (www.cielodrive.com/archive/linda-kasabian-describes-sex-orgy-mansons-power). Accessed March 29, 2021.

216 'Terminally ill Manson follower dies in prison,' *The Guardian*, September 25, 2009 (www.theguardian.com/world/2009/sep/25/charles-manson-susan-atkins-dies). Accessed March 28, 2021.

217 *Helter Skelter – the True Story of the Manson Murders*, by Vincent Bugliosi and Curt Gentry, W.W. Norton and Company, 2002 (first published in 1974), pp251, 316–318, 366, 442,

218 'Susan Atkins: Follower of Charles Manson Who Spent the Rest of Her Life in Jail After the Tate-LaBianca Killings,' *The Independent*, October 23, 2011 (www.independent.co.uk/news/obituaries/susan-atkins-follower-of-charles-manson-who-spent-the-rest-of-her-life-in-jail-after-the-tate-labianca-killings-1798210.html). Accessed March 28, 2021.

219 *Grand Jury Testimony: Susan Atkins*, December 5, 1969 (www.cielodrive.com/susan-atkins-grand-jury-testimony.php). Accessed March 29, 2021.

220 *Grand Jury Testimony: Susan Atkins*, December 5, 1969 (www.cielodrive.com/susan-at-

kins-grand-jury-testimony.php). Accessed March 29, 2021.

221 'Susan Atkins, Manson Follower, Dies at 61,' by Margalit Fox, *The New York Times*, September 25, 2009 (www.nytimes.com/2009/09/26/us/26atkins.html). Accessed August 14, 2020.

222 'Subsequent Parole Consideration Hearing, State of California, Board of Parole Hearings: In the matter of the Life Term Parole Consideration Hearing of: Susan Atkins,' CDC Number: W-08304, Central California Women's Facility, Corona, California, June 1, 2005.

223 'Charles Manson Biography (1934–2017),' Biography.com, March 6, 2020 (www.biography.com/crime-figure/charles-manson). Accessed August 14, 2020.

224 'Terminally ill Manson follower dies in prison,' *The Guardian*, September 25, 2009 (www.theguardian.com/world/2009/sep/25/charles-manson-susan-atkins-dies). Accessed March 28, 2021.

225 'Murderous Manson Family Shocked Nation,' History Collection, 2020 (historycollection.com/21-photographs-murderous-manson-family-shocked-nation/2/). Accessed August 14, 2020.

226 'Miss Atkins Testifies She Killed Sharon Tate,' *The New York Times*, February 10, 1971, pp17.

227 *Grand Jury Testimony: Susan Atkins*, December 5, 1969 (www.cielodrive.com/susan-at-kins-grand-jury-testimony.php). Accessed March 29, 2021.

228 'Nonfiction and Screen Adaptations led U.S. Book Sales from 2010 to 2019, according to NPD Bookscan,' *NPD*, December 18, 2019 (www.npd.com/wps/portal/npd/us/news/press-releas-es/2019/fifty-shades-of-grey-was-the-best-selling-book-of-the-decade-in-the-us-the-npd-group-says). Accessed February 15, 2021.

229 Why Are So Many Women Searching for Ultra-Violent Porn?' by Sophia Rahman, *Vice*, May 2, 2017 (www.vice.com/en/article/bm9w7v/why-are-so-many-women-searching-for-ultra-violent-porn). Accessed April 2, 2021.

230 Telephone interview with a British boxer who preferred to remain anonymous, March 29, 2021.

231 'What Lisa Knew,' by Joyce Johnson and Maury Terry, *Vanity Fair*, May 1988 (archive.vanity-fair.com/article/1988/5/what-lisa-knew). Accessed May 11, 2020.

232 Nat 11 @sheshostage', Twitter, February 27, 2020 (twitter.com/sheshostage/sta-tus/1233105535345414146). Accessed March 3, 2020.

233 Zak @homostly, Twitter, March 29, 2018 (twitter.com/homostly/sta-tus/979484280324804608). Accessed March 3, 2020.

234 *The Last Living Slut*, by Roxana Shirazi, HarperCollins, 2010, pp282.

235 *The Last Living Slut*, by Roxana Shirazi, HarperCollins, 2010, pp8, 203, 286, 300.

236 *Grand Jury Testimony: Susan Atkins*, December 5, 1969 (www.cielodrive.com/susan-at-kins-grand-jury-testimony.php). Accessed March 29, 2021.

237 *The Last Living Slut*, by Roxana Shirazi, HarperCollins, 2010, pp247 - 251.

238 *The Last Living Slut*, by Roxana Shirazi, HarperCollins, 2010, pp98.

239 *The Sexual Life of Catherine M.*, by Catherine Millet, Serpent's Tail Classics, 2014, pp10.

240 '*Atalanta Fugiens*' or '*Atalanta Fleeing*', by Michael Maier, published by Johann Theodor de Bry in Oppenheim, 1617.

241 'The Evolution of Maternal Birthing Position,' by Lauren Dundes, *American Journal of Public Health*, 77(5), May 1987, pp636–641.

242 'The Maya Midwife as Sacred Specialist: A Guatemalan Case,' by Lois Paul and Benjamin D. Paul, *American Ethnologist*, 2(4), November 1975, pp707–726.

243 'Hospital Care at Second Avenue and East 17th Street, New York City, 1894–1984,' by Henry Pinsker, David M. Novick, and Beverly L. Richman, *The Bulletin of the New York Academy of Medicine*, 60(9), November 1984, pp905–924.

244 *Obstetrics and Gynaecology in America: A History*, by Harold Speert, The American College of Obstetricians and Gynaecologists, 1980, pp85–86.

245 'Maternal History,' by Carrie Schram, *Canadian Family Physician*, 55(8), August 2009, pp787–788.

246 'A Brief History of Hospital-Based Maternity Services as Relates to the Routine Nursery Care of Normal Newborns,' by Faith Gibson, The American College of Community Midwives archives (collegeofmidwives.org/collegeofmidwives.org/legal_legislative01/HxMfryIndex01/abriefhx.htm). Accessed March 1, 2021.

247 *Family-Centered Maternity Care*, by Celeste R. Phillips, Jones and Bartlett Publishers, 2003,

pp7.

248 *La sage-femme ou le médecin: une nouvelle conception de la vie*, by Jacques Gélis, Fayard, 1988, pp305, 325.

249 'Obstetric Interventions,' *Simulation in Obstetrics, Gynaecology and Midwifery*, Flinders University of South Australia School of Medicine, Adelaide, South Australia, Australia, June 11, 2017 (basicmedicalkey.com/simulation-in-obstetrics-gynecology-and-midwifery/). Accessed October 12, 2020.

250 *Birth: A Changing Scene. Part II: A Controversial Figure of Man-Midwife*, by Anna Ostrowska, Wellcome Library, December 10, 2012 (blog.wellcomelibrary.org/2012/12/man-midwife). Accessed October 12, 2020.

251 *The Making of Man-Midwifery: Childbirth in England, 1660–1770*, by Adrian Wilson, Routledge, 2020 (first published in 1995), pp3.

252 *The History of Anaesthesia Society Proceedings*, The Association of Anaesthetists of Great Britain and Ireland, 20, January 16, 1997, pp13.

253 *Birth: A Changing Scene. Part II: A Controversial Figure of Man-Midwife*, by Anna Ostrowska, Wellcome Library, December 10, 2012 (blog.wellcomelibrary.org/2012/12/man-midwife). Accessed October 12, 2020.

254 'Hospital Care at Second Avenue and East 17th Street, New York City, 1894–1984,' by Henry Pinsker, David M. Novick, and Beverly L. Richman, *The Bulletin of the New York Academy of Medicine*, 60(9), November 1984, pp905–924.

255 *Obstetrics and Gynaecology in America: A History*, by Harold Speert, The American College of Obstetricians and Gynaecologists, 1980, pp85–86.

256 'Maternal History,' by Carrie Schram, *Canadian Family Physician*, 55(8), August 2009, pp787–788.

257 'Man-Midwifery History: 1730-1930,' by D.C. Shelton, *Journal of Obstetrics and Gynaecology*, November 2012, 32(8), pp718–23.

258 'John Snow, MD: Anaesthetist to the Queen of England and Pioneer Epidemiologist,' by Michael A.E. Ramsay, *Proceedings (Baylor University Medical Centre)*, 19(1), 2006, pp24–8.

259 *Masters of Medicine: Sir James Young Simpson and Chloroform*, by Dr Laing Gordon, Longmans, Green and Co., 1897, pp86.

260 'Chloroform: Chemical Compound,' by Francis A. Carey, *Encylopaedia Britannica*, November 2020 (www.britannica.com/science/chloroform). Accessed January 11, 2021.

261 'Methylene Chloride,' The National Institute for Occupational Safety and Health, Centres for Disease Control and Prevention, 2020 (www.cdc.gov/niosh/topics/methylenechloride/). Accessed August 17, 2020.

262 'Toxicological Profile for Carbon Tetrachloride,' Agency for Toxic Substances and Disease Registry, US Department of Health and Human Services, 2020 (www.atsdr.cdc.gov/toxprofiles/tp30-c2.pdf). Accessed August 17, 2020.

263 'Acute Neonatal Effects of Cocaine Exposure During Pregnancy,' by Charles R. Bauer, John C. Langer, Seetha Shankaran, Henrietta S. Bada, Barry Lester, Linda L. Wright, Heidi Krause-Steinrauf, Vincent L. Smeriglio, Loretta P. Finnegan, Penelope L. Maza, and Joel Verter, *Archives of Paediatric and Adolescent Medicine*, September 2005, 159(9), pp824–834.

264 *Blessed Days of Anaesthesia: How Anaesthetics Changed the World*, by Stephanie J. Snow, Oxford University Press, 2009, pp75.

265 *Obstetrics and Gynaecology in America: A History*, by Harold Speert, The American College of Obstetricians and Gynaecologists, 1980, pp138.

266 *Deliver Me from Pain: Anaesthesia and Birth in America*, by Jacqueline H. Wolf, Johns Hopkins University Press, 2009, pp67.

267 'Early Opposition to Obstetric Anaesthesia,' by A.D. Farr, *Anaesthesia*, 35(9), September 1980, pp896–907.

268 'Did the Use of Chloroform by Queen Victoria Influence its Acceptance in Obstetric Practice?' by H. Connor and T. Connor, *Anaesthesia*, 51(10), October 1996, pp955–957.

269 *The History of Anaesthesia Society Proceedings*, The Association of Anaesthetists of Great Britain and Ireland, 20, January 16, 1997, pp39–40.

270 *The History of Anaesthesia Society Proceedings*, The Association of Anaesthetists of Great Britain and Ireland, 20, January 16, 1997, pp39–40.

271 *Chemistry, Theoretical, Practical and Analytical, as Applied and Relating to the Arts and*

Manufactures (Volume 1), by Sheridan Muspratt, William Mackenzie, 1860: pp547.

272 'Did the Use of Chloroform by Queen Victoria Influence its Acceptance in Obstetric Practice?' by H. Connor and T. Connor, *Anaesthesia*, 51(10), October 1996, pp955–957.

273 *The History of Surgical Anaesthesia*, by Thomas E. Keys, Wood Library – Museum of Anaesthesiology, 1996 (originally published in 1945), pp48.

274 'Morphine-Scopolamine Anaesthesia in Obstetrics,' by Louis I. Breitstein, *California State Journal of Medicine*, June 1915, pp215.

275 'Morphine-Scopolamine Anaesthesia in Obstetrics,' by Louis I. Breitstein, *California State Journal of Medicine*, June 1915, pp215, 216.

276 '"In the Present State of Our Knowledge": Early Use of Opioids in Obstetrics,' by Donald Caton, *Anaesthesiology*, 3(82), March 1995, pp779 - 784.

277 'Chloroform,' INCHEM – Internationally Peer Reviewed Chemical Safety Information, World Health Organization, 2020 (www.inchem.org/documents/pims/chemical/pim121.htm). Accessed August 21, 2020.

278 'Placental Transfer of Opioids,' by Felegaly Reynolds, *Baillière's Clinical Anaesthesiology*, 1(4), December 1987, pp859–881.

279 'Placental Transfer: Anticholinergic,' *Open Anaesthesia*, 2020 (www.openanesthesia.org/placental_transfer_anticholinergic/). Accessed August 21, 2020.

280 *The Truth about Twilight Sleep*, by Hanna Rion, McBride, Nast and Co., 1915, pp177.

281 *The Truth about Twilight Sleep*, by Hanna Rion, McBride, Nast and Co., 1915, pp11.

282 *The Truth about Twilight Sleep*, by Hanna Rion, McBride, Nast and Co., 1915, pp362.

283 *The Truth about Twilight Sleep*, by Hanna Rion, McBride, Nast and Co., 1915, pp7.

284 'Ecological Association between Operative Vaginal Delivery and Obstetric and Birth Trauma,' by Giulia M. Muraca, Sarka Lisonkova, Amanda Skoll, Rollin Brant, Geoffrey W. Cundiff, Yasser Sabr and K.S. Joseph, *CMAJ*, 190 (24), June 18, 2018, pE734 - E741.

285 'Outcome of Forceps Delivery in a Teaching Hospital: A Two-Year Experience,' by Lopamudra B. John, S. Nischintha and Seetesh Ghose, *Journal of Natural Science, Biology and Medicine*, 5(1), January–June 2014, pp155–157.

286 'Operational Guidelines for Establishing Sentinel Stillbirth Surveillance System', Child Health Division, Ministry of Health and Family Welfare, Government of India, World Health Organisation, June 2016, pp34 (www.nhm.gov.in/images/pdf/programmes/RBSK/Operational_Guidelines/Operational_Guidelines_for_establishing_Sentinel_Stillbirth_Surveillance_System.pdf). Accessed September 9, 2020.

287 'Mom blames Newborn's Death on Doctor's Use of Forceps,' by Priscilla DeGregory, *The New York Post*, July 2, 2018 (nypost.com/2018/07/02/mom-blames-newborns-death-on-doctors-use-of-forceps). Accessed September 9, 2020.

288 'Traumatic Intracranial Haemorrhage in Firstborn Infants and Delivery with Obstetric Forceps,' by K. O'Driscoll, D. Meagher, D. Macdonald, and F. Geoghegan, *BJOG: An International Journal of Obstetrics and Gynaecology*, 88(6), June 1981, pp577–581.

289 'Neurodevelopmental and Psychosocial Risk Factors in Serial Killers and Mass Murderers,' by Clare S. Allely, Helen Minnis, Lucy Thompson, Philip Wilson, and Christopher Gillberg, *Aggression and Violent Behaviour*, 19(3), May–June 2014, pp288–301.

290 Hunterian Museum, The Royal College of Surgeons of England, 2020 (www.rcseng.ac.uk/museums-and-archives/hunterian-museum). Accessed October 12, 2020.

291 *The Making of Man-Midwifery: Childbirth in England, 1660-1770*, by Adrian Wilson, Routledge, 2020 (first published in 1995), pp3.

292 *The Truth about Twilight Sleep*, by Hanna Rion, McBride, Nast and Co., 1915, pp13.

293 *The Truth about Twilight Sleep*, by Hanna Rion, McBride, Nast and Co., 1915, p.iv.

294 'Scopolamin-Morphin Seminarcosis in the Second Thousand Deliveries in Barnes Hospital,' *The Journal of the Missouri State Medical Association*, edited by E.J. Goodwin, Volume 20, January–December 1923, pp12.

295 *State and Substate Estimates of Serious Mental Illness from the 2012-2014 National Surveys on Drug Use and Health*, by Rachel N. Lipari, Struther L. Van Horn, Arthur Hughes, and Matthew Williams, Substance Abuse and Mental Health Services Administration, US Department of Health and Human Services, 2016 (www.samhsa.gov/data/sites/default/files/report_3190/ShortReport-3190.html). Accessed October 9, 2020.

296 'Adults With AMI Reporting Unmet Need,' *2017 State Of Mental Health In America - Access To*

Care Data, Mental Health America, 2020 (www.mhanational.org/issues/2017-state-mental-health-america-access-care-data). Accessed October 9, 2020.

297 'Scopolamin-Morphin Seminarcosis in the Second Thousand Deliveries in Barnes Hospital,' *The Journal of the Missouri State Medical Association*, edited by E.J. Goodwin, Volume 20, January–December 1923, pp14.

298 'The Use of Apomorphine with Scopolamine in Labour,' by Robert R. White, *American Journal of Obstetrics and Gynaecology*, 64(1), July 1952, pp91–100.

299 'Home Births to Hospital Births: Interviews with Maori Women Who Had Their Babies in the 1930s,' by Helen Mountain Harte, *Maori Health and History*, 3(1), 2001, pp87–108.

300 *The Department of Anaesthesia, University of Cape Town, 1920 – 2000: A History*, by Nagin P. Parbhoo, 2002, pp13.

301 'What was Childbirth like in the 1960s, 1970s?' Ask Metafilter, March 27, 2016 (ask.metafilter.com/293793/What-was-childbirth-like-in-the-1960s-70s). Accessed June 29, 2020.

302 'Mothering Forums > Archives > Pregnancy and Birth Archives > Birth Professionals (Archive) > Twilight sleep – how long in use?' *Mothering*, (www.mothering.com/forum/228-birth-professionals-archive/794250-twilight-sleep-how-long-use.html). Accessed June 29, 2020.

303
'Twilight Sleep is Subject of a New Investigation,' *The New York Times*, January 31, 1915 (www.nytimes.com/1915/01/31/archives/twilight-sleep-is-subject-of-a-new-investigation.html). Accessed February 28, 2021.

304 *The Truth about Twilight Sleep*, by Hanna Rion, McBride, Nast and Co., 1915, pp15.

305 *Obstetrics and Gynaecology in America: A History*, by Harold Speert, The American College of Obstetricians and Gynaecologists, 1980, pp136.

306 'The Death of Natural Childbirth,' by David A.J. Reynolds, *The Technoskeptic*, June 27, 2018 (thetechnoskeptic.com/death-natural-childbirth/). Accessed August 17, 2020.

307 'Influential Individuals,' History of lysergic acid diethylamide, Wikipedia, 2020 (en.wikipedia.org/wiki/History_of_lysergic_acid_diethylamide#Influential_individuals). Accessed April 25, 2020.

308 Genesis 3:16, King James Bible, 2020.

309 'Accepting Pain over Comfort: Resistance to the Use of Anaesthesia in the Mid-19th Century,' R. Meyer and S.P. Desai, *Journal of Anaesthesia History*, 1(4), October 2015, pp115–121.

310 *Answer to the Religious Objections Advanced Against the Employment of Anaesthetic Agents in Midwifery and Surgery*, by James Young Simpson, Sutherland and Knox, 1847.

311 *Alleviation of Pain in Labour*, by William P. Sadler, Instructor in Obstetrics and Gynaecology, University of Minnesota, Read before the Forty-Fifth Annual Meeting of Idaho State Medical Association, Boise, Idaho, USA, August 30–September 2, 1937.

312 'Nembutal-Chloral Narcosis in Childbirth,' by F.B. Mallinson, *British Journal of Anaesthesia*, 15(3), April 1938, pp104–115.

313 'The Use of Apomorphine with Scopolamine in Labour,' by Robert R. White, *American Journal of Obstetrics and Gynaecology*, 64(1), July 1952, pp91–100.

314 'The Queen's Birth Stories of Her Children Charles, Anne, Andrew and Edward,' by Sophie Hamilton, *Hello*, July 9, 2020 (www.hellomagazine.com/healthandbeauty/mother-and-baby/2020070993163/the-queen-birth-stories-prince-charles-/). Accessed November 18, 2020.

315 *Obstetrics and Gynaecology in America: A History*, by Harold Speert, The American College of Obstetricians and Gynaecologists, 1980, pp139–140.

316 'Evidence of Overuse? Patterns of Obstetric Interventions during Labour and Birth among Australian Mothers,' by Haylee Fox, Emily Callander, Daniel Lindsay and Stephanie Topp, *BMC Pregnancy and Childbirth*, 19(226), July 2019.

317 'Fitness Trade-offs in the History and Evolution of Delegated Mothering with Special Reference to Wet-Nursing, Abandonment, and Infanticide,' by Sarah Blaffer Hrdy, *Ethology and Sociobiology*, 13(5-6), September-November 1992, pp409–442.

318 *One-Liners: A Mini-Manual for a Spiritual Life*, by Ram Dass, Harmony, 2002, pp59, 48.

319 *What's Possible?: Ayurvedic Odyssey: The Year Yoga Changed My Life*, by Mary Roberts, Lotus Press, 2018, pp63.

320 *Awakening the Buddha Within: Tibetan Wisdom for the Western World*, by Lama Surya Das, Harmony, 1998, pp328.

321 *The Imitation of Christ*, by Thomas à Kempis, translated by Richard Whitford, Peter Pauper

Press, (first published c.1486), pp7, 285, 160.

322 *Early Modern Catholicism: An Anthology of Primary Sources*, by Robert S. Miola, Oxford University Press, 2007, pp7.

323 Isaiah 56:9, King James Bible.

324 *Thus Spoke Zarathustra*, by Friedrich Nietzsche, Penguin Classics, 1974 (first published in 1883), pp43.

325 'Is it true that the SS had lampshades made from human skin in the Buchenwald concentration camp?' by Dr. Harry Stein, curator, Buchenwald and Mittelbau-Dora Foundation, 2021 (www.buchenwald.de/en/1132). Accessed April 8, 2021.

326 'Heff's Son: From Swimming in the Infamous Grotto to Holding School Trips to his Dad's Private Zoo: Hugh Hefner's Son Cooper Lifts the Lid on Growing Up in the Playboy Mansion,' by Jennifer Newton, *The Sun*, April 9, 2017 (www.thesun.co.uk/living/3293976/from-swimming-in-the-infamous-grotto-to-holding-school-trips-to-his-dads-private-zoo-hugh-hefners-son-cooper-lifts-the-lid-on-growing-up-in-the-playboy-mansion). Accessed November 28, 2020.

327 'At home with a teenage BILLIONAIRE: Dubai Instagram star, 16, with a $1million collection of trainers shows off the family mansion - including the private ZOO,' by Natalie Corner, *The Daily Mail*, December 6, 2018 (www.dailymail.co.uk/femail/article-6463387/Inside-home-16-year-old-billionaire-rich-kid-Dubai-private-ZOO.html). Accessed April 6, 2021.

328 'The Sex-Obsessed World of Brunei,' by Maureen Callahan, *The New York Post*, May 10, 2014 (nypost.com/2014/05/10/inside-the-wacky-sex-obsessed-world-of-brunei). Accessed November 28, 2020.

329 Dan Bilzerian's Instagram account (www.instagram.com/danbilzerian). Accessed April 4, 2021.

330 "It's degrading and disgusting': Tobacco tycoon who calls himself The Candyman leads his wife around their mansion on a LEASH – as grandparents fear for the young children growing up in a house where guests party naked,' By Daniel Piotrowski, Lucy-Mae Beers and Liam Quinn, *The Daily Mail*, May 19, 2015 (www.dailymail.co.uk/news/article-3086227/It-s-degrading-disgusting-Grandparents-wife-Australian-Hugh-Hefner-dubbed-Candyman-slam-picture-granddaughter-led-leash-fear-CHILDREN-growing-party-mansion.html). Accessed April 4, 2021.

331 'Travers "Candyman" Beynon is slammed for posting an ad looking for a "bubbly and attractive" live-in girlfriend just before International Women's Day – and the role comes with some VERY strict rules,' by Karen Ruiz, *The Daily Mail*, March 7, 2020 (www.dailymail.co.uk/news/article-8085743/Tobacco-tycoon-Travers-Candyman-Beynon-taking-applications-new-girlfriend.html). Accessed April 5, 2021.

332 'Life of the Party,' by Trent Dalton, *Weekend Australian*, March 26, 2019 (www.theaustralian.com.au/weekend-australian-magazine/supercars-sex-machines-money-to-burn-the-gold-coasts-candyman/news-story/99bb6828e1d2d8e275c980cfef9b6693). Accessed April 8, 2021.

333 'Sex-Dimorphic Face Shape Preference in Heterosexual and Homosexual Men and Women,' by Aaron N. Glassenberg, David R. Feinberg, Benedict C. Jones, Anthony C. Little & Lisa M. DeBruine, *Archives of Sexual Behaviour*, 39(6), December 2010, pp1289–1296.

334 "Straight-Acting Gays': The Relationship Between Masculine Consciousness, Anti-Effeminacy, and Negative Gay Identity,' by Francisco J. Sánchez and Eric Vilain, *Archives of Sexual Behaviour*, 41(1), February 2012, pp111–119.

335 "Hey man, how's u?': Masculine Speech and Straight-Acting Gay Men Online,' by Charlie Sarson, *Journal of Gender Studies*, 29(8), November 2020, pp897–910.

336 'Personal Characteristics, Sexual Behaviours, and Male Sex Work: A Quantitative Approach,' by Trevon D. Logan, *American Sociological Review*, 75(5), October 2010, pp679–704.

337 "Straight-Acting Gays': The Relationship Between Masculine Consciousness, Anti-Effeminacy, and Negative Gay Identity,' by Francisco J. Sánchez and Eric Vilain, *Archives of Sexual Behaviour*, 41(1), February 2012, pp111–119.

338 Telephone interview with Mark Bittlestone, June 10, 2021.

339 Genesis 1:26-28, English Standard Bible.

340 16:8, The Clear Quran, translated by Dr Mustafa Khattab, Quran.com. Accessed December 1, 2020.

341 Genesis 2:18, English Standard Bible, 2016.

342 *The Torture Garden*, by Octave Mirbeau, translated by Alvah Bessie, Bookkake London,

2021(first published in 1899), pp118

343 From my interviews with Horst Bleicher, 2007.

344 *Exceptional Spaces: Essays in Performance and History*, by Della Pollock, University of North Carolina Press, 1998, pp236.

345 'Unattainable Standards of Beauty: Temporal Trends of Victoria's Secret Models from 1995 to 2018,' by Mayra B. Maymone, Melissa Laughter, Jaclyn B. Anderson, Eric A. Secemsky, and Neelam A. Vashi, *Aesthetic Surgery Journal*, 40(2), February 2020, pNP72–NP76.

346 'Unattainable Standards of Beauty: Temporal Trends of Victoria's Secret Models from 1995 to 2018,' by Mayra Bc Maymone, Melissa Laughter, Jaclyn B. Anderson, Eric A. Secemsky, and Neelam A. Vashi, *Aesthetic Surgery Journal*, 40(2), February 2020, pNP72–NP76.

347 *Heaven and Hell*, by Emanuel Swedenborg, E-Bookarama, 2007 (originally published in 1758), pp20-21.

348 *The Torture Garden*, by Octave Mirbeau, translated by Alvah Bessie, Bookkake London, 2021 (first published in 1899), pp186.

349 'Tommy Lee: "Sheer Fucking Stupidity" Helped Motley Crue Succeed,' by Dave Lifton, *UltimateClassicRock*, October 27, 2020 (ultimateclassicrock.com/tommy-lee-sheer-fing-stupidity). Accessed April 5, 2021.

350 1:05 minutes in, *The Dirt*, directed by Jeff Tremaine and based on *The Dirt: Confessions of the World's Most Notorious Rock Band*, by Neil Strauss, Tommy Lee, Mick Mars, Vince Neil and Nikki Sixx, Netflix, 2019.

351 *To Throw Away Unopened*, by Viv Albertine, Faber and Faber, 2018, pp74.

352 'Scarred: Armie Hammer's Ex Paige Lorenze Shares Disturbing Photo of Actor's Initial 'Carved into Her Pubic Area with a KNIFE',' by Eve Wagstaff, *The Sun*, January 23, 2021 (www.thesun.co.uk/tvandshowbiz/13825942/armie-hammer-paige-lorenze-disturbing-photo-carved-pubic-knife). Accessed January 25, 2021.

353 *London Fields* trailer (londonfieldsfilm.com/). Accessed November 20, 2020.

354 Manifesto del Futurismo, Wikipedia (Italia), October 9, 2020 (it.wikipedia.org/wiki/Manifesto_del_Futurismo). Accessed October 11, 2020.

355 Translation of *Il Manifesto del Futurismo* from the Italian my own. October 11, 2020.

356 '*Prometheus* Review: More than Just an *Alien*,' By David Edelstein, *New York Magazine*, June 8, 2012 (www.vulture.com/2012/06/movie-review-prometheus-alien-prequel.html). Accessed January 20, 2021.

357 '*Prometheus* Review: More than Just an *Alien*,' By David Edelstein, *New York Magazine*, June 8, 2012 (www.vulture.com/2012/06/movie-review-prometheus-alien-prequel.html). Accessed January 20, 2021.

358 *Lectures on Ethics*, by Immanuel Kant, translated from the German by Louis Infield, Methuen and Co., 1930, pp164, 182.

359 *Octopus!: The Most Mysterious Creature in the Sea*, by Katherine Harmon Courage, Penguin, 2014, pp199–200.

360 *Sexual Personae: Art and Decadence from Nefertiti to Emily Dickinson*, by Camille Paglia, Vintage Books, 1991 (first published in 1990), pp17, 42.

361 *The Dialectic of Sex: The Case for Feminist Revolution*, by Shulamith Firestone, Verso (Kindle edition), 2015 (originally published in 1970).

362 *The Dialectic of Sex: The Case for Feminist Revolution*, by Shulamith Firestone, Verso (Kindle edition), 2015 (originally published in 1970).

363 *The Dialectic of Sex: The Case for Feminist Revolution*, by Shulamith Firestone, Verso (Kindle edition), 2015 (originally published in 1970).

364 *In the Darkroom*, by Susan Faludi, William Collins, 2016, p57.

365 'Death of a Revolutionary,' by Susan Faludi, *The New Yorker*, April 8, 2013 (www.newyorker.com/magazine/2013/04/15/death-of-a-revolutionary). Accessed November 19, 2020.

366 'Childhood Trauma and Psychosis: The Genie Is Out of the Bottle,' by Paul Hammersley, John Read, Stephanie Woodall and Jacqueline Dillon, *Journal of Psychological Trauma*, 6(2 - 3), 2008, pp7–20.

367 'Child Sexual Abuse and Schizophrenia,' by J. Read and P. Hammersley, *The British Journal of Psychiatry*, 186(1), January 2005, pp76.

368 'An Extra-Uterine System to Physiologically Support the Extreme Premature Lamb,' by Emily A. Partridge, Marcus G. Davey, Matthew A. Hornick, Patrick E. McGovern, Ali Y. Mejaddam,

Jesse D. Vrecenak, Carmen Mesas-Burgos, Aliza Olive, Robert C. Caskey, Theodore R. Weiland, Jiancheng Han, Alexander J. Schupper, James T. Connelly, Kevin C. Dysart, Jack Rychik, Holly L. Hedrick, William H. Peranteau, and Alan W. Flakea, *Nature Communications*, 8, April 2017, pe15112.

369 'Jerry Lewis: Not Funny,' *People*, October 29, 1998 (people.com/celebrity/jerry-lewis-not-funny). Accessed April 10, 2021.

370 'Article 8: A Private and Family Life,' Liberty UK, 2020 (www.libertyhumanrights.org.uk/right/a-private-and-family-life). Accessed December 6, 2020.

371 'Dephasing in Electron Interference by a 'Which-Path' Detector,' by E. Buks, R. Schuster, M. Heiblum, D. Mahalu, and V. Umansky, *Nature*, 391, February 26, 1998, pp871–1874.

372 'Extricating Yourself from Attachment,' by Ram Dass, (www.ramdass.org/extricating-yourself-from-attachment). Accessed April 5, 2021.

373 *Deliver Me From Pain: Anaesthesia and Birth in America*, by Jacqueline H. Wolf, Johns Hopkins University Press, 2009, pp8.

374 March 28, 1974 to December 22, 1989.

375 '30 Years Ago, Romania Deprived Thousands of Babies of Human Contact. Here's What's Become of Them,' by Melissa Fay Greene, *The Atlantic*, July/August 2020 (www.theatlantic.com/magazine/archive/2020/07/can-an-unloved-child-learn-to-love/612253). Accessed December 2020.

376 'Enid Bagnold: A Biography,' *Encounter*, Volume 67, 1986, pp64.

377 '13 Times Princess Diana Said Exactly What Every Mother is Thinking,' by Erin Hill, *People*, July 1, 2018 (people.com/royals/princess-diana-quotes-motherhood). Accessed April 8, 2021.

378 'L'enfant qui ne sourit pas,' by Veronique Dasen, *Revue Archéologique*, 2, 2017, pp261–283.

379 'Psychobiological Roots of Early Attachment,' by Myron A. Hofer, *Current Directions in Psychological Science*, 15(2), April 2006, pp84–88.

380 'The Queen and Prince Philip: Their Love Story, in Quotes,' by Hannah Furness, *The Telegraph*, April 10, 2021 (www.telegraph.co.uk/royal-family/2021/04/10/queen-prince-philip-love-story-quotes). Accessed April 10, 2021.

381 *American Psycho*, by Bret Easton Ellis, Picador, 2014, (first published in 1991), pp271.

382 *The Last Love Song: A Biography of Joan Didion*, by Tracy Daugherty, St Martin's Press, 2015, pp270.

383 'The New Rules of Society Romance … According to Gillian, Peter and Jemima,' by Anna Pasternak, *The Telegraph*, February 17, 2021 (www.telegraph.co.uk/women/life/gillian-peter-andjemima-can-tells-us-new-high-society-dating). Accessed February 18, 2021.

384 *The Making of Them: The British Attitude to Children and the Boarding School System*, by Nick Duffell, Lone Arrow Press, 2000, pp52, 21.

385 *Speaking of Psychology: The Mental Price of Affluence*, American Psychological Association, Episode 18, December 2014 (www.apa.org/research/action/speaking-of-psychology/affluence). Accessed September 5, 2020.

386 'Children of the Affluent: Challenges to Well-Being,' by Suniya S. Luthar and Shawn J. Latendresse, *Current Directions in Psychological Science*, 14(1), February 2005, pp49 – 53.

387 'Chloroform in Childbirth? Yes, Please, the Queen Said,' by Ellen Barry, *The New York Times*, May 6, 2019 (www.nytimes.com/2019/05/06/world/europe/uk-royal-births-labor.html). Accessed June 28, 2020.

388 'About,' Anna Pasternak's personal website, 2021 (www.annapasternak.co.uk/about). Accessed April 12, 2021.

389 *Encyclopaedia of Women in American History: Volumes I - III*, edited by Joyce Appleby, Eileen K. Cheng, Joanne L. Goodwin, Routledge, 2002, pp395.

390 *The Truth about Twilight Sleep*, by Hanna Rion, McBride, Nast and Co., 1915, pp8–9.

391 *Deliver Me from Pain: Anaesthesia and Birth in America*, by Jacqueline H. Wolf, Johns Hopkins University Press, 2009, pp100.

392 *American Dolorologies: Pain, Sentimentalism, Biopolitics*, by Simon Strick, State University of New York Press, 2014, pp71. (Quote attributed to Thomas Denman.)

393 *Deliver Me from Pain: Anaesthesia and Birth in America*, by Jacqueline H. Wolf, Johns Hopkins University Press, 2009, pp79.

394 *Twilight Sleep*, by Edith Wharton, Virago Modern Classics, 2008 (first published in 1927), Kindle edition.

395 *The Bonfire of the Vanities*, by Tom Wolfe, Picador, pp12.

396 'Morphine-Scopolamine Anaesthesia in Obstetrics,' by Louis I. Breitstein, *California State Journal of Medicine*, June 1915, pp215, 216.

397 'Twilight Sleep: Its Advantages and Disadvantages,' by George Blacker, *The Lancet*, 191(4934), March 23 1918, pp430–432.

398 'Twilight Sleep – The Brutal Way Some Women Gave Birth In The 1900s,' by Sam McCulloch, *BellyBelly*, June 5, 2018 (www.bellybelly.com.au/birth/twilight-sleep). Accessed September 9, 2020.

399 'Minimiser Bras Guide: Want to draw less attention to your chest? A minimiser bra has the capability of reducing breast projection by up to two inches for a more flattering silhouette under clothes. The specially-designed cups redistribute the breast tissue to fit evenly all over the cup to create the illusion of a smaller bust,' Linda's Online, 2020 (lindasonline.com/pages/minimizer-bras-guide). Accessed September 14, 2020.

400 'The Minimiser: The underwired bra reduces your bust size optically by one cup size,' Triumph, 2020 (uk.triumph.com/bras/minimiser). Accessed September 14, 2020.

401 *Coco Chanel: The Legend and the Life*, by Justine Picardie, HarperCollins, 2010, pp284.

402 *Becoming Anorexic: A Sociological Study*, by Muriel Darmon, Routledge, 2016, pp40.

403 'Karl Lagerfeld on His Mother, €3 Million Cat, and Being a 'Fashion Vampire',' by Amy Larocca, *The Cut*, March 31 2015 (www.thecut.com/2015/03/lagerfeld-on-his-mother-3-million-cat-more.html). Accessed July 5, 2020.

404 'Karl Lagerfeld's last words: the designer on his beloved pet cat, his disciplinarian mother and welcoming ghosts into his home,' by Justine Picardie, *Harper's Bazaar*, September 2018 (www.harpersbazaar.com/uk/fashion/fashion-news/a26403290/the-master-karl-lagerfeld). Accessed July 5, 2020.

405 'Sex And Drugs,' by Lauren Milligan, *British Vogue*, March 19, 2010 (www.vogue.co.uk/article/karl-lagerfeld-talks-sex-and-fur-to-vice). Accessed February 4, 2021.

406 'Karl Lagerfeld Weighs in on Model Debate: 'No-one Wants to See Curvy Women',' *Der Spiegel*, October 14 2009 (www.spiegel.de/international/zeitgeist/karl-lagerfeld-weighs-in-on-model-debate-no-one-wants-to-see-curvy-women-a-654945.html). Accessed July 5, 2020.

407 *Edie: American Girl*, by Jean Stein, Grove Press, 1994 (originally published in 1982), pp115.

408 *Edie: American Girl*, by Jean Stein, Grove Press, 1994 (originally published in 1982), pp296.

409 *Ciao! Manhattan*, directed by David Weisman and John Palmer, Agita Productions, 2010 (Originally released in 1972).

410 *Edie: American Girl*, by Jean Stein, Grove Press, 1994 (originally published in 1982), pp367.

411 *Edie: American Girl*, by Jean Stein, Grove Press, 1994 (originally published in 1982), pp421.

412 *How to Murder Your Life*, by Cat Marnell, Ebury, 2018, pp342.

413 'Proof That Americans are Lying about Their Sexual Desires,' by Sean Illing, *New York Magazine*, September 30, 2018 (www.vox.com/conversations/2017/6/27/15873072/google-porn-addiction-america-everybody-lies). Accessed August 14, 2020.

414 *Family Fortunes: Men And Women of the English Middle Class, 1780-1850*, by Leonore Davidoff and Catherine Hall, University of Chicago Press, 1991, pp27.

415 *Gender, Sex, and Subordination in England, 1500-1800*, by Anthony Fletcher, Yale University Press, 1999, pp183.

416 *Queen Victoria: A Portrait*, by Giles St. Aubyn, Sinclair-Stevenson, 1991, pp160, 167.

417 'SS Officer the Father of a British Princess,' *The New York Times*, April 16, 1985, pp6 (www.nytimes.com/1985/04/16/world/ss-officer-the-father-of-a-british-princess.html). Accessed March 1, 2021.

418 'Princess Michael of Kent: I would not Breastfeed in Public,' *The Telegraph*, December 10, 2014 (www.telegraph.co.uk/news/uknews/theroyalfamily/11285627/Princess-Michael-of-Kent-I-would-not-breastfeed-in-public.html). Accessed September 13, 2020.

419 *The Great Gatsby*, by F. Scott Fitzgerald, Wordsworth Editions Limited, 1993 (first published in 1925), pp13.

420 'Lonely Prince: How Charles felt the Queen was a 'cold and distant' mother – but she didn't want to 'burden' him with duties as a boy,' by Becky Pemberton, *The Sun*, December 17, 2019 (www.thesun.co.uk/fabulous/10570024/prince-charles-the-queen-cold-distant-mother-royal-duties-boy). Accessed September 13, 2020.

421 'Princess Diana gave birth to Wills standing up as Charles held her, reveals natural childbirth

activist Sheila Kitzinger who advised Lindo wing ahead of royal birth,' by Sheila Kitzinger, *The Daily Mail*, May 1, 2015 (www.dailymail.co.uk/femail/article-3064807/Princess-Diana-gave-birth-Wills-standing-Charles-held-reveals-natural-childbirth-activist-SHEILA-KITZINGER-advised-Lindo-wing-ahead-royal-birth.html). Accessed September 13, 2020.

422 *Churchill: Walking with Destiny*, by Andrew Roberts, Penguin, 2018, pp14.

423 *Edie: American Girl*, by Jean Stein, Grove Press, 1994 (originally published in 1982), pp56.

424 *Under My Skin: Volume One of My Autobiography, to 1949*, by Doris Lessing, Davey, 2001, pp10.

425 'Her Story: Doris Lessing,' *BBC World Service*, 2009.

426 *The Golden Notebook*, by Doris Lessing, HarperCollins, 1993 (originally published in 1962), pp577.

427 *Selfish, Shallow, and Self-Absorbed: Sixteen Writers on the Decision Not to Have Kids*, by Meghan Daum, Picador, 2016, pp105.

428 *The Bolter*, by Frances Osborne, Virago, 2004.

429 'Idina Sackville: The Haunted Queen of Happy Valley,' by Frances Osborne, *The Telegraph*, May 21, 2008 (www.telegraph.co.uk/news/features/3636698/Idina-Sackville-the-haunted-queen-of-Happy-Valley.html). Accessed March 1, 2021.

430 'Slains Castle and the Hays of Erroll,' *Aberdeen Civic Society Newsletter*, No. 48, December 2004.

431 *The Bolter: Idina Sackville, the Woman who Scandalised 1920s Society and became White Mischief's Infamous Seductress*, by Frances Osborne, Virago, 2008, pp132.

432 *The Bolter: Idina Sackville, the Woman who Scandalised 1920s Society and became White Mischief's Infamous Seductress*, by Frances Osborne, Virago, 2008, pp226.

433 *The Bolter: Idina Sackville, the Woman who Scandalised 1920s Society and became White Mischief's Infamous Seductress*, by Frances Osborne, Virago, 2008, pp136.

434 'Daddy,' *Ariel*, by Sylvia Plath, Faber and Faber, 2010 (first published in 1965), Kindle edition.

435 'Daddy,' *Ariel*, by Sylvia Plath, Faber and Faber, 2010 (first published in 1965), Kindle edition.

436 'This Day in History: Sylvia Plath and Ted Hughes Meet', History.com, 2020 (www.history.com/this-day-in-history/sylvia-plath-and-ted-hughes-meet). Accessed July 6, 2020.

437 *Red Comet: The Short Life and Blazing Art of Sylvia Plath*, by Heather Clark, Penguin, 2021, pp928.

438 'Written Out of History,' by Yehuda Koren and Eilat Negev, *The Guardian*, October 19, 2006 (www.theguardian.com/books/2006/oct/19/biography.tedhughes). Accessed April 11, 2021.

439 'Son of poets Sylvia Plath and Ted Hughes kills himself,' by Stephen Bates, *The Guardian*, March 23 2009 (www.theguardian.com/books/2009/mar/23/sylvia-plath-son-kills-himself). Accessed July 6, 2020.

440 *The Bell Jar*, by Sylvia Plath, Faber and Faber, 2005 (originally published in 1963), pp59.

441 *The Bell Jar*, by Sylvia Plath, Faber and Faber, 2005 (originally published in 1963), pp61.

442 *Sylvia Plath: A Biography*, by Linda Wagner-Martin, Lume Books, 2015 (first published in 1987), Kindle edition.

443 *The Bell Jar*, by Sylvia Plath, Faber and Faber, 2005 (originally published in 1963), pp162–163.

444 *Red Comet: The Short Life and Blazing Art of Sylvia Plath*, by Heather Clark, Penguin, 2021, pp274, 307.

445 *The Bell Jar*, by Sylvia Plath, Faber and Faber, 2005 (originally published in 1963), pp212.

446 'Exploring Women's Preferences for Labour Epidural Analgesia,' by Mary Ann Stark, *The Journal of Perinatal Education*, Spring 2003, 12(2), pp16 - 21.

447 'The Association between Household Socioeconomic Status, Breastfeeding, and Infants' Anthropometric Indices,' by Marjan Ajami, Morteza Abdollahi, Forouzan Salehi, Wilna Oldewage-Theron, and Yasaman Jamshidi-Naeini, *International Journal of Preventative Medicine*, 9, October 2018, pp89.

448 *Monstrous Motherhood: Eighteenth-Century Culture and the Ideology of Domesticity*, by Marilyn Francus, Johns Hopkins University Press, 2013, pp219.

449 'Nanny Families, New Inequalities and 'Good Care',' by Sara Eldén and Terese Anving, *Transforming Society*, June 8, 2019 (www.transformingsociety.co.uk/2019/08/06/nanny-families-new-inequalities-and-good-care). Accessed June 28, 2020.

450 *The State Nobility: Elite Schools in the Field of Power*, by Pierre Bourdieu, Polity Press, 1998, pxiv.

451 'Maternal Neglect: Oxytocin, Dopamine and the Neurobiology of Attachment,' by Lane Strathearn, *Journal of Neuroendocrinology*, 23(11), November 2011, pp1054 – 1065.

452 'I hate being a mom and I don't love my baby,' by throwaway90868, Reddit, October 11, 2015

(www.reddit.com/r/Parenting/comments/3oc1px/i_hate_being_a_mom_and_i_dont_love_my_baby). Accessed May 5, 2020.

453   '"I Was a Starter Wife": Inside America's Messiest Divorce,' by Justine Musk, *Marie Claire*, September 10, 2010 (www.marieclaire.com/sex-love/a5380/millionaire-starter-wife/). Accessed August 27, 2020.

454   'Elon Musk's Approach to Work-Life Balance Really is from Mars,' by Virginia Heffernan, *Yahoo! News*, March 9, 2013 (news.yahoo.com/elon-musk-s-approach-to-work-life-balance-really-is-from-mars-222036805.html). Accessed August 27, 2020.

455   '"Elon Musk," a Biography by Ashlee Vance, Paints a Driven Portrait,' by Dwight Garner, *The New York Times*, May 12, 2015 (www.nytimes.com/2015/05/13/books/elon-musk-a-biography-by-ashlee-vance-paints-a-driven-portrait.html). Accessed August 27, 2020.

456   *The Rise and Fall of the British Nanny*, by Jonathan Gathorne-Hardy, Faber and Faber, 2015, pp19.

457   'Maternal Status Regulates Cortical Responses to the Body Odour of Newborns,' by Johan N. Lundström, Annegret Mathe, Benoist Schaal, Johannes Frasnelli, Katharina Nitzsche, Johannes Gerber, and Thomas Hummel, *Frontiers in Psychology*, 5(4), September 2013, pp597.

458   *Queen Victoria: A Portrait*, by Giles St. Aubyn, Sinclair-Stevenson, 1991, pp167.

459   'Mother-Infant Neonatal Separation: Some Delayed Consequences,' by P.H. Leiderman and M.J. Seashore, *Ciba Foundation Symposium*, 33, January 1975, pp213–239.

460   'Early Contact Versus Separation: Effects on Mother-Infant Interaction One Year Later,' by K. Bystrova, V. Ivanova, M. Edhborg, A.S. Matthiesen, A.B. Ransjö-Arvidson, R. Mukhamedrakhimov, K. Uvnäs-Moberg, and A.M. Widström, *Birth*, 36(2), June 2009, pp97–109.

461   *'Shattered Nerves': Doctors, Patients, and Depression in Victorian England*, by Janet Oppenheim, Oxford University Press, 1991.

462   'The Use of Phencyclidine (CI-395) in Obstetric Procedures: A Preliminary Communication,' by Joe G. Camilleri, *Anaesthesia*, 17(4), October 1962 (associationofanaesthetists-publications.onlinelibrary.wiley.com/doi/pdf/10.1111/j.1365-2044.1962.tb13497.x). Accessed January 11, 2021.

463   'Twilight Sleep – The Brutal Way Some Women Gave Birth In The 1900s,' by Sam McCulloch, BellyBelly, June 5, 2018 (www.bellybelly.com.au/birth/twilight-sleep/). Accessed September 9, 2020.

464   'Maternity Care (US Navy, 1963),' US National Library of Medicine, 2019 (www.youtube.com/watch?v=1MZxtMOcO2o). Accessed August 18, 2020.

465   *Thus Spoke Zarathustra*, by Friedrich Nietzsche, East India Publishing Company, 2019 (first published in 1883), pp42.

466   'New Directions in Understanding How the Pelvic Floor Prepares for and Recovers from Vaginal Delivery,' by Ingrid Nygaard, *American Journal of Obstetrics and Gynaecology*, 213(2), August 2015, p121–122.

467   *Pain: The Science of the Feeling Brain*, By Abdul-Ghaaliq Lalkhen, Atlantic Books, 2021, pp2.

468   'Amelioration of Scopolamine-Induced Learning and Memory Impairment by ꞵ-Pinene in C57BL/6 Mice,' by Gil-Yong Lee, Chan Lee, Gyu Hwan Park, and Jung-Hee Jang, *Evidence-Based Complementary and Alternative Medicine*, 1, November 2017, pp1–9.

469   'Effects of Diazepam and Scopolamine on Storage, Retrieval and Organisational Processes in Memory,' by M.M. Ghoneim and S.P. Mewaldt, *Psychopharmacologia*, 44, January 1975, pp257–262.

470   'Twilight Sleep: Its Advantages and Disadvantages,' by George Blacker, *The Lancet*, 191(4934), March 1918, pp430–432.

471   *The Truth about Twilight Sleep*, by Hanna Rion, McBride, Nast and Co., 1915, pp115.

472   'Twilight Sleep: Its Advantages and Disadvantages,' by George Blacker, *The Lancet*, 191(4934), March 1918, pp430–432.

473   'Twilight Sleep: Its Advantages and Disadvantages,' by George Blacker, *The Lancet*, 191(4934), March 1918, pp430–432.

474   'Twilight Sleep: Its Advantages and Disadvantages,' by George Blacker, *The Lancet*, 191(4934), March 1918, pp430–432.

475   *The Truth about Twilight Sleep*, by Hanna Rion, McBride, Nast and Co., 1915, pp116.

476   Susan Slear, 'Twilight Sleep – The Brutal Way Some Women Gave Birth In The 1900s,' by Sam McCulloch, BellyBelly, June 5, 2018 (www.bellybelly.com.au/birth/twilight-sleep/).

Accessed September 9, 2020.

477 'Why Rape and Trauma Survivors Have Fragmented and Incomplete Memories,' by James Hopper and David Lisak, *Time*, December 9, 2014 (time.com/3625414/rape-trauma-brain-memory/). Accessed August 15, 2020.

478 Diane Faris, 'Twilight Sleep – The Brutal Way Some Women Gave Birth In The 1900s,' by Sam McCulloch, BellyBelly, June 5, 2018 (www.bellybelly.com.au/birth/twilight-sleep/). Accessed September 9, 2020.

479 *Pain: The Science of the Feeling Brain*, by Abdul-Ghaaliq Lalkhen, Atlantic Books, 2021, pp182.

480 *Sex in the World of Myth*, by David Leeming, Reaktion, 2020, pp99.

481 'Self Portrait with Inez,' by Saul Leiter, 1947, *Early Black and White by Saul Leiter*, Steidl, 2014.

482 'Hollywood's Eve by Lili Anolik, review: the 'lewd angel' who lived on cocaine, cigarettes and sex with Harrison Ford,' by Roger Lewis, *The Telegraph*, April 5 2020.

483 'Why Marcel Duchamp Played Chess with a Naked Eve Babitz,' by Alina Cohen, Artsy.net, May 16, 2019 (www.artsy.net/article/artsy-editorial-marcel-duchamp-played-chess-naked-eve-babitz). Accessed April 8, 2020.

484 'Choosing the Cover of Push the Sky Away,' by Nick Cave, The Red Hand Files, March 2019 (www.theredhandfiles.com/choosing-the-cover-of-push-the-sky-away). Accessed May 8, 2021.

485 'Pablo Picasso: Women are Either Goddesses or Doormats,' by Mark Hudson, *The Telegraph*, April 8 2016 (www.telegraph.co.uk/art/artists/pablo-picasso-women-are-either-goddesses-or-doormats). Accessed April 9, 2020.

486 *The Woman Who Says No: Françoise Gilot on Her Life with and without Picasso*, by Malte Herwig, Ankerherz Verlag, 2015, pp2.

487 *Sex in the World of Myth*, by David Leeming, Reaktion, 2019, pp42.

488 Aristotle (384–322 BC): Philosopher and Scientist of Ancient Greece,' by P.M. Dunn, *Archives of Disease in Childhood: Foetal and Neonatal Edition*, 91(1), January 2006, pF75-7.

489 'Why Hospitals Started Displaying Newborn Babies Through Windows: How Peering at Babies through Glass Became a Feel-Good Staple of American Maternity Wards,' by Hannah Fagen, *Smithsonian Magazine*, July 25, 2017 (www.smithsonianmag.com/history/why-hospitals-started-displaying-newborn-babies-through-windows-180964186). Accessed April 29, 2020.

490 'A Brief History of Hospital-Based Maternity Services as Relates to the Routine Nursery Care of Normal Newborns,' by Faith Gibson, The American College of Community Midwives archives (collegeofmidwives.org/collegeofmidwives.org/legal_legislative01/HxMfryIndex01/abriefhx.htm). Accessed March 1, 2021.

491 'Anaclitic Depression: An Inquiry into the Genesis of Psychiatric Conditions in Early Childhood, II,' by René A. Spitz and Katherine M. Wolf, *The Psychoanalytic Study of the Child*, 2(1), 1946, pp313–342.

492 'Infant Depression: Nature Seeking Nurture,' by Paul V. Trad, *Jefferson Journal of Psychiatry*, 5(1), January 1987, pp16.

493 'The Sacred Hour: Uninterrupted Skin-to-Skin Contact Immediately After Birth,' by Raylene Phillips, *Newborn and Infant Nursing Reviews*, 13(2), June 2013, pp67–72

494 'Livingstone Hospital,' *Dartford Hospital Histories*, 2020 (dartfordhospitalhistories.org.uk/livingstone/livingstone-introduction/). Accessed October 17, 2020.

495 'Historic Timeline of Obstetric Anaesthesia,' by Alistair G. McKenzie, *Oxford Textbook of Obstetric Anaesthesia*, edited by Vicki Clark, Marc Van de Velde, and Roshan Fernando, Oxford University Press, 2016.

496 'Sister Morphine,' by the Rolling Stones (words and music by Marianne Faithfull, Mick Jagger and Keith Richards, 1971).

497 *Co-Sleeping and SIDS: A Guide for Health Professionals*, The Lullaby Trust, UNICEF, 2019 (www.unicef.org.uk/babyfriendly/wp-content/uploads/sites/2/2016/07/Co-sleeping-and-SIDS-A-Guide-for-Health-Professionals.pdf). Accessed May 9, 2021.

498 'Maternity Care (US Navy, 1963),' US National Library of Medicine, 2019 (www.youtube.com/watch?v=1MZxtMOcO2o). Accessed August 18, 2020.

499 'Anaesthetic Ether,' *Meyler's Side Effects of Drugs (Sixteenth Edition): The International Encyclopaedia of Adverse Drug Reactions and Interactions*, 2016, pp383.

500 'Diethyl Ether,' by F. Monticelli, *Encyclopaedia of Toxicology (Third Edition)*, 2014, pp138–139.

501 'Ethers,' Health and Safety Department, The University of Edinburgh, 2020 (www.ed.ac.uk/

health-safety/guidance/hazardous-substances/ethers). Accessed September 2, 2020.

502 'Morphine Sulphate,' PIPER - Paediatric Infant Perinatal Emergency Retrieval, The Royal Children's Hospital Melbourne, 2020 (www.rch.org.au/piper/neonatal_medication_guidelines/Morphine_Sulphate/). Accessed August 18, 2020.

503 'Tetrachloroethylene (Perchloroethylene),' *Health Effects Notebook for Hazardous Air Pollutants*, United States Environmental Protection Agency, 2020 (www.epa.gov/sites/production/files/2016-09/documents/tetrachloroethylene.pdf). Accessed August 18, 2020.

504 'Promethazine Pregnancy and Breastfeeding Warnings,' Drugs.com, June 16, 2020 (www.drugs.com/pregnancy/promethazine.html). Accessed August 19, 2020.

505 'Lidocaine Hydrochloride: Pregnancy,' National Institute for Health and Care Excellence, 2020 (bnf.nice.org.uk/drug/lidocaine-hydrochloride.html#pregnancy). Accessed August 18, 2020.

506 'Pre-anaesthesia, Anaesthesia, Analgesia, and Euthanasia,' by Paul Flecknell and Ronald P. Wilson, *Laboratory Animal Medicine (Third Edition)*, 2015 (www.sciencedirect.com/topics/neuroscience/thiobarbiturates). Accessed August 22, 2020.

507 'Maternal and Fetal Acid-Base Chemistry: A Major Determinant of Perinatal Outcome,' by L. Omo-Aghoja, *Annals of Medical and Health Sciences Research*, 4(1), January-February 2014, pp8–17.

508 'Pentobarbital (injection),' C.S. Mott Children's Hospital Health Library, 2020 (www.mottchildren.org/health-library/d00335a1). Accessed August 18, 2020.

509 'Physician-assisted Suicide: Ongoing Challenges for Pharmacists,' by Jennifer Fass and Andrea Fass, *American Journal of Health-System Pharmacy*, 68(9), May 2011, pp846–849.

510 'The Effects of Meperidine Analgesia during Labour on Foetal Heart Rate,' by Leila Sekhavat and Shecoofah Behdad, *International Journal of Biomedical Science*, March 2009, 5(1), pp59 – 62.

511 'Respiratory Arrest and Prolonged Respiratory Depression after One Low, Subcutaneous Dose of Alphaprodine for Obstetric Analgesia: A Case Report,' by J.D. Fuller and W.R. Crombleholme, *The Journal of Reproductive Medicine*, February 1987, 32(2), pp149–151.

512 'Tetracaine Hydrochloride,' Drugs.com, October 22, 2019 (www.drugs.com/pro/tetracaine.html). Accessed August 19, 2020.

513 'Effect of Anaesthesia on the Developing Brain: Infant and Foetus,' by D.B. Andropoulos, *Foetal Diagnostic Therapy*, 43, 2018, pp1–11.

514 'Smack and the Society Junkie: Sean Thomas on the Aristocratic Addicts of Narcotics Anonymous, Chelsea,' by Sean Thomas, *The Independent*, September 24, 1994 (www.independent.co.uk/life-style/smack-and-the-society-junkie-sean-thomas-on-the-aristocratic-addicts-of-narcotics-anonymous-chelsea-1451013.html). Accessed December 23, 2020.

515 'Looking Back at Royal Births throughout History,' by Sam Dangremond, *Town and Country*, May 6, 2019 (www.townandcountrymag.com/society/tradition/g19724335/royal-births-history/). Accessed August 22, 2020.

516 'The Future of General Anaesthesia in Obstetrics,' by R.S. Chaggar and J.P. Campbell, *BJA Education*, 17(3), March 2017, pp79 - 83.

517 'd-Tubocurarine in Caesarean Section,' by T. Cecil Gray, *British Medical Journal*, 1(4500), April 1947, pp444–445.

518 'The Use of Scopolamine, Morphine, Atropine, and Similar Drugs by Hypodermic Injection before Inhalation Anaesthesia,' by Dudley W. Buxton, *Section of Anaesthetics*, March 3, 1911.

519 'Excessive Sweating following Intrathecal μ Agonists: Effective Atropine Management,' by Alaa Mazy, *Egyptian Journal of Anaesthesia*, 32(3), July 2016, pp397 – 402.

520 'Atropine,' by A.L. Scott, *Encyclopaedia of Toxicology (Third Edition)*, 2014 (www.sciencedirect.com/topics/neuroscience/atropine). Accessed August 22, 2020.

521 'The Maternal Brain and its Plasticity in Humans,' by Pilyoung Kim, Lane Strathearn, and James E. Swain, *Hormones and Behaviour*, 77, January 2016, pp113–123.

522 'Maternal Plasma Levels of Oxytocin during Physiological Childbirth – a Systematic Review with Implications for Uterine Contractions and Central Actions of Oxytocin,' by Kerstin Uvnäs-Moberg, Anette Ekström-Bergström, Marie Berg, Sarah Buckley, Zada Pajalic, Eleni Hadjigeorgiou, Alicja Kotłowska, Luise Lengler, Bogumila Kielbratowska, Fatima Leon-Larios, Claudia Meier Magistretti, Soo Downe, Bengt Lindström, and Anna Dencker, *BMC Pregnancy and Childbirth*, 19(285), August 2019 (clok.uclan.ac.uk/34336/1/12884_2019_Article_2365.pdf). Accessed May 26, 2021.

523 'Maternal Plasma Levels of Oxytocin during Physiological Childbirth – a Systematic Review

with Implications for Uterine Contractions and Central Actions of Oxytocin,' by Kerstin Uvnäs-Moberg, Anette Ekström-Bergström, Marie Berg, Sarah Buckley, Zada Pajalic, Eleni Hadjigeorgiou, Alicja Kotłowska, Luise Lengler, Bogumila Kielbratowska, Fatima Leon-Larios, Claudia Meier Magistretti, Soo Downe, Bengt Lindström, and Anna Dencker, *BMC Pregnancy and Childbirth*, 19(285), August 2019 (clok.uclan.ac.uk/34336/1/12884_2019_Article_2365.pdf). Accessed May 26, 2021.

524 'Executive Summary of Hormonal Physiology of Childbearing: Evidence and Implications for Women, Babies, and Maternity Care,' by Sarah J. Buckley, *Journal of Perinatal Education*, 24(3), 2015, pp145–153.

525 'Acute Scopolamine Treatment Decreases Dopamine Metabolism in Rat Hippocampus and Frontal Cortex,' by Maurizio Memo, Cristina Missale, Luca Trivelli, and Pier Franco Spano, *European Journal of Pharmacology*, 149(3), May 1988, pp367–370.

526 'Scopolamine,' Drugs and Lactation Database, National Centre for Biotechnology Information, US National Library of Medicine, October 31, 2018 (www.ncbi.nlm.nih.gov/books/NBK501482/). Accessed August 17, 2020.

527 'Self-Soothing Behaviours with Particular Reference to Oxytocin Release Induced by Non-Noxious Sensory Stimulation,' by Kerstin Uvnäs-Moberg, Linda Handlin, and Maria Petersson, *Frontiers in Psychology*, 5(1529), January 2015, pp1–16.

528 'Social Behaviour, Hormones and Adult Neurogenesis,' by Maya Opendak, Brandy A. Briones, and Elizabeth Gould, *Frontiers in Neuroendocrinology*, 41, April 2016, pp71–86.

529 'How Stress Can Influence Brain Adaptations to Motherhood,' by Pilyoung Kim, *Frontiers in Neuroendocrinology*, 60, January 2021, p.100875.

530 'FDA Pregnancy Categories,' *Chemical Hazards Emergency Medical Management*, U.S. Department of Health and Human Services, 2020 (chemm.nlm.nih.gov/pregnancycategories.htm). Accessed August 22, 2020.

531 'From Arrow Poison to Neuromuscular Blockers,' by T.C.K. Brown, *Paediatric Anaesthesia*, 23(9), September 2013, pp865–7.

532 'Intravenous Administration of d-Tubocurarine and Pancuronium in Foetal Lambs,' by D.H. Chestnut, C.P. Weiner, C.S. Thompson, and G.L. McLaughlin, *American Journal of Obstetrics and Gynaecology*, 160(2), February1989, pp510–513.

533 'Reactive Airway Disease,' by Malcolm Packer, *Anaesthesia Secrets (Fourth Edition)*, edited by James Duke, Mosby, 2010, pp270.

534 'GABA: A Pioneer Transmitter That Excites Immature Neurons and Generates Primitive Oscillations,' by Yehezkel Ben-Ari, Jean-Luc Gaiarsa, Roman Tyzio, and Rustem Khazipov, *Physiological Reviews*, 87(4), October 2007, pp1215–1284.

535 'ABM Clinical Protocol #15: Analgesia and Anaesthesia for the Breastfeeding Mother,' by Anne Montgomery and Thomas W. Hale and the Academy of Breastfeeding Medicine, *Breastfeeding Medicine*, 7(6), December 2012, pp547–553.

536 'Pethidine - A Little Shot Of Something Not So Nice,' by Beverley A. Lawrence Beech, *AIMS Journal*, 10(1), 1993 (www.aims.org.uk/journal/item/pethidine#:~:text=Pethidine%20is%20a%20synthetic%2C%20addictive,during%20the%20Second%20World%20War). Accessed March 1, 2021.

537 'Behavioural Effects of Norpethidine, a Metabolite of Pethidine, in Rats,' by J.L. Plummer, G.K. Gourlay, P.L. Cmielewski, J. Odontiadis, and I. Harvey, *Toxicology*, 95(1-3), January 1995, pp37–44.

538 'Norpethidine (Opioid Analgesics),' by Dhanalakshmi Koyyalagunta, *Pain Management*, 2, 2007, pp939–964.

539 'Pharmacological Methods of Pain Relief,' by Margaret Yerby, *Pain in Childbearing: Key Issues in Management*, edited by Margaret Yerby, Bailliere Tindall, 2000, pp117.

540 'Childbirth Drugs Found to Affect Babies,' by Victor Cohn, *The Washington Post*, January 16, 1979 (www.washingtonpost.com/archive/politics/1979/01/16/childbirth-drugs-found-to-affect-babies/5e19d40b-2ebe-4db7-bcc8-460d04ea6cda/). Accessed August 18, 2020.

541 'Holly,' Episode 11, Season 2, *The Handmaid's Tale*, screenplay by Bruce Miller and Kyra Snyder, directed by Daina Reid, June 27, 2018.

542 'Dear Meghan, if you're going to have a California home birth, take my advice,' by Teresa Fitzherbert, *The Telegraph*, April 10, 2021 (www.telegraph.co.uk/luxury/kids/dear-meghan-going-have-california-home-birth-take-advice). Accessed April 14, 2021.

543 'A Conversation with 30 Rock's Tina Fey', by Caroline Ryder, *Women's Health*, January 25, 2007 (www.womenshealthmag.com/life/a19932123/tina-fey-interview). Accessed May 20, 2021.

544 'Butorphanol Tartrate', *Science Direct*, 2021 (www.sciencedirect.com/topics/medicine-and-dentistry/butorphanol-tartrate). Accessed May 20, 2021.

545 'Butorphanol Pregnancy and Breastfeeding Warnings', Drugs.com, January 28, 2021 (www.drugs.com/pregnancy/butorphanol.html). Accessed May 20, 2021.

546 'Anaesthesia and the Developing Nervous System: Advice for Clinicians and Families', by Neil S. Morton, *BJA Education*, 15(3), June 2015, pp118–122.

547 'Anaesthesia for Non-Obstetric Surgery during Pregnancy,' by Madhusudan Upadya and P.J. Saneesh, *Indian Journal of Anaesthesia*, 60(4), April 2016, pp234–241.

548 'Effect of Anaesthesia on the Developing Brain: Infant and Foetus', by D.B. Andropoulos, *Foetal Diagnostic Therapy*, 43, 2018, pp1–11.

549 'Dexmedetomidine and Ketamine Show Distinct Patterns of Cell Degeneration and Apoptosis in the Developing Rat Neonatal Brain,' by Carlo Pancaro, B. Scott Segal, Robert W. Sikes, Zainab Almeer, Roman Schumann, Ruben J. Azocar, and James E. Marchand, *The Journal of Maternal-Foetal and Neonatal Medicine*, 29(23), December 2016, pp3827–3833.

550 'Potential Mechanism of Cell Death in the Developing Rat Brain Induced by Propofol Anaesthesia, by Vesna Pešić, Desanka Milanović, Nikola Tanić, Jelena Popić, Selma Kanazir, Vesna Jevtović-Todorović, and Sabera Ruždijić, *International Journal of Developmental Neuroscience*, 27(3), May 2009, pp279–287.

551 'General Anaesthetics and Neurotoxicity: How Much Do We Know?' by Vesna Jevtvovic-Todorovic, Anaesthesiology Clinics, 34(3), September 2016, pp439–451.

552 'Isoflurane Exposure for Three Hours Triggers Apoptotic Cell Death in Neonatal Macaque Brain,' by K.K. Noguchi, S.A. Johnson, G.A. Dissen, L.D. Martin, F.M. Manzella, K.J. Schenning, J.W. Olney, and A.M. Brambrink, *British Journal of Anaesthesia*, 119(3), September 2017, pp524–531.

553 'Prevalence of Benzodiazepines and Benzodiazepine-Related Drugs Exposure before, during and after Pregnancy: A Systematic Review and Meta-Analysis,' by Babette Bais, Nina M. Molenaar, Hilmar H. Bijma, Witte J.G. Hoogendijk, Cornelis L. Mulder, Annemarie I. Luik, Mijke P. Lambregtse-van den Berg, and Astrid M. Kamperman, *Journal of Affective Disorders*, 269, May 2020, pp18–27.

554 'Ketamine Anaesthesia during the First Week of Life can Cause Long-Lasting Cognitive Deficits in Rhesus Monkeys,' by M.G. Paule, M. Li, R.R. Allen, F. Liu, X. Zou, C. Hotchkiss, J.P. Hanig, T.A. Patterson, W. Slikker Jr, and C. Wang, *Neurotoxicology and Teratology*, 33(2), March-April 2011, pp220–230.

555 'Anaesthesia and the Developing Nervous System: Advice for Clinicians and Families', by Neil S. Morton, *BJA Education*, 15(3), June 2015, pp118–122.

556 'What do Recent Human Studies Tell Us about the Association between Anaesthesia in Young Children and Neurodevelopmental Outcomes?' by J.D. O'Leary and D.O. Warner, *British Journal of Anaesthesia*,119(3), September 2017, pp458–464.

557 'FDA Drug Safety Communication: FDA Review Results in New Warnings about Using General Anaesthetics and Sedation Drugs in Young Children and Pregnant Women,' US FDA, December 14, 2016 (www.fda.gov/drugs/drug-safety-and-availability/fda-drug-safety-communication-fda-review-results-new-warnings-about-using-general-anesthetics-and). Accessed January 6, 2021.

558 'General Anaesthetics and Neurotoxicity: How Much Do We Know?' by Vesna Jevtvovic-Todorovic, *Anaesthesiology Clinics*, 34(3), September 2016, pp439–451.

559 'Neonatal Pain Management: Still in Search of the Holy Grail,' by Karel Allegaert and John N. van den Anker, *International Journal of Clinical Pharmacology and Therapeutics*, 54(7), July 2016, pp514–523.

560 'Use of Analgesic and Sedative Drugs in the NICU: Integrating Clinical Trials and Laboratory Data,' by Xavier Durrmeyer, Laszlo Vutskits, Kanwaljeet J.S. Anand, and Peter C. Rimensberger, *Paediatric Research*, 67(2), February 2010, pp117–127.

561 'Morphological Features of the Neonatal Brain following Exposure to Regional Anaesthesia during Labour and Delivery', by Marisa N. Spann, Dana Serino, Ravi Bansal, Xuejun Hao, Giancarlo Nati, Zachary Toth, Kirwan Walsh, I-Chin Chiang, Juan Sanchez-Peña, Jun Liu, Alayar Kangarlu, Feng Liu, Yunsuo Duan, Satie Shova, Jane Fried, Gregory Z. Tau, Tove S.

Rosen, Bradley S. Peterson, *Magnetic Resonance Imaging*, 33(2), February 2015, pp213–221.

562 'Early Childhood General Anaesthesia Exposure and Neurocognitive Development,' by L. Sun, *British Journal of Anaesthesia*, 105 (Supplement 1), December 2010, pp.i61- i68.

563 'Neurodevelopmental Implications of the Use of Sedation and Analgesia in Neonates,' by Andrew Davidson and Randall P. Flick, *Clinical Perinatology*, 40(3), September 2013, pp559 - 73.

564 'Association between Newborns' Breastfeeding Behaviours in the First Two Hours After Birth and Drugs Used For Their Mothers in Labour,' by Zeinab Hemati, Mehri Abdollahi, Saba Broumand, Masoumeh Delaram, Mahboobeh Namnabati, and Davood Kiani, *Iranian Journal of Child Neurology*, 12(2), Spring 2018, pp33 – 40.

565 'Beyond Labour: The Role of Natural and Synthetic Oxytocin in the Transition to Motherhood,' by Aleeca F. Bell, Elise N. Erickson, and C. Sue Carter, *Journal of Midwifery and Women's Health*, 59(1), January 2014, pp35 – 42.

566 Dorothy Sweatt, 'Twilight Sleep – The Brutal Way Some Women Gave Birth In The 1900s,' by Sam McCulloch, *Belly Belly*, June 5, 2018 (www.bellybelly.com.au/birth/twilight-sleep/). Accessed September 9, 2020.

567 Telephone interview with Miranda Snow, August 30, 2020.

568 'Individualised, Supportive Care Key to Positive Childbirth Experience, says WHO,' World Health Organisation, February 15, 2018 (www.who.int/mediacentre/news/releases/2018/positive-childbirth-experience/en/). Accessed September 6, 2020.

569 'Regional Variations in Childbirth Interventions in the Netherlands: A Nationwide Explorative Study,' by A. E. Seijmonsbergen-Schermers, D. C. Zondag, M. Nieuwenhuijze, T. Van den Akker, C. J. Verhoeven, C. Geerts, F. Schellevis, and A. De Jonge, *BMC Pregnancy and Childbirth*, 18(1), June 2018, pp192.

570 'Medication use in pregnancy: a cross-sectional, multinational web-based study,' by A. Lupattelli, O. Spigset, M. J. Twigg, K. Zagorodnikova, A. C. Mårdby, M. E. Moretti, M. Drozd, A. Panchaud, K. Hämeen-Anttila, A. Rieutord, R. Gjergja Juraski, M. Odalovic, D. Kennedy, G. Rudolf, H. Juch, A. Passier, I. Björnsdóttir, and H. Nordeng, *British Medical Journal Open*, January 2014, pp4:e004365

571 'Chronic Pain Prevalence and Exposures during Pregnancy,' by Shona L. Ray-Griffith, Bethany Morrison, and Zachary N. Stowe, *Pain Research and Management*, 2, August 2019, pp1 – 7.

572 'Prenatal Exposure to Acetaminophen and Risk for Attention Deficit Hyperactivity Disorder and Autistic Spectrum Disorder: A Systematic Review, Meta-Analysis, and Meta-Regression Analysis of Cohort Studies,' by Reem Masarwa, Hagai Levine, Einat Gorelik, Shimon Reif, Amichai Perlman, and Ilan Matok, *American Journal of Epidemiology*, 187(8), August 2018, pp1817 - 1827.

573 'Associations between Acetaminophen Use during Pregnancy and ADHD Symptoms Measured at Ages 7 and 11 Years,' by John M. D. Thompson, Karen E. Waldie, Clare R. Wall, Rinky Murphy, Edwin A. Mitchell, ABC study group Collaborators, *PLoS ONE*, 9(9), September 2014, pp.e108210.

574 *Pain: The Science of the Feeling Brain*, By Abdul-Ghaaliq Lalkhen, Atlantic Books, 2021, pp148.

575 'Chronic Pain during Pregnancy: A Review of the Literature,' by Shona L. Ray-Griffith, Michael P. Wendel, Zachary N Stowe, and Everett F Magann, *International Journal of Women's Health*, 10, April 2018, pp153 – 164.

576 *Pain: The Science of the Feeling Brain*, By Abdul-Ghaaliq Lalkhen, Atlantic Books, 2021, pp259.

577 'Chronic Pain during Pregnancy: A Review of the Literature,' by Shona L. Ray-Griffith, Michael P. Wendel, Zachary N Stowe, and Everett F Magann, *International Journal of Women's Health*, 10, April 2018, pp153 – 164.

578 'The Importance of Generating More Data on Cannabis Use in Pregnancy,' by Anick Bérard, *Nature Medicine*, 26(10), October 2020, pp1515 – 1516.

579 'Prenatal Cannabis Exposure - The 'First Hit' to the Endocannabinoid System,' by Kimberlei A. Richardson, Allison K. Hester, and Gabrielle L. McLemore, *Neurotoxicology and Teratology*, 58, November - December 2016, pp5 - 14.

580 'Cannabis Use during Pregnancy: Pharmacokinetics and Effects on Child Development,' by Kimberly S. Grant, Rebekah Petroff, Nina Isoherranen, Nephi Stella, and Thomas M. Burbacher, *Pharmacology and Therapeutics*, 182, February 2018, pp133 – 151.

581 'Cannabis Use during Pregnancy and Postpartum,' by Sophia Badowski and Graeme Smith, *Canadian Family Physician*, 66(2), February 2020, pp98 – 103.

582 'U.S. Surgeon General's Advisory: Marijuana Use and the Developing Brain,' Office of the US Surgeon General, 2019 (www.hhs.gov/surgeongeneral/reports-and-publications/addiction-and-substance-misuse/advisory-on-marijuana-use-and-developing-brain/index.html). Accessed February 28, 2021.

583 'Lasting Impacts of Prenatal Cannabis Exposure and the Role of Endogenous Cannabinoids in the Developing Brain,' by Chia-Shan Wu, Christopher P. Jew, and Hui-Chen Lu, *Future Neurology*, 6(4), 2011, pp459 – 480.

584 'Cannabis and the Developing Brain: Insights into Its Long-Lasting Effects,' by Yasmin L. Hurd, Olivier J. Manzoni, Mikhail V. Pletnikov, Francis S. Lee, Sagnik Bhattacharyya and Miriam Melis, *Journal of Neuroscience*, 39(42), October 2019, pp8250 – 8258.

585 'Associations Between Prenatal Cannabis Exposure and Childhood Outcomes: Results From the ABCD Study,' by Sarah E. Paul, Alexander S. Hatoum, Jeremy D. Fine, Emma C. Johnson, Isabella Hansen, Nicole R. Karcher, Allison L. Moreau, Erin Bondy, Yueyue Qu, Ebony B. Carter, Cynthia E. Rogers, Arpana Agrawal, Deanna M. Barch, and Ryan Bogdan, *JAMA Psychiatry*, 78(1), 2021, pp64 - 76.

586 'Foetal Disposition of Delta 9-Tetrahydrocannabinol (THC) during Late Pregnancy in the Rhesus Monkey,' by J. R. Bailey, H. C. Cunny, M. G. Paule, and W. Slikker Jr , *Toxicology and Applied Pharmacology*, 90(2), September 1987, pp315 - 321.

587 'A Cannabinoid Analogue of Δ9-Tetrahydrocannabinol Disrupts Neural Development in Chick,' by Delphine Psychoyos, Basalingappa Hungund , Thomas Cooper, and Richard H. Finnell, *Developmental and Reproductive Toxicology*, 83(5), October 2008, pp477 - 488.

588 'U.S. Surgeon General's Advisory: Marijuana Use and the Developing Brain,' Office of the US Surgeon General, 2019 (www.hhs.gov/surgeongeneral/reports-and-publications/addiction-and-substance-misuse/advisory-on-marijuana-use-and-developing-brain/index.html). Accessed February 28, 2021.

589 'Association between Self-reported Prenatal Cannabis Use and Maternal, Perinatal, and Neonatal Outcomes,' by Daniel J. Corsi, Laura Walsh, Deborah Weiss, Helen Hsu, and Darine El, *JAMA*, 322(2), July 2019, pp145 - 152.

590 'Circulating Endocannabinoid Concentrations and Sexual Arousal in Women,' by Carolin Klein, Matthew N. Hill, Sabrina C.H. Chang, Cecilia J. Hillard, and Boris B. Gorzalka, *Journal of Sexual Medicine*, June 2012, 9(6), pp1588 – 1601.

591 'Endocannabinoid Signalling Directs Peri-Implantation Events,' by H. Wang, H. Xie, and S. K. Dey, *The AAPS journal*, 8(2), June 2006, E425–E432.

592 'Endocannabinoids and Immune Regulation,' by R. Pandey, K. Mousawy, M. Nagarkatti, and P. Nagarkatti, *Pharmacological Research*, 60(2), August 2009, pp85 – 92.

593 'Lasting Impacts of Prenatal Cannabis Exposure and the Role of Endogenous Cannabinoids in the Developing Brain,' by Chia-Shan Wu, Christopher P. Jew and Hui-Chen Lu, *Future Neurology*, 6(4), July 1, 2011.

594 'Maternal Cannabis Use alters Ventral Striatal Dopamine D2 Gene Regulation in the Offspring,' by Jennifer A. DiNieri, Xinyu Wang, Henrietta Szutorisz, Sabrina M. Spano, Jasbir Kaur, Patrizia Casaccia, Diana Dow-Edwards, and Yasmin L. Hurd, *Biological Psychiatry*, 70(8), October 15, 2011, pp763 - 769.

595 'Long Term Consequences of Illegal Drug Use during Pregnancy,' by Koenraad Smets, *International Archives of Paediatrics and Neonatology*, January 1, 2020, pp1 – 3.

596 'What Does Cannabis Do to the Brain before Birth?' by Stefano Musardo and Camilla Bellone, *eLife*, 7, September 2018, p.e41229.

597 'Depressive Symptoms Linked to Rapid Kidney Function Decline: Press Release,' American Society of Nephrology, May 28, 2021 (www.asn-online.org/about/press/releases/ASN_PR_20210528_CJASN.Release.Qin.F.pdf). Accessed May 30, 2021.

598 'Associations Between Prenatal Cannabis Exposure and Childhood Outcomes: Results from the ABCD Study,' by Sarah E. Paul, Alexander S. Hatoum, Jeremy D. Fine, Emma C. Johnson, Isabella Hansen, Nicole R. Karcher, Allison L. Moreau, Erin Bondy, Yueyue Qu, Ebony B. Carter, Cynthia E. Rogers, Arpana Agrawal, Deanna M. Barch, and Ryan Bogdan, *JAMA Psychiatry*, 78(1), September 2021, pp64 - 76.

599 'Cannabis Use During Pregnancy and Its Relationship with Foetal Developmental Outcomes and Psychiatric Disorders. A Systematic Review,' by Carlos Roncero, Isabel Valriberas-Herrero, Marcela Mezzatesta-Gava, José L. Villegas, Lourdes Aguilar, and Lara Grau-López,

Reproductive Health, 17(1), February 2020, pp25 - 33.

600 'Demographic, Emotional and Social Determinants of Cannabis Use in Early Pregnancy: The Generation R Study,' by Hanan el Marroun, Henning Tiemeier, Vincent W. V. Jaddoe, Albert Hofman, Johan P. Mackenbach, Eric A. P. Steegers, Frank C. Verhulst, Wim van den Brink, Anja C. Huizink, *Drug and Alcohol Dependence*, 98(3), December 1, 2008, pp218 - 226.

601 'Maternal Cannabis Use in Pregnancy and Child Neurodevelopmental Outcomes,' by Daniel J. Corsi, Jessy Donelle, Ewa Sucha, Steven Hawken, Helen Hsu, Darine El-Chaâr, Lise Bisnaire, Deshayne Fell, Shi Wu Wen, and Mark Walker, *Nature Medicine*, 26(10), August 2020, pp1536 – 1540.

602 'Cannabis Use During the Perinatal Period in a State with Legalized Recreational and Medical Marijuana: The Association Between Maternal Characteristics, Breastfeeding Patterns, and Neonatal Outcomes,' by Tessa L Crume, Ashley L. Juhl, Ashley Brooks-Russell, Katelyn E. Hall, Erica Wymore, and Laura M. Borgelt, *Journal of Paediatrics*, 197, June 2018, pp90 - 96.

603 'Cannabis Use during Pregnancy and Postpartum,' by S. Badowski and G. Smith, *Canadian Family Physician*, 66(2), February 2020, pp98 – 103.

604 'Trends in Self-Reported and Biochemically Tested Marijuana Use Among Pregnant Females in California From 2009–2016,' by Kelly C. Young-Wolff, Lue-Yen Tucker, Stacey Alexeeff, Mary Anne Armstrong, Amy Conway, Constance Weisner, and Nancy Goler, *JAMA*, 318(24), December 26, 2017, pp2490 – 2491.

605 'The Cannabinoid Content of Legal Cannabis in Washington State Varies Systematically Across Testing Facilities and Popular Consumer Products,' by Nick Jikomes and Michael Zoorob, *Scientific Reports*, 8(1), March 2018, pp4519.

606 'Changes in Cannabis Potency Over the Last Two Decades (1995-2014): Analysis of Current Data in the United States,' by Mahmoud A. ElSohly, Zlatko Mehmedic, Susan Foster, Chandrani Gon, Suman Chandra, and James C. Church, *Biological Psychiatry*, 79(7), April 2016, pp613 - 619.

607 'Demographic, Emotional and Social Determinants of Cannabis Use in Early Pregnancy: The Generation R Study,' by Hanan el Marroun, Henning Tiemeier, Vincent W. V. Jaddoe, Albert Hofman, Johan P. Mackenbach, Eric A. P. Steegers, Frank C. Verhulst, Wim van den Brink, and Anja C. Huizink, *Drug and Alcohol Dependence*, 98(3), December 1, 2008, pp218 - 226.

608 *Women and Drugs: Drug Use, Drug Supply and Their Consequences - World Drug Report 2018*, United Nations Office on Drugs and Crime (www.unodc.org/wdr2018/prelaunch/WDR18_Booklet_5_WOMEN.pdf). Accessed July 4, 2020.

609 'Recommendations from Cannabis Dispensaries About First-Trimester Cannabis Use,' by Betsy Dickson, Chanel Mansfield, Maryam Guiahi, Amanda A. Allshouse, Laura M. Borgelt, Jeanelle Sheeder, Robert M. Silver, and Torri D. Metz, *Obstetrics and Gynaecology*, 131(6), June 2018, pp1031-1038.

610 'Neonatal Behavioural Correlates of Prenatal Exposure to Marihuana, Cigarettes and Alcohol in a Low Risk Population,' by P. A. Fried and J. E. Makin, *Neurotoxicology and Teratology*, 9(1), January - February 1987, pp1 - 7.

611 'Association between Stillbirth and Illegal Drug Use and Smoking during Pregnancy,' by M. W. Varner, R. M. Silver, C. J. Rowland Hogue, M. Willinger, C.B. Parker, V. R. Thorsten, R. L. Goldenberg, G. R. Saade, D. J. Dudley, D. Coustan, B. Stoll, R. Bukowski, M. A. Koch, D. Conway, H. Pinar, U. M. Reddy, and the Eunice Kennedy Shriver National Institute of Child Health and Human Development Stillbirth Collaborative Research Network, *Obstetrics and Gynaecology*, 23(1), January 2014, pp113 – 125.

612 'Association of Depression, Anxiety, and Trauma with Cannabis Use During Pregnancy,' by Kelly C. Young-Wolff, Varada Sarovar, Lue-Yen Tucker, Nancy C. Goler, Stacey E. Alexeeff, Kathryn K. Ridout, and Lyndsay A. Avalos, *JAMA Network Open*, 3(2), February 2020, pp.e1921333.

613 'Reasons for Substance Use Continuation and Discontinuation during Pregnancy: A Qualitative Study,' by Kiri A. Latuskie, Naomi C. Z. Andrews, Mary Motz, Tom Leibson, Zubin Austin, Shinya Ito, and Debra J. Pepler, *Women and Birth*, 32(1), February 2019, pp.e57 - e64.

614 'I love him so much #willienelson #smokeweedeveryday #fangirl', Zia McCabe, Instagram, December 24, 2020 (www.instagram.com/p/CJMrw49BBHl). Accessed May 24, 2021.

615 Online interview with Zia McCabe, May 3, 2021.

616 'Verbal Memory Performance and Reduced Cortical Thickness of Brain Regions Along the

Uncinate Fasciculus in Young Adult Cannabis Users,' by Nina Levar, Alan N. Francis, Matthew J. Smith, Wilson C. Ho, and Jodi M. Gilman, *Cannabis and Cannabinoid Research*, 3(1), March 2018, pp56 – 65.

617 'Limbic-Visual Attenuation to Crying Faces Underlies Neglectful Mothering,' by Inmaculada León, María José Rodrigo, Wael El-Deredy, Cristián Modroño, Juan Andrés Hernández-Cabrera, and Ileana Quiñones, *Scientific Reports*, 9(1), April 2019, pp6373.

618 'Perceived Quality of Maternal Care in Childhood and Structure and Function of Mothers' Brain,' by Pilyoung Kim, James F. Leckman, Linda C. Mayes, Michal-Ann Newman, Ruth Feldman, and James E. Swain1, *Developmental Science*, 13(4), July 2010, pp662 – 673.

619 'The Maternal Brain and its Plasticity in Humans,' by Pilyoung Kim, Lane Strathearn, and James E. Swain, *Hormones and Behaviour*, 77, January 2016, pp113 – 123.

620 'Effect of Oxytocin on Craving and Stress Response in Marijuana-Dependent Individuals: A Pilot Study,' by Aimee L. McRae-Clark, Nathaniel L. Baker, Megan Moran-Santa Maria, and Kathleen T. Brady, *Psychopharmacology*, 228(4), August 2013, pp623 – 631.

621 'Smoking weed during pregnancy,' mariahgarrett, Reddit, January 25, 2017 (www.reddit. com/r/Treeparents/comments/5pxwhy/smoking_weed_during_pregnancy). Accessed May 24, 2021.

622 *Guilty: Liberal 'Victims' and Their Assault on America*, by Ann Coulter, 2009, pp39, 38, 44.

623 'Epidemiology of Medications Use in Pregnancy,' by Martina Ayad and Maged M. Costantine, *Seminars in Perinatology*, 39(7), November 2015, pp508 – 511.

624 'Cholinergic Modulation of the Hippocampal Region and Memory Function,' by Juhee Haam and Jerrel L. Yake, *Journal of Neurochemistry*, 142 (Supplement 2), August 2017, pp111 – 121.

625 'Comparative Study on the Effect of Anticholinergic Compounds on Sweating,' by Walter B. Shelley and Peter N. Horvath, *The Journal of Investigative Dermatology*, 16(4), April 1951, pp267 – 274.

626 'Anticholinergics,' International Hyperhidrosis Society, 2021 (www.sweathelp.org/hyperhidrosis-treatments/medications.html). Accessed January 18, 2021.

627 'Activation of Olfactory Cortex in Newborn Infants After Odour Stimulation: A Functional Near-Infrared Spectroscopy Study,' by Marco Bartocci, Jan Winberg, Carmelina Ruggiero, Lena L Bergqvist, Giovanni Serra and Hugo Lagercrantz, *Paediatric Research*, 48(1), July 2000, pp18 – 23.

628 'Activation of Olfactory Cortex in Newborn Infants After Odour Stimulation: A Functional Near-Infrared Spectroscopy Study,' by Marco Bartocci, Jan Winberg, Carmelina Ruggiero, Lena L Bergqvist, Giovanni Serra and Hugo Lagercrantz, *Paediatric Research*, 48(1), July 2000, pp18 – 23.

629 'Olfaction and Human Neonatal Behaviour: Clinical Implications,' by J. Winberg and R. H. Porter, *Acta Paediatrica*, 87(1), January 2007, pp6 - 10.

630 *Smells: A Cultural History of Odours in Early Modern Times*, by Robert Muchembled, translated by Susan Pickford, Polity, 2020 (first published as *La civilisation des odeurs: XVIe – début XIXe siècle* in 2017), pp6.

631 'Chemical Communication and Mother-Infant Recognition,' by Stefano Vaglio, *Communicative and Integrative Biology*, 2(3), May - June 2009, pp279 – 281.

632 'Does the Newborn Baby Find the Nipple by Smell?' by H. Varendi, R. H. Porter and J. Winberg, *The Lancet*, 344(8928), October 1994, pp989 - 990.

633 'Olfaction and Human Neonatal Behaviour: Clinical Implications,' by J. Winberg and R. H. Porter, *Acta Paediatrica*, 87(1), January 2007, pp6 - 10.

634 'Chemical Communication and Mother-Infant Recognition,' by Stefano Vaglio, *Communicative and Integrative Biology*, 2(3), May - June 2009, pp279 – 281.

635 'The Olfactory Critical Period is Determined by Activity-Dependent Sema7A/PlxnC1 Signalling within Glomeruli,' by Nobuko Inoue, Hirofumi Nishizumi, Rumi Ooyama, Kazutaka Mogi, Katsuhiko Nishimori, Takefumi Kikusui, and Hitoshi Sakano, *eLife*, 10, March 2021; pp.e65078.

636 'Self-Soothing Behaviours with Particular Reference to Oxytocin Release Induced by Non-Noxious Sensory Stimulation,' by Kerstin Uvnäs-Moberg, Linda Handlin, and Maria Petersson, *Frontiers in Psychology*, 5(1529), January 2015, pp1 - 16.

637 'The Olfactory Critical Period is Determined by Activity-Dependent Sema7A/PlxnC1 Signalling within Glomeruli,' by Nobuko Inoue, Hirofumi Nishizumi, Rumi Ooyama, Kazutaka

Mogi, Katsuhiko Nishimori, Takefumi Kikusui, and Hitoshi Sakano, *eLife*, 10, March 2021; pp.e65078.

638 'The Functional Neuroanatomy of Maternal Love: Mother's Response to Infant's Attachment Behaviours,' by Madoka Noriuchi, Yoshiaki Kikuchi, and Atsushi Senoo, *Biological Psychiatry*, 63(4), February 2008, pp415 - 423.

639 'Early Childhood Deprivation is Associated with Alterations in Adult Brain Structure despite Subsequent Environmental Enrichment,' by Nuria K. Mackes, Dennis Golm, Sagari Sarkar, Robert Kumsta, Michael Rutter, Graeme Fairchild, Mitul A. Mehta, Edmund J. S. Sonuga-Barke, and on behalf of the ERA Young Adult Follow-up team, *PNAS*, 117(1), January 2020, pp641 - 649.

640 'Plato and Aristotle on the Exposure of Infants at Athens,' by G. van N. Viljoen, *Acta Classica*, 2, 1959, pp58 - 69.

641 'Aristotle (384-322 BC): Philosopher and Scientist of Ancient Greece,' by P. M. Dunn, *Archives of Disease in Childhood: Foetal and Neonatal Edition*, 91(1), January 2006, p.F75 - 77.

642 "Not worth the Rearing': The Causes of Infant Exposure in Ancient Greece,' by Cynthia Patterson, *Transactions of the American Philological Association (1974 - 2014)*, 115, 1985, pp103 - 123.

643 'Recognition of Maternal Axillary Odours by Infants,' by Jennifer M. Cernoch and Richard H. Porter, *Child Development*, 56(6), December 1985, pp1593 - 1598.

644 'Unravelling the Mystery of Vernix Caseosa,' by Gurcharan Singh and G Archana, *Indian Journal of Dermatology*, 53(2), 2008, pp54 – 60.

645 'Initiative to Improve Exclusive Breastfeeding by Delaying the Newborn Bath,' by Heather Condo DiCioccio, Candace Ady, James F. Bena and Nancy M. Albert, *Health Care Improvement and Evaluation*, 48(2), March 2019, pp189 - 196.

646 'WHO Recommendation on Bathing and Other Immediate Postnatal Care of the Newborn,' World Health Organisation, February 17, 2018 (extranet.who.int/rhl/topics/newborn-health/care-newborn-infant/who-recommendation-bathing-and-other-immediate-postnatal-care-newborn). Accessed August 22, 2020.

647 'First Bathing Time of Newborn Infants after Birth: A Comparative Analysis,' by Duygu Gözen, Sinem Y. Çaka, Selda A. Beşirik, and Yıldız Perk, *Journal for Specialists in Paediatric Nursing*, 24(2), April 2019, p.e12239

648 'Neural Control of Maternal Behaviour and Olfactory Recognition of Offspring,' by Keith M. Kendrick, Ana P. C. Da Costa, Kevin D. Broad, Satoshi Ohkura, Rosalinda Guevara, Frederic Lévy and E. Barry Keverne, *Brain Research Bulletin*, 44(4), 1997, pp383 - 395.

649 'Olfactory Regulation of Maternal Behaviour in Mammals,' by F. Lévy, M. Keller and P. Poindron, *Hormones and Behaviour*, 46(3), September 2004, pp284 - 302.

650 'Maternal Prefrontal Cortex Activation by Newborn Infant Odours,' by Shota Nishitani, Saori Kuwamoto, Asuka Takahira, Tsunetake Miyamura, and Kazuyuki Shinohara, *Chemical Senses*, 39(3), March 2014, pp195 – 202.

651 'Why is the Prefrontal Cortex So Important?' University College Dublin's School of Psychology Lab, December 17, 2018 (ucdneuropsychologylab.wordpress.com/2018/12/17/why-is-the-prefrontal-cortex-so-important/). Accessed August 23, 2020.

652 'A Comparative Volumetric Analysis of the Prefrontal Cortex in Human and Baboon MRI,' by T. McBride, S. E. Arnold, and R. C. Gur, *Brain, Behaviour and Evolution*, 54(3), September 1999, pp159 - 166.

653 'Morphometric Methods for Studying the Prefrontal Cortex in Suicide Victims and Psychiatric Patients,' by G. Rajkowska, *Annals of the New York Academy of Sciences*, 836 (1), December 1997, pp253 – 268.

654 'Dorsolateral Prefrontal Cortex N-acetylaspartate/ Total Creatine (NAA/tCr) Loss in Male Recreational Cannabis Users,' by D. Hermann, A. Sartorius, H. Welzel, S. Walter, G. Skopp, G. Ende, K. Mann, *Biological Psychiatry*, 61(11), June 2007, pp1281 – 1289.

655 'Brain Structure and Functional Connectivity Associated with Pornography Consumption: The Brain on Porn,' by Simone Kühn and Jürgen Gallinat, *JAMA Psychiatry*, 71(7), July 2014, pp827 - 834.

656 'Prefrontal Structural and Functional Brain Imaging findings in Antisocial, Violent, and Psychopathic Individuals: A Meta-Analysis,' by Yaling Yang and Adrian Raine, *Psychiatry Research: Neuroimaging*, 174(2), November 2009, pp81 – 88.

657 'Impairment of Social and Moral Behavior Related to Early Damage in Human Prefrontal

Cortex,' by S. W. Anderson, A. Bechara, H. Damasio, D. Tranel, and A. R. Damasio, *Nature Neuroscience*, 2(11), November 1999, pp1032 – 1037.

658 'Prefrontal Cortical Volume in Childhood-Onset Major Depression Preliminary Findings,' by Carla L. Nolan, Gregory J. Moore, Rachel Madden, Tiffany Farchione, Marla Bartoi, Elisa Lorch, Carol M. Stewart, and David R. Rosenberg, *Archives of General Psychiatry*, 59(2), February 2002, pp173 - 179.

659 Pornography Addiction: A Neuroscience Perspective, by Donald L. Hilton Jr and Clark Watts, *Surgical Neurology International*, 2, February 2011; pp19.

660 'Relationship Between Drug Use and Prefrontal-Associated Traits,' by Marcello Spinella, *Addiction Biology*, 8(1), March 2003, pp67 - 74.

661 'Drawing the Developmental Landscape of the Human Prefrontal Cortex by Single-Cell RNAseq,' by Xiaoqun Wang, Institute of Biophysics, Chinese Academy of Sciences, March 15, 2018 (english.ibp.cas.cn/rh/rp/201803/t20180315_190734.html). Accessed August 23, 2020.

662 'Q&A Focusing on Mothering through Breastfeeding when Accrediting New Leaders – Removing Separation as a Barrier, La Leche League International, 2020 (www.llli.org/qa-focusing-on-mothering-through-breastfeeding-when-accrediting-new-leaders-removing-separation-as-a-barrier/#Babies). Accessed August 27, 2020.

663 'Preparation for Fatherhood: A Role for Olfactory Communication during Human Pregnancy?' by C. Allen, K. D. Cobey, J. Havlíček, F. P. Singleton, A. C. Hahn, C. N. Moran, and S. C. Roberts, *Physiology and Behaviour*, 206, July 2019, pp175 - 180.

664 'Chemical Communication and Mother-Infant Recognition,' by Stefano Vaglio, *Communicative and Integrative Biology*, 2(3), May - June 2009, pp279–281.

665 'Olfactory Comfort and Attachment Within Relationships,' by Melanie L. Shoup, Sybil A. Streeter, and Donald Mcburney, *Journal of Applied Social Psychology*, 38(12), November 2008, pp2954 – 2963.

666 'What is Love? Understanding The Process of Human Mate Selection,' by Stephanie Liffland, *The PIT Journal*, Cycle 5, 2014 (pitjournal.unc.edu/article/what-love-understanding-process-human-mate-selection). Accessed September 1, 2020.

667 *Smells: A Cultural History of Odours in Early Modern Times*, by Robert Muchembled, translated by Susan Pickford, Polity Press, 2020 (first published as *La civilisation des odeurs: XVIe – début XIXe siècle* in 2017), pp21.

668 'A Review of the Relevance and Validity of Olfactory Bulbectomy as a Model of Depression,' by Andrew Harkin, John P. Kelly and Brian E. Leonard, *Clinical Neuroscience Research*, 3(4-5), December 2003, pp253 - 262.

669 'How One Punch to the Head Turned My Friend, INXS Singer Michael Hutchence, into a Monster,' by Adrian Deevoy, *Event Magazine*, September 28, 2019 (www.dailymail.co.uk/home/event/article-7507359/How-one-punch-head-turned-friend-Michael-Hutchence-monster.html). Accessed June 2, 2021.

670 'Michael Hutchence Lost his Sense of Smell – and It All Went Downhill from There,' by Kate Mossman, *New Statesman*, October 9, 2019 (www.newstatesman.com/culture/music-theatre/2019/10/michael-hutchence-lost-his-sense-smell-and-it-all-went-downhill-there). Accessed September 1, 2020.

671 'Olfactory Dysfunction Predicts 5-Year Mortality in Older Adults,' by Jayant M. Pinto, Kristen E. Wroblewski, David W. Kern, L. Philip Schumm, and Martha K. McClintock, *PLoS ONE*, October 2014 (journals.plos.org/plosone/article?id=10.1371/journal.pone.0107541). Accessed June 3, 2021.

672 'The Nose That Never Knows,' by Elizabeth Zierah, *Slate*, July 8, 2008 (slate.com/technology/2008/07/the-miseries-of-losing-the-sense-of-smell.html). Accessed June 2, 2021.

673 'Olfactory Regulation of Maternal Behaviour in Mammals,' by F. Lévy, M. Keller and P. Poindron, *Hormones and Behaviour*, 46(3), September 2004, pp284 - 302.

674 'Importance of Noradrenergic Mechanisms in the Olfactory Bulbs for the Maternal Behaviour of Mice,' by C. Dickinson and E. B. Keverne, *Physiology and Behaviour*, 43(3), 1988, pp313 – 316.

675 *The Role of Psychological Ownership and the Technology Acceptance Model in Teachers' Continuance Intention of a Virtual Learning Environment*, by Joanne Yim Sau Ching, Faculty of Arts and Social Science, University Tunku Abdul Rahman, June 2019, pp53 (eprints.utar.edu.my/3554/1/The_role_of_psychological_ownership_and_the_technology_acceptance_model_in_teachers%E2%80%99_continuance_intention_of_a_virtual_learning_environment.pdf). Accessed

May 26, 2021.

676 'Scopolamine,' Drugs and Lactation Database, *National Centre for Biotechnology Information*, US National Library of Medicine, October 31, 2018 (www.ncbi.nlm.nih.gov/books/NBK501482). Accessed August 17, 2020.

677 'Births: Final Data for 2018,' by Joyce A. Martin, Brady E. Hamilton, Michelle J.K. Osterman, and Anne K. Driscoll, *National Vital Statistics Reports*, 68(13), November 27, 2019 (www.cdc. gov/nchs/data/nvsr/nvsr68/nvsr68_13-508.pdf). Accessed September 12, 2020.

678 'The Current Environment,' *National Maternity Services Plan*, Australian Government Department of Health 2011 (www1.health.gov.au/internet/publications/publishing.nsf/Content/ pacd-maternityservicesplan-toc~pacd-maternityservicesplan-chapter2). Accessed September 12, 2020.

679 'Examining Caesarean Section Rates in Canada Using the Modified Robson Classification,' by Jing Gu, Sunita Karmakar-Hore, Mary-Ellen Hogan, Hussam M.Azzam, Jon F. R. Barrett, Adrian Brown, Jocelynn L. Cook, Venu Jain, Nir Melamed, Graeme N. Smith, Arthur Zaltz, and Yana Gurevich, *Journal of Obstetrics and Gynaecology Canada*, 42(6), June 2020, pp757 - 765.

680 'The Increasing Trend in Caesarean Section Rates: Global, Regional and National Estimates: 1990 - 2014,' byAna Pilar Betrán, Jianfeng Ye, Anne-Beth Moller, Jun Zhang, A. Metin Gülmezoglu, and Maria Regina Torloni, edited by Hajo Zeeb, *PLoS One*, 11(2), February 2016, p.e0148343.

681 'FIGO Position Paper: How to Stop the Caesarean Section Epidemic,' by Gerard H. A. Visser, Diogo Ayres-de-Campos, Eytan R. Barnea, Luc de Bernis, Gian Carlo Di Renzo, Maria Fernanda Escobar Vidarte, Isabel Lloyd, Anwar H. Nassar, Wanda Nicholson, P. K. Shah, William Stones, Luming Sun, Gerhard B. Theron, and Salimah Walani, *The Lancet*, 392(10155), October 2018, pp1286 - 1287.

682 'Rate of C-Sections Is Rising at an 'Alarming' Rate, Report Says,' by Michaeleen Doucleff, *NPR*, October 12, 2018 (www.npr.org/sections/goatsandsoda/2018/10/12/656198429/rate-of-c-sections-is-rising-at-an-alarming-rate). Accessed September 12, 2020.

683 'Rate of C-Sections Is Rising at an 'Alarming' Rate, Report Says,' by Michaeleen Doucleff, *NPR*, October 12, 2018 (www.npr.org/sections/goatsandsoda/2018/10/12/656198429/rate-of-c-sections-is-rising-at-an-alarming-rate). Accessed September 12, 2020.

684 'Rate of C-Sections Is Rising at an 'Alarming' Rate, Report Says,' by Michaeleen Doucleff, *NPR*, October 12, 2018 (www.npr.org/sections/goatsandsoda/2018/10/12/656198429/rate-of-c-sections-is-rising-at-an-alarming-rate). Accessed September 12, 2020.

685 'The Impact of Caesarean Delivery Rate on Hospital Revenue,' by Yunping Li, Mingpin Hu, Yun Xia, Yuhuan Wang, Philip E. Hess, Lingqun Hu, *The Anaesthesiology Annual Meeting*, American Society of Anaesthesiologists, October 26, 2016 (www.asaabstracts. com/strands/asaabstracts/abstract.htm?year=2015&index=14&absnum=4032). Accessed September 12, 2020.

686 'Then and Now: 1814 – 1914,' by Dr John F. Fergus, *The Glasgow Medical Journal*, 20, February 1920, pp70.

687 'The British Journal of Anaesthesia: An Informal History of the First 25 Years,' by J. Norman, *British Journal of Anaesthesia*, 88(3), March 2002, pp445 - 450.

688 'A Profile of Anaesthesia Practice Patterns,' by Margo L. Rosenbach and Jerry Cromwell, *Health Affairs*, 7(4), Autumn 1988, pp118 – 131.

689 'Anaesthesia Salaries Are Increasing – But for How Long?' Medical Business Management blog, June 8, 2017 (mbmps.com/anesthesia-salaries-increasing-long/). Accessed October 27, 2020.

690 'Anaesthesiologist Supply and Demand: Trends within the Specialty,' by Tony Mira, *Anaesthesia Business Consultants*, July 2, 2018 (www.anesthesiallc.com/publications/anesthesia-provider-news-ealerts/1138-anesthesiologist-supply-and-demand-trends-within-the-specialty). Accessed October 27, 2020.

691 'How Does a Hospital Make Money?' by Samuel H. Steinberg, *Physicians News Digest*, November 16, 2006 (physiciansnews.com/2006/11/16/how-does-a-hospital-make-money/). Accessed November 11, 2020.

692 'Trends and State Variations in Out-of-Hospital Births in the United States, 2004 - 2017,' by Marian MacDorman and Eugene Declercq, *Birth*, 46(2), June 2019, pp279 – 288.

693 'Is the Rising Rage of Caesarean Sections a Result of More Defensive Medicine?' by Benjamin

P. Sachs, *Cover of Medical Professional Liability and the Delivery of Obstetrical Care: Volume II: An Interdisciplinary Review* (www.ncbi.nlm.nih.gov/books/NBK218658/pdf/Bookshelf_NBK218658.pdf). Accessed November 2, 2020.

694 'Birth Injury and Infant Mortality Rates Continue to Rise in the U.S.,' by Maggie Novak, *The Libertarian Republic*, August 5, 2019 (thelibertarianrepublic.com/birth-injury-and-infant-mortality-rates-continue-to-rise-in-the-u-s/). Accessed September 12, 2020.

695 *The Annals of the Scottish Society of Anaesthetists 2009*, pp10 (www.ssa.scot/wp-content/uploads/2017/08/SSA_Annals_2009.pdf). Accessed November 2, 2020.

696 'Global, Regional, and National Incidence, Prevalence, and Years Lived with Disability for 310 Diseases and Injuries, 1990 – 2015: A Systematic Analysis for the Global Burden of Disease Study 2015,' by GBD 2015 Disease and Injury Incidence and Prevalence Collaborators, *The Lancet*, 388(10053), October 2016, pp1545 - 1602.

697 *The Annals of the Scottish Society of Anaesthetists 2009*, pp10 (www.ssa.scot/wp-content/uploads/2017/08/SSA_Annals_2009.pdf). Accessed November 2, 2020.

698 'Is the Rising Rage of Caesarean Sections a Result of More Defensive Medicine?' by Benjamin P. Sachs, *Cover of Medical Professional Liability and the Delivery of Obstetrical Care: Volume II: An Interdisciplinary Review* (www.ncbi.nlm.nih.gov/books/NBK218658/pdf/Bookshelf_NBK218658.pdf). Accessed November 2, 2020.

699 'Is Regional Anaesthesia Better than General Anaesthesia for Caesarean Section?' by J. Bowring, N. Fraser, S. Vause, and A. E. P. Heazell, *Journal of Obstetrics and Gynaecology*, 26(5), July 2006, pp433 - 434.

700 'General Anaesthesia for Caesarean Section,' by Alan McGlennan and Adnan Mustafa, *Continuing Education in Anaesthesia Critical Care and Pain*, 9(5), October 2009, pp148 – 151.

701 'Maternity Services Monthly Statistics March 2018: Experimental statistics,' June 28, 2018, British National Health Service (digital.nhs.uk/data-and-information/publications/statistical/maternity-services-monthly-statistics/march-2018). Accessed August 31, 2020.

702 *The Double Image*, by Anne Sexton, *The Complete Poems*, Houghton Mifflin, 1999, copyright Linda Gray Sexton, 1981;

703 'Maternal Anaesthesia and Foetal Neurodevelopment,' by A. Palanisamy, *International Journal of Obstetric Anaesthesia*, 21(2), April 2012, pp152 - 162.

704 'Effects on the Foetus and Newborn of Maternal Analgesia and Anaesthesia: A Review,' by Judith Littleford, *Canadian Journal of Anaesthesia*, 51(6), June - July 2004, pp586 - 609.

705 'Beyond Labour: The Role of Natural and Synthetic Oxytocin in the Transition to Motherhood,' by Aleeca F. Bell, Elise N. Erickson, and C. Sue Carter, *Journal of Midwifery and Women's Health*, 59(1), January 2014, pp35 – 42.

706 'Epidural, Spinal Anaesthesia Safe for Caesarean Deliveries, Study Finds,' Press Release for The American Society of Anaesthesiologists, October 8, 2015 (www.asahq.org/about-asa/newsroom/news-releases/2015/10/press-release-epidural). Accessed August 31, 2020.

707 'Postoperative Opioid Use After Caesarean Delivery,' by Megan Lawlor, Kristen J. McQuerry, Jenny Tan, Corinne Williams, Wendy Hansen, and Agatha S. Critchfield, *Obstetrics and Gynaecology*, 131(1), May 2018, p.156S.

708 'Opioids in Breast Milk: Pharmacokinetic Principles and Clinical Implications,' by Shinya Ito, *The Journal of Clinical Pharmacology*, 58(S10), October 2018, p.S151 - S163.

709 'Pharmacogenetics of Neonatal Opioid Toxicity Following Maternal Use of Codeine During Breastfeeding: A Case–Control Study,' by P. Madadi, C. J. D. Ross, M. R. Hayden, B. C. Carleton, A. Gaedigk, J. S. Leeder, and G. Koren, *Clinical Pharmacology and Therapeutics*, 85(1), January 2009, pp31 - 35.

710 *Drugs and Lactation Database*, Morphine National Centre for Biotechnology Information, U.S. National Library of Medicine, July 20, 2020 (www.ncbi.nlm.nih.gov/books/NBK501237). Accessed August 31, 2020.

711 'Stunted Microbiota and Opportunistic Pathogen Colonisation in Caesarean-Section Birth,' by Yan Shao, Samuel C. Forster, Evdokia Tsaliki, Kevin Vervier, Angela Strang, Nandi Simpson, Nitin Kumar, Mark D. Stares, Alison Rodger, Peter Brocklehurst, Nigel Field and Trevor D. Lawley, *Nature*, (574), September 2019, pp117 – 121.

712 'Breastfeeding and the Risk of Maternal Cardiovascular Disease: A Prospective Study of 300 000 Chinese Women,' by S. A. E. Peters, L. Yang, Y. Guo, Y. Chen, Z. Bian, J. Du, J. Yang, S. Li, L. Li, M. Woodward, and Z. Chen, *Journal of the American Heart Association*, 6(6), June 2017,

p.e006081.

713 'Ovarian Cancer Risk is Reduced by Prolonged Lactation: A Case-Control Study in Southern China,' by Dada Su, Maria Pasalich, Andy H. Lee, and Colin W. Binns, *The American Journal of Clinical Nutrition*, 97(2), February 2013, pp354 – 359.

714 'Breastfeeding and Breast Cancer Risk Reduction: Implications for Black Mothers,' by Erica H. Anstey, Meredith L. Shoemaker, Chloe M. Barrera, Mary Elizabeth O'Neil, Ashley B. Verma, and Dawn M. Holman, *American Journal of Preventative Medicine*, 53(3 Supplement 1), September 2017, S40 – S46.

715 'Breastfeeding in the 21st century: Epidemiology, Mechanisms, and Lifelong Effect,' by Professor Cesar G. Victora, Rajiv Bahl, Professor Aluísio J. D. Barros, Giovanny V. A. França, Professor Susan Horton, Julia Krasevec, Professor Simon Murch, Mari Jeeva Sankar, Neff Walker, Nigel C. Rollins, The Lancet Breastfeeding Series Group, *The Lancet*, 387(10017), January – February 2016, pp475 - 490.

716 'Breast Cancer and Breastfeeding: Collaborative Reanalysis of Individual Data from 47 Epidemiological Studies in 30 Countries, Including 50302 Women with Breast Cancer and 96973 Women without the Disease,' by the Collaborative Group on Hormonal Factors in Breast Cancer, *The Lancet*, 360(9328), July 2002, pp187 - 195.

717 'Stemming the Global Caesarean Section Epidemic,' *The Lancet*, 392(10155), October 2018, pp1279.

718 'Partial Restoration of the Microbiota of Caesarean-Born Infants via Vaginal Microbial Transfer,' by M. Dominguez-Bello, K. De Jesus-Laboy, N. Shen, et al. *Nature Medicine*, (22), February 2016, pp250 – 253.

719 'Stunted Microbiota and Opportunistic Pathogen Colonisation in Caesarean-Section Birth,' by Yan Shao, Samuel C. Forster, Evdokia Tsaliki, Kevin Vervier, Angela Strang, Nandi Simpson, Nitin Kumar, Mark D. Stares, Alison Rodger, Peter Brocklehurst, Nigel Field and Trevor D. Lawley, *Nature*, (574), September 2019, pp117 – 121.

720 'Gender Differences in Autoimmune Disease,' by S. T. Ngo, F. J. Steyn, and P. A. McCombe, *Frontiers in Neuroendocrinology*, 35(3), August 2014, pp347 - 369.

721 'Stunted Microbiota and Opportunistic Pathogen Colonisation in Caesarean-Section Birth,' by Yan Shao, Samuel C. Forster, Evdokia Tsaliki, Kevin Vervier, Angela Strang, Nandi Simpson, Nitin Kumar, Mark D. Stares, Alison Rodger, Peter Brocklehurst, Nigel Field and Trevor D. Lawley, *Nature*, (574), September 2019, pp117 – 121.

722 *Progress in Autoimmune Diseases Research: Report to Congress*, National Institutes of Health, U.S. Department of Health and Human Services, March 2005, pp4.

723 *Breastfeeding in the 21st Century*, The World Health Organization, 2020, pp2 (www.who.int/pmnch/media/news/2016/breastfeeding_brief.pdf). Accessed May 8 2020.

724 'There's 'an Explosion' of Food Allergies - but What's Behind the Boom?' by Harry de Quetteville, *The Telegraph*, February 8, 2020 (www.telegraph.co.uk/news/0/explosion-food-allergies-behind-boom). Accessed May 8, 2020.

725 'There's 'an Explosion' of Food Allergies - but What's Behind the Boom?' by Harry de Quetteville, *The Telegraph*, February 8, 2020 (www.telegraph.co.uk/news/0/explosion-food-allergies-behind-boom). Accessed May 8, 2020.

726 'Asthma Death Toll in England and Wales is the Highest this Decade: New Data Shows Asthma Deaths have Increased by a Third in the Last Decade as Asthma UK Calls on the NHS to Urgently Tackle Issues with Basic Asthma Care,' *Asthma UK*, August 9, 2019 (www.asthma.org.uk/about/media/news/press-release-asthma-death-toll-in-england-and-wales-is-the-highest-this-decade). Accessed May 8, 2020.

727 'Number of People Living with Diabetes Doubles in Twenty Years,' *Diabetes UK*, February 27, 2018 (www.diabetes.org.uk/about_us/news/diabetes-prevalence-statistics). Accessed May 8, 2020.

728 'The Relationship of Prenatal Antibiotic Exposure and Infant Antibiotic Administration with Childhood Allergies: A Systematic Review,' by Ruth Baron, Meron Taye, Isolde Besseling-van der Vaart, Joanne Ujčič-Voortman, Hania Szajewska, Jacob C. Seidell, and Arnoud Verhoeff, *BMC Paediatrics*, 20(1), June 2020, pp312.

729 'Allergic Diseases and Asthma: A Global Public Health Concern and a Call to Action,' by Ruby Pawankar, *World Allergy Organization Journal*, 7(1), May 2014, pp7 - 12.

730 *Progress in Autoimmune Diseases Research: Report to Congress*, National Institutes of Health, U.S.

Department of Health and Human Services, March 2005, pp4.

731 'Sex Differences in Autoimmune Disease from a Pathological Perspective,' by DeLisa Fair-weather, Sylvia Frisancho-Kiss, and Noel R. Rose, *The American Journal of Pathology*, 173(3), September 2008, pp600 – 609.

732 'Global, Regional, and National Incidence, Prevalence, and Years Lived with Disability for 354 Diseases and Injuries for 195 Countries and Territories, 1990–2017: A Systematic Analysis for the Global Burden of Disease Study 2017,' by the GBD 2017 Disease and Injury Incidence and Prevalence Collaborators, Global Health Metrics, *The Lancet Journal*, 392(10159), November 10, 2018, pp1789 – 1858.

733 'Sex Differences in Autoimmune Disease from a Pathological Perspective,' by DeLisa Fair-weather, Sylvia Frisancho-Kiss, and Noel R. Rose, *The American Journal of Pathology*, 173(3), September 2008, pp600 – 609.

734 'Are you #Autoimmune Aware?: Report for Parliamentarians into Autoimmune Conditions,' British Society for Immunology, November 2018 (www.immunology.org/sites/default/files/connect-immune-research-are-you-autoimmune-report.pdf). Accessed May 9, 2020.

735 'Are you #Autoimmune Aware?: Report for Parliamentarians into Autoimmune Conditions,' British Society for Immunology, November 2018 (www.immunology.org/sites/default/files/connect-immune-research-are-you-autoimmune-report.pdf). Accessed May 9, 2020.

736 'Scopolamine Effects on Functional Brain Connectivity: A Pharmacological Model of Alzhei-mer's Disease,' by R. Bajo, S. Pusil, M. E. López, L. Canuet, E. Pereda, D. Osipova, F. Maestú and E. Pekkonen, *Scientific Reports*, 5(9748), July 2015.

737 'The Cholinergic Neurotransmitter System in Human Memory and Dementia: A Review,' by Michael D. Kopelman, *Quarterly Journal of Experimental Psychology*, 38(4), November 1986, pp535 – 573.

738 'Trends in the Incidence and Prevalence of Alzheimer's Disease, Dementia, and Cognitive Impairment in the United States,' by Walter A. Rocca, Ronald C. Petersen, David S. Knop-man, Liesi E. Hebert, Denis A. Evans, Kathleen S. Hall, Sujuan Gao, Frederick W. Unverzagt, Kenneth M. Langa, Eric B. Larson, and Lon R. Whitel, *Alzheimer's and Dementia*, 7(1), January 2011, pp80 – 93.

739 'Dementia Incidence Increased 117 Percent Globally from 1990 to 2016,' by Emma Nichols, *Healio*, December 13, 2018 (www.healio.com/news/psychiatry/20181213/dementia-inci-dence-increased-117-globally-from-1990-to-2016). Accessed January 20, 2021.

740 'Oxytocin Effects in Mothers and Infants during Breastfeeding,' by Kerstin Uvnäs Moberg and Danielle K. Prime, *Infant*, 9(6), 2013, pp201 - 206.

741 'Oxytocin Effects in Mothers and Infants during Breastfeeding,' by Kerstin Uvnäs Moberg and Danielle K. Prime, *Infant*, 9(6), 2013, pp201 - 206.

742 *Mankind in the Making*, by H. G. Wells, BiblioBazaar, 2007 (first published in 1903), pp79.

743 *The Second Sex*, by Simone de Beauvoir, Modern Library, 1968 (first published in 1949), pp513.

744 *The Second Sex*, by Simone de Beauvoir, Modern Library, 1968 (first published in 1949), pp515.

745 *The Second Sex*, by Simone de Beauvoir, Modern Library, 1968 (first published in 1949), pp513.

746 ('Biographers have been hard on de Beauvoir for what looks like a case of sordid 'grooming' [some of her students, whom she seduced and then passed on to Jean-Paul Sartre], as well as unprofessional conduct. It is hard to tell what motivated her, since she seemed indifferent to both women [among others] much of the time'), *At The Existentialist Café: Freedom, Being, and Apricot Cocktails*, by Sarah Bakewell, Chatto and Windus, 2016, pp138.

747 ('A source close to Maxwell says she spoke glibly and confidently about getting girls to sexually service Epstein, saying this was simply what he wanted, and describing the way she'd drive around to spas and trailer parks in Florida to recruit them. She would claim she had a phone job for them, 'and you'll make lots of money, meet everyone, and I'll change your life.' The source continues, 'Ghislaine was in love with Jeffrey the way she was in love with her father. She always thought if she just did one more thing for him, to please him, he would marry her.' Maxwell had one other thing to tell this woman: 'When I asked what she thought of the underage girls, she looked at me and said, 'They're nothing, these girls. They are trash'"), 'Unravelling the Mystery of Ghislaine Maxwell, Epstein's Enabler,' by Vanessa Grigoriadis,

Vanity Fair, August 12, 2019 (www.vanityfair.com/news/2019/08/the-mystery-of-ghislaine-maxwell-epstein-enabler).

748 'Childbirth and Infancy in Greek and Roman Antiquity,' by Véronique Dasen, *A Companion to Families in the Greek and Roman Worlds*, edited by Beryl Rawson, Wiley-Blackwell, 2010, pp293.

749 'Childbirth and Infancy in Greek and Roman Antiquity,' by Véronique Dasen, *A Companion to Families in the Greek and Roman Worlds*, edited by Beryl Rawson, Wiley-Blackwell, 2010, pp293.

750 *Queen Victoria: A Portrait*, by Giles St. Aubyn, Sinclair-Stevenson, 1991, pp167.

751 'Cruelty in Maternity Wards,' by Gladys Denny Schultz, *Ladies Home Journal*, May 1958, pp44.

752 'Why I Held out for Brad,' *Elle* (UK), February 2007.

753 'Be Honest: Newborns Are So Boring It Hurts,' by Kimmie Fink, *Romper*, February 14, 2018 (www.romper.com/p/be-honest-newborns-are-so-boring-it-hurts-8194868). Accessed June 15, 2021.

754 'Singing, Sharing, Soothing – Biopsychosocial Rationales for Parental Infant-Directed Singing in Neonatal Pain Management: A Theoretical Approach,' by A. Ullsten, M. Eriksson, M. Klässbo, and U. Volgsten, *Music and Science*, 1, June 2018, pp1 - 13.

755 'Should Neonates Sleep Alone?' by Barak E. Morgan, Alan R. Horn, and Nils J. Bergman, *Biological Psychiatry*, 70(9), August 2011, pp817 - 825.

756 'Care Practice #6: No Separation of Mother and Baby, With Unlimited Opportunities for Breastfeeding,' by Jeannette Crenshaw, *Journal of Perinatal Education*, 16(3), Summer 2007, pp39 – 43.

757 'Psychobiological Roots of Early Attachment,' by Myron A. Hofer, *Current Directions in Psychological Science*, 15(2), April 2006, 84 – 88.

758 'Attachment and Emotion Regulation Strategies in Predicting Adult Psychopathology,' by Katherine Pascuzzo, Ellen Moss, and Chantal Cyr, *Sage OPEN*, July - September 2015, pp1 – 15.

759 'Friedrich Wilhelm Joseph von Schelling,' *Stanford Encyclopaedia of Philosophy*, October 22, 2001 (plato.stanford.edu/entries/schelling). Accessed June 13, 2021.

760 'Infant Visual Recognition Memory,' by Susan A. Rose, Judith F. Feldman and Jeffery J. Jankowski, *Developmental Review*, 24(1), March 2004, pp74 - 100.

761 *Inconsolable: How I Threw My Mental Health Out with the Diapers*, by Marrit Ingman, Seal Press, 2005, pp76.

762 'How to Win Friends and Influence People: The Marilyn Manson Interview,' *Mouth*, by Antonella Gambotto-Burke, Broken Ankle Digital, 2013 (Kindle edition).

763 *The Long, Hard Road out of Hell*, by Marilyn Manson with Neil Strauss, Plexus, 2009 (first published in 1998), pp12, 33, 60, 61.

764 'Evan Rachel Wood and four other women accuse Marilyn Manson of abuse,' by Ben Beaumont-Thomas, The Guardian, February 1, 2021 (www.theguardian.com/music/2021/feb/01/evan-rachel-wood-and-four-other-women-accuse-marilyn-manson-of-abuse). Accessed June 14, 2021.

765 *The Long, Hard Road out of Hell*, by Marilyn Manson with Neil Strauss, Plexus, 2009 (first published in 1998), pp12, 33, 60, 61.

766 *Acid for the Children: The Autobiography of Flea, the Red Hot Chili Peppers Legend*, by Flea, Headline (Kindle edition), 2019.

767 *Edvard Munch: Behind the Scream*, by Sue Prideaux, Yale University Press, 2005, pp200.

768 *Munch and Photography*, by Arne Eggum, Yale University Press, 1990, pp16.

769 *Edvard Munch: Behind the Scream*, by Sue Prideaux, Yale University Press, 2005, pp31 – 32.

770 'A History of the Medical Mask and the Rise of Throwaway Culture,' by Bruno J. Strasser and Thomas Schlich. *The Lancet*, 396(10243), July 2020, pp19 – 20.

771 *Baroness Orczy's The Scarlet Pimpernel: A Publishing History*, by Sally Dugan, Routledge, 2016, pp1.

772 'Zorro: Fictional Character,' by Peter Sanderson, *Encyclopaedia Britannica*, 2013 (www.britannica.com/topic/Zorro-fictional-character). Accessed June 16, 2021.

773 'Male Doctors Are Disappearing from Gynaecology. Not Everybody is Thrilled About It,' by Soumya Karlamangla, *The Los Angeles Times*, March 7, 2018 (www.latimes.com/health/la-me-male-gynos-20180307-htmlstory.html). Accessed June 16, 2021.

774 'Silent (adj),' *Online Etymology Dictionary*, 2001 - 2021 (www.etymonline.com/word/silent). Accessed June 16, 2021.

775 *Women and Drugs: Drug Use, Drug Supply and Their Consequences - World Drug Report 2018*,

United Nations Office on Drugs and Crime (www.unodc.org/wdr2018/prelaunch/WDR18_Booklet_5_WOMEN.pdf). Accessed July 4, 2020.

776 'Face Perception and Processing in Early Infancy: Inborn Predispositions and Developmental Changes,' by Francesca Simion and Elisa Di Giorgio, *Frontiers in Psychology*, 6(969), July 2015, pp1 – 11.

777 'Infants Process Faces Long Before They Recognise Other Objects, Stanford Vision Researchers Find,' by Max McClure, *Stanford Report*, December 11, 2012 (news.stanford.edu/news/2012/december/infants-process-faces-121112.html). Accessed June 16, 2021.

778 'Face Perception and Processing in Early Infancy: Inborn Predispositions and Developmental Changes,' by Francesca Simion and Elisa Di Giorgio, *Frontiers in Psychology*, 6(969), July 2015, pp1 – 11.

779 'Face Perception and Processing in Early Infancy: Inborn Predispositions and Developmental Changes,' by Francesca Simion and Elisa Di Giorgio, *Frontiers in Psychology*, 6(969), July 2015, pp1 – 11.

780 'Identifying the Brain's Own Facial Recognition System,' by Elizabeth Norton, *Science*, October 23, 2012 (www.sciencemag.org/news/2012/10/identifying-brains-own-facial-recognition-system). Accessed June 16, 2021.

781 'Fusiform Gyrus,' by Shahab Shahid, *Ken Hub*, October 29, 2020 (www.kenhub.com/en/library/anatomy/fusiform-gyrus). Accessed June 16, 2021.

782 'Where Does the Legend of the Mummy Come From?' by Oliver Pfeiffer, BBC History, April 21, 2017 (www.bbc.com/culture/article/20170420-where-does-the-legend-of-the-mummy-come-from). Accessed September 4, 2020.

783 ''A Woman is a Woman, if She had been Dead Five Thousand Centuries!': Mummy Fiction, Imperialism and the Politics of Gender,' by Nolwenn Corriou, *Miranda*, November 2015 (doi.org/10.4000/miranda.6899). Accessed September 4, 2020.

784 *The Jewel of Seven Stars - The Most Complete Version Ever Published: Includes the Endings from the Original First Edition and the Revised Second Edition*, by Bram Stoker, CreateSpace, 2009, pp.119, 88, 92, 157, 159, 52.

785 *The Jewel of Seven Stars - The Most Complete Version Ever Published: Includes the Endings from the Original First Edition and the Revised Second Edition*, by Bram Stoker, CreateSpace, 2009, pp.119, 88, 92, 157, 159, 52.

786 ''A Woman is a Woman, if She had been Dead Five Thousand Centuries!': Mummy Fiction, Imperialism and the Politics of Gender,' by Nolwenn Corriou, *Miranda*, November 2015 (doi.org/10.4000/miranda.6899). Accessed September 4, 2020.

787 *Smith and the Pharaohs and Other Tales*, by H. Rider Haggard, Independent, 2020, pp22, 23, 24.

788 *Smith and the Pharaohs and Other Tales*, by H. Rider Haggard, Independent, 2020, pp21.

789 *Mummies around the World: An Encyclopaedia of Mummies in History, Religion and Popular Culture*, edited by Matt Cardin, ABC-CLIO, 2014, p.xviii.

790 'Scopolamin-Morphin Seminarcosis in the Second Thousand Deliveries in Barnes Hospital,' *The Journal of the Missouri State Medical Association*, edited by E. J. Goodwin, 20, January - December 1923, pp127.

791 'Cruelty in Maternity Wards,' by Gladys Denny Schultz, *Ladies Home Journal*, May 1958, pp44.

792 'Cruelty in Maternity Wards,' by Gladys Denny Schultz, *Ladies Home Journal*, May 1958, pp44.

793 *World War Z: An Oral History of the Zombie War*, by Max Brooks, Duckworth, 2019, pp1, 2, 10.

794 'Fast Zombie Scream (What It Really Is),' @Jirachi74, *YouTube*, October 2, 2010 (www.youtube.com/watch?v=1rhqAcCoSBQ). Accessed January 9, 2021.

795 'Ketamine: An Update for Obstetric Anesthesia,' by Yuying Tang, Renyu Liu, and Peishan Zhao, *Translational Perioperative and Pain Medicine*, 4(4), September 2017, pp1 - 12.

796 'Effects of Ketamine on Sensory Perception: Evidence for a Role of N-Methyl-D-Aspartate Receptors,' by I. Oye, O. Paulsen, and A. Maurset, *The Journal of Pharmacology and Experimental Therapeutics*, 260(3), March 1992, pp1209 - 13.

797 'We Asked People About the K-Holes that Changed Their Lives,' by Gavin Butler, *Vice*, November 6, 2017 (www.vice.com/en/article/d3dxzq/we-asked-people-about-the-k-holes-that-changed-their-lives). Accessed January 11, 2021.

798 'Ketamine: An Update for Obstetric Anesthesia,' by Yuying Tang, Renyu Liu, and Peishan Zhao, *Translational Perioperative and Pain Medicine*, 4(4), September 2017, pp1 - 12.

799 'Ketamine,' *London Friend*, 2020 (londonfriend.org.uk/ketamine). Accessed January 11, 2021.

800 'Intravenous Ketamine during Spinal and General Anaesthesia for Caesarean Section: Systematic Review and Meta-Analysis,' by M. Heesen, J. Boehmer, E. C. V. Brinck, V. K. Kontinen, S. Kloehr, R. Rossaint, and S. Straube, *Acta Anaesthesiologica Scandinavica*, 59(4), April 2015, pp414 - 426.

801 'Inside the Mind of Jeffrey Dahmer: Serial Killer's Chilling Jailhouse Interview,' *Inside Edition* (1993), November 27, 2018 (www.youtube.com/watch?v=iWjYsxaBjBI). Accessed January 24, 2021.

802 *Passage of Darkness: The Ethnobiology of the Haitian Zombie*, by Wade Davis, University of North Carolina Press, 2000, pp99.

803 'Dahmer's Inferno,' by Brian Masters, *Vanity Fair*, 1991 (www.vanityfair.com/style/1991/11/jeffrey-dahmer-dennis-nilsen-serial-killer). Accessed January 24, 2021.

804 'Dahmer's Inferno,' by Brian Masters, *Vanity Fair*, 1991 (www.vanityfair.com/style/1991/11/jeffrey-dahmer-dennis-nilsen-serial-killer). Accessed January 24, 2021.

805 *The Shrine of Jeffrey Dahmer*, by Brian Masters, Hodder and Stoughton, 2020 (first published in 1993), pp21.

806 *The Truth about Twilight Sleep*, by Hanna Rion, McBride, Nast and Co., 1915, pp335.

807 Susan Slear, 'Twilight Sleep – The Brutal Way Some Women Gave Birth In The 1900s,' by Sam McCulloch, *Belly Belly*, June 5, 2018 (www.bellybelly.com.au/birth/twilight-sleep). Accessed September 9, 2020.

808 'Twilight Sleep – The Brutal Way Some Women Gave Birth In The 1900s,' by Sam McCulloch, *Belly Belly*, June 5, 2018 (www.bellybelly.com.au/birth/twilight-sleep). Accessed September 9, 2020.

809 'Twilight Sleep – The Brutal Way Some Women Gave Birth In The 1900s,' by Sam McCulloch, *Belly Belly*, June 5, 2018 (www.bellybelly.com.au/birth/twilight-sleep). Accessed September 9, 2020.

810 *Three Essays on the Theory of Sexuality*, by Sigmund Freud, translated by James Strachey, Martino Fine Books, 2011 (originally published in 1905), pp24, 50.

811 'Looking Through the Bushes: The Disappearance of Pubic Hair,' by Roger Friedland, *The Huffington Post*, June 13, 2011 (www.huffpost.com/entry/women-pubic-hair_b_875465). Accessed January 4, 2021.

812 'Pubic Hair Removal Practices in Cross-Cultural Perspective,' by Lyndsey K. Craig and Peter B. Gray, *Cross-Cultural Research*, 53(2), April 2019, pp215 – 237.

813 'The Prickly History of Pubes in Porn,' by Shawn Binder, *Vice*, November 17, 2015 (www.vice.com/en/article/3dx9dn/the-prickly-history-of-pubes-in-porn). Accessed January 4, 2021.

814 'The History of Female Hair Removal,' Women's Museum of California blog, November 22, 2017 (womensmuseum.wordpress.com/2017/11/22/the-history-of-female-hair-removal/). Accessed January 4, 2021.

815 'Birth and the Bush: Untangling the Debate Around Women's Pubic Hair,' by Natalie Jolly, *Birth Issues in Perinatal Care*, 44(1), March 2017, pp7 – 10.

816 'Routinely Shaving Women in the Area around the Vagina on Admission to Hospital in Labour,' by V. Basevi and T. Lavender, *Cochrane Database of Systematic Reviews*, 11, November 14, 2014, Article CD001236.

817 'Birth and the Bush: Untangling the Debate Around Women's Pubic Hair,' by Natalie Jolly, *Birth Issues in Perinatal Care*, 44(1), March 2017, pp7 – 10.

818 'Routinely Shaving Women in the Area around the Vagina on Admission to Hospital in Labour,' by V. Basevi and T. Lavender, *Cochrane Database of Systematic Reviews*, 11, November 14, 2014, Article CD001236.

819 *Smells: A Cultural History of Odours in Early Modern Times*, by Robert Muchembled, translated by Susan Pickford, Polity Press, 2020 (first published in 2017 as *La civilisation des odeurs (XVIe – début XIXe siècle)*, pp75.

820 'Popularity of Breast Searches,' *PornHub*, August 10, 2017 (www.pornhub.com/insights/breast-searches). Accessed January 5, 2021.

821 'New Hampshire Now Least Religious State in U.S.,' by Frank Newport, *Gallup*, February 4, 2016 (news.gallup.com/poll/189038/new-hampshire-least-religious-state.aspx). Accessed January 5, 2021.

822 'Percentage of Infants Breastfed at Six Months,' Centres for Disease Control and Prevention,

September 28, 2020 (www.cdc.gov/breastfeeding/data/facts.html). Accessed January 5, 2021.

823 'Popularity of Breast Searches,' *PornHub*, August 10, 2017 (www.pornhub.com/insights/breast-searches). Accessed January 5, 2021.

824 'Percentage of Infants Breastfed at Six Months,' Centres for Disease Control and Prevention, September 28, 2020 (www.cdc.gov/breastfeeding/data/facts.html). Accessed January 5, 2021.

825 'Mental Health Diagnoses by State,' by Shira Feder, *Insider*, February 12, 2020 (www.insider.com/how-mental-health-conditions-affect-each-state-suicide-depression-anxiety-2020-2). Accessed January 5, 2021.

826 'Where Hate Groups Are Concentrated in the U.S.,' by Richard Florida, *Bloomberg News*, March 15, 2018 (www.bloomberg.com/news/articles/2018-03-15/the-geography-of-hate-groups-in-the-u-s). Accessed January 5, 2021.

827 'About,' Torture Garden, 2020 (www.torturegarden.com/about). Accessed October 9, 2020.

828 'The Rubber Maid's Dress,' by Ben Westwood, Vivienne Westwood Blog, April 14, 2017 (blog.viviennewestwood.com/the-rubber-maids-dress). Accessed October 10, 2020.

829 'Interview: Vivienne Westwood,' by Caterina Minthe, *Vogue Arabia*, May 7, 2013 (en.vogue.me/archive/faces_of_fashion/interview-vivienne-westwood). Accessed October 9, 2020.

830 'Tongue splitting risks significant blood loss and nerve damage, warn surgeons,' Royal College of Surgeons of England, Aug 3, 2018 (www.rcseng.ac.uk/news-and-events/media-centre/press-releases/tongue-splitting-statement/). Accessed October 11, 2020.

831 'Ripped my stocking because I'm a useless monster that doesn't deserve nice things.' @erotic.funeral, Instagram, September 11, 2020 (www.instagram.com/p/CFAjPSxl8rp/). Accessed September 13, 2020.

832 (www.instagram.com/p/CEpZx4UFhHF). Accessed September 13, 2020.

833 (www.instagram.com/p/CBOii8Ophfs/). Accessed September 13, 2020.

834 *S.E.X.*, by Madonna (words and music by Larry Darnell Griffin, Madonna Ciccone, Maureen Anne McDonald, and Tobias Gad, Sony/ATV Music Publishing/ Warner Chappell Music, 2015).

835 *Skin Tight: Rubbermen, Macho Fetish and Fantasy*, by Tim Brough, Nazca Plains, 2006, pp13.

836 My Life in Sex: 'My Rubber Fetish has Enriched my Life', *The Guardian*, September 21, 2018 (www.theguardian.com/lifeandstyle/2018/sep/21/my-rubber-fetish-has-enriched-my-life). Accessed October 9, 2020.

837 'Sexuality in the 21st Century: Leather or Rubber? Fetishism Explained,' by Antonio Ventriglio, P.S. Bhat, Julio Torales, and Dinesh Bhugrad, *Medical Journal Armed Forces India*,75(2), April 2019, pp121 – 124.

838 'Fetishism: Psychopathology and Theory,' by S. Darcangelo, *Sexual Deviance: Theory, Assessment, and Treatment*, edited by D. R. Laws and W. T. O'Donohue, Guilford Press, 2008, pp108 - 118.

839 'Sexuality in the 21st Century: Leather or Rubber? Fetishism Explained,' by Antonio Ventriglio, P.S. Bhat, Julio Torales, and Dinesh Bhugrad, *Medical Journal Armed Forces India*,75(2), April 2019, pp121 – 124.

840 'Sexuality in the 21st Century: Leather or Rubber? Fetishism Explained,' by Antonio Ventriglio, P.S. Bhat, Julio Torales, and Dinesh Bhugrad, *Medical Journal Armed Forces India*,75(2), April 2019, pp121 – 124.

841 'Robert Mapplethorpe: Framing a Sexual Revolution,' by Levi Prombaum, Guggenheim Museum, May 31, 2019 (www.guggenheim.org/blogs/checklist/robert-mapplethorpe-framing-a-sexual-revolution). Accessed October 17, 2020.

842 *Joe / Rubberman*, by Robert Mapplethorpe, 1978 (www.getty.edu/art/collection/objects/255576/robert-mapplethorpe-joe-rubberman-american-1978/). Accessed October 18, 2020.

843 'Robert Mapplethorpe's Violent Light,' by Adam Wray, *Ssense*, 2017 (www.ssense.com/en-gb/editorial/culture/robert-mapplethorpes-violent-light). Accessed October 17, 2020.

844 'Devaluation of the Human Love Object: Heterosexual Rejection as a Possible Antecedent to Fetishism,' by R. A. LaTorre, *Journal of Abnormal Psychology*, 89(2), April 1980, pp295 - 298.

845 'Sadomasochism in the Perversions: Some Thoughts on the Destruction of Reality,' by J. Chasseguet-Smirgel, *Journal of the American Psychoanalytical Association*, 39(2), 1991, pp399 - 415.

846 'Deviance as History: The Future of Perversion,' by W. Simon, *Archives of Sexual Behaviour*, 23(1), February 1994, pp1 - 20.

847 *Fetishism, Psychoanalysis, and Philosophy: The Iridescent Thing*, by Alan Bass, Routledge, 2017, pp1.

848 'Sadomasochism in the Perversions: Some Thoughts on the Destruction of Reality,' by J. Chasseguet-Smirgel, *Journal of the American Psychoanalytical Association*, 39(2), 1991, pp399 - 415.

849 *The Enduring Kiss: Seven Short Lessons on Love*, by Massimo Recalcati, Polity Press, 2021, p26, 56.

850 *Rubber: Some Facts on Its History, Production, and Manufacture*, P. W. Barker, United States Foreign and Domestic Commerce Bureau, January 1936, pp14 – 16.

851 'The Air Tractor,' *Edinburgh Monthly Journal of Medical Science*, February 1849, pp556.

852 *Obstetrics and Gynaecology in America: A History*, by Harold Speert, The American College of Obstetricians and Gynaecologists, 1980, pp209.

853 *Brought to Bed: Childbearing in America, 1750-1950*, by Judith Walzer Leavitt, Oxford University Press, 1988, pp273.

854 'The History of Surgical Gloves,' *Past Medical History*, September 19, 2019 (www.pastmedical-history.co.uk/the-history-of-surgical-gloves/). Accessed September 10, 2020.

855 *The Truth about Twilight Sleep*, by Hanna Rion, McBride, Nast and Co., 1915, pp335.

856 *Brought to Bed: Childbearing in America, 1750-1950*, by Judith Walzer Leavitt, Oxford University Press, 1988, pp61.

857 *Brought to Bed: Childbearing in America, 1750-1950*, by Judith Walzer Leavitt, Oxford University Press, 1988, pp162-3.

858 'Red Rubber Midwives' Apron, English: 1940-1955,' Science Museum: Collections, 2020 (collection.sciencemuseumgroup.org.uk/objects/co96640/red-rubber-midwives-apron-aprons). Accessed October 11, 2020.

859 'Soft Forceps,' by D.F. Roshan, B. Petrikovsky, L. Sichinava, B.J. Rudick, A. Rebarber, and S. D. Bender, *International Journal of Gynaecology and Obstetrics*, 88(3), March 2005, pp249 – 252.

860 'Prevalence and Outcomes of Breast Milk Expressing in Women with Healthy Term Infants: A Systematic Review,' by Helene M. Johns, Della A. Forster, Lisa H. Amir, and Helen L. McLachlan, *BMC Pregnancy Childbirth*, 13, November 2013, pp212.

861 *A Few Glimpses of Midwifery, 1936 – 1971: Barratt Maternity Home, Northampton*, by Elizabeth E. Wilson, September 14, 1984, pp2 (www.northamptongeneral.nhs.uk/Services/Our-Clini-cal-Services-and-Departments/Obstetrics-and-Gynaecology/Maternity/Downloads/Barratt-MaternityHome.pdf). Accessed October 11, 2020.

862 'History of Tube Feeding: An Overview of Tube Feeding: From Ancient Times to the Future,' by Ronni Chernoff, *Nutrition in Clinical Practice*, 21(4), August 2006, pp408 - 410.

863 'Obituary for Dr Herbert Barrie: Pioneer in the care of premature babies who developed new techniques for resuscitation and rewarded his team with champagne,' *The Times*, May 8, 2017 (www.thetimes.co.uk/article/dr-herbert-barrie-7kxt7jj6d). Accessed October 11, 2020.

864 *A Few Glimpses of Midwifery, 1936 – 1971: Barratt Maternity Home, Northampton*, by Elizabeth E. Wilson, September 14, 1984, pp6 (www.northamptongeneral.nhs.uk/Services/Our-Clini-cal-Services-and-Departments/Obstetrics-and-Gynaecology/Maternity/Downloads/Barratt-MaternityHome.pdf). Accessed October 11, 2020.

865 'Catheter Use in Gynaecological Practice,' by Nosheen Aslam and Paul A. Moran, *The Obstetrician and Gynaecologist*, 16(3), July 2014, pp161 – 168.

866 'Flooring Choices for Newborn ICUs,' by R. D. White, *Journal of Perinatology*, 27, November 2007, p.S29–S31.

867 'The Olfactory Critical Period is Determined by Activity-Dependent Sema7A/PlxnC1 Signalling within Glomeruli,' by Nobuko Inoue, Hirofumi Nishizumi, Rumi Ooyama, Kazutaka Mogi, Katsuhiko Nishimori, Takefumi Kikusui, and Hitoshi Sakano, *eLife*, 10, March 2021; pp.e65078.

868 'Olfaction Scaffolds the Developing Human from Neonate to Adolescent and Beyond,' by Benoist Schaal, Tamsin K. Saxton, Hélène Loos, Robert Soussignan, and Karine Durand, *Philosophical Transactions of the Royal Society B: Biological Sciences*, 375(1800), April 2020, p.B37520190261.

869 *Rubber: Some Facts on its History, Production, and Manufacture*, P. W. Barker, United States Foreign and Domestic Commerce Bureau, January 1936, pp14 – 16.

870 My interview with fetish impresario Tim Woodward (www.timwoodward.org), October 9, 2020.

871 'Looking Back at 25 Years of BDSM at Europe's Biggest Fetish Club,' by Cliff Joannou, Vice, April 19, 2016 (www.vice.com/en/article/gqkxj3/25-year-torture-garden). Accessed June 19,

2021.

872 *The Anthem Anthology of Victorian Sonnets: Volume 1*, edited by Michael J. Allen, Anthem Press, p11.

873 'Charles Goodyear: American inventor,' *Encyclopaedia Britannica*, 2020 (www.britannica.com/biography/Charles-Goodyear). Accessed October 16, 2020.

874 'The Story of the Condom,' by Fahd Khan, Saheel Mukhtar, Ian K. Dickinson, and Seshadri Sriprasad, *Indian Journal of Urology*, 29(1), January - March 2013, pp12 – 15.

875 'Charles Goodyear - The Life and Discoveries of the Inventor of Vulcanized India Rubber,' *Scientific American: Supplement*, 787, January 31, 1891.

876 'Artificial Nipple by Elijah Pratt of New York, New York,' United States Patent Office, August 4, 1845 (patentimages.storage.googleapis.com/38/e9/db/f9b6278ee3970e/US4131.pdf). Accessed October 9, 2020.

877 'Baby Comforter by Christian W. Meinecke of Jersey City, New Jersey,' United States Patent Office, September 18, 1900 (patentimages.storage.googleapis.com/3a/69/e9/ee5b44850ff543/USD33212.pdf). Accessed October 10, 2020.

878 *Mama: Love, Motherhood and Revolution*, by Antonella Gambotto-Burke, Pinter and Martin, 2015 (Kindle edition).

879 'The Relationship of Bottle Feeding and Other Sucking Behaviours with Speech Disorder in Patagonian Pre-Schoolers,' by Clarita Barbosa, Sandra Vasquez, Mary A Parada, Juan Carlos Velez Gonzalez, Chanaye Jackson, N David Yanez, Bizu Gelaye, and Annette L Fitzpatrick, *BMC Paediatrics*, 9, October 2009, pp66.

880 'The Impact of Pacifier Use on Breastfeeding: A Prospective Cohort Study,' by A. M. Vogel, B. L. Hutchison, and E. A. Mitchell, *Journal of Paediatrics and Child Health*, 37(1), February 2001, pp58 - 63.

881 'Early Weaning: Implications to Oral Motor Development,' by Flávia Cristina Brisque Neiva, Débora Martins Cattoni, José Lauro de Araújo Ramos, and Hugo Issler, *Journal of Paediatrics*, 79(1), January - February 2003, pp7 - 12.

882 'Breast Feeding, Bottle Feeding, and Non-Nutritive Sucking; Effects on Occlusion in Deciduous Dentition,' by D. Viggiano, D. Fasano, G. Monaco, and L. Strohmenger, *Archives of Disease in Childhood*, 89(12), December 2004, pp1121 - 1123.

883 'Tongue Strength: Its Relationship to Tongue Thrusting, Open-Bite, and Articulatory Proficiency,' by James P. Dworkin and Richard A. Culatta, *Journal of Speech and Hearing Disorders*, 45(2), May 1980, pp277 - 282.

884 'Breast-Fed Infants Process Speech Differently From Bottle-Fed Infants: Evidence from Neuroelectrophysiology,' by Melissa Ferguson and Peter J. Molfese, *Developmental Neuropsychology*, 31(3), 2007, pp337 - 347.

885 'The Influence of Infant Diet on Early Developmental Changes in Processing Human Voice Speech Stimuli: ERP Variations in Breast and Milk Formula-Fed Infants at 3 and 6 Months After Birth,' by R. T. Pivik, Roscoe A. Dykman, Hongkui Jing, Janet M. Gilchrist and Thomas M. Badger, *Developmental Neuropsychology*, 31(3), 2007, pp279 - 335.

886 'The Effects of Infant Feeding on Speech Quality,' by F. E. Broad, *The New Zealand Medical Journal*, 76(482), July 1972, pp28 - 31.

887 'Further Studies on the Effects of Infant Feeding on Speech Quality,' by F. E. Broad, *The New Zealand Medical Journal*, 82(553), December 1975, pp373 - 376.

888 'The Impact of Nonverbal Ability on Prevalence and Clinical Presentation of Language Disorder: Evidence from a Population Study,' by Courtenay Frazier Norbury, Debbie Gooch, Charlotte Wray, Gillian Baird, Tony Charman, Emily Simonoff, George Vamvakas, and Andrew Pickles, *Journal of Child Psychology and Psychiatry and Allied Disciplines*, 57(11), November 2016, pp1247 - 1257.

889 *Special Educational Needs in England: January 2019*, The Department for Education, (assets.publishing.service.gov.uk/government/uploads/system/uploads/attachment_data/file/814244/SEN_2019_Text.docx.pdf). Accessed October 19, 2020.

890 'The Impact of Nonverbal Ability on Prevalence and Clinical Presentation of Language Disorder: Evidence from a Population Study,' by Courtenay Frazier Norbury, Debbie Gooch, Charlotte Wray, Gillian Baird, Tony Charman, Emily Simonoff, George Vamvakas, and Andrew Pickles, *Journal of Child Psychology and Psychiatry and Allied Disciplines*, 57(11), November 2016, pp1247 - 1257.

891   'Children's Development of Semantic Verbal Fluency during Summer Vacation versus during Formal Schooling,' by Ida Rosqvist, Olof Sandgren, Ketty Andersson, Kristina Hansson, Viveka Lyberg-Åhlander, and Birgitta Sahlén, *Logopedics Phoniatrics Vocology*, 45(3), October 2020, pp134 - 142.

892   *Statistics on Voice, Speech, and Language*, US Department of Health and Human Services, 2016 (www.nidcd.nih.gov/health/statistics/statistics-voice-speech-and-language). Accessed October 19, 2020.

893   'Schoolbook Simplification and Its Relation to the Decline in SAT-Verbal Scores,' by Donald P. Hayes, Loreen T. Wolfer, and Michael F. Wolfe, *American Educational Research Journal*, 33(2), June 1996, pp489 - 508.

894   'A Preliminary Study on the Relationship between Characteristics of TV Content and Delayed Speech Development in Young Children,' by Kanako Okuma and Masako Tanimura, *Infant Behaviour and Development*, 32(3), June 2009, pp312 - 321.

895   'Redefining the Survival of the Fittest: Communication Disorders in the 21st Century,' by Robert J. Ruben, *The Laryngoscope*, 110(2), February 2000, pp241.

896   'Socio-Demographic Associations with Digit and Pacifier Sucking at 15 Months of Age and Possible Associations with Infant Infection,' by K. North Stone, P. Fleming, and J. Golding, *Early Human Development*, 60(2), December 2000, pp137 - 148.

897   'Pacifiers' Effects upon Play and Separations from the Mother for the One-Year-Old in a Novel Environment,' by Jane S. Halonen and Richard H. Passman, *Infant Behaviour and Development*, 1, January 1978, pp70 - 78.

898   *Dummies for Suckers: A Comprehensive User Guide*, by Beck and Matt Stanton, ABC Books, 2020

899   'Exclusive Breastfeeding Changes in Brazil Attributable to Pacifier Use,' by Gabriela Buccini, Rafael Pérez-Escamilla, Elsa Regina Justo Giugliani, Maria Helena Benicio, and Sonia Isoyama Venancio, *PLoS ONE*, 13(12), December 2018, p.e0208261.

900   'Rubber in the Automotive Industry. From the Viewpoint of the Rubber Technologist,' by S. M. Cadwell, R. A. Merrill, C. M. Sloman, and F. L. Yost, *Rubber Chemistry and Technology*, 14(2), 1941, pp378 – 385.

901   *The Three Eras of 'The Cal'*, Pirelli, 2019 (pirellicalendar.pirelli.com/en/the-three-eras-of-the-cal). Accessed September 10, 2020.

902   'High Fashion Quotient Marks 2015 Pirelli Calendar,' by David Yi, *WWD*, July 24, 2014 (wwd.com/wwd-publications/wwd/2014-07-24-2097280/). Accessed September 10, 2020.

903   'Self Portrait as Cherry Pie,' *Luncheon*, October 11, 2020 (www.instagram.com/p/CGNgla-lAa3z). Accessed February 11, 2021.

904   *Lou, NYC*, by Robert Mapplethorpe, 1978 (collections.lacma.org/node/2233366). Accessed October 18, 2020.

905   *Phillip Prioleau*, by Robert Mapplethorpe, 1982 (www.getty.edu/art/collection/objects/256118/robert-mapplethorpe-phillip-prioleau-american-negative-1982-print-1990/). Accessed October 18, 2020.

906   *Joe, N.Y.C.*, by Robert Mapplethorpe, 1978 (www.getty.edu/art/collection/objects/254555/robert-mapplethorpe-joe-nyc-american-1978/). Accessed October 18, 2020.

907   *White Gauze*, by Robert Mapplethorpe, 1984 (www.artnews.com/wp-content/uploads/2011/08/web05-11-at-mapple-gauze.jpg). Accessed October 18, 2020.

908   *Dominick and Elliot*, by Robert Mapplethorpe, 1979 (www.nationalgalleries.org/art-and-artists/90693/dominick-and-elliot). Accessed October 18, 2020.

909   *Fist Fuck / Double*, by Robert Mapplethorpe, 1978 (www.alisonjacquesgallery.com/exhibitions/141/works/artworks9630/). Accessed October 18, 2020.

910   *Self Portrait with Whip*, by Robert Mapplethorpe, 1978 (www.artsy.net/artwork/robert-mapplethorpe-self-portrait-with-whip). Accessed October 18, 2020.

911   *Double Fist Fuck*, by Robert Mapplethorpe, 1978 (www.alisonjacquesgallery.com/exhibitions/141/works/artworks9630); *Fist Fuck, Single*, by Robert Mapplethorpe, 1978 (collections.lacma.org/node/2233387).

912   *The Sex Doll: A History*, by Anthony Ferguson, McFarland (Kindle edition), 2014.

913   'In Every Dream Home a Heartache,' by Roxy Music (words and music by Bryan Ferry, 1973).

914   'Married to a Doll: Why One Man Advocates Synthetic Love,' by Juliet Beck, *The Atlantic*, September 6, 2013 (www.theatlantic.com/health/archive/2013/09/married-to-a-doll-why-one-man-advocates-synthetic-love/279361/). Accessed October 16, 2020.

915 Telephone interview with Nancy Kulp's best friend, June 22, 2021.

916 "She is More than Plastic': Married Japanese Man 'Finds Love' with a Sex Doll - Which He Takes Shopping, on Romantic Days Out and Even Bathes,' by Martha Cliff, *The Daily Mail*, June 27, 2016 (www.dailymail.co.uk/femail/article-3661804/Married-Japanese-man-claims-finally-love-sex-doll.html). Accessed October 17, 2020.

917 'Feeling Scared During Sex: Findings from a U.S. Probability Sample of Women and Men Ages 14 to 60,' Debby Herbenick, Elizabeth Bartelt, Tsung-Chieh (Jane) Fu, Bryant Paul, Ronna Gradus, Jill Bauer, and Rashida Jones, *Journal of Sex and Marital Therapy*, 45(5), 2019, pp424 - 439.

918 'Feeling Scared During Sex: Findings from a U.S. Probability Sample of Women and Men Ages 14 to 60,' Debby Herbenick, Elizabeth Bartelt, Tsung-Chieh (Jane) Fu, Bryant Paul, Ronna Gradus, Jill Bauer, and Rashida Jones, *Journal of Sex and Marital Therapy*, 45(5), 2019, pp424 - 439.

919 'Sexual Masochism Disorder with Asphyxiophilia: A Deadly Yet Underrecognised Disease,' by Anna Coluccia, Mario Gabbrielli, Giacomo Gualtieri, Fabio Ferretti, Andrea Pozza, and Andrea Fagiolini, *Case Reports in Psychiatry*, September 2016, pp5474862.

920 'The Fatal, Hateful Rise of Choking during Sex,' by Anna Moore and Coco Khan, *The Guardian*, July 25, 2019 (www.theguardian.com/society/2019/jul/25/fatal-hateful-rise-of-choking-during-sex). Accessed November 14, 2020.

921 'Sexual Scripts and the Sexual Behaviour of Men and Women Who Use Pornography,' by Ana J. Bridges, Chyng F. Sun, Matthew B. Ezzell, and Jennifer Johnson, *Sexualisation, Media and Society*, October – December 2016, pp1 – 14.

922 '*Women's Health* Media Kit,' Hearst Magazine Media, 2020 (www.womenshealthmediakit.com). Accessed February 28, 2020.

923 'Choking as a Sex Move - Is It for You?' by Molly Triffin, *Women's Health*, March 23, 2016 (www.womenshealthmag.com/sex-and-love/a19938109/choking-during-sex). Accessed March 2, 2021.

924 'Everything You Need to Know about Erotic Asphyxiation,' by Kimberly Holland, *Healthline*, May 29, 2019 (www.healthline.com/health/healthy-sex/erotic-asphyxiation#solo-vs-partner). Accessed November 14, 2020.

925 *The Medical Realities of Breath Control Play*, by Jay Wiseman, GreeneryPress, 1997.

926 'Why are More and More Young Women Getting Choked during Sex?' by Dan Savage, *City Pages*, September 9, 2020 (www.citypages.com/arts/why-are-more-and-more-young-women-getting-choked-during-sex/572358321). Accessed November 14, 2020.

927 'Foetal-to-Maternal Signalling in the Timing of Birth,' by Carole R. Mendelson, Alina P. Montalbano, and Lu Gaoa, *Journal of Steroid Biochemistry and Molecular Biology*, 170, June 2017, pp19 – 27.

928 'Labour Induction Basics: What Causes Labour to Begin?' *National Partnership for Women and Families*, 2021 (www.childbirthconnection.org/giving-birth/labor-induction/basics). Accessed August 15, 2020.

929 'Maternal Stress and Obstetric and Infant Outcomes: Epidemiological Findings and Neuro-endocrine Mechanisms,' by Marie-Paule Austin and Leo Leader, *Australia and New Zealand Journal of Obstetrics and Gynaecology*, 40(3), August 2000, pp331 - 337.

930 'Endocrinology of Parturition', by Sunil K. Kota, Kotni Gayatri, Sruti Jammula, Siva K. Kota, S. V. S. Krishna, Lalit K. Meher, and Kirtikumar D. Modi , *Indian Journal of Endocrinology and Metabolism*, January-February 2013, 17(1), pp50 – 59.

931 'The Childhood Asthma Epidemic,' by G. Russell, *Thorax*, 61(4), April 2006, pp276 – 278.

932 'Epidemiology of Asthma in Children and Adults,' by Shyamali C. Dharmage, Jennifer L. Perret, and Adnan Custovic, *Frontiers in Paediatrics*, 7, June 2019, pp246.

933 'The Allergy Epidemics: 1870–2010,' by Thomas A.E. Platts-Mills, *The Journal of Allergy and Clinical Immunology*, 136(1), July 2015, pp3 – 13.

934 'Asthma-Related Deaths,' by Gennaro D'Amato, Carolina Vitale, Antonio Molino, Anna Stanziola, Alessandro Sanduzzi, Alessandro Vatrella, Mauro Mormile, Maurizia Lanza, Giovanna Calabrese, Leonardo Antonicelli, and Maria D'Amato, *Multidisciplinary Respiratory Medicine*, 11, October 2016, pp37.

935 'Elective Caesarean Section: Its Impact on Neonatal Respiratory Outcome,' by Ashwin Ramachandrappa and Lucky Jain, *Clinics in Perinatology*, 35(2), June 2008, pp373.

936 *Alleviation of Pain in Labour*, by William P. Sadler, Instructor in Obstetrics and Gynaecology, University of Minnesota, Read before the Forty-Fifth Annual Meeting of Idaho State Medical Association, Boise, Idaho, USA, August 30 - September 2, 1937.

937 *My Mother Wants Me Dead*, by carolesdaughter (words and lyrics Thea Taylor, Arista Records/ Sony Music 2020).

938 'Fact Sheet: Preterm Birth,' World Health Organisation, February 19, 2018 (www.who.int/ news-room/fact-sheets/detail/preterm-birth). Accessed November 14, 2020.

939 'News Release: Individualized, Supportive Care Key to Positive Childbirth Experience, says WHO,' World Health Organisation, February 15, 2018 (www.who.int/mediacentre/news/ releases/2018/positive-childbirth-experience/en/). Accessed November 14, 2020.

940 'Epidural Analgesia in Labour and Neonatal Respiratory Distress: A Case-Control Study,' by Manoj Kumar, Sue Chandra, Zainab Ijaz, and Ambikaipakan Senthilselvan, *Archives of Disease in Childhood: Foetal and Neonatal Edition*, 99(2), March 2014, p.F116-9.

941 'Neonatology and Obstetric Anaesthesia,' by Ward Platt, *Archives of Disease in Childhood: Foetal and Neonatal Edition*, 99(2), March 2014, p.F98.

942 'Pharmacokinetics and Transplacental Distribution of Fentanyl in Epidural Anaesthesia for Normal Pregnant Women,' by Elaine Christine Dantas Moisés, Luciana de Barros Duarte, Ricardo de Carvalho Cavalli, Vera Lúcia Lanchote, Geraldo Duarte, and Sérgio Pereira da Cunha, *European Journal of Clinical Pharmacology*, 61(7), August 2005, pp517 – 522.

943 'Can I Really Handle Labour and Delivery Pains?' by Kira Weier, *Health Partners*, 2020 (www. healthpartners.com/blog/labor-and-delivery-pains). Accessed November 11, 2020.

944 'The Effects of Fentanyl for Pain Relief during Childbirth,' *PAINWeek*, July 2, 2020 (www.pain-week.org/media/news/effects-fentanyl-pain-relief-during-childbirth). Accessed November 11, 2020.

945 'Neonatal Safety of Maternal Fentanyl during Labour,' by M. Kokki, S. Westeren-Punnonen, H. Hautajärvi, S. Heinonen, M. Mazzei, S. Määttä, E. Paalanen, and H. Kokki, *British Journal of Anaesthesia*, 115(4), October 2015, pp636 – 638.

946 'Cardiac Arrest from Tramadol and Fentanyl Combination,' by Shalini Nair and Tony Thomson Chandy, *Indian Journal of Anaesthesia*, 59(4), April 2015, pp254 – 255.

947 'Remifentanil versus Fentanyl for Intravenous Patient-Controlled Labour Analgesia: an Observational Study,' by Radhika Marwah, Samah Hassan, Jose C. A. Carvalho, and Mrinalini Balki, *Canadian Journal of Anaesthesia*, 59(3), March 2012, pp246 - 254.

948 'Increased Cell Proliferation in the Rat Anterior Cingulate Cortex following Neonatal Hypoxia: Relevance to Schizophrenia,' by Evelin L. Schaeffer, Franziska Kuˊhn, Angelika Schmitt, Wagner F. Gattaz, Oliver Gruber, Thomas Schneider-Axmann, Peter Falkai, and Andrea Schmitt, *Journal of Neural Transmission*, 120(1), January 2013, pp187 – 195.

949 'The Impact of Intrapartum Analgesia on Infant Feeding,' by Sue Jordan, Simon Emery, Ceri Bradshaw, Alan Watkins, and Wendy Friswell, *BJOG: An International Journal of Obstetrics and Gynaecology*, 112(7), July 2005, pp927 - 934.

950 *An Introduction to the Principles of Morals and Legislation*, by Jeremy Bentham, Clarendon Press, 1907 (first published in 1789), pp311.

951 'Effective Management of Breathlessness: A Review of Potential Human Rights Issues,' by Metin Başoğlu, *European Respiratory Journal*, 49(5), May 2017, p.1602099.

952 'Effective Management of Breathlessness: A Review of Potential Human Rights Issues,' by Metin Başoğlu, *European Respiratory Journal*, 49(5), May 2017, p.1602099.

953 'What is Respiratory Distress Syndrome in Premature Babies?' by Donna Freeborn, Heather Trevino, and Liora C. Adler, University of Rochester Medical Centre Rochester, 2020 (www. urmc.rochester.edu/encyclopedia/content.aspx?contenttypeid=90&contentid=P02371). Accessed November 14, 2020.

954 'Fear Network Model in Panic Disorder: The Past and the Future,' by Chien-Han Lai, *Psychiatry Investigation*, 16(1), January 2019, pp16 – 26.

955 'WHO Global Report on Trends in Prevalence of Tobacco Smoking 2000-2025 - Second Edition,' World Health Organisation, 2018 (apps.who.int/iris/bitstream/handle/10665/27269 4/9789241514170-eng.pdf?ua=1). Accessed March 2, 2021.

956 'Association of High-Potency Cannabis Use With Mental Health and Substance Use in Adolescence,' by Lindsey A. Hines, Tom P. Freeman, Suzanne H. Gage, Stanley Zammit, Matthew Hickman, Mary Cannon, Marcus Munafo, John MacLeod, and Jon Heron, *JAMA Psychiatry*,

77(10), May 2020, pp1044-1051.

957 *World Drug Report: 2018 – Executive Summary, Conclusions, and Policy Implications*, United Nations, June 2018 (www.unodc.org/wdr2018/prelaunch/WDR18_Booklet_1_EXSUM.pdf). Accessed November 15, 2020.

958 'Cannabis,' Alcohol, Drugs and Addictive Behaviours Unit, World Health Organisation, 2020 (www.who.int/teams/mental-health-and-substance-use/alcohol-drugs-and-addictive-behaviours/drugs-psychoactive/cannabis). Accessed November 15, 2020.

959 'Electronic Cigarette and Vaping should be Discouraged during the New Coronavirus SARS-CoV-2 Pandemic,' by Emilie Javelle, *Archives of Toxicology*, 94(6), April 2020, pp1 – 2.

960 *The Cigarette Century: The Rise, Fall, and Deadly Persistence of the Product That Defined America*, by Allan M. Brandt, Basic Books, 2009, pp487.

961 *My Booky Wook*, by Russell Brand, Hodder, 2008, pp16, 112, 113, 226, 88.

962 'A Century of Smoking in Women's History,' Department of Nursing, University of Southern California, 2021 (nursing.usc.edu/blog/womens-history-smoking/). Accessed February 6, 2021.

963 *Women and Smoking: A Report of the Surgeon General*, Centres for Disease Control and Prevention, March 2001 (www.ncbi.nlm.nih.gov/books/NBK44311). Accessed February 6, 2021.

964 *The Handmaid's Tale*, by Margaret Atwood, Vintage, 1996 (originally published in 1985), pp25.

965 'Epidemiology of Anxiety Disorders in the 21st Century,' by Borwin Bandelow and Sophie Michaelis, *Dialogues in Clinical Neuroscience*, 17(3), September 2015, pp327 – 335.

966 *Depression and Other Common Mental Disorders: Global Health Estimates 3*, World Health Organisation, 2017 (apps.who.int/iris/bitstream/handle/10665/254610/WHO-MSD-MER-2017.2-eng.pdf). Accessed December 10, 2020.

967 'Generalised Anxiety Disorder Across the Globe,' by Ayelet Meron Ruscio, Lauren S. Hallion, Carmen C. W. Lim, Sergio Aguilar-Gaxiola, Ali Al-Hamzawi, Jordi Alonso, Laura Helena Andrade, Guilherme Borges, Evelyn J. Bromet, Brendan Bunting, José Miguel Caldas de Almeida, Koen Demyttenaere, Silvia Florescu, Giovanni de Girolamo, Oye Gureje, Josep Maria Haro, Yanling He, Hristo Hinkov, Chiyi Hu, Peter de Jonge, Elie G. Karam, Sing Lee, Jean-Pierre Lepine, Daphna Levinson, Zeina Mneimneh, Fernando Navarro-Mateu, José Posada-Villa, Tim Slade, Dan J. Stein, Yolanda Torres, Hidenori Uda, Bogdan Wojtyniak, Ronald C. Kessler, Somnath Chatterji, and Kate M. Scott, *JAMA Psychiatry*, 74(5), May 2017, pp465 - 475.

968 'Psychiatric Symptoms in Acute Respiratory Distress Syndrome Survivors: A One-Year National Multi-Center Study,' by Minxuan Huang, Ann M. Parker, O. Joseph Bienvenu, Victor D. Dinglas, Elizabeth Colantuoni, Ramona O. Hopkins, and Dale M. Needham, *Critical Care Medicine*, 44(5), May 2016, pp954 – 965.

969 'The Temptation of Drugs is a Bitch,' by Flea, *Time*, February 22, 2018 (time.com/5168435/flea-temptation-drug-addiction-opioid-crisis). Accessed June 14, 2021.

970 *Monkey Mind: A Memoir of Anxiety*, by Daniel Smith, Simon and Schuster, 2013, pp26.

971 *Joe, N.Y.C.*, by Robert Mapplethorpe, 1978 (www.getty.edu/art/collection/objects/254555/robert-mapplethorpe-joe-nyc-american-1978/). Accessed November 16, 2020.

972 '*Do You Know What It Feels Like to Drown?*: Strangulation as Coercive Control in Intimate Relationships,' by Kristie A. Thomas, Manisha Joshi, and Susan B. Sorenson, School of Social Policy and Practice University of Pennsylvania Scholarly Commons, 2014 (repository.upenn.edu/cgi/viewcontent.cgi?article=1190&context=spp_papers). Accessed November 21, 2020.

973 '*Do You Know What It Feels Like to Drown?*: Strangulation as Coercive Control in Intimate Relationships,' by Kristie A. Thomas, Manisha Joshi, and Susan B. Sorenson, School of Social Policy and Practice University of Pennsylvania Scholarly Commons, 2014 (repository.upenn.edu/cgi/viewcontent.cgi?article=1190&context=spp_papers). Accessed November 21, 2020.

974 'Moors murderer Ian Brady: the making of a monster,' by Marc Horne, *The Times*, November 2 2019 (www.thetimes.co.uk/article/the-making-of-a-monster-jdcstxp86). Accessed September 15, 2020.

975 *Scottish Midwives 1916-1983: The Central Midwives Board for Scotland and Practising Midwives*, by Lindsay Reid, A thesis submitted for the degree of PhD to the University of Glasgow, Centre for the History of Medicine and the School of Nursing and Midwifery, October 2002, pp133.

976 '"I Want to See Mummy": Ian Brady's Chilling Audio Tape Recording of 10-Year-Old Victim's Last Moments,' *The Telegraph*, May 16, 2017 (www.telegraph.co.uk/news/0/want-see-mummy-ian-bradys-chilling-audio-tape-recording-10-year). Accessed November 24, 2020.

977   *Ian Brady: The Untold Story of the Moors Murders*, by Alan Keightley, Pavilion Books (Kindle edition), 2017, pp15.

978   'Ian Brady had locked cases of his belongings removed before death,' by Frances Perraudin and Imogen Cooper, *The Guardian*, September 21, 2017 (www.theguardian.com/uk-news/2017/sep/21/moors-murderer-ian-brady-died-of-natural-causes-coroner-rules). Accessed June 29, 2021.

979   'ECHOES OF EVIL Ex-Cop Haunted by Sick Tape Recording of Ian Brady's Youngest Victim Lesley Ann Downey Pleading for Her Life with Little Drummer Boy Playing in the Background,' by Sam Christie, *The Sun*, May 16, 2017 (www.thesun.co.uk/news/3571032/ian-brady-tape-recording-youngest-victim-lesley-ann-downey/). Accessed November 24, 2020.

980   *Ian Brady: The Untold Story of the Moors Murders*, by Alan Keightley, Pavilion Books (Kindle edition), 2017, pp196.

981   "'I used to ask him why he kept strangling me so much and he told me he was practising on me': Myra Hindley reveals how 'Nazi' Ian Brady abused her in unseen private papers she handed over on her death-bed,' by Darren Boyle, *The Daily Mail*, September 20, 2018 (www.dailymail.co.uk/news/article-6188733/Myra-Hindley-reveals-Ian-Brady-raped-strangled-abused-her.html). Accessed November 24, 2020.

982   *The Shrine of Jeffrey Dahmer*, by Brian Masters, Coronet, 1993, pp26.

983   'Bendectin and Birth Defects: I. A Meta-Analysis of the Epidemiologic Studies,' by P. M. McKeigue, S. H. Lamm, S. Linn, and J. S. Kutcher, *Teratology*, 50(1), July 1994, pp27 - 37.

984   *The Shrine of Jeffrey Dahmer*, by Brian Masters, Coronet, 1993, pp26.

985   'Dahmer's Inferno,' by Brian Masters, *Vanity Fair*, 1991 (www.vanityfair.com/style/1991/11/jeffrey-dahmer-dennis-nilsen-serial-killer). Accessed January 24, 2021.

986   'Claustrophobia,' *Etymology Online*, 2001 - 2021 (www.etymonline.com/word/claustrophobia). Accessed February 23, 2021.

987   *Bright Air, Brilliant Fire: On the Matter of the Mind*, by Gerald M. Edelman, BasicBooks, 1992.

988   *Ian Brady: The Untold Story of the Moors Murders*, by Alan Keightley, Pavilion Books (Kindle edition), 2017, pp55.

989   *Art Therapy for Psychosis: Theory and Practice*, edited by Katherine Killick, Routledge, 2017, pp11.

990   'Disruption of Affectional Bonds and Its Effects on Behaviour,' by John Bowlby, *Journal of Contemporary Psychotherapy*, 2(2), Winter 1970, pp75 – 86.

991   'Developmental Consequences and Biological Significance of Mother–Infant Bonding,' by Kazutaka Mogi, Miho Nagasawa, and Takefumi Kikusui, *Progress in Neuro-Psychopharmacology and Biological Psychiatry*, 35(5), July 2011, pp1232 – 1241.

992   'Early Environmental Predictors of the Affective and Interpersonal Constructs of Psychopathy,' by Maria T. Daversa, *International Journal of Offender Therapy and Comparative Criminology*, 54(1), February 2010, pp6 – 21.

993   'Hypoglycaemia in a Newborn Baby,' Stanford Children's Health, Stanford University, 2020 (www.stanfordchildrens.org/en/topic/default?id=hypoglycemia-in-the-newborn-90-P01961). Accessed November 24, 2020.

994   'The Scientific Evidence on the Effects of Underfeeding on the Newborn Brain,' by Christie del Castillo-Hegyi, *Fed is Best*, September 9, 2016 (fedisbest.org/2016/09/the-scientific-evidence-on-the-effects-on-accidental-starvation-on-the-newborn-brain/). Accessed November 24, 2020.

995   'The Enigmatic Temporal Pole: A Review of Findings on Social and Emotional Processing,' by Ingrid R. Olson, Alan Plotzker, and Youssef Ezzyat, *Brain*, 130(7), July 2007, pp1718 – 1731.

996   *Ian Brady: The Untold Story of the Moors Murders*, by Alan Keightley, Pavilion Books (Kindle edition), 2017, pp78.

997   'Impaired Fear Conditioning Following Unilateral Temporal Lobectomy in Humans,' by K. S. LaBar, J. E. LeDoux, D. D. Spencer, and E. A. Phelps, *Journal of Neuroscience*, 15(10), October 1995, pp6846 – 6855.

998   *Ian Brady: The Untold Story of the Moors Murders*, by Alan Keightley, Pavilion Books (Kindle edition), 2017, pp343.

999   'Psychopathy and Physiological Responses to Threat of an Aversive Stimulus,' by Robert D. Hare, Janice Frazelle, and David N. Cox, *Psychophysiology*, 15(2), March 1978, pp165 – 172.

1000   'Deficient Fear Conditioning in Psychopathy: a Functional Magnetic Resonance Imaging Study,' by Niels Birbaumer, Ralf Veit, Martin Lotze, Michael Erb, Christiane Hermann,

Wolfgang Grodd, and Herta Flor, *Archives of General Psychiatry*, 62(7), July 2005, pp799 - 805.

1001 'A Mechanism for Impaired Fear Recognition after Amygdala Damage,' Ralph Adolphs, Frederic Gosselin, Tony W. Buchanan, Daniel Tranel, Philippe Schyns, and Antonio R. Damasio, *Nature*, 433, January 2005, pp68 – 72.

1002 'Sexual Sadism: Brain, Blood, and Behaviour,' by R. Langevin, J. Bain, G. Wortzman, S. Hucker, R. Dickey, and P. Wright, *Annals of the New York Academy of Sciences*, 528(1), August 1988, pp163 - 171.

1003 'Paedophilia and Temporal Lobe Disturbances, by Mario F Mendez, Tiffany Chow, John Ringman, and Geoff Twitchell, *Journal of Neuropsychiatry*, 12(1), February 2000, pp71 – 76.

1004 'Oxytocin and Early Parent-Infant Interactions: A Systematic Review,' by Naomi Scatliffe, Sharon Casavant, Dorothy Vittner, and Xiaomei Conga, *International Journal of Nursing Sciences*, 6(4), October 2019, pp445 – 453.

1005 Ian Brady: Crime Files,' *Crime and Investigation*, (www.crimeandinvestigation.co.uk/crime-files/ian-brady). Accessed November 25, 2020.

1006 'Early Childhood Deprivation is Associated with Alterations in Adult Brain Structure despite Subsequent Environmental Enrichment,' by Nuria K. Mackes, Dennis Golm, Sagari Sarkar, Robert Kumsta, Michael Rutter, Graeme Fairchild, Mitul A. Mehta, and Edmund J. S. Sonuga-Barke, *PNAS*, 117(1), January 2020, pp641 – 649.

1007 'Obituary: Ian Brady, Child Killer who Showed No Remorse for His Crimes,' *The Telegraph*, May 16, 2017 (www.telegraph.co.uk/obituaries/2017/05/16/ian-brady-obituary/). Accessed November 26, 2020.

1008 *Ian Brady: The Untold Story of the Moors Murders*, by Alan Keightley, Pavilion Books (Kindle edition), 2017, pp343 – 344.

1009 'Ian Brady: Moors Murderer 'Would Remove Feeding Tube',' *BBC News*, September 21, 2017 (www.bbc.co.uk/news/uk-england-manchester-41345128). Accessed November 24, 2020.

1010 ''An Almost Biblical Notion of Evil' – Why Ian Brady Haunts the British Psyche,' by Duncan Campbell, *The Guardian*, May 16, 2017 (www.theguardian.com/uk-news/2017/may/16/ian-brady-myra-hindley-biblical-notion-of-evil-haunt-british-psyche-moors-murders). Accessed June 29, 2021.

1011 'Moors Murderer Ian Brady: The Making of a Monster,' by Marc Horne, *The Times*, November 2, 2019 (www.thetimes.co.uk/article/the-making-of-a-monster-jdcstxp86). Accessed June 29, 2021.

1012 'Inside the Mind of The 'Celebrity' Serial Killer Ian Brady,' by Raj Persaud and Peter Bruggen, *Psychology Today*, May 16, 2017 (www.psychologytoday.com/gb/blog/slightly-blighty/201705/inside-the-mind-the-celebrity-serial-killer-ian-brady). Accessed June 29, 2021.

1013 'Ian Brady Obituary,' by Peter Stanford, *The Guardian*, May 15, 2017 (www.theguardian.com/uk-news/2017/may/15/ian-brady-obituary). Accessed November 24, 2020.

1014 *Ian Brady: The Untold Story of the Moors Murders*, by Alan Keightley, Pavilion Books (Kindle edition), 2017, pp27.

1015 'Ian Brady: I murdered children for 'existential experience',' by Gordon Rayner, *The Telegraph*, June 25, 2013 (www.telegraph.co.uk/news/uknews/crime/10141531/Ian-Brady-I-murdered-children-for-existential-experience.html). Accessed November 26, 2020.

1016 'Ian Brady Obituary,' by Peter Stanford, *The Guardian*, May 15, 2017 (www.theguardian.com/uk-news/2017/may/15/ian-brady-obituary). Accessed June 29, 2021.

1017 *Nausea*, by Jean-Paul Sartre, New Directions, 1964 (first published in 1938), pp133.

1018 Translation mine. November 27, 2020.

1019 *The Stranger* (originally published as *L'Etranger* in 1942), by Albert Camus, Knopf, 1946, pp2, 21, 75.

1020 *The Stranger* (originally published as *L'Etranger* in 1942), by Albert Camus, Knopf, 1946, pp2, 20, 21, 75, 85, 149.

1021 'Dry Heart of the Creator,' by Edward Hughes, *The Times Literary Supplement*, May 19, 2017 (www.the-tls.co.uk/articles/dry-heart-of-the-creator/). Accessed November 28, 2020.

1022 *Looking for The Stranger: Albert Camus and the Life of a Literary Classic*, by Alice Kaplan, University of Chicago Press, 2018, pp1 - 2.

1023 *Camus*, by David Sherman, Wiley-Blackwell, 2008.

1024 *London Fields*, by Martin Amis, Vintage, 2003 (originally published in 1989), pp252, 244, 318,

365.

1025 *Anna Karenina*, by Leo Tolstoy, translated by Louise and Aylmer Maude, Oxford University Press, 1939 (first published in 1875 - 1877), pp44

1026 *Lolita*, by Vladimir Nabokov, Crest, 1959 (first published in 1955), pp11, 21.

1027 'Nazism and the Occult,' by Julian Strube, *The Occult World*, edited by Christopher Partridge, Routledge, 2014, pp339.

1028 'The Occult and Comics,' by Kennet Granholm, *The Occult World*, edited by Christopher Partridge, Routledge, 2014, pp504.

1029 *The Long, Hard Road out of Hell*, by Marilyn Manson with Neil Strauss, Plexus, 2009 (first published in 1998), pp169, Acknowledgments.

1030 *Child of Satan, Child of God*, by Susan Atkins with Bob Slosser, Menelorelin Dorenay's Publishing, 2012.

1031 'Inside the Mind of Jeffrey Dahmer: Serial Killer's Chilling Jailhouse Interview,' *Inside Edition* (1993), November 27, 2018 (www.youtube.com/watch?v=iWjYsxaBjBI). Accessed January 24, 2021.

1032 *London Fields*, by Martin Amis, Vintage, 2003 (originally published in 1989), pp148, 67.

1033 *The Stranger* (originally published as *L'Etranger* in 1942), by Albert Camus, Knopf, 1946, pp58, 19, 73.

1034 *The Stranger* (originally published as *L'Etranger* in 1942), by Albert Camus, Knopf, 1946, pp127.

1035 *The Stranger* (originally published as *L'Etranger* in 1942), by Albert Camus, Knopf, 1946, pp76.

1036 *Albert Camus: From the Absurd to Revolt*, by John Foley, Routledge, 2014, pp18.

1037 *The Stranger* (originally published as *L'Etranger* in 1942), by Albert Camus, Knopf, 1946, pp128, 151.

1038 *The Stranger* (originally published as *L'Etranger* in 1942), by Albert Camus, Knopf, 1946, pp150, 151, 152, 154.

1039 'Record Awareness of Male Suicide, as Latest Stats Show 3 in 4 UK Suicides are Men,' Campaign Against Living Miserably (CALM), December 2, 2016 (www.thecalmzone. net/2016/12/record-awareness-of-male-suicide-as-latest-stats-show-3-in-4-uk-suicides-are-men/). Accessed December 4, 2020.

1040 *James Hunt: The Biography*, by Gerald Donaldson, Virgin, 2009, pp66, 319, 320, 332, 333.

1041 'Anterior Cingulate Cortex: Unique Role in Cognition and Emotion,' by Francis L. Stevens, Robin A. Hurley, Katherine H. Taber, Robin A. Hurley, L. Anne Hayman, and Katherine H. Taber, *The Journal of Neuropsychiatry and Clinical Neurosciences*, 23(2), Spring 2011, pp121 – 125.

1042 *The Causes of World War Two and the Holocaust*, by Lloyd deMause (primal-page.com/war2. htm). Accessed December 2, 2020.

1043 *German Life and Manners as seen in Saxony at the Present Day: Volume One*, by Henry Mayhew, W. H. Allen and Co., 1864, pp493 - 494.

1044 'Harsh Nazi Parenting Guidelines May Still Affect German Children of Today,' by Anne Kratzer, Scientific American, January 4, 2019 (www.scientificamerican.com/article/harsh-nazi-parenting-guidelines-may-still-affect-german-children-of-today1). Accessed February 8, 2021.

1045 'Abortion in Weimar Germany – the Debate Amongst the Medical Profession,' by Cornelie Usborne, *Continuity and Change*, 5(2), August 1990, pp199 – 224.

1046 'Abortion,' by M. Ajmal, M. Sunder, and R. Akinbinu, *Stat Pearls*, January 2020 (www.ncbi. nlm.nih.gov/books/NBK518961/). Accessed December 1, 2020.

1047 'Revealed: Teen mother went online to sell concert tickets on same day her starved baby's body was found after she had partied for six days - as her family say they are 'broken',' by Faith Ridler, *The Daily Mail*, March 27, 2021 (www.dailymail.co.uk/news/article-9409313/ Teen-mother-went-online-sell-concert-tickets-day-starved-babys-body-found.html). Accessed March 27, 2021.

1048 *Ian Brady: The Untold Story of the Moors Murders*, by Alan Keightley, Pavilion Books (Kindle edition), 2017, pp205.

1049 Book III, *Metamorphoses*, by Ovid, translated by Anthony Kline, Borders Classics, 2004, pp437 - 473.

1050 *Space Oddity*, by David Bowie (words and music by David Bowie, Onward Music, Tro-Essex Music, Westminster Music & Essex Music, 1969).

1051 '*2001: A Space Odyssey* is still the 'Ultimate Trip',' by Dennis Overbye, *The New York Times*,

May 10, 2018 (www.nytimes.com/2018/05/10/science/2001-a-space-odyssey-kubrick.html). Accessed December 15, 2020.

1052 'Stanley Kubrick Explains the Ending of *2001: A Space Odyssey* in Newly Discovered Interview,' *The Telegraph*, July 9, 2018 (www.telegraph.co.uk/films/2018/07/09/stanley-kubrick-finally-explains-ending-2001-space-odyssey-unearthed/). Accessed December 13, 2020.

1053 '2001: A Space Odyssey - Aliens and Existentialism,' Leslie Shore, *Science on Screen*, 2016 (scienceonscreen.org/programs/2016/aliens-and-existentialism). Accessed December 8, 2020.

1054 *Creazione di Adamo (The Creation of Adam)*, by Michelangelo Buonarroti, 1508 – 1512,

1055 'Stanley Kubrick on the Meaning of the Ending of 2001 in a Rare 1980 Interview,' interview by Jun'ichi Yaoi, *Eyes on Cinema*, 1980 (www.youtube.com/watch?v=er_o82OMlNM). Accessed December 8, 2020.

1056 *2001: A Space Odyssey*, by Arthur C. Clarke, Penguin, 1993 (originally published in 1968), pp26, 232.

1057 '2001: A Space Odyssey* (1968) - Star Child Scene,' *Movieclips*, January 31, 2019 (www.youtube.com/watch?v=_XuDmoP5scY). Accessed December 8, 2020.

1058 'The Colour of Medicine,' by David Pantalony, *CMAJ*, 181(6-7), September 2009, pp402–403.

1059 *AIA Guide to New York City 5*, by Norval White, the estate of Elliot Willensky and Fran Leadon, Oxford University Press, 2010, pp249.

1060 *Stanley Kubrick: A Biography*, by John Baxter, HarperCollins, 1998, pp17.

1061 'Hospital Care at Second Avenue and East 17th Street, New York City, 1894 – 1984,' by Henry Pinsker, David M. Novick, and Beverly L. Richman, *The Bulletin of the New York Academy of Medicine*, 60(9), November 1984, pp905 – 924.

1062 *IA Guide to New York City 5*, by Norval White, the estate of Elliot Willensky and Fran Leadon, Oxford University Press, 2010, pp11.

1063 'Hospital Care at Second Avenue and East 17th Street, New York City, 1894 – 1984,' by Henry Pinsker, David M. Novick, and Beverly L. Richman, *The Bulletin of the New York Academy of Medicine*, 60(9), November 1984, pp905 – 924.

1064 'An Architectural Analysis of the Film, 2001: A Space Odyssey (1968), Directed by Stanley Kubrick and Starring Keir Dullea and Gary Lockwood,' by Mehruss Jon Ahi and Armen Karaoghlanian, *Interiors*, 2012 (www.intjournal.com/0612/2001-a-space-odyssey). Accessed December 13, 2020.

1065 '2001 - The Monolith and the Message,' by Roger Ebert, *The Chicago Sun-Times*, April 21, 1968 (www.rogerebert.com/roger-ebert/2001-the-monolith-and-the-message). Accessed December 8, 2020.

1066 'Lying-In Hospital, Second Avenue (1908),' *Shorpy* (www.shorpy.com/node/6423?size=_original#caption). Accessed December 8, 2020.

1067 'Hospital Care at Second Avenue and East 17th Street, New York City, 1894 – 1984,' by Henry Pinsker, David M. Novick, and Beverly L. Richman, *The Bulletin of the New York Academy of Medicine*, 60(9), November 1984, pp905 – 924.

1068 'Fame Slept Here - in Droves,' by S. Jhoanna Robledo, *New York Magazine*, September 19, 2013 (nymag.com/realestate/features/rutherford-place-2013-9/), (images.elegran.com/2018%2F10%2F25%2F14%2F08%2F24%2F1b3336fc-2dd6-420d-9b21-6758acd2c082%2FD-SC_1494.jpg/cp/rutherford-place/305-2nd-ave_.jpg), and (www.nynesting.com/sites/default/files/rutherford_place_305_second_avenue_entrance.jpg). Accessed December 8, 2020.

1069 'Recreating the 'lying-in' month,' by Remi Harris, *Breastfeeding Matters*, 224, March / April 2018 (www.laleche.org.uk/recreating-the-lying-in-month/). Accessed December 15, 2020.

1070 'Eye Contact Detection in Humans from Birth,' by Teresa Farroni, Gergely Csibra, Francesca Simion, and Mark H. Johnson, *PNAS*, 99(14), July 2002, pp9602 - 9605.

1071 *The First Relationship: Infant and Mother*, by Daniel N. Stern, Harvard University Press, 2004, pp34.

1072 'Eye Contact Detection in Humans from Birth,' by Teresa Farroni, Gergely Csibra, Francesca Simion, and Mark H. Johnson, *PNAS*, 99(14), July 2002, pp9602 - 9605.

1073 *Francis Bacon: Revelations*, by Mark Stevens and Annalyn Swan, HarperCollins, 2021, pp11, 31, 35.

1074 ''Francis Bacon: Late Paintings,' at Gagosian, Is a Vivid Narrative,' by Ken Johnson, *New

York Times, December 3, 2015 (www.nytimes.com/2015/12/04/arts/design/francis-bacon-late-paintings-at-gagosian-is-a-vivid-narrative.html). Accessed March 19, 2021.

1075 'Inside the Mind of Jeffrey Dahmer: Serial Killer's Chilling Jailhouse Interview,' *Inside Edition* (1993), November 27, 2018 (www.youtube.com/watch?v=iWjYsxaBjBI). Accessed January 24, 2021.

1076 'The Potential of Attention,' by Jessica Cohen, *Utne Reader*, Winter 2017 (www.utne.com/mind-and-body/parapsychology-research-zm0z17wzols). Accessed December 15, 2020.

1077 'Dephasing in Electron Interference by a 'Which-Path' Detector,' by E. Buks, R. Schuster, M. Heiblum, D. Mahalu, and V. Umansky, *Nature*, 391, February 1998, pp871 – 1874.

1078 *I'll Be Your Mirror*, by the Velvet Underground and Nico (words and music Lou Reed, Oakfield Avenue Music, 1967).

1079 'Eye Contact Detection in Humans from Birth,' by Teresa Farroni, Gergely Csibra, Francesca Simion, and Mark H. Johnson, *PNAS*, 99(14), July 2002, pp9602-9605.

1080 'Depressed Mothers and Infants Are More Relaxed During Breastfeeding versus Bottle-feeding Interactions: Brief Report,'' by Tiffany Field, Miguel Diego, Maria Hernandez-Reif, Barbara Figueiredo, Shauna Ezell, and Vijaya Siblalingappa, *Infant Behaviour and Development*, 33(2), April 2010, pp241 – 244.

1081 *The First Relationship: Infant and Mother*, by Daniel N. Stern, Harvard University Press, 2004, pp34.

1082 'Prevalence, Correlates, Disability, and Comorbidity of DSM-IV Borderline Personality Disorder: Results from the Wave 2 National Epidemiologic Survey on Alcohol and Related Conditions,' Bridget F. Grant, S. Patricia Chou, Risë B. Goldstein, Boji Huang, Frederick S. Stinson, Tulshi D. Saha, Sharon M. Smith, Deborah A. Dawson, Attila J. Pulay, Roger P. Pickering, and W. June Ruan, *The Journal of Clinical Psychiatry*, 69(4), April 2008, pp533 – 545.

1083 'Children with Blindness – Major Causes, Developmental Outcomes and Implications for Habilitation and Educational Support: A Two-Decade, Swedish Population-Based Study,' by Kim de Verdier, Ek Ulla, Stefan Löfgren, and Elisabeth Fernell, *Acta Ophthalmologica*, 96(3), May 2018, pp295 – 300.

1084 'Children with Blindness – Major Causes, Developmental Outcomes and Implications for Habilitation and Educational Support: a Two-Decade, Swedish Population-Based Study,' by Kim de Verdier, Ek Ulla, Stefan Löfgren, and Elisabeth Fernell, *Acta Ophthalmologica*, 96(3), May 2018, pp295 – 300.

1085 'Autism's Direct Cause? Failure of Infant-Mother Eye Contact in a Complex Adaptive System,' by Maxson J. McDowell, *Biological Theory MIT Press*, 5(4), 2011, pp344 - 356.

1086 'Quasi-Autistic Patterns Following Severe Early Global Privation,' by Michael Rutter, Lucie Andersen-Wood, Celia Beckett, Diana Bredenkamp, Jenny Castle, Christine Groothues, Jana Kreppner, Lisa Keaveney, Catherine Lord, and Thomas G. O'Connor, *Journal of Child Psychology and Psychiatry*, 40(4), May 1999, pp537 – 549.

1087 'Autism's Direct Cause? Failure of Infant-Mother Eye Contact in a Complex Adaptive System,' by Maxson J. McDowell, *Biological Theory MIT Press*, 5(4), 2011, pp344 - 356.

1088 'Autism's Direct Cause? Failure of Infant-Mother Eye Contact in a Complex Adaptive System,' by Maxson J. McDowell, *Biological Theory MIT Press*, 5(4), 2011, pp344 - 356.

1089 'Autism's Direct Cause? Failure of Infant-Mother Eye Contact in a Complex Adaptive System,' by Maxson J. McDowell, *Biological Theory MIT Press*, 5(4), 2011, pp344 - 356.

1090 'Dahmer's Inferno,' by Brian Masters, *Vanity Fair*, 1991 (www.vanityfair.com/style/1991/11/jeffrey-dahmer-dennis-nilsen-serial-killer). Accessed January 24, 2021.

1091 '*2001: A Space Odyssey* is still the 'Ultimate Trip',' by Dennis Overbye, *The New York Times*, May 10, 2018 (www.nytimes.com/2018/05/10/science/2001-a-space-odyssey-kubrick.html). Accessed December 15, 2020.

1092 *Depression and Other Common Mental Disorders: Global Health Estimates 3*, World Health Organisation, 2017 (apps.who.int/iris/bitstream/handle/10665/254610/WHO-MSD-MER-2017.2-eng.pdf). Accessed December 10, 2020.

1093 'Suicide in England and Wales 1861–2007: A Time-Trends Analysis,' by Kyla Thomas and David Gunnell, *International Journal of Epidemiology*, 39(6), December 2010, pp1464 – 1475.

1094 *Depression and Other Common Mental Disorders: Global Health Estimates 3*, World Health Organisation, 2017 (apps.who.int/iris/bitstream/handle/10665/254610/WHO-MSD-MER-2017.2-eng.pdf). Accessed December 10, 2020.

1095 'That Gut Feeling,' by Dr. Siri Carpenter, *Monitor on Psychology*, 43(8), September 2012 (www.apa.org/monitor/2012/09/gut-feeling). Accessed December 20, 2020.

1096 *Love in Five Acts*, by Daniela Krien, translated by Jamie Bulloch, MacLehose, 2021 (first published in 2019), p228.

1097 'Birth Cohort Increases in Narcissistic Personality Traits Among American College Students, 1982 – 2009,' by Jean M. Twenge, Joshua D. Foster, *Social, Psychological, and Personality Science*, 1(1), January 2010, pp99 - 106.

1098 'Oxytocin-Gaze Positive Loop and the Coevolution of Human-Dog Bonds,' by Miho Nagasawa, Shouhei Mitsui, Shiori En, Nobuyo Ohtani, Mitsuaki Ohta, Yasuo Sakuma, Tatsushi Onaka, Kazutaka Mogi, and Takefumi Kikusui, *Science*, 348(6232), April 2015, pp333 – 336.

1099 'How to Bio-Hack Your Brain to Have Sex without Getting Emotionally Attached,' by Sirin Kale, *Vice*, August 25, 2016 (www.vice.com/en/article/59mmzq/how-to-bio-hack-your-brain-to-have-sex-without-getting-emotionally-attached). Accessed December 15, 2020.

1100 *The Pocket Guide to the Polyvagal Theory: The Transformative Power of Feeling Safe (Norton Series on Interpersonal Neurobiology)*, by Stephen W. Porges, W. W. Norton and Company, 2017, p.vii.

1101 'Selfie-image: What Have We Done to Ourselves?' by Antonella Gambotto-Burke, *The Weekend Australian*, June 12, 2020 (www.theaustralian.com.au/arts/review/selfieimage-has-social-media-turned-our-faces-into-masks/news-story/16e789d6497bec584d63d4850168bac9). Accessed December 17, 2020.

1102 *Faceworld: The Face in the Twenty-First Century*, by Marion Zilio, translated by Robin Mackay, Polity Press (first published as *Faceworld: Le visage au XXIe siècle* in 2018), 2020, pp3 - 4.

1103 'Heroin Wednesday,' by Michael Dransfield, *Collected Poems*, Australian Poetry Library (www.poetrylibrary.edu.au/poets/dransfield-michael/poems/heroin-wednesday-0712336). Accessed March 2, 2021.

1104 *Rosemary: The Hidden Kennedy Daughter*, by Kate Clifford Larson, Houghton Mifflin Harcourt, 2015, pp3.

1105 *And I Don't Want to Live This Life: a Mother's Story of Her Daughter's Murder*, by Deborah Spungen, Random House, 1996, pp10, 14, 16 – 22, 30, 31, 41.

1106 *ibid*, pp16 – 17.

1107 *ibid*, pp17 - 18.

1108 *ibid*, pp20 - 21.

1109 *ibid*, pp21 - 22.

1110 *ibid*, pp25 - 28.

1111 *ibid*, pp25 - 30.

1112 *ibid*, pp21.

1113 'That which we call a rose,' by Michael Dransfield, *Collected Poems*, Australian Poetry Library (www.poetrylibrary.edu.au/poets/dransfield-michael/poems/that-which-we-call-a-rose-0712041). Accessed July 12, 2021.

1114 *And I Don't Want to Live This Life: a Mother's Story of Her Daughter's Murder*, by Deborah Spungen, Random House, 1996, pp151, 159, 45.

1115 'Dicyclomine,' *Drugs.com*, 2020 (www.drugs.com/monograph/dicyclomine.html). Accessed January 24, 2021.

1116 'Dicyclomine: 7 Things You Should Know,' reviewed by Carmen Fookes, *Drugs.com*, November 9, 2020 (www.drugs.com/tips/dicyclomine-patient-tips). Accessed January 24, 2021.

1117 *East of England Neonatal Neuroprotection Guideline: Diagnosis and Management of Neonatal Seizures in the Term Infant*, by Topun Austin, Sam O'Hare, Circulation East of England Neonatal Neuroprotection Steering Group, Nigel Gooding, Sajeev Job, Ulrike Luedtke, East of England Neonatal ODN, NHS, 2020 (www.nnuh.nhs.uk/publication/download/seizure-guideline-diagnosis-management-of-neonatal-seizures-east-of-england-neonatal-guideline-regional-guidance). Accessed December 20, 2020.

1118 'General Anaesthetics,' by F. J. Carmichael and D. A. Haas, *Principles of Medical Pharmacology (6th edition)*, edited by H. Kalant and W. H. E. Roschlau, Oxford University Press, 1998, pp278 – 92.

1119 'The Role of the GABAA Receptor/Chloride Channel Complex in Anaesthesia,' by D. L. Tanelian, P. Kosek, I. Mody, and M. B. MacIver, *Anaesthesiology*, 78(4), April 1993, pp757 - 76.

1120 'The Role of Neurotransmitters,' by Kendra Cherry, *Very Well Mind*, November 24, 2020 (www.verywellmind.com/what-is-a-neurotransmitter-2795394). Accessed December 20,

2020.

1121 'Neonatal Blockade of GABA-A Receptors Alters Behavioural and Physiological Phenotypes in Adult Mice,' by A. A. Salari and M. Amani, *The International Journal of Developmental Neuroscience*, 57, April 2017, pp62 - 71.

1122 'GABA: A Pioneer Transmitter That Excites Immature Neurons and Generates Primitive Oscillations,' by Yehezkel Ben-Ari, Jean-Luc Gaiarsa, Roman Tyzio, and Rustem Khazipov, *Physiological Reviews*, 87(4), October 2007, pp1215 – 1284.

1123 'GABA Activation and Dopamine Suppression,' by Chloe Bennett, *News Medical*, July 18, 2019 (www.news-medical.net/health/GABA-Activation-and-Dopamine-Suppression.aspx). Accessed December 21, 2020.

1124 'GABA Activation and Dopamine Suppression,' by Chloe Bennett, *News Medical*, July 18, 2019 (www.news-medical.net/health/GABA-Activation-and-Dopamine-Suppression.aspx). Accessed December 21, 2020.

1125 'Dopamine Neurons Projecting to Medial Shell of the Nucleus Accumbens Drive Heroin Reinforcement,' by Julie Corre, Ruud van Zessen, Michaël Loureiro, Tommaso Patriarchi, Lin Tian, Vincent Pascoli, and Christian Lüscher, *eLife*, 7, October 2018, p.e39945.

1126 'Potential Mechanism of Cell Death in the Developing Rat Brain Induced by Propofol Anaesthesia, by Vesna Pešić, Desanka Milanović, Nikola Tanić, Jelena Popić, Selma Kanazir, Vesna Jevtović-Todorović, and Sabera Ruždijić, *International Journal of Developmental Neuroscience*, 27(3), May 2009, pp279 - 287.

1127 'A Brain on Cannabinoids: The Role of Dopamine Release in Reward Seeking,' by Erik B. Oleson and Joseph F. Cheer, *Cold Spring Harbour Perspectives in Medicine*, 2(8), August 2012, p.a012229.

1128 'Dopamine Neurons Projecting to Medial Shell of the Nucleus Accumbens Drive Heroin Reinforcement,' by Julie Corre, Ruud van Zessen, Michaël Loureiro, Tommaso Patriarchi, Lin Tian, Vincent Pascoli, and Christian Lüscher, *eLife*, 7, October 2018, p.e39945.

1129 'Hallucinogenic Drugs: A New Study Answers Old Questions about LSD,' by Adam L. Halberstadt, *Current Biology*, 27, February 2017, p.R139–R161.

1130 'Neuroscience of Internet Pornography Addiction: A Review and Update,' by Todd Love, Christian Laier, Matthias Brand, Linda Hatch, and Raju Hajela, edited by Andrew Doan, *Behavioural Sciences*, 5(3), September 2015 pp388 – 433.

1131 'The Role of Dopamine in the Pathophysiology of Depression,' by Boadie W. Dunlop and Charles B. Nemeroff, *Archives of General Psychiatry*, 64(3), April 2007, pp327 – 337.

1132 'Depression: Fact Sheet,' World Health Organisation, January 30, 2020 (www.who.int/newsroom/fact-sheets/detail/depression). Accessed January 19, 2021.

1133 'The Role of Dopamine in Schizophrenia from a Neurobiological and Evolutionary Perspective: Old Fashioned, but Still in Vogue,' by Ralf Brisch, Arthur Saniotis, Rainer Wolf, Hendrik Bielau, Hans-Gert Bernstein, Johann Steiner, Bernhard Bogerts, Katharina Braun, Zbigniew Jankowski, Jaliya Kumaratilake, Maciej Henneberg, and Tomasz Gos, *Frontiers in Psychiatry*, 5, May 2014, pp47.

1134 'Snoop Dogg and Seth Rogen Enjoy Smoking Weed with Each Other,' *The Howard Stern Show*, October 8, 2019 (www.youtube.com/watch?v=j2OyFTm2ycg). Accessed December 21, 2020.

1135 'How did Snoop Dogg Make his Net Worth over the Years?' by Carmen MacBeth, *FilmDaily*, September 24, 2020 (filmdaily.co/obsessions/snoop-dogg-grows-net-worth). Accessed December 21, 2020.

1136 'Seth Rogen 'Introduced Tom Cruise to Internet Porn' in 2007,' by Mike Wood, *LadBible*, August 1, 2018 (www.ladbible.com/entertainment/weird-tom-cruise-only-heard-about-internet-porn-in-2007-says-seth-rogen-20180801). Accessed December 21, 2020.

1137 'Have We Hatched the Addiction Egg: Reward Deficiency Syndrome Solution System™,' by B. W. Downs, M. Oscar-Berman, R. L. Waite, M.A. Madigan, J. Giordano, T. Beley, S. Jones, T. Simpatico, M. Hauser, J. Borsten, F. Marcelo, E. R. Braverman, R. Lohmann, K. Dushaj, M. Helman, D. Barh, S. T. Schoenthaler, D. Han, and K. Blum, *Journal of Genetic Syndromes and Gene Therapy*, 4(136), June 2013, pp14318.

1138 'Still life with hypodermic,' by Michael Dransfield, *Collected Poems*, Australian Poetry Library (www.poetrylibrary.edu.au/poets/dransfield-michael/poems/still-life-with-hypodermic-0712016). Accessed July 12, 2021.

1139 'Depression, Anxiety, Loneliness are Peaking in College Students,' by Kat J. McAlpine, *The Brink*, Boston University, February 17, 2021 (www.bu.edu/articles/2021/depression-anxiety-loneliness-are-peaking-in-college-students). Accessed February 22, 2021.

1140 'Mental Illness is Normal,' by Dr Richard Schweizer, One Door Mental Health, 2020 (www.onedoor.org.au/events-media/blog/mental-illness-is-normal). Accessed December 31, 2020.

1141 'The Rising Pandemic of Mental Disorders and Associated Chronic Diseases and Disabilities,' by M. Kramer, *Acta Psychiatrica Scandinavica*, 62(S285), September 1980, pp382 - 397.

1142 'Rising Incidence Rates of Schizophrenia among Children and Adolescents,' by Anne Dorte Stenstrøm, Erik Christiansen, Birgitte Dehlholm-Lambertsen, Peer Nøhr-Jensen, and Niels Bilenberg, *Ugeskr Laeger*, 172(31), August 2010, pp2131 - 2135.

1143 'Global Epidemiology and Burden of Schizophrenia: Findings From the Global Burden of Disease Study 2016,' by Fiona J. Charlson, Alize J. Ferrari, Damian F. Santomauro, Sandra Diminic, Emily Stockings, James G. Scott, John J. McGrath, and Harvey A. Whiteford, *Schizophrenia Bulletin*, 44(6), October 2018, pp1195 – 1203.

1144 'Brain Gamma-Aminobutyric Acid (GABA) Abnormalities in Bipolar Disorder,' by Roscoe O. Brady, Julie M. McCarthy, Andrew P. Prescot, J. Eric Jensen, Alissa J. Cooper, Bruce M. Cohen, Perry F. Renshaw, and Dost Ongürb, *Bipolar Disorders*, 15(4), June 2013, pp434 – 439.

1145 *Wild Thing: The Short, Spellbinding Life of Jimi Hendrix*, by Philip Norman, Liveright, 2020, pp311, 82, 15

1146 *Alleviation of Pain in Labour*, by Wm. P. Sadler, Instructor in Obstetrics and Gynaecology, University of Minnesota, Read before the Forty-Fifth Annual Meeting of Idaho State Medical Association, Boise, Idaho, USA, August 30 - September 2, 1937.

1147 *America's Reluctant Prince: The Life of John F. Kennedy Jr.*, by Steven M. Gillon, Dutton, 2019, pp9.

1148 *America's Queen: The Life of Jacqueline Kennedy Onassis*, by Sarah Bradford, Penguin, 2013, pp155, 191.

1149 *America's Reluctant Prince: The Life of John F. Kennedy Jr.*, by Steven M. Gillon, Dutton, 2019, pp16.

1150 'Secrets and Lies,' by Edward Klein, *Vanity Fair*, August 2003 (www.vanityfair.com/news/2003/08/john-f-kennedy-jr-carolyn-bessette-divorce-drugs-scandal). Accessed October 16, 2020.

1151 *The Kennedy Heirs: John, Caroline, and the New Generation - A Legacy of Tragedy and Triumph*, by J. Randy Taraborrelli, St Martin's Press, 2019, pp92.

1152 'Houston Died from Drowning, Coroner Says,' by Anthony McCartney, *Associated Press*, March 23, 2012 (www.yahoo.com/entertainment/news/houston-died-drowning-coroner-says-213627189.html). Accessed January 1, 2020.

1153 *Remembering Whitney: A Mother's Story of Life, Loss and the Night the Music Stopped*, by Cissy Houston, HarperCollins, 2014, pp10.

1154 'Bobbi Kristina Brown Autopsy Report Reveals She Died from 'Lobar Pneumonia',' by Shah Rahmanzadeh and Joi-Marie McKenzie, *ABC News*, March 4, 2016 (abcnews.go.com/Entertainment/bobbi-kristina-brown-autopsy-report-reveals-died-lobar/story?id=37394464). Accessed January 1, 2020.

1155 *Remembering Whitney: A Mother's Story of Life, Loss and the Night the Music Stopped*, by Cissy Houston, HarperCollins, 2014, pp168.

1156 'Can be Tamed! Miley Cyrus Reveals She's Six Months Sober after Years of Admitted Drug Use and Hard Partying,' by Rebecca Lewis, *The Sun*, June 23, 2020 (www.thesun.co.uk/tvandshowbiz/11938081/miley-cyrus-six-months-sober). Accessed January 19, 2021.

1157 *She Can't Stop: Miley Cyrus – The Biography*, by Sarah Oliver, John Blake, 2014, pp1.

1158 Kush is a Cannabis Indica strain.

1159 'Miley Cyrus Quit Smoking but Says Her Mom Is Smoking 'All the Weed I Do Not Smoke',' by Fred Topel, *Showbiz Cheat Sheet*, August 21, 2020 (www.cheatsheet.com/entertainment/miley-cyrus-quit-smoking-but-says-her-mom-is-smoking-all-the-weed-i-do-not-smoke.html). Accessed January 19, 2021.

1160 *Edie: American Girl*, by Jean Stein, Grove Press, 1994 (originally published in 1982), pp63.

1161 'Olfaction Scaffolds the Developing Human from Neonate to Adolescent and Beyond,' by Benoist Schaal, Tamsin K. Saxton, Hélène Loos, Robert Soussignan and Karine Durand, *Philosophical Transactions of the Royal Society B: Biological Sciences*, April 20, 2020 (royalsocietypublishing.org/doi/pdf/10.1098/rstb.2019.0261). Accessed August 20, 2020.

1162 'Human Foetuses Learn Odours from their Pregnant Mother's Diet,' by Benoist Schaal, Luc Marlier and Robert Soussignan, *Chemical Senses*, 25(6), December 2000, pp729 – 737.

1163 My telephone interview with Michele Kirsch, September 30, 2020.

1164 *Clean: A Story of Addiction, Recovery and the Removal of Stubborn Stains*, by Michele Kirsch, Short Books (Kindle edition), 2019.

1165 *Wishful Drinking*, by Carrie Fisher, Simon and Schuster, 2008, pp29, 12, 131, 143, 144.

1166 *My Year of Rest and Relaxation*, by Ottessa Moshfegh, Random House, 2019, p4.

1167 'Overdose,' by Michael Dransfield, *Collected Poems*, Australian Poetry Library (www.poetrylibrary.edu.au/poets/dransfield-michael/poems/overdose-0712032). Accessed March 2, 2021.

1168 'PCP Addiction and Abuse,' Addiction Centre, 2021 (www.addictioncenter.com/drugs/hallucinogens/pcp-phencyclidine). Accessed January 11, 2021.

1169 'Phencyclidine in Obstetrics,' *Anaesthesia*, 1961, pp233 (associationofanaesthetists-publications.onlinelibrary.wiley.com/doi/pdf/10.1111/j.1365-2044.1963.tb13541.x). Accessed January 11, 2021.

1170 'Chapter 122 - Anesthetic-Agent Mass Casualty Incident,' *Ciottone's Disaster Medicine (Second Edition)*, by Kinjal N. Sethuraman, Jerrilyn Jones, and K.Sophia Dyer, 2016, Pages 692 - 695.

1171 'Suxamethonium,' Queensland Board of Health, 2019 (www.health.qld.gov.au/__data/assets/pdf_file/0027/930447/nmq-suxamethonium.pdf). Accessed January 11, 2021.

1172 '60: Hyperkalemia,' *Neonatology: Management, Procedures, On-Call Problems, Diseases, and Drugs (7th edition)*, by Tricia Lacy Gomella, M. Douglas Cunningham, Fabien G. Eyal, and Deborah J. Tuttle, McGraw-Hill Education, 2013, pp415.

1173 'The Use of Phencyclidine (CI-395) in Obstetric Procedures: A Preliminary Communication,' by Joe G. Camilleri, *Anaesthesia*, 17(4), October 1962 (associationofanaesthetists-publications.onlinelibrary.wiley.com/doi/pdf/10.1111/j.1365-2044.1962.tb13497.x). Accessed January 11, 2021.

1174 'Phencyclidine: Its Transfer across the Placenta as Well as into Breast Milk,' by J. M. Nicholas, J. Lipshitz, and E. C. Schreiber, *American Journal of Obstetrics and Gynaecology*, 143(2), May 1982, pp143 - 146.

1175 'PCP Addiction and Abuse,' Addiction Centre, 2021 (www.addictioncenter.com/drugs/hallucinogens/pcp-phencyclidine). Accessed January 11, 2021.

1176 'Massive Phencyclidine Intoxication,' by Robert J. Fallis, Orm Aniline, Leslie P. Weiner, and Ferris N. Pitts Jr, *Archives of Neurology*, 39(5), May 1982, pp316.

1177 'Angel Dust: Possible Effects on the Foetus,' by Nancy L. Golden, Robert J. Sokol, and I. Leslie Rubin, *Paediatrics*, 65(1), January 1980, pp18 – 20.

1178 'The DAWN Report: Emergency Department Visits Involving Phencyclidine (PCP),' US *Substance Abuse and Mental Health Services Administration*, November 12, 2013 (www.samhsa.gov/data/sites/default/files/DAWN143/DAWN143/sr143-emergency-phencyclidine-2013.htm). Accessed January 11, 2021.

1179 'Million Dollar Ride: Crime Committed during Involuntary Scopolamine Intoxication,' by S. Reichert, C. Lin, W. Ong, C. C. Him, and S. Hameed, *Canadian Family Physician / Medecin de Famille Canadien*, 63(5), May 2017, pp369 – 370.

1180 'Barbiturates,' *DrugWise*, 2017 (www.drugwise.org.uk/barbiturates). Accessed January 4, 2021.

1181 'Controlling 'America's Opium': Barbiturate Abuse, Pharmaceutical Regulation, and the Politics of Public Health in the Early Post-war United States,' by Nicolas Rasmussen, *Journal of Policy History*, 29(4), September 2017, pp543 – 568.

1182 'Psychedelic Drugs Market Projected to Reach $6.85 Billion by 2027,' *Cision PR Newswire*, June 24, 2020 (www.prnewswire.com/news-releases/psychedelic-drugs-market-projected-to-reach-6-85-billion-by-2027--301082594.html). Accessed January 10, 2021.

1183 My telephone interview with Alan McGee, November 1, 2020.

1184 *Civilisation and Its Discontents*, by Sigmund Freud, translated by Joan Riviere, Hogarth Press and the Institute of Psycho-Analysis, 1930, pp31 – 32.

1185 *The Pocket Guide to the Polyvagal Theory: The Transformative Power of Feeling Safe (Norton Series on Interpersonal Neurobiology)*, by Stephen W. Porges, W. W. Norton and Company, 2017, p.vii.

1186 'Spencer Drives Heidi's Sister to Tears during Violent Outburst,' by Us Weekly Staff, *US Magazine*, May 12, 2010 (www.usmagazine.com/entertainment/news/spencer-drives-heidissister-to-tears-during-violent-outburst-2010125/). Accessed January 3, 2021.

1187 @my_refocused_life_adopted, Instagram, January 17, 2021 (www.instagram.com/p/CK-Ju0mVBTXj). Accessed January 17, 2021.

1188 'Opioid Overdose: Fact Sheet,' World Health Organisation, August 28, 2020 (www.who.int/news-room/fact-sheets/detail/opioid-overdose). Accessed January 13, 2021.

1189 'Overdose Death Rates,' National Institute on Drug Abuse, March 10, 2020 (www.drugabuse.gov/drug-topics/trends-statistics/overdose-death-rates). Accessed January 13, 2021.

1190 *My Year of Rest and Relaxation*, by Ottessa Moshfegh, Penguin, 2019, pp91.

1191 'carolesdaughter: 'I was drawn to extremes ... so felt like I never belonged,'' by James Hickie, *Kerrang*, May 5, 2021 (www.kerrang.com/features/carolesdaughter-i-was-drawn-to-extremes-so-felt-like-i-never-belonged). Accessed July 11, 2021.

1192 *Please Put Me in a Medically Induced Coma*, by carolesdaughter (words and lyrics Thea Taylor, Arista Records/Sony Music 2021).

1193 'Overdose Deaths Accelerating During COVID-19: Expanded Prevention Efforts Needed,' US Centers for Disease Control and Prevention, December 17, 2020 (www.cdc.gov/media/releases/2020/p1218-overdose-deaths-covid-19.html). Accessed January 10, 2021.

1194 'Meth Psychosis: How Can Meth Use Cause Psychosis and Hallucinations,' The Recovery Village (www.therecoveryvillage.com/meth-addiction/meth-psychosis). Accessed January 10, 2021.

1195 'Americans Increase LSD Use - and a Bleak Outlook for the World May Be to Blame,' by Rachel Nuwer, *Scientific American*, July 10, 2020 (www.scientificamerican.com/article/americans-increase-lsd-use-and-a-bleak-outlook-for-the-world-may-be-to-blame1/). Accessed January 9, 2021.

1196 'Opioid Overdose: Fact Sheet,' World Health Organisation, August 28, 2020 (www.who.int/news-room/fact-sheets/detail/opioid-overdose). Accessed January 13, 2021.

1197 'The Economic Costs of the U.S. Criminal Justice System,' by Tara O'Neill Hayes, *American Action Forum*, July 16, 2020 (www.americanactionforum.org/research/the-economic-costs-of-the-u-s-criminal-justice-system). Accessed February 4, 2021.

1198 'The Economic Burden of Incarceration in the United States,' by Michael McLaughlin, Carrie Pettus-Davis, Derek Brown, Chris Veeh, Tanya Renn, *Institute for Justice Research and Development* (ijrd.csw.fsu.edu/sites/g/files/upcbnu1766/files/media/images/publication_pdfs/Economic_Burden_of_Incarceration_IJRD072016_0_0.pdf). Accessed February 4, 2021.

1199 'Box Office History for Terminator Movies,' *The Numbers*, 1997 – 2021 (www.the-numbers.com/movies/franchise/Terminator#tab=summary). Accessed January 10, 2021.

1200 'Cyborgs and space,' by Manfred E. Clynes and Nathan S. Kline, *Astronautics*, September 1960 (web.mit.edu/digitalapollo/Documents/Chapter1/cyborgs.pdf). Accessed January 10, 2021.

1201 *Bright Air, Brilliant Fire: On the Matter of the Mind*, by Gerald M. Edelman, BasicBooks, 1992, pp17.

1202 'Prevalence and Risk Factors for Delirium in Critically Ill Patients with COVID-19 (COVID-D): a Multicentre Cohort Study,' by Brenda T. Pun, Rafael Badenes, Gabriel Heras La Calle, Onur M. Orun, Wencong Chen, Rameela Raman, Beata-Gabriela K. Simpson, Stephanie Wilson-Linville, Borja Hinojal Olmedillo, Ana Vallejo de la Cueva, Mathieu van der Jagt, Rosalía Navarro Casado, Pilar Leal Sanz, Günseli Orhun, Carolina Ferrer Gómez, Karla Núñez Vázquez, Patricia Piñeiro Otero, Fabio Silvio Taccone, Elena Gallego Curto, Anselmo Caricato, Hilde Woien, Guillaume Lacave, Hollis R. O'Neal Jr, Sarah J. Peterson, Nathan E. Brummel, Timothy D. Girard, E. Wesley Ely, Pratik P. Pandharipande for the COVID-19 Intensive Care International Study Group, *The Lancet Respiratory Medicine*, January 8, 2021 (www.thelancet.com/pdfs/journals/lanres/PIIS2213-2600(20)30552-X.pdf). Accessed January 10, 2021.

1203 'So Lonely I Could Die,' American Psychological Association, July 27, 2017 (www.newswise.com/articles/so-lonely-i-could-die). Accessed January 10, 2021.

1204 'Should Neonates Sleep Alone?,' by Barak E. Morgan, Alan R. Horn, and Nils J. Bergman, *Biological Psychiatry*, 70(9), November 2011, pp817 - 825.

1205 *Letter to D*, XXXXX

1206 ''Solo' Dads and 'Absent' Dads Not as Different as They Seem,' by Lindsay M. Monte, *United States Census Bureau*, November 5, 2019 (www.census.gov/library/stories/2019/11/the-two-extremes-of-fatherhood.html). Accessed January 10, 2021.

1207 'One in Five Dads Lose Contact With Children When Families Break Up, Says Survey,' *DJS Research*, November 25, 2013 (www.djsresearch.co.uk/CentralGovernmentMarket-ResearchInsightsAndFindings/article/One-in-Five-Dads-Lose-Contact-With-Children-When-Families-Break-Up-Says-Survey-01428#:~:text=According%20to%20new%20research%20 it's,children%20born%20during%20earlier%20relationships.). Accessed January 10, 2021.

1208 'So Lonely I Could Die,' American Psychological Association, July 27, 2017 (www.newswise. com/articles/so-lonely-i-could-die). Accessed January 10, 2021.

1209 'The Rise of Living Alone: How One-Person Households are Becoming Increasingly Common around the World,' by Esteban Ortiz-Ospina, *Our World in Data*, December 10, 2019 (ourworldindata.org/living-alone). Accessed January 10, 2021.

1210 'Families and Households in the UK: 2019,' British Office for National Statistics, November 15, 2019 (www.ons.gov.uk/peoplepopulationandcommunity/birthsdeathsandmarriages/ families/bulletins/familiesandhouseholds/2019). Accessed January 10, 2021.

1211 'The Rise of Living Alone: How One-Person Households are Becoming Increasingly Common around the World,' by Esteban Ortiz-Ospina, *Our World in Data*, December 10, 2019 (ourworldindata.org/living-alone). Accessed January 10, 2021.

1212 'The Rise of Living Alone and Loneliness in History,' by K. D. M. Snell, *Social History*, 42(1), January 2017, pp2 – 28.

1213 'When Will You Be Ready?' *High Priest*, by Timothy Leary, Ronin, 1968, p289.

1214 'Timothy Leary Daughter Hangs Self in Cell, Dies in Hospital,' *The Los Angeles Times*, September 6, 1990 (www.latimes.com/archives/la-xpm-1990-09-06-mn-1266-story.html). Accessed June 13, 2020.

1215 'Xbox Fan Pummelled Toddler Daughter to Death after she Knocked over his Console,' *The Daily Mail*, January 30, 2008 (www.dailymail.co.uk/news/article-511346/Xbox-fan-pum-melled-toddler-daughter-death-knocked-console.html). Accessed October 20, 2020.

1216 'The Apgar Score,' American Academy of Paediatrics - Committee on Foetus and Newborn, 644, October 2015 (www.acog.org/-/media/project/acog/acogorg/clinical/files/commit-tee-opinion/articles/2015/10/the-apgar-score.pdf). Accessed February 15, 2021.

1217 'Epidural Analgesia in Labour and Neonatal Respiratory Distress: A Case-Control Study,' by Manoj Kumar, Sue Chandra, Zainab Ijaz, and Ambikaipakan Senthilselvan, *Archives of Disease in Childhood: Foetal and Neonatal Edition*, 99(2), March 2014, pF116-9.

1218 'Group B Strep,' NHS, March 12, 2021 (www.nhs.uk/conditions/group-b-strep). Accessed July 7, 2021.

1219 'Risk Factors for Early Onset Neonatal Group B Streptococcal Sepsis: Case-Control Study,' by Sam Oddie and Nicholas D. Embleton, *British Medical Journal*, 325(7359), August 2002, pp308.

1220 'Intrapartum Antibiotics for GBS Prophylaxis Alter Colonisation Patterns in the Early Infant Gut Microbiome of Low Risk Infants,' by Jennifer C. Stearns, Julia Simioni, Elizabeth Gunn, Helen McDonald, Alison C. Holloway, Lehana Thabane, Andrea Mousseau, Jonathan D. Schertzer, Elyanne M. Ratcliffe, Laura Rossi, Michael G. Surette, Katherine M. Morrison and Eileen K. Hutton, *Scientific Reports*, 7(16527), November 2017.

1221 'Prospective Surveillance of Antibiotic Use in the Neonatal Intensive Care Unit: Results From the SCOUT Study,' by Joseph B. Cantey, Phillip S. Wozniak, Pablo J. Sánchez, *The Paediatric Infectious Disease Journal*, 34(3), March 2015, pp267 – 272.

1222 'Adverse Consequences of Neonatal Antibiotic Exposure,' by Charles M. Cotten, *Current Opinion in Paediatrics*, 28(2), April 2016, pp141 – 149.

1223 'Antibiotic Resistance Threats in the United States,' Centres for Disease Control and Prevention, 2013 (www.cdc.gov/drugresistance/pdf/ar-threats-2013-508.pdf). Accessed February 21, 2021.

1224 'Intrapartum Antibiotics for GBS Prophylaxis Alter Colonisation Patterns in the Early Infant Gut Microbiome of Low Risk Infants,' by Jennifer C. Stearns, Julia Simioni, Elizabeth Gunn, Helen McDonald, Alison C. Holloway, Lehana Thabane, Andrea Mousseau, Jonathan D. Schertzer, Elyanne M. Ratcliffe, Laura Rossi, Michael G. Surette, Katherine M. Morrison and Eileen K. Hutton, *Scientific Reports*, 7(16527), November 2017.

1225 'The Relationship of Prenatal Antibiotic Exposure and Infant Antibiotic Administration with Childhood Allergies: A Systematic Review,' by Ruth Baron, Meron Taye, Isolde Besseling-van der Vaart, Joanne Ujčič-Voortman, Hania Szajewska, Jacob C. Seidell, and Arnoud Verhoeff, *BMC Paediatrics*, 20(1), June 2020, pp312.

1226 'Pitocin (Oxytocin) Induction Risks and Side Effects,' Reiter and Walsh PC, 2010 – 2021 (www.abclawcenters.com/practice-areas/prenatal-birth-injuries/labor-and-delivery-medication-errors/pitocin-and-oxytocin). Accessed February 18, 2021.

1227 'Neonatal Hyperbilirubinemia Associated With Oxytocin Labour Augmentation,' by Manik Mani, R. L. Priyanka Chevuturi, Gita Basu Banerjee, Sumona Ghosh, Tamanna Hossain, and Suman Sahu, *IOSR Journal of Dental and Medical Sciences*, 19(3), March 2020, pp1 – 6.

1228 'Pitocin (Oxytocin Injection USP, Synthetic),' US FDA, 2020 (www.accessdata.fda.gov/drugsatfda_docs/label/2014/018261s031lbl.pdf). Accessed February 18, 2021.

1229 'Potential Dangers of Oxytocin,' AIMS Journal, 10(2), 1998 (www.aims.org.uk/journal/item/potential-dangers-of-oxytocin). Accessed February 18, 2021.

1230 'Pitocin (Oxytocin Injection USP, Synthetic),' US FDA, 2020 (www.accessdata.fda.gov/drugsatfda_docs/label/2014/018261s031lbl.pdf). Accessed February 18, 2021.

1231 'Jaundice in Newborns,' *Paediatrics and Child Health*, 4(2), March 1999, pp165 – 166.

1232 'Association of Peripartum Synthetic Oxytocin Administration and Depressive and Anxiety Disorders within the First Postpartum Year,' by Aimee R. Kroll-Desrosiers, Benjamin C. Nephew, Jessica A. Babb, Yurima Guilarte-Walker, Tiffany A. Moore Simas, and Kristina M. Deligiannidis, *Depression and Anxiety*, 34(2), February 2017, pp137 – 146.

1233 *Jaundice in Newborn Babies under 28 Days: Clinical Guideline*, NICE, 2020 (www.nice.org.uk/guidance/cg98/resources/jaundice-in-newborn-babies-under-28-days-pdf-975756073669). Accessed February 18, 2021.

1234 'Jaundice in Healthy Newborns,' La Leche League GB, 2020 (www.laleche.org.uk/jaundice). Accessed February 18, 2021.

1235 *Jaundice in Newborn Babies under 28 Days: Clinical Guideline*, NICE, 2020 (www.nice.org.uk/guidance/cg98/resources/jaundice-in-newborn-babies-under-28-days-pdf-975756073669). Accessed February 18, 2021.

1236 'Pitocin: Side Effects', By Cerner Multum, *Drugs.com*, April 24, 2019 (www.drugs.com/mtm/pitocin.html). Accessed July 2, 2020.

1237 'Uterine Hyperstimulation,' *Misoprostol*, 2020 (www.misoprostol.org/uterine-hyperstimulation). Accessed July 2, 2020.

1238 'Synthetic Oxytocin (Pitocin, Syntocinon): Unpacking the Myths and Side-Effects,' by Sarah Buckley, September 23, 2019 (sarahbuckley.com/pitocin-side-effects-part1). Accessed February 17, 2021.

1239 'Maternal Plasma Levels of Oxytocin during Physiological Childbirth – a Systematic Review with Implications for Uterine Contractions and Central Actions of Oxytocin,' by Kerstin Uvnäs-Moberg, Anette Ekström-Bergström, Marie Berg, Sarah Buckley, Zada Pajalic, Eleni Hadjigeorgiou, Alicja Kotłowska, Luise Lengler, Bogumila Kielbratowska, Fatima Leon-Larios, Claudia Meier Magistretti, Soo Downe, Bengt Lindström and Anna Dencker, *BMC Pregnancy and Childbirth*, 19(285), August 2019.

1240 Illustrated Hyperstimulation of the Uterus, Reiter and Walsh, 2021 (1q3nfm4evj5z1s-gm624e93ka-wpengine.netdna-ssl.com/wp-content/uploads/2016/08/Hyperstimulation-of-the-Uterus-and-Hypertonic-Uterine-Contractions-with-Placental-Detachment.jpg). Accessed February 20, 2021.

1241 'Exposure to Synthetic Oxytocin during Delivery and its Effect on Psychomotor Development,' by María-José González-Valenzuela Dolores López-Montiel, and Ernesto Santiago González-Mesa, *Developmental Psychobiology*, 57(8), December 2015, pp908 – 920.

1242 'Foetal Exposure to Synthetic Oxytocin and the Relationship with Pre-Feeding Cues within One Hour Post-Birth,' by Aleeca F. Bell, Rosemary White-Traut, and Kristin Rankin, *Early Human Development*, 89(3), March 2013, pp137 – 143.

1243 'Neurodevelopmental Outcomes after Initial Childhood Anaesthetic Exposure between Ages 3 and 10 Years,' by Caleb H. Ing, Charles J. DiMaggio, Andrew J. O. Whitehouse, Mary K. Hegarty, Ming Sun, Britta S. von Ungern-Sternberg, Andrew J. Davidson, Melanie M. Wall, Guohua Li, and Lena S. Sun, *Journal of Neurosurgical Anaesthesiology*, 26(4), October 2014, pp377 - 386.

1244 'General Anaesthetics and Neurotoxicity: How Much Do We Know?' by Vesna Jevtovic-Todorovic, *Anaesthesiology Clinics*, 34(3), September 2016, pp439 – 451.

1245 'Maternal Plasma Levels of Oxytocin during Physiological Childbirth – a Systematic Review with Implications for Uterine Contractions and Central Actions of Oxytocin,' by Kerstin

Uvnäs-Moberg, Anette Ekström-Bergström, Marie Berg, Sarah Buckley, Zada Pajalic, Eleni Hadjigeorgiou, Alicja Kotłowska, Luise Lengler, Bogumila Kielbratowska, Fatima Leon-Larios, Claudia Meier Magistretti, Soo Downe, Bengt Lindström and Anna Dencker, *BMC Pregnancy and Childbirth*, 19(285), August 2019.

1246 'Catecholamine and Cortisol Reaction to Childbirth,' by Siw Alehagen, Klaas Wijma, Ulf Lundberg, Bo Melin, and Barbro Wijma, *International Journal of Behavioural Medicine*, 8(1), 2001, pp50 – 65.

1247 'The Orgasmic History of Oxytocin: Love, Lust, and Labour,' by Navneet Magon and Sanjay Kalra, *Indian Journal of Endocrinology and Metabolism*, 15(Suppl3), September 2011, p.S156 – S161.

1248 'The Role of Hormones in Childbirth,' National Partnership for Women and Families, 2021 (www.childbirthconnection.org/maternity-care/role-of-hormones). Accessed February 17, 2021.

1249 'Repeated Massage-Like Stimulation Induces Long-Term Effects on Nociception: Contribution of Oxytocinergic Mechanisms,' by Iréne Lund, Y Ge, Long-Chuan Yu, Kerstin Uvnas-Moberg, Jing Wang, Cheng Yu, Mieko Kurosawa, Greta Agren, Annika Rosén, Magnus Lekman, and Thomas Lundeberg, *The European Journal of Neuroscience*, 16(2), July 2002, pp330 - 338.

1250 'Does Regular Massage from Late Pregnancy to Birth decrease Maternal Pain Perception during Labour and Birth? A Feasibility Study to Investigate a Programme of Massage, Controlled Breathing and Visualisation, from 36 Weeks of Pregnancy until Birth,' by Mary T. McNabb, Linda Kimber, Anne Haines, and Christine McCourt, *Complementary Therapies in Clinical Practice*, 12(3), August 2006, pp222 - 231.

1251 'How Much Synthetic Oxytocin is Infused during Labour? A Review and Analysis of Regimens used in 12 Countries,' by Deirdre Daly, Karin C. S. Minnie, Alwiena Blignaut, Ellen Blix, Anne Britt Vika Nilsen, Anna Dencker, Katrien Beeckman, Mechthild M. Gross, Jessica Pehlke-Milde, Susanne Grylka-Baeschlin, Martina Koenig-Bachmann, Jette Aaroe Clausen, Eleni Hadjigeorgiou, Sandra Morano, Laura Iannuzzi, Barbara Baranowska, Iwona Kiersnowska, and Kerstin Uvnäs-Moberg, *PLoS ONE*, July 2020.

1252 'Birth with Synthetic Oxytocin and Risk of Childhood Emotional Disorders: A Danish Population-based Study,' by Nicole Nadine Lønfeldt, Katrine Strandberg-Larsen, Frank Cornelis Verhulst, Kerstin Jessica Plessen, and Eli R. Lebowitz, *Journal of Affective Disorders*, 274, September 2020, pp112 – 117.

1253 'Pain in Labour: Your Hormones are Your Helpers,' by Sarah J. Buckley, *Pregnancy*, Autumn 1999 (sarahbuckley.com/pain-in-labour-your-hormones-are-your-helpers-2). Accessed February 17, 2021.

1254 'The Meaning of Labour Pain: How the Social Environment and Other Contextual Factors Shape Women's Experiences,' by Laura Y. Whitburn, Lester E. Jones, Mary-Ann Davey, and Rhonda Small, *BMC Pregnancy and Childbirth*, 17(1), May 2017, pp157.

1255 'Regional Variations in Childbirth Interventions in the Netherlands: a Nationwide Explorative Study,' by A. E. Seijmonsbergen-Schermers, D. C. Zondag, M. Nieuwenhuijze, T. Van den Akker, C. J. Verhoeven, C. Geerts, F. Schellevis, and A. De Jonge, *BMC Pregnancy and Childbirth*, 18(1), June 2018, pp192.

1256 'Maternal Body Mass Index and Use of Labour Neuraxial Analgesia: A Population-based Retrospective Cohort Study,' by Alexander J. Butwick, Cynthia A. Wong, and Nan Guo, *Anaesthesiology*, 129(3), September 2018, pp448 - 458.

1257 *From Chloroform to Epidurals: New Book by UF Physician Examines History of Labour Pain Relief*, University Of Florida Health Science Centre, March 1, 2000.

1258 'Panadeine Tablets Leaflet,' GlaxoSmithKline Consumer Healthcare, 2015 (www.hpra.ie/img/uploaded/swedocuments/PA0678-026-001-2165632-09022016121901-63590617143564250.pdf). Accessed March 2, 2021.

1259 'Use of Codeine and Tramadol Products in Breastfeeding Women - Questions and Answers: Answers to questions about certain opioid medications and their effects on breastfed infants,' *Drug Safety and Availability*, FDA, August 1, 2019 (www.fda.gov/drugs/postmarket-drug-safety-information-patients-and-providers/use-codeine-and-tramadol-products-breastfeeding-women-questions-and-answers). Accessed March 2, 2021.

1260 'Parental Drug Usage: Effects upon Chromosomes of Progeny,' by Kenneth W. Dumars,

Paediatrics, 47(6), June 1971, pp1037 – 1041.

1261 'From Cocaine to Ropivacaine: the History of Local Anaesthetic Drugs,' by Y. A. Ruetsch, T. Böni, and A Borgeat, *Current Topics in Medicinal Chemistry*, 1(3), August 2001, pp175 - 182..

1262 *Naropin 2 mg/ml, 7.5 mg/ml, 10 mg/ml Solution for Injection: Ropivacaine Hydrochloride*, package leaflet ('Information for the User'), AstraZeneca 2015 (www.medicines.org.uk/emc/files/ pil.1498.pdf). Accessed February 26, 2021.

1263 *Naropin 2 mg/ml, 7.5 mg/ml, 10 mg/ml Solution for Injection: Ropivacaine Hydrochloride*, package leaflet ('Information for the User'), AstraZeneca 2015 (www.medicines.org.uk/emc/files/ pil.1498.pdf). Accessed February 26, 2021.

1264 'From Cocaine to Ropivacaine: the History of Local Anaesthetic Drugs,' by Y. A. Ruetsch, T. Böni, and A Borgeat, *Current Topics in Medicinal Chemistry*, 1(3), August 2001, pp175 - 182..

1265 *Scully's Medical Problems in Dentistry (Seventh Edition)*, Crispian Scully, Churchill Livingstone, 2014, pp51 – 96.

1266 'The Influence of Maternal Analgesia on Neonatal Behaviour: II. Epidural Bupivacaine,' by D. B. Rosenblatt, E. M. Belsey, B. A. Lieberman, M. Redshaw, J. Caldwell, L. Notarianni, R. L. Smith, and R. W. Beard, *British Journal of Obstetrics and Gynaecology*, 88(4), April 1981, pp407 - 13.

1267 'The Influence of Maternal Analgesia on Neonatal Behaviour: II. Epidural Bupivacaine,' by D. B. Rosenblatt, E. M. Belsey, B. A. Lieberman, M. Redshaw, J. Caldwell, L. Notarianni, R. L. Smith, and R. W. Beard, *British Journal of Obstetrics and Gynaecology*, 88(4), April 1981, pp407 - 13.

1268 'Placental Structure, Function and Drug Transfer,' by Sarah K. Griffiths and Jeremy P. Campbell, *Continuing Education in Anaesthesia Critical Care and Pain*, 15(2), April 2015, pp84 – 89.

1269 'Obstetricians and the Rights of Pregnant Women,' by Howard Minkoff and Lynn M. Paltrow, *Women's Health*, 3(3), May 2007, pp315 – 319.

1270 *Under the Ivy*, by Kate Bush (words and music Kate Bush, EMI, 1985).

1271 *Thus Spake Zarathustra*, by Friedrich Nietzsche, translated by Thomas Common, Modern Library (first published in 1883), pp69.

1272 *Civilisation and Its Discontents*, by Sigmund Freud, translated by Joan Riviere, Hogarth Press and the Institute of Psycho-Analysis, 1930, pp27 – 28.

1273 *Civilisation and Its Discontents*, by Sigmund Freud, translated by James Strachey, W. W. Norton and Company, 1961 (first published in 1930), pp52.

1274 'Relationship between Physical Disability and Depression by Gender: A Panel Regression Model,' by Jin-Won Noh, Young Dae Kwon, Jumin Park, In-Hwan Oh, and Jinseok Kim, edited by Xuchu Weng, *PLoS One*, 11(11), November 2016, p.e0166238.

1275 'Depressive Symptoms in People with Disabilities; Secondary Analysis of Cross-Sectional Data from the United Kingdom and Greece,' by Elena S. Rotarou and Dikaios Sakellariou, *Disability and Health Journal*, 11(3), July 2018, pp367 – 373.

1276 *Depression and Disability: A Practical Guide*, by Karla Thompson, The North Carolina Office on Disability and Health, 2002 (fpg.unc.edu/sites/fpg.unc.edu/files/resources/other-resources/ NCODH_Depression.pdf). Accessed January 19, 2021.

1277 'Manifestations of Depression in People with Intellectual Disability,' by G. M. Marston D. W. Perry, and A. Roy, *Journal of Intellectual Disability Research*, 41(6), December 1997, pp476 – 480.

1278 'Anxiety and Depression in Parents of Disabled Children,' by Claudia Sălceanu and Mihaela Luminiţa Sandu, *Technium Social Sciences Journal*, 3, February 2020, pp141 - 150.

1279 'Randomised Controlled Trial of Effect of Intervention by Psychogeriatric Team on Depression in Frail Elderly People at Home,' by Sube Banerjee, Kim Shamash, Alastair J. D. Macdonald, and Anthony H. Mann, *British Medical Journal*, 313, October 1996, pp1058 - 1061.

1280 'Can disabled athletes outcompete able-bodied athletes?' by Christian Yates, *The Guardian*, September 7, 2016 (www.theguardian.com/sport/2016/sep/08/can-disabled-athletes-out-compete-able-bodied-athletes). Accessed January 19, 2021.

1281 'Essential Guide to Serotonin and the Other Happy Hormones in Your Body,' *Atlas*, May 27, (atlasbiomed.com/blog/serotonin-and-other-happy-molecules-made-by-gut-bacteria/#-list-of-happy-hormones). Accessed January 19, 2021.

1282 'Imaginary wife and lover,' by Michael Dransfield, *Collected Poems*, Australian Poetry Library (www.poetrylibrary.edu.au/poets/dransfield-michael/poems/imaginary-wife-and-lover-0712273). Accessed July 12, 2021.

1283 'Preterm birth,' *World Health Organisation Factsheet*, February 19, 2018 (www.who.int/news-room/fact-sheets/detail/preterm-birth). Accessed August 15, 2020.

1284 *The Eclipse: A Memoir of Suicide*, by Antonella Gambotto-Burke, Broken Ankle Digital, 2003 (Kindle edition).

1285 'From Resource Extraction to Outflows of Wastes and Emissions: The Socioeconomic Metabolism of the Global Economy, 1900–2015,' by Fridolin Krausmann, Christian Lauk, Willi Haas, and Dominik Wiedenhofer, *Global Environmental Change*, 52, September 2018, p131 - 140.

1286 'Epidemiology of Drugs Taken by Pregnant Women: Drugs that May Affect the Foetus Adversely,' by J. O. Forfar and M. M. Nelson, *Clinical Pharmacology and Therapeutics*, 14(4), July -August 1973, pp632 - 642.

INDEX